THE EMERGENT EGO

THE EMERGENT EGO

COMPLEXITY AND COEVOLUTION IN THE
PSYCHOANALYTIC PROCESS

Stanley R. Palombo, M.D.

INTERNATIONAL UNIVERSITIES PRESS, INC.
Madison   Connecticut

Library of Congress Cataloging-in-Publication Data

Palombo, Stanley R.
    The emergent ego : complexity and coevolution in the psychoanalytic process / Stanley R. Palombo.
       p.   cm.
    Includes bibliographical references and indexes.
    ISBN 0-8236-1666-5
    1. Psychoanalysis.   I. Title.
BF173.P255   1998
150.19′5—dc21   98-22827
                                                                            CIP

Manufactured in the United States of America

To my wife Patricia

CONTENTS

FOREWORD:
THE EMERGENT EGO

At the beginning of this century, psychoanalysis burst upon the intellectual scene. At the end of this century, psychoanalysis is largely held in disregard by many scientists and much of the general public. Psychoanalysis is seen as unscientific, untestable, ineffective, and expensive. Make way for pharmacology—scientific, testable, effective, and relatively inexpensive.

But the truth is deeper and more complex. Baby ducks imprint on their mothers, or on a variety of other stimuli. Human babies emerge with three million years of hominid evolution lying behind their birthright assumptions in their still forming brains. Infant rats and monkeys, deprived of adequate maternal nurturing, grow abnormal neural structures in hippocampus and amygdala, critical regions of the brain for processing emotional experience. Noninvasive studies of the frontal cortices of small children of depressed mothers show abnormal responses in the left versus right cortex when their mothers are out of sight. Normal children show activation of the left cortex. Children of depressed mothers show little or no activation.

For something like three million years, humans have been learning throughout the course of their lives. Learning modifies the neural, hormonal, and other systems whose base forms are the result of biological evolution. Abnormal base forms due to genetic variations and abnormal learning due to harmful experiences do, in fact, alter brain and body structure and function. If today we can approach some of these issues pharmacologically, that is wonderful. But chemistry remains a blunt instrument with which to remold a misshapen spirit. Learning and relearning remain central aspects of healing. Psychoanalysis remains our most subtle and refinable means of touching and caring.

How does a head work? We do not know. But we know increasingly more. And we have enhanced conceptual and experimental frameworks with which to marry our understanding of neural development, emotional development, and their abnormal variants.

If today psychoanalysis is regarded with suspicion, tomorrow or the decade after tomorrow, I predict, psychoanalysis will be regarded as a forefront arena of science. We will have developed tools to visualize brain function and abnormal function in mental illness. We will have developed tools to measure delicate changes in neural, hormonal, immunological, and other physiological functions as various forms of therapy for mental illness develop. We can expect psychoanalysis to continue telling us where to look among these functions and what to look for.

In this fine and highly original book, Dr. Stanley Palombo takes important, indeed, major steps to extend and reformulate psychoanalytic theory in such a way that it will become more effective therapeutically and more open to experimental validation. Palombo bases his extension on the emerging concepts of complex adaptive systems. A microbial community some two billion years ago was a coevolving complex adaptive system trying to thrive in its own world. Analyst and patient form a coevolving complex adaptive system as well. The interpretations of the analyst do, in fact, impinge on the self-reinforcing belief systems of the patient. Palombo calls such self-reinforcing whirlpools "attractors." In doing so, he has properly borrowed concepts from nonlinear dynamical systems. In the state spaces of such systems, states lie on trajectories that flow to subregions of the space and remain there—rather like water flowing down the sides of a mountain into different lakes. The lakes correspond to the attractors, the river drainage basins to the basins of attraction of the attractors.

Palombo formulates the concept of an "unconscious infantile attractor," a sustained belief and feeling system that closes upon itself and is relatively impervious to perturbations. The attractor is sustained by stimuli which are liable to be misinterpreted by the patient, and act as a "food set" for the attractor. Analysis proceeds as a coevolutionary process between analyst and patient in which the interpretations of the analyst lead to changes in the underlying beliefs and feelings that swirl persistently through the infantile attractor. Such changes can, hopefully, lead to the diminution of the malignant attractor and the emergence, often through phase transitionlike phenomena, of new attractors. As a successful analysis proceeds, Palombo suggests, the variety of options open to the patient increases, allowing new, more adaptive responses to his life situation.

A brief foreword is not the place to preface Palombo's entire thesis: The book accomplishes that task. A foreword is a place, however, to encourage analysts and other mental health professionals to read Palombo's work. More, it is the place to encourage a doubtful public to read and take note. The human mind is truly one of the most complex and awesome creations in the unfolding universe. As we develop more tools to visualize and measure brain and mental functioning, and more sophistication in the ways we learn, relearn and heal, analysis will reemerge as a central part of our efforts to understand and to help. Stanley Palombo's book is essential.

Stuart Kauffman, M.D.

PREFACE

There *is* something new under the sun in psychoanalysis. Despite the widespread notion that psychoanalytic theory is stale and unprofitable, it has adapted to the extraordinary developments in science since Freud's time. *The Emergent Ego* offers an approach to the psychoanalytic process based on the findings of the scientific revolution now in progress.

We are well into the second century of psychoanalysis. The world is different and psychoanalysis is different too. When I was a psychiatric resident, I was in awe of Freud's brilliance and limitless energy. I still am. Yet I knew even then that his ideas needed to be updated, as all theoretical concepts must be to survive. Herbert A. Simon's William James Lectures on artificial intelligence at Harvard in 1962 made me aware that new ways were at hand for representing the detailed operations of the psyche with much greater subtlety and precision than our rough verbal models of the time could offer.

An idea of Simon's became the germ of the theory of dreaming I developed in *Dreaming and Memory: A New Information-Processing Model* (1978). The new theory redefined the mechanism of condensation in dreams as an adaptive procedure, in conflict with the defensive activity of the dream censor described by Freud. *Dreaming and Memory* gave theoretical support to Freud's frequent observations of the constructive work done by the primary process, the apparently irrational aspect of mental life. These observations had found little support in Freud's "metapsychology," as he called his theory of mental activity. There the primary process served only as a mechanism for the discharge of accumulated psychic energy.

A better theory of the primary process would have broad implications for psychoanalytic treatment. I made an initial proposal to that effect in "The Primary Process: A Reconceptualization" (1985c). This was a beginning, but a detailed application to the clinical situation eluded me. Information theory and classical artificial intelligence did not seem powerful enough to bridge the considerable gap between Freudian metapsychology and the realities of psychoanalytic practice. Neither of these theories deals effectively with *process*. I felt that the necessary ideas were still missing from our theoretical equipment.

In the late 1980s, connectionist theories of artificial intelligence and chaos theory pointed in the right direction. Connectionism was helpful in updating my theory of dreaming (Palombo, 1992b). However, they were not adequate to fulfill the task of explaining how psychoanalytic treatment actually works. Stuart Kauffman's *Origins of Order: Self-Organization and Selection in Evolution* appeared in 1993. When I read this exciting and original book, I sensed that the conceptual key to the psychoanalytic process was at hand. I began to write *The Emergent Ego* almost immediately. While I was writing, I visited Stuart Kauffman at the Santa Fe Institute, where he worked with a group of creative scientists on complexity theory.

Kauffman took an interest in my project. He was taken by the idea that complexity theory could actually be applied to something as complex as the psychoanalytic process. We had many talks, particularly about the idea of the unconscious infantile attractor, which became the key to my model of unconscious influence on feelings and behavior. He graciously offered to try to keep me scientifically honest in my efforts to apply complexity theory and modern evolutionary theory to psychoanalytic treatment.

Many observations I had made over the years about the treatment process now came together. I saw a larger pattern into which my isolated observations could fit comfortably. Many questions about transference and countertransference that had puzzled me before seemed to answer themselves within the new framework.

The book that resulted is not a primer in psychoanalysis or psychoanalytic psychotherapy. It presupposes some prior knowledge about the aims and methods of psychoanalytic treatment. People in the mental health professions should have no difficulty with *The Emergent Ego*. But others should profit from it as well, particularly those who will not be discouraged if they miss a few details of the argument. A first-hand experience of any of Freud's writings would be helpful to the lay reader.

The mathematics is not difficult, even if it may seem unfamiliar at first in this context. Most of it can be skipped without damage to the overall thesis. My aim in including it was to satisfy readers who want to see for themselves what complexity theory is about. I have described modern evolutionary theory in what may seem unnecessary detail for a book on psychoanalysis. Modern evolutionary theory is still very new to most people, and quite different from traditional neo-Darwinism. It provides a new basis for understanding how one thing leads to another in the psychoanalytic process. This was something else I did not want the reader to have to take on faith, although the details are not essential to the argument.

Patience in reading *The Emergent Ego* will be rewarded. The major themes are approached from many angles. The larger picture will emerge for the reader who hangs in there.

Readers who think psychoanalysis is nothing but talk might profit from this book as well. I am thinking here of the scientists and philosophers of science who judge psychoanalysis today by the obsolescence of the scientific ideas Freud acquired in the nineteenth century. I challenge these intelligent people to take the time and do the work necessary to understand how psychoanalytic theory is advancing along with the rest of the scientific world.

I believe that the interaction between the psychoanalyst and the patient is one of the most complex activities that takes place between people. Fortunately, despite methodological problems caused by the need to preserve the confidentiality of the analytic relation, the course of an analysis can be followed in great detail.

In many ways, psychoanalysis can produce the most reliable data available anywhere for the study of complex processes. It is a matter of knowing what to look for and where to look for it.

I think of the *ego* as the highest level of organization of the mental contents of a mind or a psyche. Integrating disconnected contents into the ego is the business of psychoanalysis. The ego must reorganize to include its new components. The reorganized ego *emerges* from the integration and coordination of its component parts through a process of self-organization. These components are themselves organizations at a high level of *complexity*. Complexity is the state that results when many components interact to produce a collective output that is not a linear function of the input to the individual components, the whole being greater than the sum of its parts. *Coevolution* is the process through which interacting systems self-organize in order to adapt to one another. Psychoanalysis is a coevolutionary ecosystem in which the patient's self-knowledge is reorganized through his adaptation to the analyst's increasing knowledge of him.

My thanks for help in writing *The Emergent Ego* go first to Stuart Kauffman, who was always ready with comments and suggestions about the scientific content of the book and its psychological implications as well. Although Stuart read some parts of the manuscript several times over, I believe I may have slipped some scientific errors past him. I am solely responsible for any such mistakes that turn up.

Besides my talks with Stuart at the Santa Fe Institute, I spent many fruitful hours there with Murray Gell-Mann, Chris Langton, Andy Wuensche and countless others who were helpful to me in many ways. The Institute Staff gave me its enthusiastic support, although I was only a short-term visitor in Santa Fe.

John Gedo and James Grotstein read an early version of the manuscript. Their comments and suggestions encouraged me through the years it took to complete it. I discussed the book chapter by chapter with a study group of the Forum on Psychiatry and the Humanities of the Washington School of Psychiatry. I want to thank John Muller, Gordon Kirschner, Joseph Brent, Paul Kainen, Houston MacIntosh, John Stock, Wilfried ver Ecke, Macario Giraldo, Seymour Rubenfeld, and Marilyn Austin for their incisive comments. After each of our meetings I ran back to the computer to incorporate their suggestions for clarifying my thoughts and my prose.

Some of my ideas about change during the psychoanalytic process had emerged earlier in a study group of the Washington Psychoanalytic Society. Howard Benensohn, David Miller, David Joseph, David Levi, Stephen Rosenbloom, and Susan Lazar were members. Many other friends and colleagues cheered me on, among them Stanley Cavell, Bennett Simon, David Forrest, Ralph Wharton, Richard Friedman and Clarice Kestenbaum.

I want also to thank the many colleagues whose writing contributed to my understanding of the psychoanalytic process. Most are represented in the references, but sometimes I simply do not remember where a particular idea of mine originated. I apologize to anyone whose work I have neglected to cite, especially to those whose achievements were before their time, forgotten until reinvented by the Zeitgeist. Nevertheless, I believe a substantial fraction of the unattributed ideas are my own. What is most important to me is the organization of the ideas presented in *The Emergent Ego*. I claim the credit, if any is due, for that.

My wife Patricia cheerfully tolerated the expenditure of time required to write *The Emergent Ego*. Her encouragement was essential to me throughout.

1 THE EVOLUTIONARY PROCESS

Psychoanalysis as Science

The Emergent Ego is the first stage in an effort to reorganize the way we think about psychoanalysis. When I say *reorganize,* I have in mind putting together the old pieces in a new way. The objective is a more coherent theory about the psychoanalytic process and how it works. This is possible today because the sciences of complexity have given us a new perspective on the nature of the evolutionary process. Seen from the vantage point of complexity theory, a system evolves through an integrating series of reorganizations that raise it to a new level of structure and function. We will be looking at the progress of psychoanalytic treatment as an evolutionary process. (A reorganization may be the result of a random variation selected because it is better adapted to the system's environment. Or it may arise as a spontaneous outgrowth of unfolding changes in the existing organization of the system.)

We are concerned with the *therapeutic system* in psychoanalysis. This is the dyad composed of the patient and the analyst; and both patient and analyst are systems. There are systems within systems. We want to know how changes in the *ecosystem* formed by the patient and the analyst can increase the fitness of the

1

patient. My hypothesis is that adaptive change in the patient results from the *coevolution* of the therapeutic dyad in the analytic ecosystem. A better adapted ego emerges in the patient as the patient and the analyst become better adapted to one another.

The patient and the analyst are the components of the therapeutic ecosystem. Complexity theory explains how the interaction of the components of a system can give rise to the properties of the system as a whole. The system as a whole, in turn, is an environment that selects from among the properties of its components those that are fittest for maintaining the larger system. The new properties of the components lead to another round of interactions that may produce a higher level of organization in the ecosystem. The process is continuous. Over time, the component systems become better adapted to one another, and the ecosystem becomes more stable and efficient.

An increased level of adaptation by the patient is the goal of the psychoanalytic process. For the fitness of the patient to evolve, the ecosystem formed by the analytic partnership must also evolve.

Improvements in the functioning of the patient emerge when the patient's ego moves to a higher level of organization. The psychoanalytic process itself is the trajectory of the therapeutic ecosystem through a series of phase transitions.

Complexity is intrinsic to all systems that occur in nature. Nearly all objects and structures in the universe have affinities for other objects and structures at their own level of organization. The rule applies at all levels of structure, from particles and atoms to ideas and people. While there are affinities between objects at every level of organization, the nature of the affinity at each level is specific to that level. Because of these natural affinities, aggregates of objects and structures tend to be self-organizing.

The psychoanalytic process promotes the self-organizing properties of the ideas and feelings that make up the contents of the patient's mind. This happens in a hierarchical series of phase transitions. At first, only smaller disordered aggregates become organized. Then aggregates of these new organizations are themselves organized into larger units, and so on, for many generations. All of this happens in many separate and asynchronous trajectories that give rise to nonlinear change overall. In this way, the analytic process moves through a series of self-organizing events, each one based on the outcomes of many previous events at lower levels.

The application of complexity theory to the psychoanalytic process will extend the power of psychoanalytic theory to account for the full range of events, large and small, that characterize the therapeutic relationship. My main goal in this volume is to explain more clearly than has been possible before how the patient can benefit from taking part in this prolonged and intimate therapeutic interaction.

A secondary but not a trivial goal of this volume is to show that the familiar claim that psychoanalysis is "unscientific" is based on a naively reductionist bias. As we learn to conceptualize the details of the psychoanalytic process, it will become clear that psychoanalysis is a scientifically coherent procedure.

When I speak of the psychoanalytic process, I have in mind the psychoanalytic process as I describe it here. I believe this conforms closely to what one might call the standard model of psychoanalysis as practiced by most analysts. Analysts who are partisans of a particular theoretical viewpoint may not agree about this. I welcome their efforts to describe what they consider to be their own optimal therapeutic procedure at the level of detail I am attempting here. In that way we can devise hypotheses that can be tested without disrupting the analytic process.

Many other descriptions of the process have appeared before this one, each different from the others in some respects. I believe that the most valuable ideas of these models have been embedded within the model I present here. That has been my intention, at any rate, whether it has been carried out successfully or not.

My approach to the psychoanalytic process will take some readers through territory they may find unfamiliar to them. To orient those readers, let me say that my basic viewpoint arises from a theoretical tradition found within the mainstream of psychoanalytic theory. This tradition had its first clear statement as the principle of Eros in Freud's *Beyond the Pleasure Principle* (1920).

Eros for Freud was the life instinct that binds things together in the universe, contrary to the general entropic drift toward disorder. Nunberg (1931) wrote of a *synthetic function* of the ego that brings about the unification of ego operations. This function acts in a way that is similar to Freud's life instinct. Nunberg removed this synthetic function from the Freudian id, and assigned it to the ego.

Hendrick (1943) wrote of a drive to master the environment, White (1953) of a drive toward competence and efficacy. Both require synthetic activity. Fairbairn (1958) said: "I consider that the term 'analysis' as a description of psycho-analytic treatment is really a misnomer, and that *the chief aim of psycho-analytic treatment is to promote a maximum 'synthesis' of the structures into which the original ego has been split, in the setting of a therapeutic relationship with the analyst*" (p. 380; emphasis in the original).

Although I believe that Fairbairn's ideas about the relation of the ego to its various parts are too simple, I can only agree with him that psychoanalysis is a process of synthesis. Today, we can do a better job of explaining how the synthesis occurs. The synthesizing function of the psychoanalytic process is the result of its self-organizing and emergent properties. These properties are the subject matter of complexity theory.

The new stage in the development of scientific self-consciousness marked by complexity theory should be a cause for excitement among psychoanalysts. Science today is moving away from the reductionism that blunted its usefulness to psychoanalytic theory in the past. Biology is going beyond the molecular level to a new understanding of the whole organism and its detailed development through self-organizing events.

Questions of form, structure, coordination, and adaptation have come to the fore again in the life sciences. Technological and mathematical tools are now available for the analysis of the organism as a self-maintaining process rather than a static entity. As cognitive psychology and the neurosciences converge, new discoveries are being made that are narrowing the gap between the human mind and the human body.

Events determined by many interacting causes can be understood in a new and more rigorous way. Although not predictable through a simple mapping of cause into effect, they form expectable patterns as they extend in time and space. The psychoanalytic process is an expectable pattern that can be understood in these terms.

Science is now in a much better position to learn from psychoanalysis than it has been in the past. The wealth of data generated by the analyst's interaction with the patient can be organized and examined in new ways. These data illuminate the patient's most urgent and most personal concerns. The stakes are high in analysis. At risk is the ultimate success and quality of the patient's emotional life. Analysis requires a mutual commitment to the completion of the process, a deep commitment often matched in human life only in the most intimate of family relationships. These are matters of the greatest scientific interest.

The conditions of an analysis are well controlled for the observation of an interaction of such intensity and longevity. With the development of complexity theory, the data of psychoanalysis can be used to study interactions between people at very high levels of seriousness and subtlety. The data generated by the psychoanalytic process are the ideal material for these new theoretical tools to work on. Psychoanalysis is a natural laboratory of complex interactions.

For science to give anything like a *complete* account of the world, it has to apply the same vision to the most complex systems as to the simplest units of matter and energy. Human minds and brains are the most complex systems we know of. Murray Gell-Mann, the discoverer of the quark, is a Nobel laureate in physics (1969), and cofounder of the Santa Fe Institute. As he says (1994): "The point is that human psychology, while no doubt derivable in principle from neurophysiology, the endocrinology of neurotransmitters, and so forth—is also worth studying at its own level. Many people believe, as I do, that when staircases are constructed between psychology and biology, the best strategy is to work from the top down and from the bottom up" (p. 117).

The psychoanalytic process is near the top of this ladder. It offers the best perspective we have on the detailed workings of the most complex natural system in the physical universe that we know. The use of complexity theory to refine the practice of psychoanalysis should provide concrete therapeutic benefits for many people who now suffer from mental illness. It should also show the value of applying complexity theory to concrete problems in everyday life.

How Evolution Has Evolved

Trivial processes repeat themselves without change. We are concerned here with the kind of process that causes change, especially unanticipated change. The psychoanalyst works with the goal of relieving his patient's suffering, but the way in which this goal is achieved is unique to every patient. The analyst has a set of broad expectations for the analysis, and many techniques for dealing with the patient's resistance to painful conflicts. But he knows very little in advance about how the fine structure of the analytic interaction will mesh with his broad expectations.

For the patient, the changes that unfold as he discovers his unconscious wishes and fantasies are necessarily unanticipated. One source of resistance in the patient is his belief that the analyst knows exactly what will happen, and for that reason is in control of the analysis. What the patient says will not matter. The analyst must be clear that he does not know what the patient is going to say and does not know the meaning of what he actually says until the analytic process has revealed it to both of them.

The general term for a process that brings about unanticipated change is *evolution*. For many reasons, organic evolution has become the scientific paradigm for the evolutionary process in all its forms. Mendel's discovery of units of inheritance, later to be identified as the genes, gave organic evolution an advantage over other kinds of evolutionary systems. The mechanism of the genes is amenable to mathematical analysis. That makes for hard science.

Darwin's most concise definition of evolution was "descent with modification." Durham (1991), a leading cultural anthropologist, points out that:

> The success of this definition through the years—itself an impressive cultural evolutionary phenomenon—can be attributed to three of its implications. First, the phrase has general applicability: it implies that many things can evolve, not just the species of Darwin's original concern. Second, the phrase implies derivation with change or "modification" but does not presuppose any particular form or process of change. It encompasses a very large set of possible processes, not simply the natural selection that Darwin

emphasized. Third, the phrase seems to suggest nearly the full set of "systems requirements" for evolution in any given system [pp. 21–22].

Complexity theory has created a common ground for theories of organic evolution and evolution in other spheres. The psychoanalytic process is one of these other spheres. "Descent with modification" fits the psychoanalytic treatment process very snugly. In the chapters that follow I will develop the argument that psychoanalysis is an evolutionary process, and that many useful and important consequences follow from that recognition. My examples will be drawn from recent advances in the theory of organic evolution and the broadening scope of evolutionary theory in its more inclusive forms. In later chapters I will apply these ideas to some puzzling questions about the nature of the psychoanalytic process.

We will see that the psychoanalytic partners form a loosely coupled self-organizing ecosystem. The components of the ecosystem, in turn, are two tightly coupled self-organizing systems. Patient and analyst are each coevolving within the analytic ecosystem. These terms will be clarified and elaborated as we go on.

The universe itself is an evolving self-organized system. We are its components and its descendants, with modification. The big bang is the moment when the natural history of self-organizing systems and their evolution begins.

When the universe suddenly expanded, a homogeneous concentration of radiation began to cool. Matter appeared in simple and then more complex forms. A variety of new, separate, and distinct entities and combinations of entities condensed out of the cosmic radiation. New kinds of objects were formed at every scale by the combinatorial properties of the already existing objects that preceded them.

The development of more intricate structure, culminating in the life forms on our planet (and most likely others) added to the *information content* of the expanding universe. To what extent this continuing creation of new information balances the rise in entropy caused by the dispersion of the original radiation of the big bang is a matter of speculation. The story of complexification at the cosmic level is quite fascinating. It sets the stage for the emergence of life and the process of organic evolution (Schroedinger, 1944; Prigogine and Stengers, 1984; Gell-Mann, 1994).

For our purposes, however, it will be enough to begin the story of psychoanalysis as evolution with the beginnings of organic evolution. This is a richer paradigm for the kind of change that forms the increasingly complex world we belong to.

For people whose ideas on this subject were acquired a generation ago, the idea of evolution evokes images of organisms changing passively, over many eons, at much less than glacial speed. One might wonder how a process so remote from the brief lives of individual people could have anything to do with psychoanalysis.

During the last 25 years the evolution of evolutionary theory has accelerated dramatically (Depew and Weber, 1995). Many of Darwin's original ideas have survived, but others have gone the way of the dinosaurs. As the term is used today, evolution can refer to dynamic processes that operate on the scales of the very large and the very small, including the scale of our own everyday lives. Biological evolution is no longer the entire story of evolution.

Three levels of evolutionary research are now going on. On the first, we have research on organic evolution within the traditional Darwinian framework. Much remains to be learned about the way that change occurs at random by mutation and genetic recombinations in individuals. Some changes can survive because the individuals that carry them are better adapted to the chance alterations of climate and geology. In what Depew and Weber (1995) call the Newtonian framework, the organism is seen as a passive object of external forces. It has no influence on the course of events. For example, when some individuals of a species migrate to a new geographical area, in the Newtonian framework they are traditionally described as having become isolated from the rest of their species. One can just as easily see them as having selected themselves for the new conditions they encounter.

Second, modern theories of biological evolution emphasize the role of processes of self-organization in the lives of individuals and species. A mutation must be adapted to the existing organization of the genome it appears in before its phenotype has the chance to interact with the external world (Kauffman, 1993). Each newly appearing cell type in evolution must have adapted to the organization of tissues that surround it (Buss, 1987). The evolution of life before the arrival of the genetic code could only have been built from assemblies of self-organized and self-maintaining autocatalytic systems of macromolecules (Kauffman, 1993).

Third, modern evolutionary theory has expanded from this biological base to become the science of change in complex adaptive systems (CASs) generally. All living individuals are complex adaptive systems. However, many other kinds of CASs, both organic (anthills, for example) and man made (computer simulations) have features that overlap with but do not exactly replicate those of an organism. These systems evolve, however, on time scales running from minutes to eons.

Traditional Darwinian evolutionary theory and the more complexity-oriented modern view of biological evolution overlap in many ways. The modern view of biological evolution and the modern view of evolution in general overlap too. Nevertheless, controversy about whether traditional Darwinian evolution and the general modern evolutionary theory have much in common still thrives (Depew and Weber, 1995). Many traditionalists are skeptical, even those like John Maynard Smith (1982, 1994), whose contributions have stimulated much of the modern work on biological evolution. Fortunately, this debate has little significance for our purposes here. Psychoanalytic theory can profit from models developed at all three levels of evolutionary research.

On the spectrum of evolving CASs, natural life forms are bracketed on one side by adaptive computer programs (Holland, 1975, 1996; Lindgren, 1992; Ray, 1992, 1994; Koza, 1992, 1994). On the other side are systems made up of many organisms, like the slime molds, the colonies of social insects, and our own economic and social systems (Prigogine and Stengers, 1984; Gumerman and Gell-Mann, 1994). These complex entities all have interacting parts that exert a mutual influence. They evolve by adapting to environmental pressures through a change in the arrangement of these parts.

Natural selection seemed to Darwin to work most effectively on the scale of very small and gradual change, such as he believed he had observed on his famous trip to the Galapagos (Darwin, 1859; Dawkins, 1976; Weiner, 1994). In Darwin's own view, gradualism was a strong antidote to religious beliefs that called for the sudden and arbitrary intervention of supernatural forces. This idea goes back at least to Lucretius in the first century B.C. and to the pre-Socratic philosophers centuries before that.

It seemed to Darwin, and to many of his followers as well, that the slower were the changes in natural forms, the less need there would be for a designer with superhuman skills and intelligence. Some traditional Darwinians today still seem to feel that the gradualist doctrine is a bulwark against the claims of religious fundamentalists. However, Darwin's gradualism had a major problem from the beginning. The fossil record does not support it.

The fossil remains of a typical species appear suddenly, without transitional types, last for millions of years with little change, and then disappear with equal suddenness. Darwinian gradualists explained this pattern as an accident caused by frequent gaps in the fossil record. To accept this explanation, however, either in Darwin's time or now, one would have to make quite a leap of faith. One would have to believe that the random gaps in the record had eliminated all the transitional forms but spared the stable periods in the histories of every species.

Gradualism does not help to explain the radiation of many new species from a common ancestor after a mass extinction. If gradualism were the rule, the selection of many different descendants in a short period would have implied a sudden decomposition of the environment into isolated compartments. That did not happen.

The case for gradualism as an overriding principle of evolution has also been weakened in recent years by the detailed field-work of traditional Darwinians. One example is the study of the Galapagos finches and their food sources (Grant and Grant, 1992; Weiner, 1994) over nearly two decades. This work shows that natural selection causes rapid population shifts even during year-to-year fluctuations in the climate. Not only does the genetic makeup of each species change rapidly with environmental conditions, but the Grants also found an exchange of genes by related species during a major upheaval in the food supply.

Sudden changes in the environment can shift the direction of the prevailing selection pressure. When this happens, the hybridization of related species can increase the variation in the genome population. This creates an opportunity for new phenotypes to escape the adverse selection facing the existing species. A dramatic case of adaptive hybridization occurred in the Galapagos after the floods of 1983.

Thirteen closely related species of finches share a set of overlapping niches on the islands. Even so, hybrids in the Galapagos are both rare and unlikely to thrive when the weather is dry, as it usually is. After the floods caused by the super-Niño of 1983, however, cross-species matings markedly increased. Since then, two different new hybrid populations have bred more successfully than their original ancestral species.

That two species would adapt in hard times by hybridization is not what one would be led to expect by the traditional Darwinian focus on the individual organism. The Grants report that the Galapagos finches chose their mates from a neighboring species only under very harsh conditions. The existing species were at a severe disadvantage under these circumstances. Increasing genetic variation was the one possible way out of an evolutionary trap. This mating across species could not have been the effect of a shortage of mates. During the early stages of hybridization only one of each cross-mating pair of species was significantly diminished in its numbers. The intact species had its usual choice of mates within its own species. Moreover, members of the cross-mating species do not mate when paired in captivity.

The birds acted as evolutionary agents within a system larger than either the individual or the species. It is not likely that the individual birds were aware that they were increasing the numbers of their own progeny by violating the normal species boundaries. Their ability to make this choice was the result of their evolutionary histories, not their individual experience. The cross-breeding finches acted as if they were searching the gene pool in the entire ecosystem to find greater genetic variation.

The finches of the Galapagos vividly affirm the more general observation that individuals and species do not evolve in isolation. They are driven by the pressure of interactions with other members of the ecosystems they inhabit. Evolution in nature is the *coevolution* of species interacting with one another (Ehrlich and Raven, 1964).

This work also sheds some badly needed light on the origins of new species (a topic Darwin did not discuss in any detail). The systematic observation of the Galapagos finches shows that natural selection makes finer distinctions than anyone knew. Even differences of half a millimeter in the width of a finch's beak can alter the kinds of seed it can crack open and feed on. This difference can be selected for within a single generation, as dramatic shifts in rainfall change the plant population on the islands. At the same time, this work shows that natural selection of random variation by itself may not account for everything that changes. The finch's choice of an out-of-species mate when food is short is difficult to view as a random increase in the pool of variations from which the selection will be made.

The work of the Grants makes it clear that biological evolution can be rapid and wildly fluctuating, even in vertebrates. Then why is the fossil record static for the most part? This is not an easy question to answer. A common explanation is that changes in the environment fluctuate over the near term, causing changes in the phenotype to cycle through a narrow range that leaves little trace in the fossil record. This may be the case in the Galapagos, at least as far as the selection of successful beak sizes is concerned.

If the phenotype is fluctuating, then the genotype must be fluctuating too. However, it does not follow that when an earlier phenotypic form is reconstituted in response to a shift in the environment, the earlier genotype is restored as an exact copy. Adaptively neutral changes in the genotype can accumulate while the phenotype fluctuates around a stable norm. The genotype transformed in this way may be primed for speciation, given a new fluctuation in environmental conditions, though no stable phenotypic change has been evident.

Accumulated small changes in the genotype can lead to species level changes in the phenotype. This is more likely to be the result of nonlinear changes in organizational structure than a simple summation of changes that reach and cross over a fixed threshold. In the same way, many small, unremarkable changes within the psychoanalytic patient interact within him to produce a large, noticeable change in his adaptation to the analysis and to the outside world. In order to understand how change occurs in psychoanalysis, we need to understand how change takes place in naturally evolving systems generally.

In 1972, Eldredge and Gould proposed their theory of *punctuated equilibrium* (Eldredge and Gould, 1972). Their theory suggested that, in general, evolution swings from short periods of rapid and extensive change to much longer periods of relative stability or stasis. They wrote:

> Paleontology's view of speciation has been dominated by the picture of "phyletic gradualism." It holds that new species arise from the slow and steady transformation of entire populations. Under its influence, we seek unbroken fossil series linking two forms by insensible graduation as the only complete mirror of Darwinian processes; we ascribe all breaks to imperfections in the record.
>
> The theory of an allopatric (or geographic) basis for speciation suggests a different interpretation of the paleontological data. If new species arose very rapidly in small, peripherally isolated populations, then the great expectation of finely graded fossil sequences is a chimera. A new species does not evolve in the homeland of its ancestors; it does not arise from the slow transformation of all its forebears. Most breaks in the fossil record are real.
>
> The history of life is more adequately represented by a picture of "punctuated equilibria" than by the notion of phyletic gradualism. The history of evolution is not one of stately unfolding, but a story of homeostatic equilibria, disturbed only "rarely" (rather often in the fullness of time) by rapid and episodic events of speciation [p. 84].

Eldredge and Gould took the fossil record at face value. They explained the lack of transitional forms in the record by postulating very brief periods of new species formation followed by much longer periods of stasis. The transitional forms would be missing because the periods in which they existed were too short to leave an impression in the record.

According to their theory, new species formation, *speciation*, results from the sudden and rapid branching of an older line. Eldredge and Gould adopted Mayr's (1963) idea that speciation takes place primarily in small peripheral groups that have drifted away from their ancestral populations. Novel environmental conditions in these regions would lead to rapid change through natural selection.

The individuals of the peripheral group would be selected for genetic changes that improve their adaptation to the new setting. Because of the misfit between the ancestral genes and the new conditions, the selection of new forms would run its course quite rapidly. Then, when the optimally adapted new species was formed, it would stabilize and maintain its new genotype with little alteration.

While abandoning gradualism, Eldredge and Gould held to the traditional assumption that evolutionary change comes only when new external events create new pressure. A successful genotype would remain static as long as external conditions continued to be stable.

However, it is not likely that any genotype could remain static for millions of years. Either it would have to be biochemically inert or else all more adaptive mutations and genetic recombinations would have to be extinguished by adverse selection. A more plausible explanation would be that genotypic changes neutral to selection in the short term are accumulating throughout the stable period. One thinks here of the reorganization of genetic material via recombination, gene jumping, the reordering of operons and other mechanisms.

Multicelled animals whose descendants are still living today first appeared in a sudden eruption of diverse phyla and classes about 550 million years ago, during the Cambrian era. The Cambrian explosion, as it is called, spread in a (geologically) short time to cover the entire planet. The fauna of the Cambrian included more than a dozen now extinct phyla and at least that many classes of extinct arthropods (jointed invertebrates). Only four classes of arthropods have survived to modern times, although they now include 80 percent of the world's animals.

The conventional view in paleontology is that the explosion occurred because the ecology of the Cambrian was wide open. There were many empty environmental niches and no competitors for the multicellular animals. The diversity among the new animals would have increased until all the niches were filled. Then the less fit species would have been eliminated.

However, the earliest multicellular organisms, the *ediacara* of 700 million years ago, were an evolutionary dead end. Despite a lack of competition, they did not either diversify or thrive. Gould (1989) also points out that the habitats of the Cambrian fauna were not at all diverse (as they should have been according to his allopatric theory of speciation). These metazoan forms evolved on the muddy bottoms of shallow bodies of water. Yet the extraordinary variety of these animals remained quite stable in this narrow ecology for tens of millions of years.

In his more recent work, Gould (1989) has suggested that the genetic organization of the pre-Cambrian fauna affected the Cambrian explosion as much as the environmental opportunities did. He quotes Stuart Kauffman's idea that the potential for major forms of diversification would have to decrease over time as complex adaptive systems evolve.

Kauffman had argued that, as time goes by, organisms become better adapted by elaborating on their already successful basic structural blueprints, rather than by changing their basic design features. Only a 1.6 percent genetic difference accounts for the enormous adaptational differences between chimpanzees and modern humans, for example. Nevertheless, Gould did not go on to examine the internal changes in genetic structures that both limit and focus the opportunities for genetic variation. (More of this later.)

Manfred Eigen (Nobel Prize, 1967) modeled the heightening of natural selection through the self-organization of a genome and its family of mutants. Eigen (Eigen, McCaskill, and Schuster, 1988) suggested that what we usually call a species contains a spectrum of genotypes that differ slightly from the *wild type*. The wild type is the most common of these types, although it may represent only a small fraction of the total number of individual genomes. Because its genetic composition is the average by consensus of the compositions of all the other genome types, the wild type is presumed to be their source. Eigen calls this ensemble of closely related genome types a *quasi-species*. The quasi-species distribution was discovered in RNA viruses by Weissman's group (Domingo, Sabo, Tanaguchi, and Weissmann, 1978).

Eigen (1992) says:

The generation of a superior mutant, which was left to pure chance in the neo-Darwinian model, is now seen to be determined by the following causal chain.

[1] Mutants closely related to the wild type arise primarily by erroneous copying of the wild type itself. A distribution develops, in which close relatives of the wild type appear most frequently.

[2] Selective advantage can generally be expected only for relatively large mutation jumps. These cannot occur frequently by statistical fluctuation.

[3] The initial [adaptive] value-free distribution is modified by selection of preferred states within the quasi-species distribution. Functionally competent mutants, whose selection values come close to that of the wild type (though remaining below it), reach far higher population numbers than those that are functionally ineffective.

[4] An asymmetric spectrum of mutants builds up, in which mutants far removed from the wild type arise successively from intermediates. The population in such a chain of mutants is influenced decisively by the structure of the value landscape.

[5] The value landscape consists of connected plains, hills and mountain ranges. In the mountain ranges, the mutant spectrum is widely scattered, and along ridges even distant relatives of the wild type appear with finite frequency.

[6] It is precisely in the mountainous regions that further selectively superior mutants can be expected. As soon as one of these turns up on the periphery of the mutant spectrum, the established ensemble collapses. A new ensemble builds up around the superior mutant, which thus takes over the role of the wild type.

[7] The occupation of the ridges of the value mountains by efficient mutants steers the process of evolution systematically in the direction in which a higher peak is expected. This circumvents the need to try out blindly a vast number of valueless sequences [p. 25].

Here Eigen is describing the priming of a population of genomes for species change. His model does not seem to depend on the reorganization of individual genomes for its power, but this may be the explanation for the appearance of "preferred states" at step 3 and their role in step 7. When a superior mutant appears, "The existing quasi-species is destabilized; it 'evapo-rates', only to 'condense' again in a different part of the sequence space. Evolution can thus be likened to a succession of phase transitions" (Eigen, 1992, p. 29).

The adaptive landscape described by Eigen (Figure 1.1) is a good model for the associative process in psychoanalysis. Think of the patient's conscious thought, yet uninfluenced by the ana-lyst, as the wild type of the virus. The emotional intensity of the thought is its adaptive value in the analytic ecosystem. Let us call this value the *altitude* of the thought. The patient's defenses act like the force of gravity, limiting the altitude of his expression.

Figure 1.1. The adaptive landscape of a quasi-species. (From Eigen, 1992, p. 99 in *Steps Towards Life*. Reprinted by permission of Oxford University Press.)

An interaction with the analyst brings new ideas to the patient's mind. These are close relatives of the wild type. Their adaptive value at first is close to that of the wild type, perhaps a little lower. One or more of these new ideas is selected for its greater associative productivity, as judged by both the patient and the analyst. This new idea becomes the focus for further association.

As the process of association and selection continues, guided by the mutual interest of the analytic partners, the force of the patient's defenses may weaken. That is, the analytic discourse may enter territory not yet known to the patient's conscious mind, not familiar to him, not easy for him to control. The diminished gravity of the defenses raises the altitude of the discourse. More of the patient's spontaneous feeling enters into it.

A new idea takes form in the patient's mind when the discourse is elevated in this way. Such an idea supplants the original one as an independent element in his thinking. In Eigen's terms, the original wild type is supplanted. The quasi-species of conscious thought evaporate and recondense at a higher level of affect.

Of course, what we are calling the wild type in the patient's mind is not really wild at all. It is a type selected by his defenses because it was too tame to disturb the old balance of power between conflicting wishes. The new idea reorganizes the patient's consciousness by opening links to related ideas kept out of mind by his defenses.

In biological coevolution, a change in one component species of an ecosystem is the result of reciprocal changes in the genes of that species and of others that share the same environment. In psychoanalysis, a change in the patient or the analyst is the result of reciprocal changes in both the intrapsychic and interpersonal spheres. In particular, the patient's mental contents change as the contents of the analytic discourse change.

Social scientists have traditionally been cautious about applying models of evolutionary change like these to processes in which individual human beings are the atomic components of larger systems. There are several reasons for this caution. One is that the mechanisms of biological evolution, as they had been traditionally defined, seemed quite remote from any actual source of cultural or political change.

Compared with the vast discontinuities of scale in biological evolution, the scale of human life and history is compact and coherent. We do not intuitively link genetic change at the molecular level with historical events like Michelangelo's painting of the Sistine Chapel or the demise of the Soviet Union. At the larger end of the scale, the vast expanse of geological time is also quite remote from our own lives and acts.

When evolution was viewed only from a traditional Darwinian point of view, its relevance to extremely complex events that take place in a fraction of a human lifetime may have seemed doubtful. That has been changed now by the discovery that the common properties of complex systems, especially their tendencies to evolve, are similar at all scales of time and space, including the human scale.

A second and perhaps more important reason for caution about evolution as a model for change in social systems was the lack of an inner dynamic in traditional Darwinian models. The early punctuated equilibrium model followed the tradition in emphasizing outside pressure as the source of change. According to these theories, external events were the only causes of change in organisms. The organisms themselves were passive vehicles for the change.

Social scientists and humanists saw biological evolution as contrasting sharply with human events, where complex decisions are made by human agents, both individually and in large and small groups. However, organisms and people are complex adaptive systems. They are agents. They have the dynamic properties that emerge from the nonlinear interactions among their various parts. Simple models of these interactions, which are difficult to isolate and study in the natural world, have been successfully simulated on the computer for some years now. Agency is not an exclusive function of humans.

Artificial organisms in their simulated environments have evolved into new and better adapted forms simply by random mutation and selection. How these forms evolved could not have been predicted from a knowledge of the programs before they were run (e.g., Lindgren, 1992; Ray, 1992, 1994; Koza, 1994).

This work shows that evolution by mutation and natural selection is possible without novel or stressful input from the environment. Only the presence of the viable forms brought into existence by the mutations (i.e., the quasi-species) was needed to keep things going. Thus, the dynamic properties of complex adaptive systems offer an explanation for punctuated equilibrium that does not depend on ad hoc events going on in the outside world.

Another reason for caution among social scientists has been methodological. There is no distinct unit of cultural transmission, equivalent to the gene, that can be easily recognized and analyzed mathematically. Progress in quantifying cultural evolution is being made slowly. New studies of individual and cultural memory have helped. Detailed comparisons of genetic and cultural transmission (Durham, 1991) show that this problem is much more tractable than it seemed in the past.

There is a vast anthropological literature on cultural evolution. This work has anticipated much of modern evolutionary theory. Campbell (1965) says, for example, "the analogy to cultural accumulations [is not from] organic evolution per se, but from a general model [of evolutionary change] . . . for which organic evolution is but one instance" (p. 26, quoted in Durham, 1991, p. 187).

Durham argues cogently that cultural evolution and biological evolution run on parallel tracks, each of them driven by variation and selection. Cultural evolution may interact with biological evolution to enhance the effects of genetic change, or, less often, to oppose them. Cultural evolution may also have its own agenda, neutral to biology. The circumstances decide. Durham's analysis, accompanied as it is by excellent case studies, is quite compelling.

Following Dawkins (1982), Durham refers to the unit of transmission in cultural evolution as a *meme*. A meme is said by Dawkins to be "a unit of information residing in a brain. . . . This is to distinguish it from its phenotypic effects, which are its consequences in the outside world" (p. 109). A meme is apparently a unit of information at any organizational scale or level, unlike a gene, whose level is fixed. This gives the term an advantage for the description of emerging hierarchical organizations in a patient's mind during a psychoanalysis.

It makes sense to think of psychoanalysis as a special case of social or cultural change. The psychoanalytic process could be analyzed as a form of cultural evolution, grounding it in the theory of the cultural evolutionists. One important aspect of cultural evolution is paradigmatic for psychoanalysis. That is the influence by successful carriers of a cultural trait on the criteria used by their successors for the selection of other traits in the future. Psychoanalysis depends on this modification of criteria in the patient as the bootstrapping factor that leads him toward independence from the analyst. The patient is a slightly different person after each phase transitional reorganization.

However, there are also good reasons not to model the psychoanalytic process after cultural evolution. Cultural evolutionary theory is largely concerned with the influence of a few cultural leaders on their many followers. Identifying the transmitters and the conditions under which they transmit can be a complicated problem. This oblique form of cultural transmission is very different from the direct conveyance of genetic influence. Psychoanalysis is closer to the genetic model in this respect.

Influence in the psychoanalytic process can be exerted only by the two participants. The primary influencer and the primary influencee are designated by the nature of the process. What is of special interest is the need for the patient to influence the analyst to enable the analyst to help him. The fine structure of their mutual interaction is not a phenomenon that can be approached with the statistical tools of cultural anthropology. Complexity theory, with its ties to the evolutionary process in biology, offers a more useful technique.

Psychoanalysis as an Evolutionary Process

Complexity theory offers an approach to the question of units of evolutionary change that applies equally well to biological and social systems. Instead of trying to isolate a unit of transmitted substance like the gene, the theory focuses on the elements of the process of change itself, the events that cause a phase transitional reorganization. These events are critical to cultural and organic evolution alike, and to the psychoanalytic process.

Many theorists have been distracted from the study of the evolutionary process as a process by the conceptual shortcut supplied by the gene. Two important but less quantifiable influences on evolution, the development of the embryo and the interactions of organisms with each other, were put on the back burner. They were considered inconsequential when compared with the dominant role of the genes. The doctrine of gradualism decreed that there were no describable macroscopic *events* during evolutionary change, in any case. When the discoveries of Mendel were synthesized with Darwinian theory, it seemed that the phenotypic expression of the gene was a mere afterthought to the transmission of the gene. Events leading to the reorganization of the genome in evolution could be ignored. So too could the reorganization itself. The punctuated equilibrium theory, with its emphasis on the events of speciation and extinction, was the first serious threat to this dogma.

When we look at the sequence of complex adaptive systems from the least to the most complex, two striking discontinuities seem to occur at the level of human experience. One is the change from a very slow transmission of information, via the genes, to a very rapid transmission via cultural symbols and artifacts. The other is the shift from tightly coupled systems, such as the individual organism, to more loosely coupled systems, like the society or culture. Our belief in the uniqueness of human beings is often motivated by the mystery surrounding these discontinuities and their convergence in human life. (Narcissistic anthropocentrism doesn't explain everything.)

The psychoanalytic process takes place just at the focal point of this convergence. Psychoanalysts work where genetic and cultural influences meet, where the development of the individual and the development of familial and social groups intersect. If we wish to see what happens in the passage across these discontinuities, the passage that only human beings have made, psychoanalysis is a convenient place to look.

When social organizations are studied in the usual way, individual people are often treated as interchangeable atomic units, rather than as complex systems in their own right. In the study of individual development, on the other hand, social influences have often been understood primarily as external stimuli coming from outside the system under study. Traditional psychoanalytic theory followed this path. It saw the interventions of the analyst as stimuli coming from the outside, into the patient's psyche. The interactions between the patient and the analyst were not conceived as internal to a larger system with a structure that included them both.

What was missing here was the idea that the psyche of the patient on the one hand and the therapeutic relationship on the other are separate organizations at different but interacting levels of complexity. Therapeutic change results when the systems at these two levels interact. An inner reorganization of the patient's discordant parts comes about as the interactive role he takes in the analytic relationship is refined and reshaped. This is not something done by the analyst to the patient. It follows from the reorganization of the relationship as that takes place at many stages of the process.

The reciprocal effects of the patient's intrapsychic development and his interaction with the analyst occur in a setting of intimacy. Analytic treatment is a process of unfolding inner change, driven by the mutual adaptation of the patient and the analyst. As the patient and the analyst become better connected, the patient's mental organization becomes more effectively organized. As his mental structures become better connected, the patient becomes better able to adapt, both inside and outside the analysis.

One major task of the new connections created in analysis is to circumvent the pathological attractors that add such bitter intensity to the patient's emotional life. We will have much to say, further on, about these attractors. They funnel the patient's broad experience of life into small, isolated cells of morbid fantasy. New connections are needed to replace the primitive ties that close off the elements of these attractors from the current realities of the patient's world.

Psychoanalysis is a laboratory for the structure and evolution of human relationships as they change over time. Compared with the events of daily life, the conditions that frame the interaction of the patient and the analyst are unusually well controlled. Time, place, frequency, and functional roles are held as nearly constant as possible. Under these conditions, the exploration of the internal structure of the patient can proceed with a thoroughness not otherwise possible.

Kauffman's ideas in *The Origins of Order: Self-Organization and Selection in Evolution* (1993) offered a coherent account of the emergence of higher levels of organization from the interactions at lower levels. This seemed to me to be *the* most important feature of psychoanalytic treatment. Yet it had not been formulated clearly by psychoanalysts as an issue, let alone understood.

Kauffman's general point of view in *The Origins of Order* can be gathered from this condensed summary paragraph:

> In this book, therefore, I have tried to take steps toward characterizing the interaction of selection and self-organization. To some great extent, evolution is a complex combinatorial optimization process in each of the coevolving species in a linked ecosystem, where the landscape of each actor is deformed as the others move. Within each organism, conflicting constraints yield a rugged fitness landscape graced with many peaks, ridges and valleys. Two major alternative limitations to selection exist. First, selection is limited by the structure of the fitness landscape on which it acts; in many landscapes, as the organisms under selection grow more complex, the attainable optima fall toward the average features of the class of systems on which selection is acting. Second, on any landscape, a mutation–selection balance is struck; beyond some level of complexity, selection cannot hold an adapting population at the high peaks of the landscape, and the population then falls toward the average properties of the underlying class of systems. Both limitations suggest that, in sufficiently complex systems, much of the order found is that spontaneously present in the class of systems under selection. Therefore I have made bold to suggest that much of the order seen in organisms is precisely the spontaneous order in the systems of which we are composed [p. 644].

The implications of this statement will be explored in detail as we go on. Self-organization, or spontaneous order, has been the most significant missing ingredient in psychoanalytic theory, as it had been in evolutionary theory and every comprehensive scientific theory put forward before the latter part of this century.

Freud's main idea about the analytic process was simple. He thought the interpretations of the analyst would remove the barriers in the patient's mind against his awareness of his repressed

wishes. The patient's executive ego would then use this information to seek out the satisfaction of these wishes in a mature and
realistic way. This would create a restructuring from the top down,
made possible by the availability of psychic energy released when
the repression was dissolved. The restructuring itself would take
place within the patient's ego, using the feelings and memories
liberated from his unconscious. The repressed wishes would be
released along with the psychic energy that supplied the fuel for
the patient's ego. The patient's ego would then take over and
integrate the new material into itself.

In my clinical work, however, I saw the reorganization
needed for lasting change at this level of complexity taking place
both in the analytic relationship and in the psyche of the patient.
When the patient's unconscious wishes were opened to mutual
scrutiny, the patient's view of the analysis and of his way of interacting with the analyst were able to change. Corresponding
changes took place in the analyst's image of the patient. As the
analytic interaction was modified, the patient's inner representations of himself and the analyst were reorganized into more realistic schemata.

The patient's outlook on life went through a series of small
and large jumps. His associations to the repressed wishes during
the analytic hours and the content of his dreams were connected
in a feedback cycle that lasted through many sessions. I was particularly struck by the way that small bits of insight assembled themselves into larger and larger structures, organizing the patient's
memory of events into a graded hierarchy. This process seemed
to work from the bottom up.

Many analysts have been dissatisfied with the one-sidedness
of Freud's formulation. Important contributions had been made
since his death in 1939. Yet no unified theory has emerged to
account for the bottom up aspects of the analytic process. This
is not a surprise. Although coherent bottom up theories existed
in individual sciences in 1939, the idea that bottom up growth
was a feature of all natural processes was still ahead.

Kauffman was proposing a bottom up theory that made sense
at all scales in biology, from simple molecules to highly complex
organisms to ecosystems made up of many interacting species.
The psychoanalytic process takes place where the interactions of

the parts of a person become embedded in the interactions between the person and the other people around him. I thought complexity theory might be the basis for a common language linking these two very different kinds of organization.

Kauffman's work suggested that the rapid emergence of a new form need not be solely the result of a small change in the genotype that improves its fitness. The cumulative result of the rearrangements caused by the genome's own internal dynamics might contribute significantly as well.

Many viable mutations carry no adaptive advantage. Yet they are propagated because of their proximity on the genome to other genes that do confer adaptive superiority. Because of this, a genome can include genes that are adaptively neutral. Such a genome can be rearranged through recombination or gene translation, making a new configuration that incorporates previously neutral genes. Within the context of the reorganized genome, however, the previously neutral genes might confer an adaptive benefit. This would increase the overall fitness of the genome and perhaps move it a step toward the emergence of a new and fitter species.

A reorganization of this kind can occur without a change in the selection pressure from the environment. The new genetic organization could not have been selected for by the environment earlier, because it did not yet exist. This pathway to higher fitness would take advantage of the organizational properties of the already complex genome.

During a psychoanalysis, a series of internal rearrangements of the patient's mental contents can play a similar role in raising the level of his mental fitness. (These rearrangements are often seen for the first time in the patient's dreams.) A new insight can be selected as a permanent feature of the patient's psyche by his recognition that a missing piece of the puzzle has appeared. For the analyst, the patient's insight modifies and enhances his working model of the patient.

Such changes in the ecosystem formed by the patient and the analyst follow the pattern of punctuated equilibrium seen in evolutionary change of all kinds. Small differences accumulate until a turning point is reached at which the course of the analysis shifts in a new direction.

Traditional analytic teaching offers two simple explanations for such a sudden breakthrough. One is that the patient's defenses have been literally broken through, on the model of a lengthy war of attrition. The other is that the analyst has simply discovered the right interpretation after a period of trial and error. Neither of these ideas makes clear how the many small changes can prepare the patient for the interpretation that precipitates the actual shift. Moreover, traditional teaching does little to help the analyst recognize how or when these intermediate steps are leading him in the right direction. Complexity theory, on the other hand, is focused on the contributions of these modest changes to the overall process.

Modern evolutionary theory affirms the clinical intuitions of analysts about the conditions needed for their work with patients to succeed. The theory also gives them an opportunity for more precise qualitative definitions of many of these clinical intuitions. Sharper definitions can stimulate new topics for research, and help refine psychoanalytic technique.

As we move on to discuss specific models of complex systems, I would like to clarify an important point. These models can adapt and evolve only on a scale very much smaller and simpler than that of the mental and emotional world of an adult human being. I will *not* be claiming that human feeling and behavior are *no more complex* than what goes on in these much simpler systems, as a reductionist might do.

While these CASs are far simpler than a human being, they show many kinds of complex behavior. My claim is that any scientific explanation of human feelings and behavior must be *at least as complex* as an explanation of these simpler systems. Any useful theory of the psychoanalytic process has to be at least as complex as the physical, biological, and organizational processes that underlie human mental life. Since we are experiencing an outburst of new discoveries about these simpler processes, psychoanalytic theory has to be prepared to change along with them.

I do not mean to say that we have to know all the details of the physical and biological processes that underlie the workings of the mind and brain. Quite the contrary. Complexity theory allows us to draw useful conclusions about the aggregate behaviors of the parts of a system without having to know the detailed behavior of each part. However, in trying to work with the emergent behaviors of a complex system, we have to be aware of their dependence on the simpler structures from which they arise.

I believe Freud would have agreed. From the outset, he tried to build his theory on the foundations of natural science. His success as a researcher in neurology and neuroanatomy encouraged him to keep his ideas as compatible as he could make them with the science known in his time. He was very much aware that emergent behavior at the psychological level cannot be explained solely by physics or biology. Yet he knew that psychoanalytic theory could not contradict the findings of the more basic sciences.

Freud also knew that he ran the risk of incorporating the flaws in the theories of the basic sciences then current into psychoanalytic theory. In the sciences these flaws are corrected naturally as further research is done. Psychoanalysts can only protect themselves from a loss of credibility by keeping abreast of these developments and by updating their own ideas. They are responsible for the continued validity of ideas borrowed by Freud in his own day. Unfortunately, this has not been a common practice in the psychoanalytic world. Psychoanalytic theory is still burdened by the limitations of nineteenth century ideas in physics and biology.

Some simple physical models Freud used have proven to be misleading in many details when applied to mental life, for example the idea of *psychic energy*. Psychoanalysts would do well to adopt the more sophisticated models of causation developed in the basic sciences. Complexity theory is the source of the most sophisticated of these ideas at the present.

Some psychoanalysts have reacted to developments in the natural sciences by trying to cut their ties with it. Their hope is to ground their ideas about human behavior in the study of social and cultural institutions. Erik Erikson (1950), a great student of culture himself, was the first to see clearly that these approaches were not alternatives but complementary ways to study human motivations.

Other analysts have reacted to the evolution of science by denying the relevance to their work of any data not generated by the patient in the analytic hour. For some this has even included the work of developmental and cognitive psychologists.

Hartmann (1939, 1964) affirmed and extended the commitment Freud had made to the natural sciences when he wrote that psychoanalysis should strive to become a *general psychology*. This program faltered because it privileged psychoanalytic data in a way that made collaborative work with other scientists very difficult. Hartmann also wrote at a time when there was little enthusiasm beyond the psychoanalyst's office for ideas about mental structure or about complex and conflicting feelings and motives.

Psychology has made an about face on this issue in the last generation. A revolution in the cognitive sciences has been based in large part on the development of information theory and the availability of computerized models of complex systems. It has created a body of ideas and data compatible with and complementary to the psychoanalytic approach to mental activity.

Unfortunately, analysts who took this new work seriously have had little direct influence on mainstream psychoanalytic theory. Hawkins (1966), Breger (1967), Peterfreund (1971, 1983), Rosenblatt and Thickstun (1977), Rubinstein (1980), Reiser (1990) and Olds (1994) have been the most important contributors in this area. The lack of responsiveness of psychoanalysts to their work has been very costly to the profession, in my view. Psychoanalysis seems to many people outside the field to have been treading water scientifically. The decline in the prestige of psychoanalysis may be an incentive for change in this respect.

Psychoanalysts can join in this new opportunity to bring their theory of mental life up to date. However, being merely compatible with the findings of the other sciences is no longer sufficient for psychoanalytic theory. The phenomena treated by psychoanalytic theory must now be represented in a way that is at least as complex as the models of complexity generated in those other, more basic sciences.

One final note to this section. Psychoanalytic terminology, like that of other sciences, sometimes drifts away from the common language into a dialect of its own. In psychoanalytic discussions, the term *adaptation* can be used in a pejorative way to refer to the surrender of the individual's needs and wishes to the immediate demands of his environment. This usage was popularized by Fromm (1941) and others, but goes back ultimately to Freud's

idea that the ego is formed by external pressure to deny instinctual demands.

I use the term in its more customary sense, as the optimization by an organism of the opportunities available to it in its
environment. Adaptation in what follows will always mean the
optimization of opportunities that lead to greater fitness. The
patient and the analyst are adapting to one another in just this
sense during an analysis.

Therapeutic Change in Psychoanalysis

Freud explained therapeutic change in psychoanalysis as the result of a release of dammed up *psychic energy*. Psychic energy was
his term for the demands of the body on the mind for work
leading to instinctual gratification. For Freud, these demands
fueled the activity of the psychic apparatus. He thought of psychic
energy as a fluid that would successfully seek its own level (by
getting the work done) if allowed to flow freely, unobstructed by
the mechanisms of defense.

Instinctual gratification is felt as pleasure. Unrestricted pleasure seeking has its dangers. It conflicts directly with the demands
of the outside world, especially with demands arising from the
desires of other people. For that reason, psychic energy has to be
channeled during childhood development into socially acceptable forms of gratification. A child learns to postpone instinctual
pleasures until they are biologically and socially appropriate. The
structures that enforce the delay develop into the child's ego.

The ego fails to develop normally, according to Freud, when
the demand for pleasure is expressed without the usual social
inhibitions, inviting angry reprisals from the people who deal
with the child. Such a child is seriously maladapted for life in
society. In the child destined to become neurotic, on the other
hand, the mechanisms of inhibition are overactive. Psychic energy
is bottled up by elaborate defensive structures, leaving the child
unable to attend to his basic biological and emotional needs.
Freud saw the therapeutic role of psychoanalysis as the controlled
discharge of this bottled up energy in the neurotic patient. This
newly discharged energy would naturally flow into constructive
channels of pleasure seeking.

Freud saw the day-to-day work of the psychoanalyst as identifying the patient's repressed biological impulses, his hidden stores of psychic energy, in their derivative form as unconscious wishes. Equally important was the analyst's role in helping the patient become aware of his unconscious defenses against these impulses. The defenses had to be acknowledged by the patient if they were to be deprived of their power. Then the patient's ego could take over and find the appropriate channels for the energy released by the analytic process.

For Freud, the major achievement of a successful analysis was what he called *the resolution of the transference neurosis.* Transference is the reenactment by the patient of early relationships with parents and other caretakers. The analyst is assigned the loving and hating roles of the most significant of these caretakers. The patient interacts with the analyst in the present moment as he once interacted with these earliest objects of his desire and hatred.

In the analysis, these early feelings and responses become focused primarily on the analyst, rather than on the other important people in the patient's life. This is spoken of as the consolidation of the transference neurosis. Relations with other people improve, sometimes quite markedly. One patient in the second year of his analysis recited a list of victories he had achieved by asserting himself with his boss, his mother, his older brother, and his wife. "But," he said, "when I walk through this door I'm still the same schmuck I was on the first day I came here."

The analyst helps the patient recognize the distortions of his perception caused by the transference reenactment. When the patient has understood how he unconsciously identifies the analyst with his early objects, he can begin to register in a deeply emotional way that he is really quite different from them. A transference neurosis is resolved when the patient can distinguish the analyst as he really is from the internalized figures that belong to the past.

This model has been very useful to analysts. It describes many important features of the analytic process. However, for many reasons it fails to capture the full complexity of the therapeutic interaction. It makes the role of the analyst too static. Freud wrote that the analyst functions as a mirror that reflects the patient's transference distortions back to him so that he can finally see them.

But the patient is not merely exposing his impulses and defenses for analytic interpretation. Changes occur not merely in *what* the patient sees when he looks at himself in the analytic mirror, but in *how* he looks as well. He learns to approach himself in a new way, from a different angle. He learns how to interact with an unconscious part of himself he had never before acknowledged. All of this requires that the analyst be a flesh and blood presence, an active collaborator and a potential rival, not just a reflecting surface. The patient learns to see himself from these new angles by identifying with the analyst's method of working and with his motivation to work. The patient is taking in more of the analyst than just his ideas. He is taking in and incorporating the analyst's knowledge of process. His ability to use his freed up energy is not an automatic function of his ego; it is something he acquires through his interaction with the analyst over the time of the analysis.

Freud's explanation for the therapeutic effect of psychoanalysis was enhanced by the work of the object relations theorists. This approach was developed in the 1930s and 1940s in Great Britain, by Klein, Heimann, and Money-Kyrle (1955), Fairbairn (1946), Winnicott (1965), Guntrip (1961), and elaborated on both sides of the Atlantic (Greenberg and Mitchell, 1983). Object relations theory sees human development as a series of projections and internalizations, much like the assimilations and accommodations in the theory of cognitive development of Piaget.

According to this theory (much compressed and schematized here), the child develops through the internalization of relations with his caretakers. He creates internal representations of these people, his internal objects, which he uses as models for his own self-understanding and for his behavior. These representations change over the stages of his development, starting with his images of himself as helpless and of his caretakers as all powerful. His representations of self and others become more reciprocal and symmetrical as he matures.

If the caretakers fail to provide the necessary models for growth, or if the child fails to mature because of his own limitations, then his relations with people as an adult can become stereotyped and maladaptive. He is likely to project his own defective internalized object representations onto the new people he meets with and to treat them as if they were his old caretakers as he saw them when a child. New objects are assimilated to his old models.

When he treats the people in his adult life as if they were his old caretakers, they are likely to react at times as if they are. He internalizes this behavior also, adding to his already deficient self-image. If the projections of his hateful self-image are not corrected by other people, he feels confirmed in his hatefulness. The newly enhanced negative self-image will again be projected. An endless loop results.

From the object relations point of view, the analysis succeeds by exposing the inappropriateness of the projections and internalizations. To do this, the analyst must first avoid taking in the patient's projections himself. He has to keep out of the patient's loop. This gives the patient an opportunity to develop a more mature object relationship with the analyst, whose appropriate adult behavior can then be internalized.

The object relations model is an improvement on Freud's in two respects. It puts the emphasis on changes in the self-representations and internal objects that shape the patient's memory into a more stable structure. Getting new information into that structure, where it can become the basis for a new stage of self-organization, is the task of the analysis.

The object relations model also emphasizes the participation of the analyst in an emotional interaction with the patient. The maintenance of the analyst's detachment from the patient's distortions is an active process. It takes hard work for the analyst to do it. While the roles of patient and analyst are still quite distinct, the two exchange their thoughts and feelings in a way that is less asymmetrical than Freud's model would suggest.

These models of therapeutic change capture some medium and long range effects of analytic treatment. Yet neither offers an integrated picture of the process as it moves from the smallest scale to the largest. A series of moment to moment exchanges of information during the analytic hour leads eventually to a series of personality reorganizations that normally takes years to complete. In particular, the models do not give us a detailed account of the order in which the therapeutic events of the analysis are likely to occur.

When analysts get together to discuss the theory of therapeutic change, the test of a theoretical point is usually to see how well it explains a clinical example. Most often, such a discussion has to go beyond the theoretical interest to deal with the rich details of the clinical material. Even when the example illustrates the theory well enough, it more often than not evokes reservations, qualifications, refinements, and extensions in the thinking of the group.

This is partly because the theory as it exists today does not adequately account for the richness of the analytic interaction. When a group of analysts has a chance to work directly with the clinical material, the discussion has a more lively and authentic feeling. The theoretical discussion fails to capture the richness of the clinical material for another, deeper, reason, however.

Psychoanalytic theory, as it has been handed down, does not attempt to specify the detailed contents of the patient's associative structures. Nor does it deal with the question of what is accessible to his consciousness at any given moment. It is content to set a series of lower bounds on the complexity of the patient's state of mind and of his interaction with the analyst.

For example, when the patient expresses a feeling with some force, the theory says it is likely that an opposing feeling is not being expressed because it would lead to more anxiety. If a parent is depicted by the patient as either all black or all white, something significant has to be missing from the picture. If the patient denounces his or her opposite sexed parent, he or she is often suffering from unresolved feelings of guilt over an infantile love that aroused envy or jealousy.

These statements all say that whatever else is true about the patient or his situation just then, this other thing must also be true. Something important has been left out. He is presenting an incomplete picture. The reasons he has left something out are well understood in general, but the details at any moment depend on his individual personality and experience and must be elicited from him. The full story is likely to be more complex, perhaps *much* more complex, than the theory suggests.

I feel that Freud intended his mechanistic models of mental functioning to be lower bounds on complexity, rather than full explanations. This is despite his lapsing at times into language suggesting that the details of the patient's inner life would be unimportant if only the theory were understood. What he meant to be saying, I believe, was that people are dealing with a multiplicity of motivational forces, and this fact has important consequences that may be far from obvious. When motivational forces are prevented from being expressed, they do not simply vanish, as people would often like to believe. Their effects are internalized in one way or another. They modify the structure of the person's mind and body, sometimes at what seems superficially to be a great distance from the original source of the motivation.

Freud's way of using his physical and biological models continues to make sense, provided only that the physical and biological models are updated as the basic science moves ahead. This has not been the rule in the history of psychoanalytic theory. One of my goals in writing *The Emergent Ego* is to help other analysts update the models they use to understand their patients and the work they do with them. The lower bounds of complexity that psychoanalytic theory attributes to intrapsychic and interpersonal structures can be raised if we use the more sophisticated scientific models now available.

During an analysis, the patient and the analyst generate mental representations of various kinds. Reports are received from outside and from inside each of them, along with data, beliefs, opinions, fantasies, and memories. These representations are exchanged and then internalized by the recipients. The patient tries to tell the analyst everything that occurs to him; the analyst is selective about what he tells the patient. The information is never complete or precise. Through mutual adaptation, unfolding over time, the gaps in the patient's story are filled and the distortions corrected. The analyst learns how the patient's maladaptive strategies have been working. The patient learns how the analyst does his job. This knowledge coevolves during the analysis. Seen in this light, the analytic process has a finer grained and more coherent look.

2 A SAMPLING OF THE PSYCHOANALYTIC PROCESS

Coevolutionary Reorganization

A clinical example will show how evolutionary change takes place during the unfolding of the psychoanalytic process. This report emphasizes a dramatic sequence of phase transitions that occurred during the first two-and-a-half years of an analysis. These events have been chosen because they are easy to recognize as critical points in the progress of the analysis and because their effects can be clearly seen as cumulative. Of course, this is a very small sample of the analytic process. But at this point I hope only to give enough detail to illustrate my main thesis.

Richard is what psychoanalysts traditionally call "a good analytic patient." That means that he consciously strives to follow the fundamental rule of free association. He does his share of the analytic work without complaining, and generally assumes that the analyst is working to help him. The analytic process has been easier to understand with patients like Richard than with less trusting and more disturbed people. With someone like Richard the analyst knows what to expect. Surprises will be infrequent.

The analyst will not need to adapt in a dramatic way to what he encounters.

Consequently, the coevolutionary aspect of the analytic process is not in the forefront of the analyst's interaction with Richard. Patients like Richard are commonly thought of as "analyzable." This means that they can be analyzed successfully with only a minor degree of flexibility and creativity needed by the traditionally trained analyst. The analyst's view of his treatment method is required to change only in small and gradual steps during such an analysis.

The analyst still has a job to do in matching his model of the patient with the actual patient, however. He must make frequent judgments about the timing and nature of his interventions. He must know where the patient is, emotionally, in his childhood development and in the development of the analytic process. These judgments are not always easy to make. The patient is an expert at concealing his feelings from himself. The analyst can go only so far with his knowledge of people in general. Although the emphasis will be on the phase transitions going on within the patient, the analyst's thinking as he decides to intervene will be described also.

The patient, Richard, was a lapsed Roman Catholic attorney in his late thirties. He entered analysis when his chronic low-grade depression became acute. He was having frightening suicidal fantasies. These were brought on by a failing relationship with Ellen, his girl friend of four years, and by dissatisfaction with a new job he had taken to be near her. He believed that the decline of the relationship was due in part to what he thought of as his sexual inadequacy.

When not blaming himself, Richard blamed his terrible state of mind on his parents, who he felt had undermined his self-esteem throughout his life. He was the third of four siblings, with an older brother and sister and a younger brother. His parents had encouraged his older brother's artistic and academic ambitions, but paid no attention to his own. This brother had become a great success in his career.

Richard became a passive little boy, indifferent to his surroundings. He followed his brother through high school and college but did little work. He had a mediocre record in school until the last year or two of college, after his brother had left. Still, he managed somehow to be accepted by a good law school far from home. There he did well in his studies. His employment experience after graduation was not very satisfying, although sometimes better than in his new job. He was dissatisfied because his specialty, environmental law, did not pay well. But he wasn't interested in the more competitive and lucrative aspects of the law. He day dreamed obsessively about quitting law and going to medical school.

Whenever Richard's parents visited him, he went into a paralyzing rage. He was unable to talk to them openly, either when he saw them or when they telephoned. He said that his father was a bully and his mother a pushover for his father. His girl friend, Ellen, had been demoralized for some time by her mother's slow dying of cancer. Now she was preoccupied with taking care of her widowed father. Richard's sexual relationship with Ellen was in decline. He couldn't talk to her about his feelings or needs.

He did seem willing to talk to the analyst, however. His mood started to improve within a few weeks, as he described his ambivalence about his work. His new job was in a small firm under a female boss. He felt he was forced to do only menial work, with no scope for his creative imagination. When he did well at it, which was seldom, his boss would take all the credit. He thought she had some political savvy but little insight into the substantive issues he was working on.

He soon had to interrupt the analysis briefly for a business trip with his boss. He left in a state of fury about being forced to arrange the trip and to accompany her on it. When he came back, he described doing all the scut work while she did the negotiating with the high level people. He did manage to talk to lots of people and learn a lot on the trip, however. After a short while he began grudgingly to write a report on the trip. The main topic of the analysis at this time was his lack of initiative in improving his situation at work. He related this to his long history of angry withdrawal from various activities as a child.

Unexpectedly, he found himself getting excited while working on the report. He spent long hours on it, although he knew he would receive little recognition for his efforts. When it was finished, he felt very pleased. He decided to circulate the report to people outside his firm who were interested in the project for which the trip had been made. He received very high praise from someone whose work he admired. He handed the report to his boss, with some comments on the response he had received. She was unexpectedly very positive. She offered to publish it and to allow Richard extra time to do more research. He developed a new project that was entirely his own. He felt good for the first time since the analysis began.

During these early months the analyst had been listening to Richard's story empathically. He recognized that Richard's withdrawal had some adaptational value during his childhood. But he reminded him frequently of the differences between the narrow world of his family and the larger world in which he was now living. Richard took easily to this way of looking at things. His desire for the analyst's approval overrode his need to be unhappy. His pattern of associations revealed that as a child he had been quite willful in his withdrawal from the outside world. This strategy allowed him to maintain his role as a victim of his parents' incompetence and neglect. He was now willing to give this up in his eagerness to please the analyst.

During this time the analyst learned to see Richard as an intelligent and competent person able to work hard at the analytic process. This ability had been compromised for most of his life by his self-defeating neurotic strategy for keeping his desires and ambitions hidden.

Richard, in turn, could respond to an analyst who listened to him but didn't seem to be interested in exploiting his protestations of weakness and helplessness. He began to see himself as having used a great deal of ingenuity in defending himself from anxiety by remaining unrecognized and unheeded. He could take the opportunity presented by the report on his trip to assert himself in a more constructive way. Still, no breakthrough had occurred in his awareness of the unconscious impulses that caused him to hide from himself and from other people. Because of this, the analyst felt uncertain about where Richard really was.

While he was enjoying the success of his report, Richard had a disturbing dream. He began the hour by reporting his discomfort when Ellen mentioned that she was ready to get married and have children. He began to talk of other things. Then he mentioned the dream. He was having anal sex with an unidentified man. He was the aggressor, going at it in a kind of frenzy. While this was going on in the dream, he was aware that his little brother was right next door in their parents' bedroom. Richard ignored his brother in the dream.

The analyst had formed an impression that Richard's anxiety about his sexuality was a defense against oedipal issues. Richard had not engaged in homosexual activity and had very few erotic fantasies about men. This dream appeared to confirm the analyst's impression. He said, "Your indifference in the dream to your little brother's being in your parents' room reminds me of the cool reaction you reported today when Ellen told you she wanted to get married and have children."

In this intervention, the analyst linked Richard's difficulty in committing himself to Ellen with his angry reaction when his mother disengaged from him after his brother was born. Richard's response to the intervention was a series of associations illustrating his fear when his brother was a baby that he might destroy his mother by expressing his rage at her abandoning him. He became aware that his frustrating sexual inhibition with Ellen was related to the unconscious persistence of this fear, now transferred from his mother to Ellen.

Richard's first statement on the following day was a very angry, "I'd just like to tell her, 'Fuck you, Mom.' " This hour was the most animated and emotional of the analysis thus far. Richard remembered with spontaneous affect a number of events in his childhood that left him feeling abandoned by his mother and suffering from very intense separation anxiety. This avalanche of memories was much more excited and vivid than anything that had occurred before in the analysis. The breakthrough of feeling toward his mother set the stage for Richard to reconsider his identification of Ellen with her.

Two weeks later, he said that Ellen had left on one of her frequent business trips. For the first time in their four years together, he missed her. When he came home from work he was thinking how nice it would be if she were there. He thought it might be really nice to get married and get on with their lives. This would require a poignant break with the family tradition of marital discord. The remainder of the hour was spent on the pleasures and regrets he would feel in leaving the familiarity of his depressed family life behind him.

In the next hour he said he realized he had been using his problems in his relationship with Ellen as a weapon in his struggle against his parents. Anything wrong with the relationship could be blamed on them. As a result, he had been unable to enjoy Ellen as a person in her own right. If he married her and were happy, he would be letting his parents off the hook. He couldn't blame them any more for screwing him up. He acknowledged that letting go would be difficult. At his next meeting with his parents, a few weeks later, he found himself surprisingly calm. He felt sympathy for them as well as anger. He asked them searching questions about the feelings they had experienced during the traumatic events of his childhood and adolescence. His manner allowed them to respond to his queries for the first time without being defensive.

A few weeks after his parents' visit, his father sent Richard a birthday gift that he himself (father) had selected. This was an-other first. Richard was very pleased by his father's personal atten-tion to him. Two days later he had a dream that he said was unique in his experience for what he called its "gravity." In the dream he was living in a huge old house with his father and siblings. An old room in the basement, which had been kept locked up for years, was being opened so that it could be reno-vated.

In the dream, Richard was panicked, because the basement room was where he hid the remains of his mother's body after he chopped her in pieces many years before. He tried to move the body to prevent the others from finding it, but then broke down and confessed the murder to his older brother and father, who were "very understanding." His sister, when she heard, was horrified. Richard thought he was going crazy in the dream.

In this dream an important transference issue was coming more clearly into focus. Richard agreed readily when the analyst connected the opening of the basement room with the work of the analysis. Yet he kept referring to the murder of his mother as the subject of the dream, rather than the bringing to light of the murder after years of secrecy. The analyst brought this to his attention and suggested that he was still doubtful that the analysis could help him put his childhood trauma behind him, as the dream suggested he could do. He said he felt extremely relieved to have had the dream, but disappointed that in the dream he could not put the pieces of his mother back together.

A fantasy emerged in which he imagined himself able to reconstruct his idealized childhood mother if he could only keep the murder a secret and the pieces hidden. This fantasy had undermined his ability to accept Ellen's occasional failures to live up to his ideal expectations for a woman. Richard hoped the analyst could help him contain his anger at his mother and other women, as he had hoped his father could do. His fear of his competitive feelings toward his father had made this impossible, however. The positive transference to the analyst had revived this hope, but Richard still had his doubts. The analyst could become a rival too.

Phase Transitional Dreams

These dreams, and the discussions that followed Richard's reporting of them to the analyst, mark major phase transitions in the evolution of the analysis. Each dream initiated a reorganization of Richard's self image. In each of them his sexually colored rage at his mother became more open and less dangerous.

In the first of the dreams, Richard's expression of his rage was indirect, a sadistic homosexual attack on a surrogate for his little brother. The second dream contains a direct sadistic assault on his mother's body, mollified by the passage of time and by an identification with his father and older brother, who are the covictims with him of his mother's attention to the youngest brother. His sister's response in the dream identified her with the demolished mother.

In the first dream, the unknown subject of the sexual attack may also represent the analyst, although nothing in Richard's associations confirmed this idea. In the second dream, the analyst is clearly the instigator of the "renovation" that causes the discovery of the murder. The analyst is also implicated in the surprisingly mild reaction of Richard's father and brother to his confession.

These important phase transitions led Richard to a higher level of structural organization. They moved him a decisive step toward breaking his lifelong pattern of inhibited sexual ambition. Because of the dreams and their aftermath, he could acknowledge his anger and frustration with his mother and begin to separate these childhood feelings from his relationship with Ellen. He realized that his unconscious vengefulness toward his mother (as distinct from his conscious contempt) had upset his masculine self-image and his relationships with women all his life. He saw for the first time that something better could be imagined and aimed for.

As the person most responsible for the discovery, the analyst inherited many of Richard's ambivalent attitudes toward his father and brother. This was the first clear transference role established for the analyst. Like his father, he had become both a potential rival of Richard's for his mother and a sympathetic fellow victim of her narcissism and depression. The analyst's part in the discovery of Richard's murderous fantasy about his mother was met with the same ambivalent feelings.

At the critical moment in a phase transition, the technical role of the analyst may be no more than to construct a single connection that expedites a reorganization. Reaching such a moment in the analysis presupposes, of course, that much preliminary work has already been done. But once the moment has been prepared, a very narrow opening into Richard's unconscious can provide access to a whole series of buried memories.

The context makes the difference. The analyst made what seemed to him a routine interpretation, linking the baby brother in the dream to the child wanted by Ellen. He would not have predicted that the intervention could precipitate an avalanche of new associative material. Out of context, the analyst's comment might have seemed like a small step toward an understanding of the patient and his neurotic problems.

But the events of this hour had many antecedents and many ramifying connections with other events stored in Richard's memory. In this light, their power to bring about the formation of a new and richer structure in his associative organization is not so mystifying. The image of an avalanche of memories may be somewhat misleading here, however.

An avalanche in a sandpile or on a mountainside usually ends with a pileup of lifeless objects that have no obvious attraction for one another. Of course, the new pile formed by an avalanche has a structure of mutually reinforcing sand grains or boulders. But the memories that spilled out when Richard's anger at his mother became focused were interactive at a much higher level of complexity. The structure emerging from the avalanche of newly conscious memories was accordingly much more complex than the structure that had kept these memories together in Richard's unconscious. The new organization was not a repetition or replication of the simpler preavalanche structure.

What do we know about the structure of these related memories in Richard's unconscious, then? The fact that they emerged together suggests that they were originally grouped in an inaccessible region of Richard's long-term memory. The basis for the grouping was the common theme of humiliation by mother. Richard's memories of her were linked by this cognitive and emotional theme. The memories were like a set of jigsaw puzzle pieces scattered in a box. They "went together" as pieces of the puzzle, but they did not form a coherent picture of anything. The information needed to form the picture was there, but they did not possess an organization capable of constructing the picture.

Freud was intrigued by the formal difference between ideas in conscious and unconscious mental activity. He proposed (1915) that mental activity in the unconscious consisted of a juxtaposition of "thing representations." Conscious thought, in contrast, operated with "word representations." Freud's ideas about the structure of thought relied almost entirely on the example of language. This simplification led him to think that the unconscious has no structure at all. Although this assumption caused serious trouble for psychoanalytic theory, Freud was correct in pointing out that consciousness offers new opportunities for organization.

When the memories emerged within Richard's consciousness, they acquired new affinities that permitted them to organize into a different and more coherent picture of Richard's relationship with his mother throughout his early years. Richard's bad mother imago could now be seen as an object continuous in time, not just a pile of disconnected pieces. The identification of the

bad mother as a continuous object led very quickly to a reconcilia-
tion between good and bad mother imagoes as demonstrated by
Richard's new behavior toward his mother in real life. This
change seems very similar to what Melanie Klein (1940, 1946)
described as the conversion of part object relatedness to whole
object relatedness in analysis. Here we can see Klein's formulation
as a summary statement for many acts of reorganization taking
place at many structural levels.

One might be tempted to say here that Richard's memories
were reorganized by an executive agent operating through conscious thought and deliberation, with the help of the analyst's
interpretation. But the suddenness with which a reorganization
can take place shows that the analyst's intervention supplies the
keystone for an arch rather than the blueprint for a building.
The interpretation that set off Richard's avalanche of associations
to the first dream was of this character.

A keystone must fit into a precise locus in an arch. A grain
of sand can start an avalanche by falling almost anywhere on a
sandpile. The analyst's intervention must hit the target exactly,
but he has many targets to shoot at. Would any other interpretation of the dream about Richard's baby brother in the parents'
bedroom next door have caused the phase transition that followed? We don't know. Perhaps the coevolutionary process of
the analysis brought Richard and the analyst to exactly the right
place at the right time. Perhaps the time was ripe enough for
many other interventions to have had the same effect. What we
do know is that the analytic process had prepared both Richard
and the analyst for the reorganizing events that profoundly
changed his unconscious representation of his mother.

The traditional description of an analytic interpretation gives
the analyst credit for consciously understanding what is happening in the patient's unconscious. He conveys his understanding
to the patient, and the patient reacts, either by "accepting" or
"rejecting" the interpretation. Accepting may take the form of
conscious agreement, or it may be implicit in the production of
new evidence that confirms the interpretation. Rejecting may be
conscious disagreement or a failure to produce confirming evidence. Producing or failing to produce new evidence is a much
stronger indicator than the patient's conscious response.

The events in Richard's analysis suggest that the traditional description places too much weight on the analyst's conscious understanding. Richard's analyst knew that the homosexual dream made a connection between Richard's fear of women and his mother's preferring a male rival. He was expecting this connection to appear in an analyzable form at some time. He saw the dream as an opportunity to close a gap that had been visible to him from the beginning of the analysis. As it turned out, this was all he needed to know.

The analyst had little information about the way the events referred to in the imagery of the dream were organized in Richard's unconscious. This material had simply not come up in the analysis before the dream report. Therefore he had no way of predicting that his intervention would lead to a reorganization. If there was going to be a reorganization, he had no idea what form it would take. Richard's enormous rage at his mother was a surprise to him.

The analyst did not need to know any of this in advance. His intervention succeeded in this instance because he could recognize the feelings and ideas that should have been connected in Richard's mind but were not. His unconscious simulation of Richard's mental operations and Richard's developing self representation had come close enough together for a spark of recognition to jump across the interval between them.

By the rule of parsimony, I suggest that an intervention that bridges a gap between two previously isolated areas in the patient's unconscious is all the analyst needs to do to create new organizational structure in the patient. Of course, the patient and the analyst's simulation of him must have evolved together for this to work. When the point is reached, the analyst's current intellectual formulation of the patient's problem will most likely be incomplete, inaccurate, and superfluous. The analyst will have a much clearer idea about what is happening after the intervention than before.

In his response to the first dream, the analyst connected Richard's rage at being displaced by his younger brother with his fear of marrying and having children of his own. Both issues had come up during the hour, but in isolation from one another.

When the analyst said that the dream reminded him of the anxiety about Ellen's wish for children, a new area of Richard's long term memory became accessible to him. The recovery of his repressed experiences of rage at his mother was enough to change Richard's picture of his entire emotional history.

One can infer from the fact that the memories appeared as a group that the original unconscious decision to sequester them together was made at a higher level of structural organization. That is, an unconscious decision was made to repress all memories with the common theme of rageful feelings against his mother. Each memory might have been repressed individually, but an additional decision was made to repress the group. Thus, the derepression of the memories as a group indicates a phase transition at a higher structural level.

This brings up the question of scale in describing and identifying a phase transition. How much does the patient have to change before one can recognize that a phase transition has taken place? We can be sure that many smaller changes had to be made within the organization of the patient's mental contents before a turning point like those reported could have occurred.

For example, before the session in which Richard reported the dreams about his brother in his parents' bedroom, much work had been done on his undifferentiated anger at both parents. By the time of the dream, Richard had become aware that he had different reasons for being angry with each of them. They were no longer the single merged object of his wrath. This change had been gradual. It was not accompanied by new insight, by the derepression of linked memories, or by the emergence of primary process imagery. Yet this change may also be described as a phase transition, if of a lesser order.

As a rule, larger phase transitions incorporate the smaller phase transitions that precede them. The differentiation of the parental couple is rudimentary in the first dream, but quite advanced in the second. We must suppose that any new connection creates a phase transition at some level, perhaps only in a very small segment of the patient's memory structure. Many of these smaller phase transitions would have to occur below the level at which they can be observed clinically.

When enough of these subclinical reorganizations coalesce to form a larger organization, this new phase transition is clinically obvious. When Richard's parents visited, such a change was expressed in his new behavior toward them. After the first dream, the recovery of a cluster of repressed memories led to a very rapid reorganization of Richard's self-image. The content of the first dream was suddenly coordinated with a long series of earlier lower level connections made during earlier stages of the analysis. The second dream, about confessing his mother's murder, brought his awareness of unconscious fantasy to a new and higher level.

About six months after the reporting of these dreams, Richard became dramatically aware that he was no longer feeling depressed. He realized that he had become very different from the other members of his family, who, like his brother, remained caught up in their depressive ways of relating to people. He reported telling his brother about his good feelings for Ellen. He then told the analyst he felt very "solid" during this discussion, referring to his former doubts about his relationship with her.

Richard's depression had made him very undemanding of Ellen, who reacted by keeping herself at a distance when Richard became withdrawn. He worried that she could not respond to him in a more active and affectionate way now that his depression had abated. He said, "Even though I'm feeling much better about her, the relationship hasn't seemed to improve." The analyst suggested that the relationship must have improved to some degree, but that now he wanted even more from it. Richard said, "That's right, I want more!" He became momentarily euphoric about having acknowledged that he really wanted something, which he said he had never been able to do before the analysis.

Then he said, "I was afraid I was sounding like a born again Christian when I was talking to my brother about Ellen." He explained that he was referring to the zealousness of the newly converted, who can't hear what other people have to say. But he did feel reborn into a new life. The analyst pointed out that for him, an atheist, a born again Christian might be someone who was caught up in an illusion.

Richard responded to this with an image of himself he had when he started the analysis, but had not mentioned before. He had lived his whole life "shut up in an urn." He could poke his head out every once in a while and look around, but then he would be pushed back inside.

At this point the analyst might have commented on the funerary aspects of the urn. Because the remark was an association to the theme of rebirth, coming as it did right after the mention of the born again Christians, he felt that the issue was Richard's *coming back* from the dead. He said to him that being shut up in the urn must be connected with being reborn. Richard then remembered the image that had occurred to him during the much earlier session when he realized that he was coming out of his depression. He had felt as if he had been trying unsuccessfully for his entire life to get up on his water skis. When he came out of his depression, he was up on top of the water for the first time. The analyst said, "Now we can see the emergence from the water as another image of rebirth. But we need to know more about the born again Christians, who are reborn into what you would consider to be a womblike world of fantasy, while you seem reborn into the real world."

Here the analyst was doing several things at once. He was connecting Richard's images of unnatural restraint on his emotional development with the theme of rebirth. Although the images emphasized passivity, being shut in or pulled along, their deeper significance was in the danger they imputed to the aggressive component of normal growth. The analyst was already tuned in to Richard's fear of his aggression. He recognized the idea of rebirth as a solution to Richard's difficulty in separating from his mother without destroying her. He could ignore the ridicule with which Richard tried to disguise the importance of this change in his feelings. The analyst was extracting the aggressive impulse from Richard's lifelong pattern of disguise and denial.

This example shows that the analyst's identification of the patient's instinctual wish is only one part of his job. Every such wish is found in a particular stratum of the patient's ego structure (at a particular hierarchical level of his mental organization). The instinctual component of the wish is coupled to a piece of the patient's ego structure. That piece of ego structure provides a plan (a fantasy) for fulfilling the wish. The more primitive the level of the ego structure, the less adaptive the plan for fulfilling it. A fossil or an artifact is much more useful to an archaeologist when it is found in situ, along with evidence of its chronology and ecological function. In the same way, an instinctual wish is most useful to the analyst when it emerges along with a particular fantasy for fulfilling it.

For Richard, the image of rebirth represented a new solution to the problem of separating without destroying. In fact, Richard was afraid that it attenuated his aggression too much, as shown by his fear that his love for Ellen was unrealistic (born again Christianity) or merely childish. Yet its superiority to his earlier models was clear enough to evoke a spontaneous review of his history of defensive behavior. It was no accident that the wish emerged into the analytic discourse along with a new and more constructive plan for achieving it. The new plan reduced the anxiety attaching to the aggressive wishes.

Finally, the analyst was linking Richard's recovery of his capacity to grow with the events of the analytic process. Richard's solution to the problem of creating change without destroying anything was modeled on the analysis itself. The analyst's confidence that neither he nor Richard would be hurt if Richard revealed his good feelings in the analysis was a critical factor in his freedom to move forward.

Richard responded to the analyst's last remark by saying, "I bought Ellen an engagement ring the other day." He couldn't exactly remember which day. The analyst said, "That was even before you decided to marry her, according to what you've told me." Richard replied, "I'm embarrassed by my feelings for her. It's like puppy love, as if we'd just met. It seems silly to be feeling that way now." The analyst said, "Puppy love must also have something to do with rebirth." Richard went on to describe how good he was feeling about Ellen. He said the only thing that would be different if they got married was that they could have children. He was feeling much less frightened about that now.

Richard said he had wanted to tell the analyst at the outset of the session that he had bought the ring. His embarrassment about feeling hopeful had prevented him from going ahead. Feeling hopeful undermined his loyalty to his gloomy father as well as separating him from his engulfing mother. The analyst in his father's place would have ridiculed his good feeling.

The turning point in this hour came when the analyst distinguished the religious fantasies of the born again Christians from the reality of Richard's good feelings about Ellen. Richard was then able to admit that he had taken a positive step in the real world, by buying her the ring. His subsequent reference to puppy love was a temporary reversion to his old fantasy that when he separated from his mother he would be left in a childish and diminished condition.

Richard began the next hour by announcing with great enthusiasm that he was engaged to Ellen. On the evening after the last analytic session he had proposed to her, then put the ring out on the restaurant table for her while she was at the ladies' room. He said she was not surprised by the proposal but seemed shocked by the ring. Engagement rings were not fashionable in their social circle, but he wanted to make an unequivocal statement about his good feelings for her.

He noted that this was completely atypical of him. He talked about making arrangements for the wedding. He would have turned this into a huge problem in the past, he said, but now realized that all you have to do is decide what you want and do it. The analyst remarked that he was seeing his old self from the outside now. He said, "Yes, but it's still there. But it *is* different. I'm seeing it in a different way. It's a paradigm shift." *Paradigm shift* is Thomas Kuhn's popular term for a phase transitional leap in the evolution of a science (Kuhn, 1961).

Richard said, "Now I feel free just to be, just to feel. When I thought of myself stuck in the urn, the only way I could escape would have been for the urn to shatter. Then the water skiing image gave me another way out. But now the water skiing image seems too restrictive. There aren't many options when you're on water skis. Now I feel as if I'm back on dry land." The analyst said, "There was also the problem of being tied to the person who was driving the boat." Richard said, "Yes, now I've got my hands free. I can fight my demons with a sword."

He had been especially frightened of the damage he might cause his mother in the shattering of the womblike urn. This image was a more positive version of the murder and dismemberment of his mother related in the breakthrough dream months earlier. During this session, his birth imagery moved through an arresting series of images. It began with the violent breakout from the urn. Then there was the more gentle separation implied by the rising of the water skis out of the water. Then it shifted out to the unexplored territory on the dry land.

After a short time, he said, "I'd been shopping for the ring for several weeks." He described his search for a ring with a traditional setting for the diamond. He wanted the diamond worked into the design of the ring, not just sticking out of it. The analyst said, "I'm wondering about your not telling me you were shopping for the ring." Richard described a feeling that he didn't want to tell people about the ring. He hadn't told his brother or his best friend either. He wanted to do it on his own. He had felt embarrassed when he told his brother and the analyst that he was looking at houses for himself and Ellen last spring. This time it was different. He wasn't embarrassed.

The analyst said, "Perhaps your wanting to do it alone is connected with the water skiing image. Maybe you were trying to get away from the person driving the boat." Richard said, excitedly, "When you said that, the image flashed into my mind of fishing with my father when I was a kid. It was the first time I stopped sitting right next to him and found my own spot. That was a good moment for me." Richard went on to describe how much he enjoyed going fishing with his father. His older brother was too impatient to fish, and his younger brother was still too young, while his sister wasn't interested. His father seemed relaxed when they went out together. He smoked a cigar. The cigar smoke was a pleasant memory. His father often used to smoke a cigar at home on Sundays, when he wasn't caught up in the constant pressures of the family business. He could "just be." The analyst said, "So your father did have some moments when he could just be." Richard said, "Yes but when I got a little older I went off fishing by myself." The analyst said, "That must have been a bittersweet experience for you. Doing it on your own meant giving up some of the few moments you had with your father when he wasn't preoccupied."

Richard mentioned some other good times with his father, who occasionally played cards and chess with him. "But he seemed kind of bored. It wasn't the same as going fishing. We still play poker together with his friends when I come to visit.

We're both good at poker and usually win." Then he said, "I don't want my parents to have anything to do with the wedding. Not that they could do much, since they're not paying for it and they're 1200 miles away. But I don't want them interfering." The good memories of his father were suddenly overcome by bad memories of his mother's intrusiveness and his father's unwillingness to oppose her. The pull of his lifelong accommodation to his parents' depressed relationship was threatening to undo the masculine assertion that led to his buying the ring for Ellen.

The sequence in the latter part of this hour suggests that Richard was eager to identify with his father's maleness. However, he found the opportunities for doing so without a mutual experience of anxiety to be quite rare. Perhaps he was attracted to his mother's bossy manner in compensation for his father's usual anxious passivity. This might help to account for his obsessive fear when the analysis began that he was sexually inadequate.

It is striking that Richard's positive memories of a phallic father emerged for the first time in the analysis during the hour in which he told the analyst he was engaged. The engagement was made possible by the retrieval of the good feelings epitomized in the recovered memory of his going off on his own while fishing with his father. This recovered memory was reenacted, before it was remembered, when he went shopping for the wedding ring without telling the analyst about it. The analyst's remark on the significance of the reenactment prepared Richard to reexperience the memory with appropriate affect. Richard felt less anxiety when the analyst brought up the reenactment for the second time.

The cascade of good memories about his father was precipitated by the analyst's statement, "Perhaps your wanting to do it alone is connected with the water skiing image. Maybe you were trying to get away from the person driving the boat." We can see from this later material how the intervention had been prepared both by the preceding events of the hour and by the earlier events of the analysis.

The image of the water skis had first come up a number of months before. Richard had returned to it often as a marker of his progress in the analysis. Before this moment, the analyst had said nothing about the obvious connection between himself and the driver of the boat. He thought Richard might find such a reference deflating to his aspirations for independence. In this hour, Richard had for the first time voiced the thought that water-skiing was "too restrictive" and that there must be something better. This allowed the analyst to bring up the transference impli-cations of the rope, including the wide range of Richard's ambiva-lent feelings toward him. This was an opportunity the analyst had been expecting.

Richard's clear expression of his wish to have more of life when he went shopping for the ring was coupled with his defiance of the basic rule of analysis. He had held back his excitement about the ring for a number of analytic hours, indicating in this indirect way that he felt the analytic relationship was interfering with his masculine strivings.

Everything was now in place for an intervention making ex-plicit the convergence of these associative strands (making the convergence a part of the record of the analytic discourse). The precise moment of the intervention was determined by Richard's report of the shift in his attitudes about the style of the ring. The analyst was tempted to follow up on the obvious sexual symbolism of a setting that "sticks out' replaced by a setting "worked into the overall design." But this statement of Richard's was made with very little feeling, in contrast with his just previous statements about using his free hands to fight his demons. The analyst felt that Richard was slipping away from the important material about the transference interaction. His intervention brought Richard back to this charged topic, opening the way to the series of posi-tive memories about his father.

This session shows what the analytic process is like when things are going well. The associative pathways in Richard's mem-ory were converging. What was happening to Richard inside the analysis explained what was happening outside the analysis, and vice versa. Richard's sense of what he experienced and fantasized in the present illuminated his memory of similar experiences and fantasies in the past, and vice versa. Richard and the analyst were reorganizing their views of one another. Their expectations of each other were increasing reciprocally. Richard could express strong but finely shaded feelings. This is the optimal state of the psychoanalytic process, close to what I will be calling *the edge of chaos.*

The imagery that marks the series of changes in Richard's self-representation during this segment of the analysis fits closely with the major developmental issues of early childhood. His fantasy about being stuck in the urn, unable to move, embodies the passivity, the rage, and the obsessional defenses that impeded him for much of his life. The origin of such an image must have come very early in his development, perhaps as far back as the time he was learning to crawl. His imprisonment in the urn would have prevented him from moving under his own power. One has the sense of massive external constraints becoming internalized.

Although this fantasy had influenced much of Richard's emotional life, he became aware of it only when he began the analysis. The first critical stage in the emergence of this theme was the dream about the dismemberment, burial, and much later discovery of his mother's body. This dream expressed his wish to do to his mother what he felt she had done to him, namely, prevent him from developing a unified body image under the coordination and control of his own autonomous ego. He could only imagine an escape from her influence as explosive and indiscriminate. He had to hold off this overwhelming danger to his mother with rigid self-restraint.

This theme emerged in Richard's consciousness only when he could grasp the idea that there might be a better alternative. The image of the urn did not emerge in the analysis until the waterskiing image had already appeared and been assimilated. The contrast of a more autonomous self image was necessary before Richard could see his earlier view of himself as a *limitation.* Being dragged through the water on a rope allowed him more freedom than being shut inside the urn. Escape from the urn could only be catastrophic. But a constructive alternative to being submerged in the water was readily available once he was ready. All he had to do was lift himself up.

The waterskiing image also suggested that Richard was now less isolated than he had been when stuck inside the urn. A waterskier must have a well-intentioned partner in the boat. Richard must have recognized a potentiality in his father to intercede and free him from the feeling that he was completely confined and immobilized by his mother. Apparently his father had failed to live up to this potential, at least in Richard's eyes. The analyst was assigned the role of the competent father whose guidance would have helped Richard get out of his trap.

The waterskiing imagery also suggests that Richard became aware of his father's potential to intercede for him during his third or fourth year, when his motor skills were already developed. By then his body was well enough coordinated for real action. But he was still passive and dependent; his hands were still tied. In the first dream described above, Richard was engaging in a homosexual act while his mother was busy with his baby brother. His brother arrived when Richard was 2. His brother had become the immobilized but privileged baby.

The sense of the water skiing as an activity with built-in *limitations* did not appear until an even better alternative had come along, the fight with a sword against the demons on dry land. This phallic-oedipal theme supplies a newer feeling of freedom, including the freedom to love and hate his father without the fear of being engulfed by his mother. The new freedom remained fragile, however, in the last hour described above. We might say that this newest phase has just appeared on Richard's imaginative horizon.

Self-observation may be a very tepid expression for this patient's experience of himself as he became aware at this transition point of the imaginative themes that shaped his neurotic illness. He began the following analytic hour by saying that he had been thinking of the sequence of these images ever since he had left the office. He was impressed and excited by the way they encapsulated the story of his unhappy life and pointed out the route for his escape. "I really love those images," he said.

This experience of sudden self-awareness was once called *insight* in the psychoanalytic world, with positive connotations. Nowadays this term is often taken to mean a kind of intellectualized understanding without deep feelings or serious personal engagement. Richard's reporting of this experience suggests that insight is still a useful descriptive term, perhaps a term we cannot do without. An analyst can distinguish genuine insight from the sterile and intellectualized facsimile of it. This is another topic that will occupy us as we go along.

Ellen had asked Richard to help her decide how to invest some money she received as a gift from her father. Richard became obsessed with the idea of choosing just the right investments. After telling the analyst at some length about how much the research was competing with other activities, Richard said, "It must be that I have to work very hard for this money."

Richard felt that bad luck was something he deserved or else that he brought on himself, while good luck was undeserved or obtained under false pretenses. The analyst said, "Bad luck keeps you a member in good standing of your depressed family, but good luck makes you a disloyal renegade." Richard said, "Something good was always followed by something bad. I just had a bizarre memory. My family owned a waterskiing boat that had some problems. My father couldn't enjoy the boat because he was always focused on the problems. But the boat worked perfectly well most of the time." Asked why the memory seemed bizarre, he said, "It's because nothing bad really happened. It was all in my father's head."

Here we see a memory in the act of being dislodged from (or disgorged by) an *unconscious infantile attractor* that had swallowed it up many years before. This attractor is a dynamic structure in the unconscious that draws together a wide range of new experiences and transforms them into a small and narrow set of stereotyped fantasies. Waterskiing was first mentioned during the analysis as a symbol for Richard's escape from confinement in his mother's emotional womb, represented by the urn. In the new image, his father pulled him up out of the watery maternal enclosure. This allowed Richard a greater measure of independence, but at the price of having to follow unswervingly in his father's wake. This configuration became a powerful attractor for Richard's later experience with men in authority. Under the spell of the attractor, Richard saw the world from within his father's depressed and distorted view.

As Richard recognized the influence of his father's depression on him, the mythic power of this attractor started to dissipate. Richard could see that his image of himself as a water-skier under his father's tutelage came from an actual, remembered experience, rather than from a fantasy generated by the attractor. What had seemed to him to be reality (that good things are always followed by bad things) could now be seen as the twisted viewpoint of his father which Richard had adopted for himself. Now he could locate the depressed state of the world inside his father's head, rather than all around him. Richard's feeling that his actual memory was bizarre served as the marker of the transition from the distorted world of the attractor to the real world of memory. Richard's view of things was turned inside out by the reemergence of the memory, hence the feeling that the actual memory was strange. The bizarre feeling was the "pop!" as the memory broke out of the gravitational field of the infantile attractor. Richard realized that the waterskiing attractor had played a major role in binding his oedipal guilt by idealizing his father and subordinating himself.

Three weeks later Richard's mother made a long trip by herself to be present at Ellen's bridal shower. Richard said that several people told him how wonderful she was at the party. On the analyst's mind at this time was a strenuous and dangerous backpacking trip Richard's mother had just completed. Richard and Ellen had taken the same trip together a few months before. According to Richard's description of his mother as a frightened and indecisive person, this trip was completely out of character for her. Her behavior at the shower was another example of this surprising behavior. The analyst was interested in connecting these experiences, but also in linking them with Richard's fantasy that his mother would be damaged by his efforts to separate from her. He said, "You must have been underestimating your mother's potential for following in your footsteps as you've gotten better."

Richard agreed. Then he said, "It's as if I've been traveling from one mountaintop to another, with a deep valley in between. My parents were with me on the old mountaintop, but I'm climbing the new one alone. There's a new perspective. I can see other mountains ahead. Having children is the next one. That's going to be hard for me. In fact, I still can't really see it, even though Ellen has described it to me in detail. On the old mountaintop I couldn't see anything ahead of me. My parents were blocking the view. I had to beat them down before I could see anything."

Through Richard's associations, this last image developed into the idea that he was beating them down from the mountaintop into the valley, then crossing over them to get to the next mountain. The analyst asked if he was crossing over their dead bodies. Richard said, "No. I was thinking that, but it isn't right. They're not dead. I'm walking across their backs." The analyst said, "So then they can get up and follow you up the next mountain." Richard said, "It looks that way." Then, after a short silence, "You know, I've never had this perspective before. Even when the urn turned into the waterskiing, and then the island, I couldn't see very far. Now I'm up high looking down, over everything. But maybe this is still all taking place inside the urn."

He remembered philosophical discussions when he was a freshman at college about what is real and what isn't. He thought his adherence to a very stoical view of life was a defense against his depressive expectation that everything would turn sour if he allowed himself to enjoy it. He then related a dream about his ambivalence in identifying with what he called his father's skills as a handyman, like his ability to repair a broken garage door. The dream imagery indicated that this had something to do with making and raising a baby. The analyst thought this was a reference to the damage he imagined his mother suffered in giving birth to him. Since this theme did not appear in Richard's associations, the analyst thought it inappropriate to bring it up. Richard interrupted the discussion of the dream with a "weird" thought he hesitated to tell the analyst. "What if there were no Ellen," he said, "and I had been making all this up and telling it to you for the last two years?"

The imagery of peaks and valleys suggested a trajectory on a *fitness landscape,* a fundamental idea in evolutionary theory. It appeared quite spontaneously in the analytic discourse. The analyst had mentioned on several occasions that the opening of new perspectives was an aim of the analysis. He had never linked the idea of a new perspective with the imagery of a higher natural vantage point, however.

Richard imagined that to move to a new adaptive peak he would have to beat his parents down and then cross over on their backs. This fantasy adds a dynamic flavor to the abstractions of the computer simulations of adaptive landscapes. Richard's comparison of the urn with the mountain landscape may warrant a look at the urn and the other images that show a gain in his self-awareness as locations on a fitness landscape. We note the progression from the enclosed urn to a peak in a mountain range. In this progression, the horizon of Richard's fitness landscape has opened out from the rim of the urn to the view from the mountaintop. Richard's position in the landscape has also been turned inside out and upside down. He was originally at the bottom of the urn looking up. Now he was at the top of the mountain looking down.

One must be cautious about finding an equivalence between the subjective representations of a patient and the objects and events of the actual world he is trying to represent. The subject matter of a psychoanalysis is, after all, the mismatch between what the patient thinks and feels and what is really out there (*out* there in the world and *out* there in his unconscious). Richard was concerned about this too. He said in this session, "I'm afraid the changes in me are too linear," meaning too predictable, too much by the book. The analyst should be able to distinguish the distortions due to the patient's illness from the emerging reorganizations that appear when his illness is healing. At this point he felt little doubt that Richard's insight was genuine.

Mountain Climbing

Richard returned from his mountain-climbing honeymoon quite pleased with himself and with Ellen. They had gotten along well. But he had suffered a relapse of his intermittent but severe chronic lower back pain. He felt there was a connection between the back pain and his unconscious conflicts. The analyst asked if he had overexerted himself on the mountains. He didn't think so, but maybe. He described a strenuous and invigorating hiking schedule that could easily have overstressed anyone with his back condition.

The analyst wondered if Richard's fantasy about climbing over the backs of his parents to reach the next peak in his life might be relevant to the back pain. Richard said he thought it really had to do with his sexual fears. He had been determined to have intercourse with Ellen at least once every day of their trip. He managed for a while, but finally couldn't make it. "That's when my back started to bother me," he said. Exploration of

Richard's fear yielded little. Perhaps the back pain was his punishment for failing the demanding test of his heterosexuality. Richard was sure that physical stress was not the explanation.

Still, he felt good. So good, in fact, that he wanted to cut his analytic hours in half. He made it clear that this wasn't just an idea. He intended to put it into effect unilaterally and immediately.

On hearing Richard's notification that he was about to curtail the analysis just when it was demonstrating its usefulness to him, the analyst was surprised and a little dismayed. He had expected Richard's competitiveness to surface, but was caught off guard by the timing and the apparent nonnegotiability of Richard's announcement. His immediate feeling was that Richard was making a mistake, one that if carried through would deprive Richard and himself of the fulfillment afforded by a completed analysis.

Richard seemed to be preoccupied with a fear of being dominated by the analyst, whose power had just been demonstrated by the successful honeymoon. Having achieved this major goal, Richard could not imagine that there was any more that analysis could do for him. He therefore had an opportunity to diminish the analyst's influence over him by unilaterally reducing the number of hours, thereby taking charge of the analysis himself.

The analyst had two choices in dealing with this fear. He could try to show Richard that the fear was unfounded by allowing him to decide what to do, despite his own misgivings about it. Perhaps Richard would eventually realize his error on his own. Against this choice were a number of considerations. The analyst believed Richard was being directed by an unconscious oedipal transference wish to defeat him. He thought that unless he brought this wish to the surface it would become self-confirming for Richard. Richard had thus far been successful in keeping his oedipal aggression out of the analysis. The analyst felt that one more such success could be fatal to the analysis. Furthermore, the analyst believed that if he responded passively to Richard's attempt to undermine the integrity of the analysis, Richard would be left stranded on the plateau he now occupied.

Richard's mental organization had settled on a local optimum, the mountaintop landscape of his honeymoon with Ellen.

He was afraid it would all be downhill from there, as he took on the responsibilities of a husband and eventually a father. He preferred to stay where he was. The analysis now presented an obstacle to his remaining stationary at the top of this particular mountain peak. He sought to minimize the threat of the analysis by diminishing its effect on his life.

The analyst's second choice was to express his conviction that Richard could expect greater benefits from continuing the analysis just as it was and that any risk in moving forward was well worth taking. This statement would also convey that the analyst was not threatened by Richard's wish to be independent of him and that he would not abandon Richard because of it. It would address Richard's unconscious fear that his competitive transference feelings would cut him off from the analyst's help. It would tell him that the anxiety that made him fear leaving his local optimum was unfounded. If the analyst acted as if Richard's decision made sense to him, he would confirm Richard's new belief that the analysis was no longer useful. In that case the analysis would end very quickly.

On the negative side of this choice was the possibility that Richard might see the analyst's taking a strong position as evidence that he was more concerned about being in charge than about Richard's welfare. For Richard to see things this way he would have to devalue the positive changes that had already taken place. The analyst did not believe that Richard's transferential defiance would outweigh his positive feelings about the progress of the analysis. He thought the risk would be small.

The analyst chose the second option. He told Richard he thought he was avoiding an opportunity to build on the very successful work they had been doing thus far. He was again expecting something bad to follow something good, whereas something better was actually much more likely to follow, as his experience in being an analyst assured him. Perhaps some new issues were coming up that Richard felt anxious about. Competitive feelings toward the analyst were likely to arise now that he had taken such a big step forward in his own life. Richard would be giving himself a bad deal if he insisted on cutting down his hours.

Richard said he would think it over. After two more sessions he said he would go along with the analyst, but reluctantly. He was clearly quite angry that the analyst had claimed to know better than he did what was good for him. The analyst asked if that were a position his father often assumed with him. Indeed, it had been. For the first time, Richard's oedipal conflict had become an emotional issue in the transference.

The outcome of this exchange between Richard and the analyst is an example of successful coadaptation. Each of the analytic partners had to give up an illusion about the progress of the analysis. Richard was required to abandon the unconscious fantasy that he could reach a successful conclusion to his treatment without facing the frightening feelings of his oedipal rivalry with his father. The analyst had suffered from a related illusion. He imagined that he could bring Richard's repressed feelings about his father into the analysis simply by being reasonable. He learned that he had to use his authority as an experienced analyst to oppose Richard's impulse before Richard could understand his reasons for the opposition.

In giving up their conflicting fantasies about the state of the analysis, Richard and the analyst became more closely attuned. As their views of the analytic process moved closer to reality, their simulations of each other moved closer together. We can see here that a lack of information is not the only reason for an incomplete or inaccurate simulation of an analytic partner. The illusion that an analysis will be simpler, easier, or shorter can act as a powerful resistance to observation.

Richard turned to the oedipal issues at his new job, acting for a while as if he were doing so under protest. With a much larger firm, this job required him to direct the work of other people. It also gave him greater freedom in choosing his own work. After some initial hesitation, he had aggressively negotiated for the new position, which paid a bit less than his old job. He managed to get the new firm to split the difference between their original offer and his previous salary. At the time of the negotiations, the analyst had suggested that his hesitation was connected with guilt feelings directed at his father. Richard now revealed that he had felt this suggestion was the equivalent of a command to ignore his own feelings and plunge ahead despite his discomfort in asserting himself. He was now glad he had insisted on higher pay and a better title than he had been offered at first. However, since he started the job, he had alternated between elation about the new responsibilities he was given and depression about his inability to do the job perfectly. He realized that the analyst had not been asking him to disregard his own feelings but to act effectively is spite of them. He had been afraid the analyst would react in a vengeful way if he expressed his anger at the time.

Four months after the wedding, Richard still had little conscious understanding of his competitive feelings toward the analyst, however. Now he reported two dreams during successive hours. In the first dream, he was sexually attracted to his older brother's new wife. He was embracing her in the dream when his brother walked in on them and became very angry. The rivalrous aspect of Richard's sexual feelings was represented here for the first time. Richard said he now felt older than his brother, who had been in psychotherapy on and off for several years without achieving impressive results. This new feeling was very uncomfortable for Richard. It seemed to upset the order (birth and otherwise) of the family structure. His lifelong policy of letting his brother have all the public success no longer worked.

In the second dream, Richard and Ellen had moved into the analyst's house. Richard was having a session in the analyst's home office. (In reality, the analyst saw Richard in a building with many other psychiatric offices.) The analytic hour in the dream was interrupted when Ellen appeared from the shower completely naked, apparently not seeing the analyst. Richard signaled her quickly that the analyst was there and that she had to go back immediately and cover up.

Richard's associations had to do primarily with the fact that he and Ellen had just had a contract accepted for the purchase of their first house. For most of their down payment they were using money that was a gift from her father. They had been looking in a neighborhood closer to the analyst's home, but decided to stay in the area where they were currently living. In the dream, however, Richard was literally moving in on the analyst. At the same time, he was afraid the analyst would become angry and withdraw his services, just as he was afraid that his father-in-law would withdraw the money if Richard became a competitor of his.

The sudden appearance of Richard's heterosexual aggression in the context of an undisguised sexual rivalry with the analyst was a surprise. An issue for every analyst is the voyeuristic gratification he gets from hearing his patients talk about their sexual experiences. Richard's dream showed his awareness that this was something the analyst had to control. On the one hand, he was trying to get the analyst to care more about him (to take Richard into his family) by pandering to this unsavory pleasure of the analyst. On the other, he was subtly chiding the analyst for his collusion in Richard's plot (the urgent instructions to Ellen to cover herself up). Richard could admit to having a roving eye only if he could lay it on the analyst too.

The analyst had some difficulty in integrating the many issues brought up by these dreams all at once. He felt excited by the sudden breakthrough of the new material he had been expecting for some time. This excitement left him feeling vulnerable to Richard's innuendo about an illegitimate interest in his relationship with Ellen. When Richard's associations led to his father-in-law, the analyst followed by developing the oedipal theme in terms of Richard's relationships with his own parents.

He pointed out that the sexual drama of the second dream reversed the action of the first. In the earlier dream, Richard was taking away a woman who belonged to an older rival; in the second, he was exposing his own woman to an older man. He wanted to show Ellen off to the analyst, to prove his competence as a male, but at the same time he was inviting his rival to a forbidden kind of intimacy with her. He suggested that the attractive women in the dream were connected with Richard's mother and the older men with his father.

In the next session Richard reported hearing something that confirmed a disturbing story his mother had told him two years before. When Richard was 6, his father became very depressed. His mother had taken over the family affairs and was instrumental in finding a loan to establish what was to become their family business. For the next 15 years, she made many of the business decisions from behind the scenes.

Richard had dismissed this story when he had heard it from his mother about two years before. He had always been very bitter about his mother's devotion to the business, which he strongly believed had caused her to neglect his needs as a child. Now it appeared that this bitterness might have been related to his becoming aware as a child that his mother worked to keep his father emotionally intact as well as for the family's financial well-being. His mother was taking care of his father instead of him. Moreover, she was setting his father up as a model of competence for Richard to identify with, undermining Richard's ability to evaluate his father realistically. Richard's refusal to act competently as a child was both a way to protect his father and a way to show his mother that he saw through her act.

His father's response to his mother's efforts to keep the business going had been to disparage and belittle her. Richard said he now understood better how she had managed to shrug off his father's criticism and contempt for so many years. Richard had been quite happy to join in his father's condemnation of his mother as an intrusive but ineffectual busybody. He had considered her willingness to put up with this abuse as a sign of contemptible weakness. This opinion conformed with his oedipal wish and fantasy that his mother be his father's *unwilling* victim. It also supported his fantasy that his mother had so little value as an oedipal object that it would have made no sense at all to fight over her.

These dreams and the acknowledgment of his mother's role in the family business marked the third stage in the emergence of Richard's oedipal conflict. The first was marked by his fantasy that after getting his hands free from the waterski ropes he would be able to fight his demons with a sword on the dry land. This new view of himself had led to his taking an active role in his relationship with Ellen, leading to their engagement and marriage.

In the second stage he acted out his opposition to his father's authority in the transference relationship with the analyst, by announcing that he was going to reduce the frequency of his hours. In the third stage, the acting out was replaced by the dream imagery, which made the sexual aspect of the rivalry with his father explicit for the first time.

A few weeks after the dreams were reported, Richard and
Ellen were about to close on the purchase of their new house.
During a session at this time, the analyst asked Richard to change
his next appointment time for the analyst's convenience. Richard
came to the new appointment (at the end of the day instead of
early morning) complaining of fatigue and preoccupation with
his work. The hour was exceptionally unproductive, despite the
analyst's suggestions early and late in the session that Richard
might be angry about being asked to make the change.

In the following hour Richard described his puzzlement
about his lack of productivity in the previous hour. He had
thought about it at length and realized that he felt trapped by
the analyst's request for the change in schedule. On the one
hand, the request was reasonable. The analyst had made similar
changes at Richard's request. He would feel ridiculous refusing
to take the alternate appointment time. On the other hand, he
resented the fact that the analyst had put him in a position where
he would seem spiteful if he exercised his rights and refused. This
was a familiar role for him in his relationship with his father.

Richard then began to talk about how smoothly things were
going for him. He was moving ahead in his new job which was
going as well as he could hope for after only a few months. The
purchase of the house was making him feel he was establishing
himself on his own, away from his family of origin, in a clear-cut
way he had never felt before. The idea of having a family of his
own now felt quite natural to him. He and Ellen stopped using
contraception.

He felt he was entering a new, easier phase of his development. He recalled the images of the urn and the waterskis that
seemed to define the earliest stages. He said he was having trouble
characterizing the next stage. The analyst reminded him of two
images he had used to characterize that stage, fighting his
demons on the dry land with a sword and moving from peak to
peak across the backs of his parents.

Richard said, "Yes, it's so obviously an evolution, like the
evolution of man." He wondered why that hadn't occurred to
him before. Then he said he hadn't minded being away from the
family home on a recent holiday, even though his siblings and
their spouses were there. He felt perfectly at ease with Ellen's

father and her siblings. Everything had been such a struggle in the past. Now it seemed different. The analyst said, "Perhaps it was an evolutionary struggle." Richard said, "Yes, I'm not sabotaging myself the way I used to."

The next session was on the morning of the closing for the house. Richard said he was feeling great about it. He wasn't feeling anxious, although he had felt that way during the walk-through on the previous day. The house was not only for his pleasure, but also for Ellen and for the raising of a family. For that reason, getting what he wanted was less of a burden. He mentioned that a few weeks earlier he had "gotten it into his head" that he wanted an exercise bicycle. Ellen suggested he wait a while before getting it, and he went along with her. There was really no reason to postpone it, since it cost only a tiny fraction of the price of the house.

When he was in college, he wanted a bicycle. He waited for a very long time before he would let himself buy one. He finally found some excuse that made it seem as if it weren't really his idea to buy the bicycle. Then he bought it. But the only thing he really liked doing in college was playing poker. That kept him from thinking about his difficulty in meeting people and making friends. Especially in his first year. Nothing else gave him pleasure.

The previous owner of the new house was very nice about showing them around. In the basement Richard noticed an old table saw. He had always wanted to own a table saw. Now there would be room to have one. He imagined how good it would feel to be able to work in the basement with lots of room around him. He asked the owner if the saw were for sale. The owner said he had already sold it for $75.00, but wasn't sure the other person was going to pick it up. He would check.

The analyst was feeling a loss of momentum in the hour and decided to bring up an issue that was on his mind since the previous hour ended. He said, "I've been thinking about the relationship between your mood in our last hour and in the previous one. In the previous hour you were very glum about not being able to exercise your right to refuse the offer of a schedule change to make up for the hour I missed. Now I'm wondering if there weren't something about the house involved also. Perhaps you had some angry feelings about not being able to reduce your guilt by refusing to accept the house from Ellen and her father."

Richard said, "I'm thinking about burning the house down. I'm in the basement, where the wood is stored for the table saw. I'm setting it on fire." The analyst said, "I'm also reminded that your pleasure in playing poker in college was a way of identifying with your father. But there was a double edge to it, since at the same time you were defying his intention for you to get a good education. Maybe last week you were making me into a paternal authority who was forcing you to move ahead with your life whether you wanted to or not. It wasn't until we worked that through in our last session you were able to express your real enthusiasm about buying the house."

This was a much longer than usual statement for the analyst. His aim in making this intervention was to link up the transference resistance of the earlier hour with the issues current in Richard's life situation. The connecting thread was Richard's ambivalence about his father's authority. The analyst was concerned that the episode of resistance to the analysis two sessions earlier had been left too far behind to be of use in making this link.

Richard replied mischievously,

My father had a table saw too. I almost mentioned it earlier, but I didn't want to say it. He made our porch furniture 20 years ago and it's still there on the porch. I helped him build it. He let me do all kinds of things, measuring, cutting, fitting the pieces together. I really enjoyed doing it. There's a funny story about the furniture.

When Ellen and I were in Florida recently we had dinner at an expensive hotel in the most beautiful setting in the world, at least to me. Then we went out on the porch of the hotel. There it was, my father's furniture. I called him up right away and said, "I'm at the hotel and guess what!" He said, "I know, I know. That's where I got the idea for the furniture." I felt bad that he never told me. All those years I thought he had created it himself. My younger brother works with a table saw too. He makes beautiful furniture. As a matter of fact, he has my father's old table saw.

The analyst said, "Maybe it's okay to identify with your father's admirable qualities if he hands them over to you. Then you don't have to worry about your wish to grab them away from him and invite his retaliation. Perhaps one attraction of the table saw in your new house was that it was owned by an older man who could pass it on to you."

Richard said, "The whole house is part of that." The analyst said, "Yes, the closing is like the changing of the guard between the generations." Richard said, "The old owner even said that. He said the house needed new blood. I'm thinking about cutting off my foot with the table saw. That would take some acrobatics."

This final remark illustrates Richard's brand of black humor. He was mocking his father's authority by responding to the letter rather than the spirit of the previous owner's wish that he rejuvenate the life of the house. Behind the mockery was his frightening fantasy that if he mutilated himself he might comply with his father's imagined demand that he give up any competitive self-assertiveness. Self-mutilation, symbolically castration, was the only form of self-assertion open to him in this fantasy. This comes through in the implicit message to the analyst, "Not so fast. I haven't yet exhausted my right to refuse whatever I've gained from our work together."

A few days after moving into the new house Richard reported a minor but disturbing incident. He had an appointment with a plumber at the house. After waiting half an hour, he left for work. This was the second time the plumber failed to show up at the appointed hour. Richard called the plumber. His secretary, who Richard thought was his wife, berated him for not waiting. When he protested she said, "Maybe we can't help you. You seem to need a plumber who is punctual." Richard was furious. He felt falsely accused.

The analyst suggested that the woman had gotten in touch with a feeling of guilt in Richard that probably went back a long way. He said, jokingly, "I didn't murder her." He remembered crying bitterly whenever his parents went out and the baby-sitter came. He was sure his parents would never come back. He then started speculating about being sexually abused by a baby-sitter. "That would explain so much." After some further discussion of his very meager fantasies about this possibility of sexual abuse, he said, "But that's just an excuse for denying my own responsibility. Maybe they weren't such bad parents after all."

Then he said, "You know, this goes all the way back to the urn stage. I've been thinking about the stages we've talked about, the urn, the waterskiing, and the rest. Maybe all those were parts of another stage that I've been in since the analysis began, that's coming to an end now. In each of those stages I was making my parents into monsters. But they aren't monsters." The analyst reminded him that there had actually been a progressive reduction in his intolerance for his parents since the analysis began.

Richard said, "Yes, but something seems changed right now. Maybe I misinterpreted everything they did." He listed some of his personal myths of victimhood. The analyst said, "Your expecting them not to return when they went out seems like a clear example of misinterpretation."

Richard said, "I'm reminded of something you told me a long time ago, that every patient thinks his neurosis is what's interesting about him. I made everything so elaborate in order to blame my parents, when really life is pretty simple. I used to be unable to make a decision, because the pros and cons had to balance each other out. I blamed my parents for that."

In this session, Richard's self-organization has reached a new hierarchical level. From the perspective at this new level, the earlier stages of his freeing himself from his parents' influence seem to him to have taken place within a neurotic world from which he could finally see the possibility of escape. The idea that he had misinterpreted his parents' intentions precipitated a new phase transition which allowed him to see his neurosis from the outside. A new, less neurotic self emerged from this reorganization.

The analyst made the earlier remark referred to by Richard to help him see that he had a self distinct from his illness. He told Richard that while patients often considered their neuroses to be works of art, one neurosis was actually very much like another. What was interesting was the individual person hidden behind the stereotyping of his neurotic defenses. Richard was able to see the point of the analyst's comment in a new way as his more competent and more observant self emerged through the analytic process.

Richard's new hope that he could separate himself from his neurosis led him to exaggerate the change in perspective brought about by the latest phase transition and to play down the work he had accomplished in the analysis prior to that point. When the analyst pointed this out to him, Richard was able to focus more realistically on the sudden change in viewpoint he was experiencing.

This initial segment of Richard's analysis shows how a successful psychoanalysis evolves through a series of phase transitions as the patient and the analyst adapt to the new information they receive from one another. For the patient the adaptation is usually manifest through his spontaneous associations to the analyst's interventions. The analyst adds a level of conscious reflection and reprocessing to his unconscious attunement to the patient. At this point Richard's analysis was far from completion, but the analytic process was firmly established.

We have seen that a major phase transition, precipitated by the culminating phase transitional interpretation, increases the patient's inner connectedness, moves his overall functioning in the analysis nearer the edge of chaos, improves his fitness, opens new connections to sequestered areas of long-term memory, and allows new, more effective behaviors to emerge. The culminating interpretation is not a large-scale synthesis of unconscious material, as one might have expected, but an interpretation of fairly limited scope that completes a reorganization of the patient's mental contents taking place over a period of time.

Because the analyst's simulation of the patient becomes more accurate through the series of phase transitions, his fitness to be the analyst for this patient is also increased.

Culminating interpretations able to open a large region of memory are infrequent. Small avalanches that reorganize a localized area of memory are much more common. This pattern creates a tremendous hardship for researchers who take a purely linear approach to the sequence of events in an analysis.

Of course, in an analysis, as in any evolutionary process, culminating events are few and far between. I have focused my discussion of Richard primarily on these events because of their theoretical and practical interest. The analyst's activity in promoting the evolutionary process has been my major concern. It would be a mistake to construe this as an attempt to describe what is typical of the day-to-day texture of the analytic process. The activity of the analyst is appropriate only when the timing is right for a process-enhancing intervention.

Richard was asked later on to read the manuscript of this chapter to see whether he thought the analyst's efforts to disguise his identity were sufficient. He included this paragraph with his suggestions about confidentiality:

I have only one overall comment, which is that I think you sell yourself short by not providing more of a perspective on the time that elapsed between and during the different phases of treatment. I have come to recognize the shift that occurs in my understanding of a particular problem, from "intellectual" to "emotional." However, only over time and after developing trust in you was I able to verbalize enough intellectually understood problems and off-the-cuff memories to obtain an emotional understanding of them. I came to appreciate your relatively scarce and usually well-timed comments. Perhaps previous chapters in your book make it clear that the conditions for success were created over time, but the condensation of phases in this chapter did not give me that sense.

3 METABIOLOGY

Artificial Life or Metabiology

Modern evolutionary theory inspired the founding of the Santa Fe Institute in 1984. Christopher Langton organized the first in a series of biennial Workshops on Artificial Life in 1987. The Proceedings of these conferences (Langton, 1989; Langton, Taylor, Farmer, and Rasmussen, 1992) give a broad overview of the serious work being done today in this new field of applied complexity theory. Contributions to the Workshop were made by physicists, biologists, economists, and social scientists.

Artificial life is often misunderstood as a program for replicating life forms found in nature with manmade or artificial versions. If this were so, the artificial life project could only succeed in creating a very small and hardly significant *subset* of lifelike phenomena. Artificial life forms would be valued by the closeness of their approximation to natural organisms. They are not close.

The research objectives in artificial life research are both more modest and much more ambitious. The goal is to create a *superset* of lifelike forms, a superset that includes terrestrial organisms and artificial life as two of many possible member sets

(Langton, 1989, 1992). Natural life forms elsewhere in the universe, whatever they are, are also members of the superset. *Metabiology* would be a more accurate term for the study of this superset than artificial life. The work of the metabiologist is a generalization from biological life in the same way that non-Euclidean geometry is a generalization from the familiar geometry of our daily world (Fontana and Buss, 1994).

None of this presupposes that artificial lifelike forms are alive in the same sense as biological organisms, or that they could ever be. What is of interest here is that artificial life research finds patterns and processes in the logic of organic evolution that can tell us how CASs in general evolve. Among these CASs are large and small systems created by the interactions of individual people. Psychoanalysis is one.

From the perspective of metabiology, one can ask new questions about biological systems. For example, what processes are common to the two kinds of lifelike forms we now know? They have similar formal structures, but are made of very different materials. What are the essential ingredients of lifelike processes in the broad sense? What aspects of terrestrial life are due to historical accidents limited to this planet? Are there inherent limits to the lifelike behavior of life forms not based on carbon chemistry?

Some essential processes of life can now be simulated on computers. Others are likely to appear. These simulations synthesize what Von Neumann (1966) and Monod (1971) thought of as the logic of natural life, rather than the material instantiation of actual organisms.

Biological organisms have several essential capacities, including, at a minimum, these four: (1) To maintain and repair themselves by incorporating and metabolizing spare parts and energy sources from the environment. (2) To adapt to environmental change by evolving to higher levels of fitness. (3) To reproduce their store of genetic information. (4) To develop new individuals from that information.

These capacities can now be found in artificial organisms living in the memory of a laptop computer.

Some of these essential functions can be carried out by other complex adaptive systems that are not organisms, but are made up of living components, a beehive or the British Empire, for example. These CASs do not reproduce as organisms do. At the other end of the spectrum, CASs created on the computer are many orders of magnitude simpler than the simplest biological organisms. They lack most of an organism's facilities for interacting with its surroundings. But all these complex adaptive systems share the capacity to evolve.

People, as we know, are among the most complex of complex adaptive systems. Intimate human relationships that endure are open systems requiring a constant interchange of energy and information. The partners in a relationship must adapt continually if the relationship is to survive. This is especially true of the therapeutic relationship in psychoanalysis, where the threat of stereotyping and stagnation is greater than usual. The psychoanalytic partnership must also evolve to survive. Otherwise, every move toward the edge of chaos would add to the anxiety of the partners. *Intimacy* is the capacity of a relationship to evolve *toward* the edge of chaos.

The Origin of Life

Much of the mystery in the evolution of complex structures is epitomized by the problem of the origin of life, the second great reorganization of matter in the universe after the big bang. Traditional Darwinian theories assume the chance formation of a self-replicating genome, usually thought to be a large molecule of RNA. Laboratory experiments, however, have had little success in finding conditions that could bring about the step-by-step polymerization of nucleotides needed for self-replication. This would be a preliminary step necessary to the production of an amino acid code. Traditional Darwinism cannot explain the origin or even the very existence of a complex genome whose random variations could be sorted by natural selection.

Morowitz (1992) argues from biochemical evidence that three distinct phases of molecular evolution were required before the first cell could form. He pictures this development as the formation of three concentric shells of molecular types, with a narrow gateway leading from each shell to the next outer shell.

The first shell was composed of organic compounds containing carbon, hydrogen, oxygen, phosphorus, and sulfur, polymerized to form carbohydrates and lipids. These compounds self-organized into closed membranous vesicles, in which other kinds of reactions could safely take place.

The gateway from the first to the second shell was the incorporation of nitrogen into the simple sugars within these vesicles, to form the amino acids (see Figure 3.1). Polymerization of the amino acids created biologically active proteins in the second shell. Opening the gateway from the second to the third shell was the formation of the nucleotide bases from the amino acids. In the third shell, these nucleotides were polymerized into the nucleic acid macromolecules.

Each of the three phases required a higher level of energy and a period of stabilization before the next phase could begin. The functions associated with each shell, (1) structuralization, (2) enzyme catalysis, and (3) information storage, emerged one after the other during these three stages of evolution and reorganization. Later evolutionary change created the new organizational structures of the prokaryotic cell (algae and bacteria), the nucleated eukaryotic cell, and in the end, organisms with many cells.

Kauffman (1993) and others have shown that many functions of a living system have to be present long before the capacity to form a self-replicating genome can even begin to evolve. The most important of these capacities is self-maintenance. Any system able to generate a nucleic acid genome must start as a self-maintaining system of nucleotides and polynucleotides, the basic components of the future genome. The genome evolves only if stable conditions support consistent selection of longer and longer polymers. Peptides and polypeptides would have to be included in the system if the genetic code were to evolve along with the physical structure of the genome.

For such a system to be stable, it must be able to maintain itself in spite of perturbations. It must be able to replace constituents lost through the action of disintegrative processes, both internal and external. These constituents would have to include polymers of many different sizes with highly specific structures. How could such a system form and how could it maintain itself?

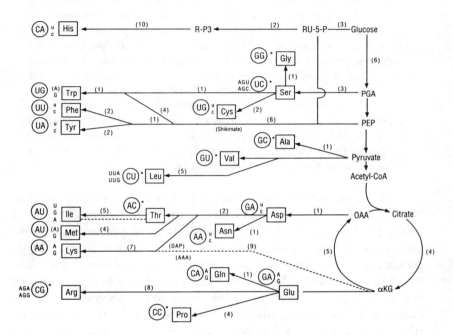

Figure 3.1. The gateway to the second shell in prebiotic evolution. Pathways from Intermediary Metabolites to Amino Acids. Outlines of general synthetic pathways of the coded amino acids. The first two bases are circled for clarity. Numbers in brackets indicate the number of steps in the pathways. An alternative pathway for lysine synthesis is indicated by a dashed line; ∝KG, ∝-ketoglutarate; OOA, oxaloacetic acid; PEP, phosphoenolpyruvate; PGA, phosphoglycerate; R-P3, 5-phosphoribosyl pyrophosphate; Ru-5-P, ribulose-5-phosphate; * is used for "any base." (From Morowitz, 1992, p. 169 in *Beginnings of Cellular Life*. Reprinted by permission of Yale University Press. © 1992 by Yale University Press; adapted from Taylor and Coates, The code within the codons. *Biosystems*, Volume 22, pages 177–187, 1989. Reprinted with permission from Elsevier Science.)

Kauffman gives us an answer to this question, which he links with his own exposition of modern Darwinism:

> [This new view] is based on the discovery of an expected phase transition from a collection of polymers that do not reproduce themselves to a slightly more complex collection of polymers which do jointly catalyze their own reproduction. In this theory of the origin of life, it is not necessary that any molecule reproduce itself. Rather, a collection of molecules has the property that the last step in the formation of each molecule is catalyzed by some molecule in the system. The phase transition occurs when some critical complexity level of molecular diversity is surpassed. At that critical level, the ratio of reactions among the polymers to the number of polymers in the system passes a critical value. A connected web of catalyzed reactions linking the polymers arises and spans the molecular species in the system. This web constitutes the crystallization of catalytic closure such that the system of polymers becomes collectively self-reproducing [p. 285].

The critical fact here is that the number of possible reactions between the polymers grows faster than the number of polymers inside the vesicles. Once a large enough set of polymers accumulates in a circumscribed physical space, their collective catalytic powers are sufficient to generate all of the members of the set. Kauffman calculates that each reaction between two polymers of the set will be catalyzed by at least one other polymer if the set contains 10^9 or more polymers. Crossing this threshold causes a phase transition in the organization of the set, which then becomes an *autocatalytic set*. Within an autocatalytic set, the creation of larger polymers forms a positive feedback loop that leads to the creation of still larger polymers.

Autocatalytic sets do not reproduce in the way that living organisms do. They maintain themselves by regenerating any components they lack. Because of the positive feedback loop of autocatalysis, they grow in complexity. Associations of components, subsets of the autocatalytic set, become stable in themselves. These associations have their own emergent properties.

At some later point, in a manner not yet well understood, the macromolecules produced by autocatalytic sets of peptides and polynucleotides became associated systematically to form the genetic code. One clue to the evolution of the code is that the most common amino acids are associated with the simplest nucleotide codons made up of the most common nucleotide bases, C and G (Eigen, 1992). The evolution of the genetic code might be described by saying that the code crystallized, with its emergent properties, in a phase transition from the primordial prebiotic soup. Kauffman refers to the emergence of the autocatalytic set in the passage quoted above as, "a phase transition from a collection of polymers which do not reproduce themselves to a slightly more complex collection of polymers which do jointly catalyze their own reproduction." A *phase transition* is an abrupt change of state from one degree of organization to another. Changes of state in the physical systems we see around us are phase transitions. The melting of ice and the boiling of water are the most familiar examples. These are changes in the organizational structure of the water molecules.

Kauffman and other biologists use the idea of the phase transition to refer to abrupt *changes of organization* with the emergence of new properties in complex systems. Many physicists are quite comfortable extending the idea of a phase transition to even the most complex of phenomena.

Michio Kaku (1994), an important contributor to superstring theory, writes enthusiastically of self-organizing events at individual and social scales as phase transitions. He lists the developmental phases of childhood described by Piaget and Erikson as phase transitions, and also such massive social and political processes as the French Revolution.

Phase transition is really too weak a term to describe this degree of reorganization (Kauffman, 1993). In a physical phase transition, the organization changes but the physical units of the organization do not. The water molecules in ice and steam are still the same water molecules. But at the level of biological organization new component entities appear along with the new organizations. (New macromolecular types are produced when an autocatalytic set crystallizes out of the soup, for example.)

One might call these superphase transitions, or reorganizational transitions. Turchin (1977) suggests the term *metasystem transition*. In a metasystem transition, a new system is created at a higher level of organization than that of the original systems entering the transition. The phase transitions we observe in psychoanalysis are all metasystem transitions. For the sake of brevity, however, I will continue to call them phase transitions, with the understanding that this term has the expanded scope just described.

The idea of the phase transition as a critical moment in the evolution of organizations makes the origin of life integral to the evolution of life. It makes the development of increasingly complex structures intelligible as a normal process in the natural world. For the psychoanalyst, it means that the process of change in analytic treatment shares its basic features with all other kinds of progressive change in nature. Any advance in the understanding of process and organization can contribute to the analyst's understanding of the events taking place in his office. The idea of the phase transition as the unit of change in the analytic process is one main theme of *The Emergent Ego*.

Of particular interest to the analyst is the fact that self-organized behavior is a basic property of the material world. Its occurrence in psychoanalysis is not an oddity, but something that links the analytic process to a universal hierarchy of organizational activity. Fontana and Buss (Fontana, 1992; Fontana and Buss, 1993, 1994) have used the computer to study self-organized behavior in a simple form. Their system is similar to a chemical flow reactor, but instead of ions and molecules the interacting units are algebraic expressions in the computer memory.

Fontana calls his system *algorithmic chemistry,* or Alchemy for short (see Figure 3.2). It illustrates the spontaneous evolution of higher level organizations in autocatalytic sets of algebraic expressions. Since this work is important for the understanding of increasingly complex organizations as they evolve, I will describe it here in some detail.

Each of Fontana's algebraic expressions is a function that acts on another expression to form a new expression as a product. An expression can be applied to an expression identical to itself or to an expression that is different. While each expression acts as a function, it is also a substrate for other functional expressions that can be applied to it. A thousand or more expressions, each different and each randomly generated, are made to interact in a computational flow reactor.

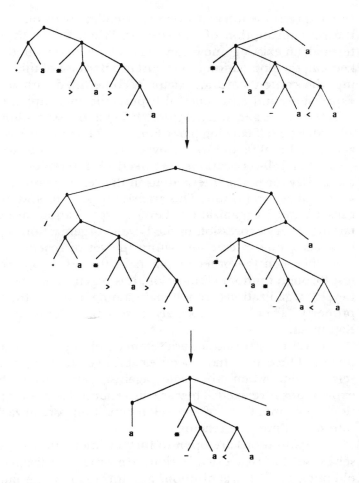

Figure 3.2. Interacting expressions in Alchemy. Interaction between algorithms. Two algorithmic strings (top) represented as trees interact by forming a new algorithmic string (middle) that corresponds to a function composition. The new root with its two branches and '-operators is the algorithmic notation for composing the functions. The interaction expression is evaluated according to the semantics of the language and produces an expression (bottom) that represents a new function. (From Fontana, 1992, in C. Langton, *Artificial Life:* Volume II, 1992, p. 174. © 1992 Addison-Wesley Publishing Company Inc. Reprinted by permission of Addison-Wesley Longman Inc.)

Expressions interact when they collide with one another in the random motion of the reactor. When a new expression is formed, an existing one is randomly eliminated from the reactor, keeping the population level constant. Because of this steady mixing, the contents of the reactor become filled with self-copying expressions and ensembles of hypercyclically coupled functions. A *hypercycle* (Eigen and Schuster, 1977) is an association of mutually catalytic self-copying pairs. Fontana refers to this level of interaction as Level 0, and to the hypercycles as Level 0 structures.

When self-replications are selectively filtered out of the reactor as they form, the interactions in the reactor proceed through a new phase transition. This transition produces what Fontana calls a Level 1 organization. Level 1 organizations are self-maintaining. Every expression in the Level 1 organization is produced by at least one interaction within the set of reactions that take place between the other members of the set. If one member is lost through random elimination, it is regenerated by the others. Level 1 organizations are self-maintaining, because they have this property. They are autocatalytic sets like those described by Kauffman.

Level 1 organizations are self-maintaining but not self-reproducing. Once they have been established, they maintain themselves even when the rule against self-copying by single expressions is relaxed. They are also robust when foreign expressions (not members of the self-maintaining organizations) are introduced into the reactor.

Organizations are open to further interaction among themselves, so that new organizations are produced frequently from old ones. Level 1 organizations also form families. A family is the set of distinct self-maintaining organizations generated by any single organization in the reactor. An isolated family is closed under interaction, but individual expressions in a multifamily group do interact.

Two unrelated Level 1 organizations (not members of the same family) can also interact. When they do, they produce expressions whose types are members of each of the parent Level 1 organizations. Often, though not always, they also produce expressions that are not members of either parent organization. The further interaction of the original parent organizations with these nonmember products can then lead to a second phase transition producing a new kind of Level 2 metaorganization.

Nonmember products, called the "glue" by Fontana, are essential to the formation of structures at Level 2. The glue acts as a catalyst for transformations *between* the Level 1 organizations that are not possible *within* the organizations themselves. However, the glue is not self-maintaining in isolation. The presence of the parent Level 1 organizations is required to replenish it.

Let us imagine the analyst and the patient to be Level 1 organizations encountering one another to form a Level 2 analytic ecosystem. Then the analogue of Fontana's glue is the record in the memories of the patient and the analyst of the discourse produced by their interaction. This analytic discourse is the shared experience that holds the two individual organizations together. It is the material basis for the coadaptive transformations that take place within both parties. The analytic discourse remains accessible to either party though the constant interactions that update and expand it.

In the alchemical soup, progressions from Level 0 to Level 1 and from Level 1 to Level 2 organizations are evolutionary progressions. Evolutionary change in this system is possible without either reproduction or the selection of the fittest offspring. The process that leads interactions of Level 0 expressions to form Level 1 organizations is a coevolutionary process. Level 1 organizations coevolve to form Level 2 organizations.

Evolution in Fontana's system is not like Darwinian evolution, which is based on reproduction and selection. But the output of the flow reactor is very similar to the stages of prebiotic evolution described by Kauffman and Morowitz. Fontana's algorithmic chemistry gives a new formal status to Kauffman's insight into the evolutionary role of autocatalytic sets.

Between them, Kauffman and Fontana have shown that: (1) traditional Darwinian theory cannot logically account for the fact that complex self-reproducing life forms exist in nature; and (2) there is a logically (computationally) coherent alternative that can.

To deny evolutionary status to self-maintaining organizations that increase in complexity through mutual interaction would be to cut down the concept of evolution at its roots.

When a psychoanalysis ends, only one patient and one analyst remain. They have not reproduced. But they have evolved, as has the ecosystem they form. Many other evolving nonbiological systems, such as those that make up political, economic, cultural, and linguistic groups, share some but not all of their defining traits with the living world. The important common trait of these systems, from the psychoanalyst's point of view, is the evolutionary emergence of ever more complex self-maintaining structures.

The self-maintenance of these structures keeps the analysis moving forward in the direction of optimal complexity. As the contents of the patient's mind become more organized, new hierarchical structures are stabilized. These new structures in turn create a new viewpoint for the patient's powers of self-observation. *Self-observation,* as I use the term here, is not dispassionate scientific observation, but the deeper kind of self-knowledge that comes from seeing ourselves as if through another's self-interested eyes.

Self-maintenance is essential to structures and organizations that arise during an evolutionary process. When organisms evolve, self-maintenance is supplemented by the reproductive process. In psychoanalysis, a different method of self-maintenance fixes the newly formed structures in permanent memory. But I am getting ahead of the story. More needs to be said about complex adaptive systems before we go on.

Simplicity and Complexity

A complex adaptive system evolves through the nonlinear interactions of its component parts. That is a serviceable working definition of a CAS. But how is the complexity of a CAS related to our more usual ideas about complexity? In this section I will explore the nature of complexity through its companion concept of simplicity. In everyday language, complexity is a relative term. An irreducible aspect of its meaning is the contrast with simplicity. However the relation between simplicity and complexity in nature is not that of a binary opposition.

The holistic properties emerging at the top organizational level of a CAS are often simpler than the sum of the individual properties of its components at the lower levels. The behavior of a whole person, for example, is simpler in many ways than the sum of the behaviors of his or her various organs or appetites. In psychoanalytic treatment, the resolution of a patient's conflicting wishes leaves him feeling that his life is *simpler*.

Gell-Mann (1994) warns of a danger, in the rush to study complexity, of neglecting the simplifying aspects of emergent organizations. He suggests the term *plectics* to encompass the range of possible forms, from simple to complex, encountered in the natural and manmade worlds. Plectics is derived from *plek*, the common Proto-Indo-European root of sim*ple* and com*plex*. The original meaning of the root is *to fold*. (It appears in such paired English words as imply and implicate, comply and complicate, reply and replicate.) A simple object has a single layer of substance, while a complex system is a manifold.

Gell-Mann is surely correct about the importance of the unity achieved through emergence. The gain in the organizational power of the patient's psyche that gives analysis its therapeutic value is due to the integration of the new structures that emerge during the analysis. Wholeness implies simplicity of a certain kind. However, common usage tells us that not all simplicities imply wholeness. A person who is well put together is considered a whole person but not a simple person. Psychoanalysis tries to bring about the emergence of wholeness in a person who is internally divided or conflicted.

One way of exploring the notion of simplicity is through information theory. Can the simplicity or complexity of an object be specified by the compactness of its description (Gell-Mann, 1992, 1994)? Attempts have been made to define the complexity of an object or system as the length of an algorithm able to generate the object. How long is the shortest algorithm that can produce it? (Of course, by asking about the length of the algorithm one avoids asking about the *complexity* of the algorithm, which would lead to an infinite regression.)

This procedure seems to work up to a point, but has severe limitations. Consider the object in question to be a function that transforms a given input to a given output. How many commands would a computer program need to execute to produce the transformation? How many lines or symbols or bits would be needed to output a result as complex as the object? The fewer the rules, lines, symbols, or bits, the simpler the object.

Take the output of a computer program. In machine language, this would be a linear series (a string) of ones and zeros. An extremely simple output would be a uniform sequence of either symbol. The program would only have to PRINT ZERO (or ONE) and REPEAT to specify either of these cases. An alternation of ones and zeroes would require a longer program, PRINT ZERO, PRINT ONE, and REPEAT. Call this program ALT. ALT forms a pattern of ones and zeros. Knowing the pattern and the current symbol (one or zero) being put out, one could predict each additional symbol in the sequence. The information inherent in the pattern is *compressed* by the program.

Many such patterns, large and small, can be superimposed, so that very intricate sequences may be formed. The greater the size and number of superimposed patterns, the longer the program will be. As the distributions of the ones and zeros become more varied when the intricacy of the pattern increases, the information required to locate each symbol in the sequence also increases. As this goes on, the output of the program is developing more structure.

Up to this point, when the program is still short compared with the length of the output, everything moves together in the same direction. The complexity (program length), the formation of structure and the information content all increase together. However, new cycles can be added to the pattern indefinitely. The length of the program may finally approach the length of the output. When this point is reached, the program can no longer compress the information in the pattern.

The structure of the sequence has melted away. It looks now as if it had been produced by random coin flips. Has the output reached a point of maximal complexity? Not in any realistic sense. For all practical purposes, we can replace this very long program with a much simpler one that merely says FLIP A COIN and REPEAT. Lacking both a coherent pattern and the power to predict, all random sequences are functionally identical although informationally unique. The peak level of complexity coincides with the maximum of structure, not the maximum of information content.

When the level of algorithmic complexity is low, we find a regularly repeating pattern, like the black and white keys on a piano. A program with about a half-dozen commands would suffice to produce this pattern. It could be done, using only PRINT ONE, PRINT ZERO, and ALT, with some parentheses thrown in. A more complex output string would be the melodic line of Beethoven's ninth symphony, if it were transcribed for the piano and then printed out as the sequence of black and white notes that resulted. Where every note is consciously placed, as it is here, there would be many rule governed patterns. Rules of musical tonality, of sonata and symphonic form, of Beethoven's stylistic preferences, would all apply. Yet there would remain many decisions about the placement of notes that are unique to this piece.

But notice that the emergent properties of these more complex patterns also have simple descriptions at higher levels of organization. "The pattern of black and white keys on a piano" is one, and "the pattern of black and white keys you would get if you transcribed Beethoven's ninth symphony for the piano" is another. "Beethoven's ninth symphony" is not just a name, like "The Apassionata," or "The Eroica," but a descriptive term for the conjunction of two evolutionary systems. One system is the evolution of the symphonic form, which originated in the middle of the eighteenth century, about the time when Beethoven was born. Another is Beethoven's evolution as a composer of symphonies, which revolutionized the form. The ninth symphony, his final effort in the grand orchestral style, was his most notable experiment of this kind. Because of Beethoven's innovation in this work, the introduction of human voices in its final movement, the ninth symphony is often called "The Chorale Symphony."

In traditional psychoanalytic theory, simple descriptions at higher levels of organization are often used when detailed information at lower levels is scarce. "The negative transference," "the Oedipus complex," and "the therapeutic alliance" are typical of the terms at this level of discussion. The gains in compactness of description and ease of reference are counterbalanced by a corresponding vagueness about the actual situation they apply to.

To describe the pattern of notes in Beethoven's ninth is not really to understand the symphony. Understanding comes only in listening to the music. Psychoanalysts often feel that one must listen to the music of psychoanalysis to know what it is about. The analogy goes only so far. Listening to Beethoven is not a means to some other end, as psychoanalytic treatment is, but an end in itself.

Yet there are parallels. We tend not to be aware (or to care) that moments of harmonic reorganization in a musical composition are phase transitions. Unless we are students of music, we do not ordinarily think of the individual components of the ninth symphony as they existed in Beethoven's mind before being organized into the symphony itself. But the ninth symphony had a history. Beethoven's Chorale Fantasy, an orchestral piece with voices, was written many years earlier. The theme of the Chorale Fantasy evolved into the similar but more forceful theme of the final movement of the ninth symphony. The restructuring of the Chorale Fantasy into the Chorale Symphony generated a phase transition at a very high level of complexity.

The behavior of an emergent organization is unified, integrated, and coordinated in relation to the sum of the behaviors of its parts. It functions in the larger world as a whole thing, an agent with its own interests to protect. This integrated behavior may be simple when compared with the *total* of disconnected behavior that its components display on their own. Of course, the emergent behavior is *not* simpler than the behavior of a *single* component of the system from which it emerges.

The functional range of emergent properties and behaviors is not simple either. Although a whole person is simpler as an entity than the sum of his individual parts, he can accomplish much more in his interactions with the external world than the sum of his parts can. The ability of a complex system to influence the outside world is highly correlated with its inner integrity.

In Plato's *Phaedo,* Socrates argues for the immortality of the soul as he is about to die. A close reading of *Phaedo* shows that Socrates is actually making a subtle argument for the reality of the emergent properties of a person seen as a living system of lifeless parts. Socrates' psychological vocabulary is quite different from ours (Simon, 1978; Padel, 1992). The emotional issue of the moment, his death sentence, casts the question of life after death into prominence. But the deeper philosophical content of the dialogue is the simplicity of the emergent properties of a hierarchical system.

Socrates praises the *psyche* for its unity, its purity, and its ability to maintain itself unchanged despite changes in the body parts and appetites that belong to it. *Psyche,* the word for soul in Plato's fourth century Greek, originally seems to have meant *breath.* It is the word used in Homer to designate the living substance of a person as it *physically* leaves his body when death occurs.

Psyche can also mean ghost or shade in Homer. But the psyche after death is merely the shadow or pale imitation of the person from whom it has been separated. Achilles makes this clear in the Odyssey, when Odysseus asks him what his existence in Hades is like. Achilles says he would rather be the meanest peasant scratching at the surface of the earth than the king of the underworld.

Between Homer and Plato, psyche took on a meaning much like that of the inner fluids that convey feelings in Greek literature of the fifth century B.C.E., fluids like blood, bile, spinal fluid, semen, *thumos* (force), and *menos* (anger). These concepts suggest some part function that moves through channels within the body. It was not until Plato that psyche takes on the meaning of the essential self, the individual essence or identity.

Socrates compares the psyche with the attunement of a string on the *kithaira* to a particular mode. The string of the musical instrument is like the body. It performs its musical function only when it is tuned and played. Socrates' point is that the attunement continues to exist as a pattern even when the string is out of tune and silent. The musician can bring it to life again whenever he applies his plectrum to the well-tuned string and divides it to form a harmonic ratio. Similarly, the soul continues to exist even when the body is dead.

Phaedo and his grieving friends are not convinced that this argument implies the immortality of the soul. Indeed it does not. What it implies is that the emergent properties of the person can be identified and described even when the system that produced them, the body, is no longer present or functioning. Socrates' then suggests a connection between psyche and *kleos,* reputation or fame. His reputation is an emergent property of his life as a philosopher. It is immortal in the minds of his disciples and in their works, which will last long after Socrates himself is gone.

In *Crito,* a dialogue that just precedes *Phaedo,* Socrates is adamant in his refusal to corrupt his reputation by breaking the law of Athens and escaping into exile. His argument against breaking the law is significant for our discussion here. He insists that the emergent properties of the democratic polis have a higher value than the interests of any individual in the community, *even when the democratic decision is unjust.*

Breaking the law would thwart the democratic political system, whose preservation is a greater good for Socrates even than justice for the individual. Socrates wishes to preserve the simplicity and stability of democracy against the anarchy that had been spread throughout Greece by the Peloponnesian War, which had ended in a great defeat for Athens.

A major difference between the psyche conceived as breath and the psyche conceived as soul is that the psyche as soul is an agent, a system that acts on its own behalf. An autocatalytic set is an agent, as are all CASs, but a sandpile in a state of self-organized criticality is not. The soul, as Socrates imagines it, is the quality of agency that characterizes a living person. When it is missing, when the body is dead, no person is present.

Although the definition of an agent is universal, the scope of its agency is always limited by circumstances. The simulated organisms of an experiment in artificial life are agents within the domain of their particular computer program, but not in the natural world. An autocatalytic set is an agent in a cell or in a chemostat, but not when it is splashed on the floor of the laboratory. A person may be an agent in one context, but a patient (one who suffers or is acted upon) in another.

In hierarchical systems, an entity formed at one level of organization may act as an agent at that level, yet function as a component subordinated to another agent at a higher level. In other words, the scope of its agency is limited by its place in the hierarchy. Every agent is functionally indivisible at its own level, no matter how complex its inner organization. When it acts on its own behalf, the *it* in question is singular. This means that every agent is simple in Gell-Mann's sense, no matter how complex its structure.

Socrates made a logical error when he supposed that the property of agency in a person can continue to exist after the nonagent part of the person has been buried. He reasoned that since a person equals a body and a soul together, the remainder when the body is subtracted from the person is the soul. But the body and soul need each other to function; neither can exist alone. An organization cannot exist without members. It *is* an organization *of* members.

Socrates' reputation is quite another matter. It exists in the minds of other people, influencing them in a variety of ways. It has no direct relation to Socrates' body, alive or dead, except that Socrates must have lived to have created a reputation. Socrates' reputation is the product of the emergent organization of his various parts, but not the organization itself.

The psychoanalytic process is employed in the hope of transforming patients into agents, whole person agents (Schafer, 1976). This is another way of saying that the id will be transformed into the ego. A patient asks for analytic treatment because he is acting contrary to his own interests, in a manner not necessarily known to him. That is, he is acting only in part as an agent.

Freud's innovation here was to suggest that an *It*, a functionally dead or foreign body, can be sequestered within the *I* that normally signifies the presence of an agent. He saw that in this situation the usual relation of a live agent to a dead body can be reversed, so that it may be the id that seems alive and the ego dead. The dead It can usurp the activity of the living I.

The paradox can be explained if one views the whole person as a Jacksonian hierarchy of organizational levels. Each level is made up of agents, taking action on their own level but subordinated to agents at higher levels, like the citizens of Socrates' democracy. When all is well, a person acts as a single and unified agent. Only the highest level of organization, the soul or *Seele* as Freud called it, can interact with other people. In mental illness, the hierarchy breaks down. Normally subordinate systems now govern the outward behavior of the ill person. They have been decoupled from the hierarchy.

The analytic process is designed to create or restore a harmonious integration of these subordinate agents into a whole person. As a rule, an agency at a higher level cannot act coherently in its own behalf until its component agents are themselves functioning successfully. Self-organization is difficult in a set of poorly functioning agents.

The bottom-up aspect of the analytic process organizes small units of function into larger units. The larger units *emerge* from the self-organization of their components. The analyst helps the patient find the missing pieces needed for the self-organization of his psyche to proceed. The pieces are agents at their own level of organization, but subordinate components of the new entity that emerges when the next round of self-organization takes place.

The newly emergent organization has a built-in top down view of its components. Their visibility increases, even as (or perhaps because) the newly emergent structure limits the scope of their agency. The functioning of any agent is more clearly seen from a higher level, in its position as the component of an organization above it in the hierarchy. The patient's observation of his functioning in the analytic relationship opens the way to new movement in the analysis.

Bottom up and top down interactions keep alternating in the analytic process. The reorganization that creates a new level of functioning often leads to a fuller exploration of its components on the lower level. New information about the component elements is likely to be discovered for the first time from the perspective of a higher level. This new information may in turn cause a further reorganization at the higher level.

When the analytic patient remembers what it is he had been repressing, a new story or picture emerges. The new story or picture contains gaps and empty spaces, of course, but the story itself carries information that narrows down the range of events that might be expected to fill the gaps. This information will act as a probe of the patient's long term memory (LTM). With the discovery of the missing links in LTM, the patient's picture of himself becomes more coherent. The possibilities are narrowed again. The cycle repeats.

Schafer advocated a focus in analysis on the functioning of the patient as a whole person. This was a very constructive suggestion, in my view. He argued that the emergence of ego structure is a regular feature of the psychoanalytic process. Many analysts had assumed along with Freud that an "intact" ego structure is a precondition for analysis. Schafer was suggesting that wholeness and simplicity belong together.

However, Schafer seemed to deny the agency of the various components of the whole person, minimizing the significance of psychic conflict. He saw the attribution of agency to conflicting motives as destructive to the integrity of the patient's self-image (cf. Rosenblatt and Thickstun, 1977, for a different view). But the wholeness of the patient's self-image depends on the incorporation of its parts into a hierarchical arrangement. To deny the agency of its components is simply to drive them underground again.

The Natural History of Complex Systems

The evolution of complex systems began when the universe expanded from a point of infinite temperature and density, which has been cooling ever since. As the universe cooled, ever more highly organized structures emerged from the original homogeneous concentration of radiation. At some point in the expansion, matter emerged as quarks and gluons (or their even simpler precursors). The early stages of this evolution are easy to identify—quarks and gluons joined to make protons and neutrons, which in turn made atomic nuclei, which made atoms. Atoms formed molecules, and then biological macromolecules, the protista, the eukaryotes, and the efflorescence of multicellular life. It is a story of successive escalations in complexity that created larger, more intricate, and more diversified interactive systems.

The properties of complex systems can be observed in our own everyday world even in a pile of sand. Per Bak, Tang, and Wiesenfeld (1988) studied the formation and behavior of sandpiles. They modeled the fall of individual sand grains on a flat surface from a fixed point above the surface. As a sandpile grows beneath the fixed point, its sides become steeper and steeper, until a critical state is reached. When the sides of the pile can no longer support the addition of one more grain, the next one dropped on the pile causes an avalanche. They found that the extent of the avalanche was quite variable. A single grain might just slide to the bottom of the pile. An avalanche might dislodge just a few grains, or many, or even a considerable fraction of the pile.

The piles reached what Bak et al. called a state of *self-organizing criticality*. As each grain fell, it came to rest at some convenient place on the pile, where it might be called on to support the next falling grain. Eventually, the pile as a whole reached the critical state in which it supported the maximum number of grains for its area on the supporting surface. The sandpile had self-organized to an unstable critical state. When another grain was added, and the critical threshold surpassed, the organization of the pile broke down.

The sizes of the avalanches were neither random nor uniform. Avalanches of all sizes occurred. However, the magnitudes of the avalanches were inversely proportional to the frequencies of occurrence for each size, following a power law. Small avalanches were common. Large avalanches were rare. Plotting each avalanche by its magnitude and frequency yielded a self-similar fractal graph. This power law relationship is typical of natural events that result from the buildup of structural tension. Earthquakes, volcanic eruptions, cloud formations, and solar flare activity all follow a power law.

Self-organized criticality in a sandpile is just at the threshold of complexity in the natural world. Yet it already shows the pattern of punctuated equilibrium we see in biological evolution. The relation between the sizes of biological extinction events and their frequencies is very close to the pattern of avalanches in a sandpile (Raup, 1992; Kauffman, 1993). It is also similar to the pattern that we see in the progressive reorganization of the patient's mental contents in psychoanalytic treatment.

In Richard's analysis, the first intervention described in chapter 2 fell like a grain of sand on the by then supercritical state of his unconscious mental organization. The analyst made a connection between two negative feelings expressed during the hour. One was Richard's angry reaction to his brother's presence in his parents' bedroom in his dream; his negative feeling about having children with Ellen was the other. This small addition to Richard's store of information about his angry feelings launched an avalanche of angry associations. These concerned his experience of his mother's neglect after his younger brother had arrived. These associations led eventually to the dream in which he confessed to having murdered and dismembered his mother's body.

The complex systems found in nature and studied by Bak do not adapt to the world around them, but their complexity is inherited by all complex adaptive systems. Other approaches to the study of complex systems are illuminating. Langton's (1992) work on *cellular automata* has been very influential. A cellular automaton is a lattice of parallel computing elements that can take one of a finite set of values. Each value puts the element in a particular state. States succeed each other as the simulation proceeds. The value of the state of each element is computed from the values of its next door neighbors (including its own value) in the *previous* state of the system. Langton (1992) defines a cellular automaton in this way:

> Formally, a cellular automaton is a D-dimensional lattice with a finite state automaton (FSA) residing at each lattice site. Each automaton takes as input the states of the automata within some *finite, local* region of the lattice, defined by a neighborhood template N, where $N = < D$. The size of the neighborhood template, $[N]$, is just the number of lattice points covered by N. By convention, an automaton is considered a member of its own neighborhood [p. 43].

Cellular automata (CAs) were invented by Von Neumann (1966) and Ulam in their search for a self-reproducing artificial organism in the 1940s. Conway's celebrated Game of Life is the most famous and familiar example of a cellular automaton. (The acronyms may be confusing here: CAs are cellular automata, but CASs are complex adaptive systems.)

The Game of Life takes place on a two-dimensional grid of cells, represented as a matrix on the computer screen, but in principle infinite in extent. The transition rules of the game are extremely simple. Each cell has two states, on and off. If a cell is on, and either two or three of its eight nearest neighbors are also on, then the cell stays on after the next computation. If the cell is off and three of its neighbors in its three by three-element neighborhood are on, then it turns on in the next generation. In all other cases the cell is off in the next round.

When the game is initiated by a random selection of on and off cells, several groups of connected on cells remain after the first generation. Most of these die out quickly, but some persist for long periods or even (in principle) forever. Some groups produce *gliders,* groups of five cells that move diagonally across the grid to infinity if not obstructed by other patterns. "Glider guns" that produce a steady stream of gliders can be arranged to form a digital computer on the grid (Berlecamp, Conway, and Guy, 1982).

The Game of Life computer is a Turing machine. It can compute anything computable by the most powerful supercomputer, given enough time and a large enough grid. Remarkably, such a complex mechanism can be constructed from the three simple transition rules that define the Game of Life. No better demonstration is needed of the organizational power of complex interactions in large arrays of simple parts.

Langton produced a self-replicating cellular automaton for which each cell had only eight possible states. Langton's CAs needed a few hundred squares on the grid to reproduce. Von Neumann had needed 29 states and 200,000 squares for his self-replicating CA. Self-replication in cellular automata was not nearly as difficult as it had seemed. Still, Langton was interested in even more basic properties of cellular automata. He began studying the simplest family of CAs, those with only one dimension.

A one-dimensional CA is just a row of cells. The state of each cell in the next generation is determined by the current state of its neighbors. A one-dimensional CA with two states can be represented by a sequence of zeros and ones, a bit string. An advantage in studying one-dimensional CAs is that the temporal sequence of their states can be laid out spatially in the second dimension on a computer screen. Langton was interested in exploring the space of possible rules for determining the on or off status of each cell in the next generation.

He used a neighborhood of five cells, a central cell and the two beside it on either side. Each cell could take four possible states (three on and one off). The number of possible configurations of states for the five cells in the neighborhood is 4^5 or 1024. Four to the 1024th power (10^{600}) is the number of different rules that can be used to specify the state of a cell in the next generation. (The age of the universe in seconds is about 10^{39}.) Each of these rules can be expressed as a string of 1024 ones and zeros. One fourth of the states determined by these rules are zero, or off, the other three fourths, 1, 2, or 3, are on.

An initial string of 128 cells was created with random state assignments. When one of the 10^{600} transition rules, also chosen at random, was applied to each cell in the initial string, a new string was generated. The same rule was then applied to the new string and each of its successors. The sequence of new strings formed a two-dimensional configuration in which patterns developing over time could be viewed.

Langton found a striking relationship between the pattern of ones and zeros that made up the transition rule and the complexity of the bit strings it generated. He tested a set of 24 bit rules selected at random from the rule space. When the ratio of zeros to ones in the rule string was very high, the on cells died out in the first few generations. When the ratio of ones to zeros was very high, the successor states were uniformly turned on.

As the mixture of ones and zeros in the rule string approached the point equidistant from these extremes, where zeros and ones were evenly balanced, something unexpected happened. Moving from the predominantly zero rule strings toward the point where ones and zeros are equally distributed, cycles began to build up during the sequence of generations. At first these were just cycles of one state, simple repetitions. The value of a particular cell repeated itself indefinitely, forming a vertical line on the computer screen.

Then, a little closer to the midpoint, more complicated periodic structures arose from small groups of cells in the initial bit string. These structures repeated themselves after two to four generations. As the midpoint approached, new structures began to appear that repeated only after hundreds of generations. These structures were made up of smaller units, a few cells wide, that repeated, but not exactly, every few dozen generations.

The columns of evolving structure, called *transients*, moved diagonally at a much slower pace than their vertical movement on the time scale. Transients often collided, sending off gliders to be intercepted by other transients, as in the Game of Life. As the size of the cycles increased, so did the number of generations which each sequence went through before finally dying. This number reached into the thousands, and asymptotically approached infinity at the midpoint.

Moving toward the midpoint from the other extreme, where the rules were made up predominantly of ones, transients developed slowly once again, this time from within a chaotic background. They became more and more structured (less chaotic) as they approached the midpoint. First the smaller and then the larger patterns in the transients appeared after beginning as a featureless jumble. The spike at the midpoint was the locus of differentiation and structure when approached from either side. At the two extremes Langton found first rigid order and then chaotic disorder.

Watching the computer screen while a one-dimensional CA evolves is like watching the atoms of Lucretius falling through the void. Lucretius pictured the world as made up of atoms falling forever through empty space in parallel streams. At rare intervals, one of the atoms swerved and struck a neighbor, making possible the more complex combinations that we see in the macroscopic world.

The diagonal movement of the more complex transients on the screen (the gliders) brings to mind the *clinamen* or swerving of atoms that Lucretius described in his poem, *The Order of Things*. Lucretius saw the clinamen as a motion that is necessary to give the universe form, but not predictable from the prior states of the model. This is like the motion of complex systems with nonlinear dynamics, whose emergent properties are determined by lower level laws but are not predictable from those laws.

Langton's work with the one-dimensional CA was, in effect, a quantification of the clinamen. Ilya Prigogine (Nobel Prize, 1977) had seen this pattern evolve in the nonlinear dynamics of some chemical systems (Prigogine and Stengers, 1984). The clinamen is graphically portrayed in a one-dimensional CA. In this simple system, Langton had isolated a narrow strip of highly differentiated activity, just where the regime of periodically ordered behavior collided with the zone of chaos. Following Packard (1988), Langton called this narrow zone *the edge of chaos* (see Figure 3.3).

$\lambda = 0.45$ $\lambda = 0.50$ $\lambda = 0.55$

Figure 3.3. Transients near the edge of chaos. (From C. Langton, *Artificial Life:* Volume II, 1992, p. 53. © 1992 Addison-Wesley Publishing Company Inc. Reprinted by permission of Addison-Wesley Longman Inc.)

Wolfram (1986) had ranked the behaviors of cellular automata in four classes: (I) rigid order, (II) periodic order, (III) chaotic disorder, and (IV) highly individualized and differentiated behavior. Langton showed that Wolfram's class IV behavior occurred at the edge of chaos, between classes II and III. (The edge of chaos is not necessarily a straight line, as in a one-dimensional CA, but can be a curving and sometimes discontinuous path through phase space.) The Wolfram classes were not just ad hoc categories, but a measure of distance from the edge of chaos.

Several $K = 5$ rules (rules operating on 5 cell neighborhoods) have been discovered that create one-dimensional cellular automata with only two states, capable of doing universal computation. One such rule was evolved by a computer program using the genetic algorithm (Holland, 1975). Although organisms do not seem to require universal computational powers to maintain themselves, their computational needs are still quite high. These powers are readily available in complex systems.

The edge of chaos in cellular automata marks a *phase transition* between order and chaos. At the phase transition, new entities (transient formations) appear in great profusion. The edge of chaos is where the interesting action is. Complicated structures poised between order and disorder are generated at the phase transition.

The "good psychoanalytic hour" (Kris, 1951) is the unusual analytic session in which thoughts and feelings come together for the patient in a new and more complex way. Could the good hour be an hour in which a phase transition occurs in the organization of the patient's mental contents? We will see later on why this seems very likely. Several of Richard's hours described in chapter 2 showed the analysis moving at the boundary between order and chaos, where phase transitional reorganization was taking place.

Complex Adaptive Systems (CASs)

The class of complex adaptive systems includes all living things, all organizations of living things, and a growing number of computer programs. Complex adaptive systems are self-organized, like the sandpile. Unlike the sandpile, their structures can change in response to environmental pressures. The patient and the analyst are each complex adaptive systems. They share with other such systems a set of properties that determine the most basic aspects of their behavior. Each of them has many component parts, each part with a degree of independence from the larger system (the person) they belong to. The parts interact within each system in a dynamic nonlinear way. The patterns they form cannot be predicted by the usual methods of mathematical analysis.

Complex adaptive systems are open to the world around them. To maintain or improve their internal structures, they extract energy and information from the outside world. They work constantly, in fact, to maintain a state of disequilibrium with their entropy-drenched surroundings.

Inside a complex adaptive system, many kinds of organization are possible. For example, all components of a system need not interact with all other components. Each variant pattern of connectedness may be unique. A fully connected system tends to be chaotic (disordered), because too much is happening within it at one time. At the edge of chaos, only a fraction of the components are usually turned on.

The organization of a CAS, its pattern of interaction, is dynamic. It responds to changes both external to the system (climate changes or the threat of new predators) and internal to it (mutation and recombination). These changes reorganize the components of the system so that it is better able to maintain itself under the new conditions.

An adaptive system responds in a way that improves its fitness for maintaining itself in the environment. The environment confronts it with a set of physical and organizational constraints, and, in the biological world, with a population of other systems with conflicting interests. *Adaptation is possible only when the pattern of connections within a system can change.* Bak (1994) says, "Fitness is a synonym for self-consistent integration into a highly integrated complex or critical state by any part of the system."

Complex adaptive systems have become well known for their *emergent properties and behavior.* Emergent properties appear at all levels in the organization of matter, whenever a set of components organizes to become a system. The properties of a system

are spoken of as emergent when the properties of their components individually are neither necessary nor sufficient for them
to arise. For example, the properties of molecules are emergent
with respect to the properties of the atoms they are composed
of. In complex adaptive systems this effect is magnified many
times over.

Emergence is a concept with deep roots in human experience. One of the primitive assumptions underlying the concept
of *making,* a basic category of human activity (Lakoff and Johnson, 1980) is that "the object comes out of the substance." Making is the special case of *doing* in which a new object appears as
a result of the action. "You can make ice out of water by freezing
it" (p. 73), is a typical example. "I made a statue out of clay"
(p. 73), is another.

In everyday speech, the roles of objects and substances can
be extended to mental or behavioral states. For example, the new
object can be an action, and the substance a state of mind, as in,
"He shot the mayor out of desperation" (p. 75). In all of these
cases, the emerging object results from an action planned and
executed by a conscious human agent. An emergent organization
"made out of" its components is an exception to this general
rule of language.

It is still difficult for many people to think of the making of
a new object without a conscious human (or superhuman) agent
working at it from the top level down. The idea of new properties
emerging without the act of a conscious agent has an uncanny
feel to it. Complexity theory shows us that in the world of nature
new objects are made through the nonlinear interactions of objects that already exist. These new objects include associations of
human beings whose interactions produce results that cannot be
accurately predicted.

For the broad class of complex adaptive systems, emergent
properties and behaviors result from the reorganization of their
parts into new kinds of structures with novel functions.
Crutchfield (1994) says, "A process undergoes emergence if at
some time the architecture of information processing has
changed in such a way that a distinct and more powerful level of
intrinsic computation has appeared that was not present in earlier
conditions" (p. 9). Here Crutchfield is pointing out that the

emergence of a new organization is a computation over the unorganized components. Thus a computer simulation mimics the intrinsic computation of self-organizing matter.

Complex adaptive systems must interact with their environments to survive. They extract information from the activity going on around them and compute adaptive responses to it. A patient in analysis gets better when new ways of gathering information about himself emerge from a more effectively connected mental organization. We see how a reorganization of his mental contents can make previously unconscious information available for processing in a new context.

A complex adaptive system with a great many interacting components and little structure is slow to adapt. Communication from one end of the system to the other can only occur through repeated interactions between adjacent components. Opportunities for error are numerous. If a CAS is to respond quickly to its environment, hierarchical structures are needed to coordinate and unify the responses of each of its components (Huberman, 1989). The time it takes for a system without hierarchical structures to adapt to a new environmental constraint grows exponentially with the number of its parts.

Huberman simulated a system of 10 agents, each of them capable of behaving according to two different plans or strategies. A goal was introduced that required each of the 10 agents to use one of its two strategies. When the simulation was run, the system remained in its original configuration for a long time. Then the system made a very sharp and sudden transition to the optimal mix of strategies for solving the problem.

Huberman compared this finding with the punctuated equilibrium found in the fossil record. One of the most important implications for him was that:

> [A] large collection of computational agents in an open system will not spontaneously generate adaptive behavior when the introduction of constraints produces metastable configurations. In such situations, either more sophisticated procedures are needed, or a global agent has to exist in order to (a) become aware of the advantage produced by another fixed point [a new combination of strategies]; and (b) to induce a coordinated action whereby

processes simultaneously change their ESS [Evolutionary Stable Strategy, i.e., the original mix of strategies] [1989, p. 128; brackets added].

The global agent that becomes aware of the advantages of a new mix of strategies in Huberman's simulation plays the role of the observing ego in a psychoanalytic patient. The original agents become the components of the global agent, if and when a global agent emerges from the coevolutionary dynamics of the situation. In the course of his analysis, Richard was able to observe larger and larger units in his representations of himself and his objects.

Adaptive evolution takes place when hierarchical structures arise that coordinate the lower level agents, so that an agent at a higher level can respond to a change in the environment. In the psychoanalytic process, improvement takes place when the repressed contents of the patient's memory and self-image are coordinated by new structures emerging at a higher level. Richard's analysis is notable for the spontaneous verbal articulation of these new inner structures.

To function, these new higher level structures must include an awareness of the repressed mental contents and their psychological effects. As Huberman's experiment shows, this awareness of components is an inherent property of the higher level organization itself. In thinking about the psychoanalytic process, we would do well to note the fine gradations of awareness that emerge spontaneously with these higher levels of organization. There is no need for a homunculus to appear suddenly to observe the inner workings of the patient's mind. The patient's observing ego is itself an *emergent hierarchical organization*. In Crutchfield's (1994) terms, once again, "The architecture of information processing has changed in such a way that a distinct and more powerful level of intrinsic computation has appeared that was not present in earlier conditions" (p. 9).

A central concern of the analyst is to strengthen the patient's powers of self-observation, his ability to observe and compute what he thinks and feels. The analyst's part is to promote the emergence of the new mental structures that make this kind of advance possible.

Traversing the Fitness Landscape

During the psychoanalytic process, the role of mutation is played by the changes *within each participant* that arise from the *interaction of their separate views* of themselves and the world. These changes are not stored in a separate and segregated structure like the genome, to be transmitted as a unit. The connection weights at the synapses on the dendrites of neurons in the brain are modified by events, as they are in an artificial neural network. (The connectedness of the neurons in the brain may be modified as well as the weights of the synapses, although this effect is not yet clearly understood.)

However, the genome is still a convenient unit for exploring the features of evolutionary change. For example, a simple model for studying the interaction of structural change with adaptive success is the *adaptive landscape* of Wright (1931). The adaptive landscape is a many dimensional graph that shows the effect of a series of single gene mutations on the fitness of an organism. (We saw the usefulness of the adaptive landscape in Eigen's description of self-organization in the genome ensemble of the retroviruses, pp. 15–17.)

Kauffman (1993) used a simple computer model to explore important properties of the adaptive landscape—he refers to it as the *fitness landscape*. His results show why the evolution of self-organization in the patient's inner world has to be nonlinear.

The genome in his model has N genes, with 2 possible values or *alleles* per gene. This structure can be represented in the computer as a string of ones and zeros. There are 2^N possible genotypes represented by strings of length N. When these 2^N genotypes are connected to one another by N edges, they form an N-dimensional cube. The distance between genotypes can be measured by the number of vertices that separate them on the N-dimensional lattice formed by the edges of the cube.

In Kauffman's model, mutations occur randomly among the genes, but only one gene at a time is affected. A series of mutations in a single gene traces a path in this N-dimensional space.

The fitness landscape is usually visualized as an undulating surface of fitness values with a number of peaks and valleys. A

mutation in a single gene moves a genotype to an adjacent location on the surface of the landscape within the genotype space.
This new position may have a higher or lower adaptive level.

Adaptive mutations are those that increase the fitness of the
genotype, moving the location of the genotype to a higher value
on the landscape. Under the pressure of natural selection then,
the genotype eventually takes an uphill walk via a series of single
gene mutations toward a local optimum. The combination of
mutation and selection pressure leads the genotype to a higher
level of fitness.

Such a series of mutations forms a connected path on the
surface of the landscape. The path reaches an endpoint at a local
optimum, when there are no single gene mutations left that can
increase the fitness of the genotype. Other combinations of
genes, at a distance greater than one, may be able to produce a
more fit genotype, but those combinations cannot be found
through a single gene mutation.

As an illustration, we can take a simple genome with only
three genes (see Figure 3.4). Its eight possible genotypes are connected in the same pattern as the vertices of a cube. Each genotype has three nearest neighbors, three more distant neighbors,
and one most distant neighbor on the opposite corner of the
cube. Each of the eight genotypes has its own fitness value. There
can be as many as four local optima in this system, depending on
the fitness values and their distribution on the cube. A genotype
space that forms a cube with only one local optimum has a smooth
fitness landscape. On a cube with four local optima, the landscape
is very rugged.

In the more general case, if the number of genes, N, is very
large, and if the fitness of each gene is independent of all the
others, then the differences in fitness between adjacent genotypes
are small. The landscape has a single peak and a smooth surface.
When the fitness value of a gene is influenced by the characteristics of neighboring genes, however, the number of peaks and
valleys in a region goes up. The landscape becomes more rugged.
The average number of genes influencing a single gene in such
a system is referred to as K, the degree of connectedness within
the system. As K increases, the landscape becomes more rugged.
On a very rugged landscape the peaks are steeper and there are

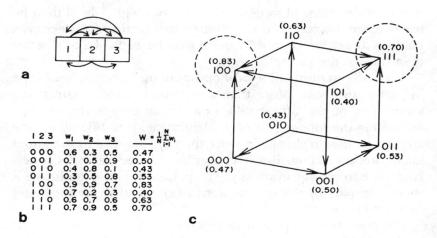

b

1 2 3	w_1	w_2	w_3	$W = \frac{1}{N}\sum_{i=1}^{N} w_i$
0 0 0	0.6	0.3	0.5	0.47
0 0 1	0.1	0.5	0.9	0.50
0 1 0	0.4	0.8	0.1	0.43
0 1 1	0.3	0.5	0.8	0.53
1 0 0	0.9	0.9	0.7	0.83
1 0 1	0.7	0.2	0.3	0.40
1 1 0	0.6	0.7	0.6	0.63
1 1 1	0.7	0.9	0.5	0.70

Figure 3.4. Fitness landscape for three genes with two alleles. (*a*) Assignment of $K = 2$ epistatic inputs to each site. (*b*) Assignment of fitness values to each of the three genes with random values for each of the eight combinations of $K + 1$ alleles bearing on genes 1, 2, and 3. These fitness values then assign a fitness to each of the $2^3 = 8$ possible genotypes as the mean value of the fitness contributions of the three genes. (*c*) Fitness landscape on the three-dimensional Boolean cube corresponding to the fitness values of the eight genotypes in (*b*). Note that more than one local optimum exists. (From *The Origins of Order: Self-Organization and Selection in Evolution* by Stuart A. Kauffman, 1993, p. 42. Copyright © 1993 by Oxford University Press, Inc. Used by permission of Oxford University Press, Inc.)

more of them. A smooth landscape has few peaks and gentle slopes. If the landscape is too smooth, change will be very slow. If it is too rugged, adaptive changes come rapidly but are much diminished in amplitude. Sequences of adaptive mutations leading to a local optimum will be very short. An intermediate level of ruggedness gives the system its best opportunity for significant change at a reasonable pace.

The psychoanalytic process also has its optimal degree of ruggedness. The danger of an analysis foundering on a local optimum is considerable. At a local optimum the patient feels that he has improved, but that any further change will only return him to an earlier state of discomfort. Lacking a view of himself that includes states of well-being at an even higher level than he has reached, he may convince himself that further treatment is a waste of time. He cannot imagine that he could be any better than he is at the moment.

A CAS can move off a local optimum on its fitness landscape in one of two ways. More than one mutation can occur at the same time, or the fitness values on the landscape can change, deforming the topography of the landscape. It is difficult for the analytic patient to change in more than one way at a time without major stress ensuing. But it is possible for the patient's fitness landscape to change gradually. The patient's fitness landscape is shaped in part by the expectations of the analyst for his better functioning.

A myth often repeated in psychoanalytic circles is that the analyst should expect nothing from the patient. Otherwise, it is said, the patient will try to meet the analyst's expectations at the expense of his own autonomy. The analyst will be intruding on the patient's unconscious fantasies and deflecting the spontaneous flow of his associations. If the analyst can only hold himself back from interfering with the patient's free associations, everything will be revealed eventually.

Two things are wrong with this idea. First of all, the analyst creates an expectation whenever he opens his mouth, and often when he doesn't. Every interpretation presupposes that the patient is ready to deal with the content of the interpretation. It does not escape the patient that this is an expectation he may fail to fulfill.

Even more significantly, the spontaneous flow of the patient's associations cannot move beyond the nearest local optimum. Apart from a serious setback, only a change in the analyst's expectations can move the patient beyond that point. Most of the time, the analyst expects that as the patient reveals more of his unconscious mental life, his capacity to handle interpretations of more sensitive issues increases with it. Most of the time the analyst is right about this. But not when the patient has reached a local fitness optimum.

For the patient to go further, he has to be willing to experience anxiety as he moves away from his current local optimum to seek a higher level of functioning. The patient is more likely to take the risk if the analyst makes his own expectations for further change explicit to the patient. He can do so by pointing out the problems left unsolved at the current optimum.

This activity by the analyst can have a mutative effect on the patient. But it has to be modulated in a way that causes the patient a minimum loss of self-esteem. The analyst has to remind the patient that the need for further movement reflects his successful climb up the fitness landscape, even if it has led him to a temporary dead end at a local optimum.

In this situation, the landscape cannot be too smooth, or the patient will not be able to leave the local optimum. He will either go around in circles near the peak or else break off the treatment. If the landscape is too rugged, the patient may suffer a serious loss of self-esteem as he feels himself bounced from a local peak into a valley where his frustration seems likely to be unending.

Richard's discovery of the fitness landscape was serendipitous. As an attorney, Richard had no experience of fitness landscapes in his work. The analyst had not introduced any theoretical ideas into the analytic discourse. Richard's rich imagination was able to apply the very basic metaphor of an up and down journey to his progress in the analysis. His own contribution was to place his parents in the landscape. They were standing in front of him on the first mountain, obscuring his view of a better future. When he was able to descend from this local optimum, they were at the bottom of the valley, their backs forming a bridge on which he crossed over a stream to the next peak.

This last image alludes in a specific way to the help the analyst had provided Richard in his descent from the first local optimum, the help that allowed him to risk the anxiety he knew he would feel on coming down to the valley. The analyst had shown him that he could use his anger toward his parents to trace out a major source of unconscious confusion in his childhood experience. Richard had believed that the anger could only be destructive. Now he had a constructive use for his parents that preserved them from the effects of his anger. Once this change occurred, he could feel the anger without being afraid that it would disrupt or destroy his search for a better life.

Kauffman (1993) shows that the ruggedness of a fitness landscape depends on the size of the population and the degree of its connectedness. Its ruggedness is a function of both the total number of components in the system, N, and the number of individual components connected to and interacting with each other component, K. For a fixed N, the ruggedness of the landscape increases with K, which measures the degree of connectedness among the communicating components of the mutating system. Orderly evolutionary change for any system takes place at an optimal intermediate level of ruggedness. (This can be compared with the optimal level of complexity at the edge of chaos in CAs, although the concepts are not identical.)

On a smooth or correlated fitness landscape, one with few peaks and valleys, the values of each genotype are predictable from the fitness values of its nearest neighbors. These are the neighboring genotypes that differ by just a single gene. On a completely uncorrelated landscape (one with a high density of peaks), the fitness of neighbors have less relation to one another. A correlated landscape is smooth, with perhaps only one peak. A relatively uncorrelated landscape is rugged, with many peaks and valleys.

The fitness of a gene is usually influenced by its structural context in the genotype. On a linear structure like a chromosome, each gene is adjacent to two others. These adjacent genes often have an influence on the expression of the gene between them; so may other genes adjacent to those two. K once again indicates the *connectedness* of the genome, the number of other genes in the system influencing each individual gene.

How far can a series of single gene mutations move through the fitness landscape of an organism? Kauffman showed that in a network of linear genotypes with two alleles at each gene site, the number of local optima increases rapidly as K increases relative to N (as the landscape becomes more rugged). At the same time the average fitness of the local optima declines toward the mean fitness of all the genotypes in the space.

When every component is connected with every other, and $K = N - 1$, the fitness landscape is uncorrelated and connections are indistinguishable. The optimal value of K, the value that gives the highest average fitness value for local optima, is at the boundary between correlated (low K) and uncorrelated (high K) landscapes. All of this assumes that the fitness values of the individual genotypes remain constant. In a coevolutionary context, the fitness values of a member system vary when those of its neighbors vary, though not in a linear way.

The idea of a genotype can be generalized to any system whose structure is based on stored information. This would include the traditional biological genome that does not vary with the life experience of the organism that carries it. But it also includes CASs that can be reorganized by the interaction of their parts when new information is available to them. The states of mind of a psychoanalytic patient fall into this latter category.

Gell-Mann's more general term that includes the genotype is the *schema*. The word has been widely used in developmental psychology since Piaget (1937) introduced it to describe the successive cognitive structures acquired by a child as it grows. Gell-Mann (1994) says: "The common feature of all these processes is that in each one a complex adaptive system acquires information about the environment, identifying regularities in that information, condensing those regularities into a "schema" or model, and acting in the real world on the basis of that schema" (p. 17).

A biological genome changes slowly over many generations, in response to new information coming from the environment (but think of the Galapagos finches). Schemata in other CASs can change more quickly, like the pattern of synaptic weights in a neural network, for example. Ackley and Littman (1994) are even moved to say that "natural life was forced to adopt a Darwinian scheme, in essence, because it was constrained to arise spontaneously from a chemical system. By contrast, in deliberately constructed artificial evolutionary systems, Lamarckian evolution can be both easy to implement and far more effective" (p. 3).

This is true of the schemata in all man-made complex adaptive systems, including social and political systems. The American Constitution is a good example of such a schema. It can be modified when new experience indicates, but not easily enough to lead to chaotic behavior. The founding fathers were able to locate the edge of chaos in political life on only their second attempt.

Changes in a patient during analysis are like mutations in a biological genome. The great majority of them take place at a level analogous to the genotypic level in organic evolution. That is, they are small structural changes in the patient's self- and object-representations, difficult to observe directly. They might not be visible at all in the analytic fossil record, the bare written transcript of a recorded analytic session.

Movement from one local fitness optimum to another occurs only if the fitness of the genome declines sufficiently for it to cross a valley to the slope of a local optimum at a higher level. For the patient, this temporary loss of fitness is a regression he suffers for the sake of further exploration and growth. But the patient has to be able to tolerate such a regression even when he cannot feel fully confident that it will be temporary.

The patient can escape more easily from a local optimum if the landscape changes, so that the descent from his current location is less abrupt. This can be the case if the analyst modifies his own behavior appropriately. Technical questions that come up in supervision and in case conferences are almost always about the appropriate way to deform the patient's fitness landscape to facilitate further movement. This can only be done within the context of the analytic relationship at a particular moment. Even when done with tact, a change of direction by the analyst may leave the patient feeling betrayed or abandoned before he is able to realize the benefits it will bring.

A major question for the analyst is how to respond to the regression that accompanies the patient's descent from a local optimum. The analyst has to avoid encouraging the patient to fall to a dangerously low level of fitness before he resumes his upward movement toward a higher peak. But he cannot discourage the beginnings of a positive movement toward a new optimum, either. Whether the patient feels able to risk the regression depends in part on the sensitivity of the analyst. This in turn reflects the success thus far of the coevolutionary process as it has developed during the analysis.

The concept of the local optimum offers a structural explanation for some of the difficulty that patients have in giving up old ways to make room for newer and more effective adaptations. *In a complex adaptive system, resistance to change is built into the process of change itself.* This resistance may be quite distinct from the specific actions of the patient's defense mechanisms.

Coevolution

In an intimate two-person system, like the psychoanalytic treatment situation, the fitness of one person depends to a great degree on the behavior of the other. Like the bee and the flower, or the fox and the rabbit, the two are interdependent. Adaptive interdependence tends to accelerate evolutionary change, as each adapting system adapts to changes in the other. This condition is called *coevolution*.

The patient and the analyst are two interacting self-organized systems. Each of these systems is made up in turn of many connected interacting components. The interacting systems adapt over time to changes in each other's behavior in their shared ecosystem. When this process is successful, each system in the ecosystem evolves to an optimal degree of internal connectedness as well as to a higher level of fitness (Kauffman, 1993, 1995). Coevolutionary change in the analyst's view of the patient is the mechanism that keeps an analysis from stagnating on the patient's local optimum.

A system evolving in a particular environment alters the fitness values of other systems sharing the environment. Examples include symbiosis, parasitism, insect pollination, and predators and their prey. Increased power and speed in a predator makes its natural prey relatively less fit, unless the prey also becomes able to run fast enough to compensate for the change in its coevolutionary partner.

Evolving species deform the fitness landscapes of the species with which they interact. When coupled in an ecosystem, so that changes in each deform the fitness landscapes of the others, they coevolve. The mutual deformation of fitness landscapes loosens the tendency of each system to adhere to its current local optimum. Freud (1937b) explained the obstacles created by local optima as due to "the adhesiveness of the [patient's] libido." (We shall see, however, that the ecosystem as a whole can reach an equilibrium that limits further change to its component species.) Here Freud took a different direction from Darwin, who emphasized that the major influences in any organism's environment are other organisms. The analyst's simulation of the patient is the most salient factor in the patient's analytic environment.

The analyst's increasing knowledge of the patient makes it possible for him to tilt the adaptive landscape so that the patient can move in the direction of a higher peak. This is what usually happens when the analyst conveys his belief that the patient's ability to adapt has risen beyond his neurotically diminished expectations.

A dramatic example of this occurred in Richard's analysis when he returned from his honeymoon. Having attained a major goal, Richard was afraid to tempt fate any further. He wanted to reduce his analytic hours, clearly intending an early exit. When the analyst would not endorse this decision, Richard continued to come as before, but with angry protestations. Analysis of the anger led to a much deeper understanding of his ambivalent feelings and fantasies about his father.

Coevolution in nature is a process of finer and finer approximations to an ideal state of adaptation. A well-studied example is that of the cuckoo and its hosts, the species of birds in whose nests it lays its eggs (Davies and Brooke, 1991). There are four varieties of cuckoo in Great Britain, each of which deposits its eggs in the nest of a different species of bird. There the cuckoo chicks are hatched and raised by the host species. Three of the four cuckoo varieties lay eggs that look very similar to those of the host. The host accepts the similar cuckoo egg, but ejects other eggs that are different from its own.

The fourth species of host, the dunnock or hedge sparrow, is different. It is tolerant of eggs placed in its nest that are quite unlike its own. The dunnock cuckoo seems to know about this. The eggs it lays in dunnock nests bear no resemblance to dunnock eggs. This situation can be explained if the dunnock cuckoo has only recently begun exploiting the dunnock, so that the dunnock had not yet evolved an antipathy to cuckoo eggs and an urge to expel them. The proportion of dunnock nests parasitized by the cuckoos is smaller than that of the other three hosts, also suggesting that the dunnock may be a more recent cuckoo victim.

The dunnock behaves like other birds with no experience of parasitism, which are generally accepting of strange eggs in their nests. As a result of its experience with cuckoos, one can expect the dunnock to evolve the same intolerance to strange eggs that the other cuckoo hosts have done. One can also expect the dunnock cuckoo to evolve an egg that resembles the egg of the dunnock when this happens.

The British cuckoos and their hosts are coevolving. As it happens, one can easily predict the next stage in their contest. In Central Europe, cuckoo host species eject any eggs that are not *exactly* like their own. In retaliation, the European cuckoos have evolved eggs that are indistinguishable from the host eggs.

This series of increasingly refined specializations is characteristic of coevolution. Each partner becomes more and more attentive and reactive to the actions and intentions of the other. Actions become more specifically designed to evoke a desired response. The result, depending on the motives of the partners, can be an escalating arms race or a finely tuned collaboration.

In the case of the cuckoo and its hosts, the contest is a zero sum game. What is good for the cuckoo is bad for the host, and vice versa. As they coevolve, each of them improves its ability to counteract the improvements in the other. They each adapt more effectively to the struggle between them. The net result, however, is that neither improves its position relative to the other. They have to keep running as fast as they can to stay in the same place, like the Red Queen in *Alice in Wonderland.*

When the partners are coevolving toward a situation that benefits both of them, as the bees and the flowers have done, then the partnership itself gains in fitness as well as the individual participants. This is also what happens in psychoanalysis. The interests of the patient and the analyst are convergent, although in some ways quite distinct from one another. Some patients, of course, begin their treatment with serious doubts that psychoanalysis could be anything other than a zero sum game.

In the course of psychoanalytic therapy, the patient's view of the analyst, and the analyst's model of the patient, in both conscious and unconscious versions, evolve in tandem. The therapeutic process brings about a series of modifications, of the patient's views of himself and the analyst, and of the analyst's views of the patient. Whether the analyst's view of himself also has to change has been debated within the psychoanalytic community. In recent years, more and more attention has been paid to the changes in the analyst's self-image that result from his continuing analysis of his countertransference to the patient. We will see that this is actually an essential aspect of the dynamics of the analytic process.

The setting of the psychoanalyst's office is designed for coevolutionary change. The therapeutic ecosystem is insulated as far as it can be from outside stimulation and influence. It has a fixed meeting schedule that maximizes its inner continuity and its autonomy from outside events. The frequency of psychoanalytic sessions allows more time to be spent on events internal to the therapeutic ecosystem, and less (proportionately) on the events taking place outside.

This arrangement frees the patient and the analyst to develop their models of each other with a minimum of distraction. The changes in these models are often large at first, then more and more gradually refined. We will be looking in detail at the coevolutionary interaction of patient and analyst.

4 COMPLEX ADAPTIVE SYSTEMS

Tierra: Artificial Evolution

An evolving complex adaptive system small enough to be understood in every detail is Thomas Ray's Tierra (1992), a simulation made up of artificial organisms that reproduce. As simple as it is, Tierra produces evolutionary behavior that is self-organized, self-similar, and unpredictable in the details of its moment to moment changes.

The organisms that populate Tierra are independent programs competing for processor time and memory space. They live in a virtual computer that prevents them from escaping into the memory of the actual computer where they could turn into viruses. The virtual computer uses a special set of instructions created by Ray that make the organisms robust enough to survive even when random mutations strike them.

Within the virtual computer is a region of empty memory space called "the soup." A single self-reproducing artificial organism is introduced into the soup. This organism, called *the ancestor*, contains a sequence of 80 instructions that cause it to copy itself. The organism first measures its own length, then copies itself into an empty memory space of the same length, and finally detaches

119

itself from its now independent offspring. (One of Tierra's own ancestors is John Holland's famous *genetic algorithm* [1975].)

Random mutations create new organisms with altered sequences and numbers of instructions. Some of these mutated forms are able to reproduce, but most of them are not. The successful daughter organisms multiply until about 80 percent of soup capacity is reached, about 360 organisms (see Figure 4.1).

By the time the soup is filled, it contains about 20 different sizes of organisms (size is number of instructions). These 20 sizes come in about 160 different genotypic variations (sequences of instructions). When the soup capacity is saturated, the oldest organism is killed by a mechanism called the "reaper." The strict chronological order of the reaper queue is modified slightly according to the success of the organisms in executing their instructions. Those that succeed with two of the most difficult instructions are moved one place down on the queue. An organism that generates an error in execution is moved up one place toward an earlier death.

The size classes of the organisms in Tierra have some properties reminiscent of the properties of distinct species in biological life. They are few in comparison with the number of genotypes created by mutation. One would expect the viability of a Tierra organism undergoing a change in its number of instructions to be lower than that of an organism undergoing a change in instruction sequence only. The ancestor organism was originally designed with the idea that all of its instructions were essential. Although the evolution of the Tierra culture proves that this is not so, the loss of an instruction poses a greater threat than a reshuffling of the existing genotype.

Members of a Tierra size class can be identified from the outside, as it were, by counting the number of instructions. The observer does not have to know the identities of the individual instructions to do this. In this respect, a size class resembles a biological species identified only from its morphology in the fossil record.

At first, the ancestor reproduces itself exactly. Then an increasing number of viable genotypic variations appears. Some time after that, new species (sizes) appear. These have 79 or 81 instructions. The first stable groups that differ considerably in

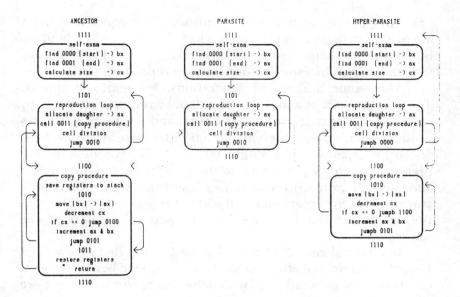

Figure 4.1. Genomes of Tierra organisms. Metabolic flow chart for the ancestor, parasite, hyperparasite, and their interactions: ax, bx and cx refer to CPU registers where location and size information are stored. [ax] and [bx] refer to locations in the soup indicated by the values in the ax and bx registers. Patterns such as 1101 are complementary templates used for addressing. Arrows outside of boxes indicate jumps in the flow of execution of the programs. The dotted-line arrows indicate flow of execution between creatures. The parasite lacks the copy procedure; however, if it is within the search limit of the copy procedure of a host, it can locate, call, and execute that procedure, thereby obtaining the information needed to complete its replication. The host is not adversely affected by this informational parasitism, except through competition with the parasite, which is a superior competitor. Note that the parasite calls the copy procedure of its host with the expectation that control will return to the parasite when the copy procedure returns. However, the hyperparasite jumps out of the copy procedure rather than returning, thereby seizing control from the parasite. It then proceeds to reset the CPU registers of the parasite with the location and size of the hyperparasite, causing the parasite to replicate the hyperparasite genome thereafter. (From Ray, 1992, in C. Langton, *Artificial Life:* Volume II, 1992, p. 381. © 1992 Addison-Wesley Publishing Company Inc. Reprinted by permission of Addison-Wesley Longman Inc.)

size from the ancestor are the *parasites*. They typically contain about 45 instructions. A parasite has lost its own copy instructions, but is able to adapt to this lack by taking control of the copy sequence of an ancestorlike organism to reproduce itself.

After some millions of generations, *hyperparasites* appear. These organisms, of about size 80, adapt by recapturing the copy sequence commandeered by a parasite, and redirecting it to reproduce themselves. Later still, *social hyperparasites* are evolved. Social hyperparasites, of length 60, can only reproduce in the presence of another organism of the same type. *Hyperhyperparasites,* only 27 instructions long, can insert themselves between a pair of social hyperparasites in the act of reproduction. They use the reproductive cycles of the hyperparasites to replicate themselves.

In a typical run of 40 or 50 I analyzed, the first new species (size class) appeared after 80,000 instructions had been executed, or about 100 generations. By 560,000 instructions, there were already 4 species. Then a rapid burst of new speciation began, so that five more new species appeared by the execution of the 800,000th instruction. A long lull followed. At 2.16 million, a new burst, slower than the first, added five more, bringing the total to 14 species at 2.8 million. The fifteenth species did not appear until 4.57 million, the sixteenth at 5.36. Another burst began with the seventeenth at 6.16 million. By 6.4 million there were already 20 species.

At 10 million there were 22 species; at 15 million 25. By 20 million a rough maximum of 28 had been reached. The number of species then drifted slowly downward, through many small fluctuations, until at 110 million there was only 20 again. This level remained stable for another billion instructions or more. This is the typical pattern of punctuated equilibrium.

Each run of the program was different in detail, but all followed this pattern. Short periods of rapid variation in the sizes of the dominant species alternated with much longer periods of relative stability. As the runs become longer, the periods of speciation were more and more widely separated. Neither the number of new species created in each burst nor the time consumed by a burst increased. The time lag between bursts of speciation lengthened in rough proportion to the age of the entire system. This pattern is reproduced on each run, though it is never exactly the same. And it happens, as Ray says, "without asteroids."

The parallel between Tierra and the stages of metazoan evolution from the Cambrian explosion until modern times is rather uncanny. As in the Cambrian era, the pattern of punctuated equilibrium in Tierra is already well established before the ecological niche of the organisms is at all chose to saturation. The burst of diversification that marked the Cambrian period is modeled in the early stages of a Tierra run. Then, as in the later history of the Cambrian fauna, the less successful species are weeded out. But even this longer term stability is subject to sudden reversal.

As the generations go by in Tierra, the reproductive efficiency of the organisms increases. The size of the genome becomes smaller on average. The number of instructions executed during a replication decreases too, even faster than genome size. The reproductive cycle of the organism evolves to ever greater compactness and efficiency. A highly evolved organism of length 22 replicates itself by executing 146 instructions, a ratio of 6.6 executions per instruction. At length 80, the ancestor needs 839 executions, a ratio of 10.5.

The key to this pattern of punctuated equilibrium is the changing genotype pool. The number of distinct genotypes is about eight times the number of species or size classes at any moment. The genotype pool is constantly changing, accumulating new variations that lead after a period of time to bursts of speciation. In the fossil record too, an active latency period between genotype change and species change may be enough to explain the long periods of stasis we observe. The asteroids may simply tip over a genotypic array already heavily tilted to one side.

As Casti (1993) has put it, "The Tierra exercise was the first ever to definitively demonstrate that the process of evolution is independent of a particular material substrate. It can take place just as easily among a population of computer programs competing for memory space in a machine as it can among populations of carbon-based organisms competing to survive in an earthly environment" (pp. 20–21).

The success of the Tierran ecosystem as a whole can be measured by the higher reproductive efficiency of the entire set of organisms that comprise it. From the point of view of the ecosystem, the various species are coevolving in a way that optimizes the reproductive efficiency of the mix of organisms as a whole. But the efficiency of the individual organisms increases along with the efficiency of the whole ecosystem. Greater efficiency is a collaborative result for the whole ecosystem.

Tierra shows that evolution through variation and selection is not confined to the terrestrial life we know; it is a blueprint for change in all complex adaptive systems, of whatever origin or composition. In the psychoanalytic process, as it evolves over time, the less fit components of both the patient and the analyst systems lose their influence. They become integrated into their own larger systems through the coevolutionary process that integrates the ecosystem as a whole. The information content of these unfit parts becomes more available to the analytic discourse as their influence on the participants fades away.

The Evolution of Individuals

Analytic treatment often includes long, drawn out, uneventful stretches that end with a sudden and rapid breakthrough of repressed material. These breakthroughs are often thought by psychoanalysts to happen when the patient's defenses crumble after a long process of attrition. But the attrition metaphor covers over and obscures the process of reorganization actually taking place.

The characteristic therapeutic event of every psychoanalytic hour is the release of previously repressed mental content. A breakthrough is a more active and creative event, from the patient's side of the equation, than the breaking down of defensive structures would suggest. The emergence of the repressed material results from a phase transitional change in the patient's mental contents. The phase transition occurs when the connectedness of the system reaches a critical level that permits the patient a higher degree of self-observation. New properties, behaviors, organizational features, and information processing capacities emerge when his point of view is elevated in this way.

The concept of emergence is difficult to define because it seems to imply a subjective observer or evaluator of the newly emergent properties (Crutchfield, 1994). Doubts can arise about the observer's objectivity and his ability to recognize emergence at various scales and under differing conditions. For example, the scale of reorganization might be so small that any concurrent emergent properties would be below the observer's threshold of observation.

At the low end of the scale in the psychoanalytic process, moment to moment changes are often very difficult to observe. However, it is usually quite obvious that the emergence of a major insight in the patient is coupled with a reorganization of mental contents that had been sequestered in the unconscious for years or decades.

Traditional psychoanalytic theory does a very sketchy job of relating the texture of psychoanalytic work from hour to hour with the emergence of significant change in the patient's inner mental structures. What psychoanalysts need is a way to think about how small, even unobservable, changes in the moment to moment analytic interaction can lead to larger, stable, observable changes in the patient. If the large scale changes are emergent, what are they emerging from?

This issue in psychoanalysis is analogous to the problem in evolutionary theory resolved by modern Darwinism. Some changes in the genotype of an organism that cannot be observed macroscopically give rise to quite salient changes in its phenotype, while others have no overt expression at all.

In the laboratory, genotypic changes can now be specified precisely as alterations in the nucleic acid sequences of a gene. But changes in a single gene usually cannot be recognized in the properties of the whole organism, either in the fossil record or in a living species. (Blue eyes and wrinkled peas are the exceptions, not the rule.) Even the observation of a phenotypic change depends to some degree on the subjective criteria of the observer. The identification of a new phenotype can involve an irreducible degree of arbitrariness.

The observation of change in the psychic functioning of the psychoanalytic patient can also be obscured by his defenses. The patient's verbal productions may be filled with circumlocutions, meanderings, temporary regressions, false hopes and fears. What seems to be a change may be a fiction meant to win the approval of the analyst. But after a series of what seem like false starts and digressions (sometimes a very long series), an observable improvement will usually appear. The change may be seen in many areas of the patient's life, including the patient's dreams, his attitudes toward his parents, his dealings with people in his current life, and his relationship with the analyst.

What was happening during the period prior to the change, when nothing appeared to be happening? We can consider at least three possibilities:

1. Nothing really did happen. The observed change was due to the sudden discovery of a critical clue that turned everything around.
2. Small changes (in the patient's unconscious mental life) were taking place all along. The observable change occurred when the sum of these smaller changes reached a threshold value.
3. Small, unconscious changes were taking place all along. The interaction of the effects of these small, invisible changes led to a reorganization that produced the clearly observable change. The final small change of the series precipitated the sudden appearance of this reorganization.

The third formulation combines the virtues of the other two. The large scale change is a real change, not just a threshold phenomenon. Yet it results from the buildup of many small changes. The buildup to a reorganization is nonlinear, accounting for the fact that the length of time required for the reorganization is not predictable. A single event finally tips the balance, but this event may be very small compared with the change that follows. If this final event had taken place before the series of small unobservable changes, no reorganizational effect would have emerged.

But is the observation of the observable change reliable? The two observers present at an analysis may have criteria for recognizing significant change that differ considerably. This can be a troubling issue. If the phase transition is a result of the coevolutionary interaction of these two observers, however, one can assume that the change is a real change only if the patient and the analyst are both aware of it. The analyst has the more external and objective viewpoint. But an increase in the patient's level of self-organization would have to include, ipso facto, an increase in his powers of self-observation. Having both external and internal observers for a phase transitional change means that psychoanalysis has a unique set of data for observing the phenomena of coevolution.

Acts of self-observation by the patient tend to be cumulative when not isolated by repression. When the patient's powers of self-observation increase, his chances for further emergent organizational change increase along with them. As the patient learns to observe his mental contents and their connections, the extent and variety of possible changes expand. Thus there is a natural order to the sequence of such changes, each change being inclusive of previous ones.

Self-observation does not occur automatically when the patient experiences a sudden discharge of feeling and fantasy he has been unaware of. The patient has to have a position outside (or on the edge of) an avalanche of feeling in order to observe it rather than to be swept away by it. As in Robert Frost's poem, "one step backward taken" is what makes the difference. It is not always an easy step for the patient. Unconscious infantile attractors pull the patient back into the painful material, often leaving him in a state of terror or bewilderment. Unconscious attractors will be looked at in detail as we go on.

The expansion of the patient's *observing ego* is very closely linked with other signs of increasing inner connectedness. The patient's observing ego is itself an emergent property of his ego organization as a whole. As his mental contents become better connected, his capacity for self-observation also increases. This happens not continuously, but in observable increments of varying size and comprehensiveness.

But wait. According to psychoanalytic folklore, patients can feel better without knowing why they feel better. They may improve, it is said, without insight into the analytic process that helps them improve. I doubt that this is actually so. Perhaps we should take a closer look at such reports. The patient who claims he doesn't know how he's gotten better is likely to be denying his own healing role in the analytic process. He is still defending himself from unconscious feelings of guilt in this way. The analyst who accepts this kind of testimony from a patient has to be colluding in his denial and indulging in a bit of therapeutic grandiosity of his own. Transference and countertransference feelings and fantasies have yet to be resolved.

Improvements in the patient's personal relationships and in his work life are important indications of progress in the analysis, but they are reported to the analyst at second hand. Increments of self-observational power are usually accompanied by new insights into the patient's way of relating to the analyst. The analyst has the advantage of observing the interaction for himself.

An expansion of self-observational capacity is almost always a reliable sign of therapeutic progress. Every increase in the patient's powers of self-observation entails the emergence of higher level connectedness and organization. The emergent properties of the new organizational structures should be observable to both the patient and the analyst.

When a phase transition occurs in analysis, the patient becomes able to see himself in a new and different way. A more coherent self-image comes with each reorganization, at whatever scale. Feelings, fantasies, and memories that were isolated and insulated from each other before the phase transition now fit together in a more consistent shape. Internalized objects who seemed all good or all bad to the patient become more three dimensional. Things that had to be hidden from the analyst now can be told.

However, one can easily imagine a caricature of the phase transitional event just described. What we would see in this case would be the analyst making an observation, and the patient then constructing a pseudo-self-observation modeled on the analyst's remarks. If a defensive maneuver can be imagined, the analyst can be sure some patients will use it. Those who are very concerned about pleasing the analyst are prone to this distortion. Freud (1911) was very concerned about the patient's ability to supply this kind of pseudo-corroboration. He was right to be.

Analysts are often warned during their training about the dangers of mistaking the patient's effort to comply with the analyst's wishes for therapeutic progress. However, I have noticed that analysts are also liable to overcompensate for this tendency on the part of compliant patients. They may even fail to recognize insight that is quite authentic when trying to avoid being taken in.

The reorganization process relocates the patient's defenses within his larger mental space. This allows the defenses to be circumvented rather than broken down. The military imagery Freud often used for the analyst's role in the overcoming of the patient's defenses may have been seriously misleading in this regard.

A middle-aged male analytic patient reported this dream.

> I was running with the ball on a football field. My team was running along with me, but the other team came up and blocked my way. I turned to lateral the ball to a teammate, but I fumbled it and it bounced over to him. He picked up the ball, and, instead of running the way I was going, he ran in the opposite direction, under the goal post and right out of the stadium. He got on a motorcycle and drove it around the stadium and came in behind the other team through the end of the stadium we had been going for. He put the ball in the end zone and scored a touchdown that way.

During the previous analytic session this patient had made a very important discovery. After discussing a series of dreams, the analyst had hypothesized that his father had been emotionally blackmailing him in his early childhood years. According to this theory, his father was off having an affair while leaving the patient feeling responsible for his mother's very serious depression. This struck a chord with the patient, who produced a number of corroborating memories. He felt he was forced to take responsibility for his mother's unhappiness or else risk the loss of his father, the only sane person in the family. This helped to explain his lifelong feeling of intense guilt and anger over any dissatisfaction with him expressed by the women in his life.

He saw the football dream as a reference to this recent interaction with the analyst. The analyst's interpretation had allowed him to "get behind his parents" by passing the ball to the analyst, who was able to go around the opposition. He identified the opposing team with his own defenses against seeing his parents as they really were, and giving up his grandiose ideas about saving their marriage. His feeling in the dream that his teammate the analyst was acting in a ridiculous way expressed his frequent impatience with the peculiar indirectness of the analytic process. But finding an apparently ridiculous way to get around the patient's defenses is the primary route of the psychoanalytic process.

The football dream accompanied a major reorganization of this patient's view of his position in his family. Phase transitions like this one can occur in many regions of the psychic organization and at many hierarchical levels. The extent of the reorganization naturally varies according to the level of the hierarchy affected. In his later writings (1937a), Freud spoke of a certain kind of phase transition as a *construction*. In describing what he meant by a construction, however, Freud emphasized the actions of the analyst rather than the changes taking place within the patient as a result of their interaction.

A phase transition is a spontaneous change within the patient, in the coevolutionary context of the analytic process. A construction, in Freud's description, is something made by the analyst and adopted by the patient. A phase transition can reorganize any or all of the contents in a given region of the psyche. A construction, as described by Freud, has to do more specifically with the historical record of traumatic events in the patient's early life.

A phase transition is not something that can be reversed by a patient's will, although it can be denied or disavowed. It is an integral part of him. A construction, as Freud describes it, is a hypothesis of the analyst's. The patient can take it or leave it. A phase transition is the natural product of the evolutionary process at work in the analytic relationship. A construction, in Freud's description of it, appears to be an ad hoc creation of the analyst.

Despite these differences of emphasis, the phenomenon Freud called a construction has the essential characteristics of a phase transition. Freud's analyst-centered point of view made it difficult for him to see the construction as a product of coevolution, that is, as an event generated by the analytic process itself.

The sequence of phase transitions that take place during the unfolding of the analytic process traces a trajectory through a space of possible mental states. The emergence of an organizational change creates a *bifurcation* in this trajectory. The bifurcation is like the branching of a new species in evolution. The old species or organizational phase is not transformed directly into the new one. Instead, the two species continue to coexist until one or the other establishes a clear adaptive advantage in their shared territory. This is like the emergence of a new wild type in Eigen's quasispecies.

In the same way, a breakthrough in analysis is followed by a period of consolidation in which the old and new phase structures wage a struggle for dominance. The patient is like a subject watching a Necker cube turn itself inside out in front of him. Only an accumulation of further evidence can stabilize the new structure.

During this period of consolidation, which may be long and tedious, insights are *worked through*. The old and new structures are competing attractors for the patient's self-representation. New input can shift the patient quite suddenly from one attractor to the other. The consistency of the analyst's interventions is a major factor in stabilizing the new and more complex self-organization that emerges from the phase transition.

Whereas Freud (1914) thought of the working through period as a single phase occupying the middle period of an analysis, we see now that every phase transition has its own working through period. At any moment, several phase transitions can be undergoing consolidation at different hierarchical levels. The lengths of time needed for consolidation may be very different, depending on the hierarchical levels involved. The sum of these many consolidation periods would resemble a complex wave form, with many frequencies and amplitudes superimposed on one another.

If we think in terms of superimposed phase transitions, however, the processes of consolidation that were taking place at different organizational levels would be interacting with one another. The summation of these processes, although fully deterministic, would be nonlinear and not predictable. As far as the progress of the analysis is concerned, the nonlinearity is beneficial. Successful conflict resolution at the lower levels, during the working through phases, bubbles up to act as input for the consolidation of transitions at the higher levels. Serendipity is a byproduct of nonlinear systems as they self-organize.

When a new organization replaces an older one, the loss of repressive control by the older maladaptive defensive structures seems to follow a power law pattern. Derepressed material appears in large and small bursts of free association. The size of these bursts looks to this clinical observer to be inversely proportional to their frequency during the course of an analysis.

This is like the pattern of extinctions in organic evolution. Changes in climate and geology deform the fitness landscapes of all species and their genotypes to some degree. At any given time, the fitness of some living species will decrease to the extinction level. But mass extinctions also occur. As many as 96 percent of ocean dwelling species disappeared during the catastrophic Permian extinction that took place 250 million years ago. The species that managed to survive that calamity produced many viable mutants, some of which climbed to newer and higher levels of fitness in the ecological niches left vacant. These events sharply reduced the genetic diversity among the dominant organisms after the crash.

The rapid radiation of the survivor species after an extinction punctuates the usual slow development of new species. Major extinctions and speciations like the Permian occur very rarely, minor ones with considerable frequency. The paleontological data are sparse, but they approximate the power law relationship predicted by Kauffman (1993). A power law, or a close approximation to it, seems likely to underlie the nonlinear pattern of change in analytic patients. This is an important topic for clinical research.

An analytic breakthrough at a high level of organization is usually accompanied by a strong subjective feeling in the patient. If the breakthrough involves the extinction of a maladaptive defensive strategy, the patient is likely to feel it as a new outburst of energy. This has traditionally been thought of as the release of dammed up psychic energy. But it is much more likely to be the subjective sense of a sudden radiation of new and more effective strategies into niches occupied in the recent past by extinguished maladaptive behaviors.

Fitness and Internal Connectedness

Organization evolves naturally as connections are made in large systems with many components, like the human memory. Kauffman (1993) modeled a simple case with N isolated components, represented by points. Edges connecting pairs of points were added to the system one by one at random. Some of these isolated pairs combined to form a number of small connected subsets. A message sent through a fragmented network like this would be unlikely to arrive at its destination (see Figure 4.2).

When the number of edges, E, reached half the number of components, $E = N/2$, the system went through an abrupt phase transition. From a collection of small and separate internally connected subsets, a single giant connected subset emerged, to which almost all the components of the system belonged. A message would now have a good chance of getting through.

When the number of edges equaled the number of components $(E = N)$, another phase transition took place. Cyclic subsets (loops) of all lengths began to appear within the giant subset. A message would be almost certain to arrive at this point. However, if the network were allowed to become fully connected, the message would likely be slowed down or even lost in a maze of intersections.

Piaget and others have noted the development of percolating cognitive networks in the thoughts of the growing child. These networks make possible the reversible symbolic operations of the 6- and 7-year-old. A similar effect occurs in psychoanalysis, where the emergence of reversible operations in fantasy is a critical step toward recovery. New connections are built up when the patient's conscious fantasy life incorporates the unconscious material previously kept out of awareness. These new connections can bridge the discontinuities caused in the past by the patient's defensive strategies.

In very large highly connected networks, chaotic disorder is commonplace. Kauffman used Boolean (two valued) networks with random connections to study this problem. The connections in a Boolean network can be thought of as either positive or negative, excitatory or inhibitory, 1 or 0. Each component of the network has an output of 1 or 0 determined by the pattern of its inputs. These patterns are identical with the rules of a cellular automaton. A CA with only two states is a Boolean network, though not usually randomly connected. In a random Boolean network, connections are made by chance, without any preordained structure. The output rule for each component is also selected at random.

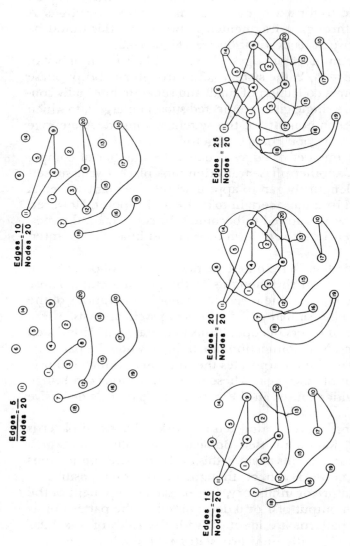

Figure 4.2. Phase transition forming a giant component. Random graphs for a fixed number of points N connected at random by an increasing number of edges E. For large values of N, as E/N increases past a threshold of 0.5, most points become connected in one gigantic component. As E/N passes 1.0, cycles of all lengths begin to emerge. (From *The Origins of Order: Self-Organization and Selection in Evolution* by Stuart A. Kauffman, 1993, p. 308. Copyright © 1993 by Oxford University Press, Inc. Used by permission of Oxford University Press, Inc.)

A random Boolean network has N components. K inputs reach each component from its neighbors. In a fully random network, K would also be random. Because Kauffman was interested in the relation between K and the degree of order in a network, however, he compared networks with different fixed values of K. He found that the degree of order was sensitively dependent on K (see Figure 4.3).

At $K = 0$ all components are isolated from one another. At $K = N$, every component is connected to every other one and to itself. Kauffman found that random Boolean networks become chaotic very quickly at $K = > 2$. At $K < 2$, a network is frozen. At $K = 2$, it is ordered but near the edge of chaos. If K is varied smoothly from 0 to N, a phase transition from frozen to chaotic behavior occurs at $K = > 2$.

The input pattern of a random Boolean network at time t_0 generates a new configuration or state at time t_1. Each network can move through a number of such configurations before having to return to a state it previously encountered. For $K = 2$, the number of states in each cycle increases slowly, as the square root of N. Even in very large networks with $K = 2$, the number of states in a cycle rises very slowly. A network of a million components has a cycle of only 1000 states. If state cycles of neurons were used to represent events in the external world, then a network of a million neurons would contain 1000 representations that could easily be distinguished. This would be about the right size for the functional unit of the human brain. Such a network could be searched in a reasonable amount of time. But only if K were equal to 2. If K were greater than 2, the number of states in a cycle would increase exponentially with N. A network with a million components would have 10^{36} states per cycle.

However, two conditions can be imposed on random Boolean networks with $K > 2$ that change their behavior to that of $K = 2$ networks (Kauffman, 1993). As a result, it is possible to order the behavior of a large network with $K > 2$ without having to decrease the value of K. This finding may be of use for understanding the organization of the neural networks underlying human memory, where K is known to be high.

One condition is the addition of *canalizing* input rules to the otherwise random mix. A canalizing rule has at least one input

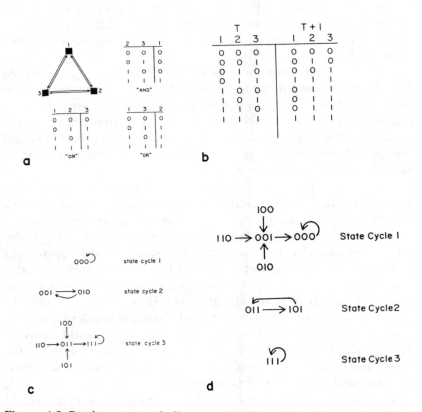

Figure 4.3. Boolean network diagram. (*a*) The wiring diagram in a Boolean network with three binary elements, each an input to the other two. (*b*) The Boolean rules of (*a*) rewritten to show, for all $2^3 = 8$ states at time T, the activity assumed by each element at the next time moment $T + 1$. Read from left to right this figure shows the successor state for each state. (*c*) The state transition graph, or behavior field, of the autonomous Boolean network of (*a*) and (*b*), obtained by showing state transitions to successor states connected by arrows. (*d*) Effects of mutating the rule of element 2 from "Or" to "And." (From *The Origins of Order: Self-Organization and Selection in Evolution* by Stuart A. Kauffman, 1993, p. 189. Copyright © 1993 by Oxford University Press, Inc. Used by permission of Oxford University Press, Inc.)

that by itself can determine the output of the rule. AND and OR are canalizing rules. A single input of 0 to a component using an AND rule forces an output of 0, no matter what the other input may be. An input of 1 to an OR rule determines the output to be 1, regardless of the other input. Canalizing rules channel the information they take in by narrowing the range of possible outputs (see Figure 4.4).

When a Boolean network contains a sufficient number of canalizing rules, chains of connected canalizing rules percolate from one end of the network to the other. Percolating chains of connected AND or OR rules give order to a network, as in the randomly connected $K = 2$ network. In the cell nucleus, networks

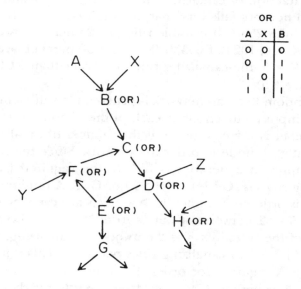

Figure 4.4. A canalizing network. Forcing structure among binary elements governed by the Boolean "Or" function. The forcing 1 value propagates down the structure and around the forcing loop, which eventually is frozen into the forced state with 1 values at all elements around the loop. The loop then radiates fixed forced 1 values downstream. (From *The Origins of Order: Self-Organization and Selection in Evolution* by Stuart A. Kauffman, 1993, p. 204. Copyright © 1993 by Oxford University Press, Inc. Used by permission of Oxford University Press, Inc.)

of regulatory genes that turn structural genes on and off are governed by canalizing rules (Kauffman, 1993). Kauffman suggests that biological systems may in general rely on canalizing rules to guide their regulatory processes.

Networks with $K = 2$ are ordered because 12 of the 16 possible rules for 2 inputs, each with one of two values, are canalizing rules. The number of possible rules for such a system is 2 raised to the 2^K power, where K is the number of inputs to each of the elements or components in the network. (An example of a noncanalizing rule with $K = 2$ is EXCLUSIVE OR, one or the other but not both, which requires a 1 in either of its two inputs but not in both. Neither input alone can determine the output of EXCLUSIVE OR.)

The fraction of canalizing rules among all possible rules in a random network falls very sharply as K increases. When $K = 3$, only 64 of the 256 (2^8) possible rules, or 25 percent, are canalizing. For $K = 4$, 1024 of 65536 (2^{16}), or 1.56 percent, are canalizing. For $K = 5$, the canalizing rules are fewer than 0.01 percent (see Figure 4.5).

A random Boolean network is ordered if a sufficient number of the K input connections to each of the N nodes is canalizing. This number is $C * N$, where C is the number of canalizing rules needed at each node to order the network. Since the total number of inputs in a network is $N * K$, the required fraction of canalizing rules is $(C * N) / (N * K)$ or C/K. A random Boolean network is ordered if a fraction $> = C/K$ are canalizing rules.

For $K = 2$ networks, C varies from > 1 to < 1.5. Since 75 percent of the rules in a $K = 2$ network are canalizing, there are 1.5 N ($3/4 * N * 2$) canalizing rules per node. This is more than the 1.4 + N required for order. For random Boolean networks with $K = 3$ or higher, C can vary from 1.3+ to nearly 2. Only 25 percent of the rules in a random $K = 3$ network, or 0.75 N, are canalizing, when $1.3 - 1.95$ N are required for order. For $K > 3$ the deficit of canalizing rules is far worse. An RBN with $K = 3$ or higher is naturally chaotic, but it can be ordered by nonrandomly raising its average number of canalizing input rules per node to C.

In his book, *Neural Darwinism* (1987), Gerald Edelman suggests that the neurons in the cerebral cortex of a human fetus

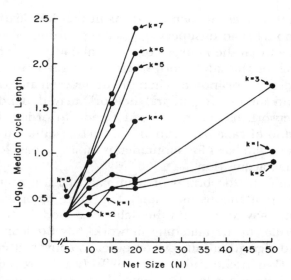

Figure 4.5. Order and chaos in random Boolean networks. Log_{10} median cycle lengths in random networks with K ranging from 1 to 7. Cycle lengths grow less than linearly for $K = 1$ and $K = 2$ but exponentially for $K > 3$. The slopes are predicted moderately well by the mean-field theory. (From *Ensemble Modeling* by Gelfand and Walker, 1984. Reprinted by permission of Marcel Dekker. Also from *The Origins of Order: Self-Organization and Selection in Evolution* by Stuart A. Kauffman, 1993, p. 197. Copyright © 1993 by Oxford University Press, Inc. Used by permission of Oxford University Press, Inc.)

are connected randomly until the fetus is exposed to actual experience. As events begin to register, random networks of neurons whose structures match the structures of the events being experienced are reinforced. Networks are not designated in advance to represent particular events. Networks that match events are combined to form representations of categories at many levels. Networks that have not been matched to experience become isolated and atrophied.

Edelman's model appears to many biologists to give too little emphasis to connections among neurons functionally preprogrammed by the genes. The model also ignores the increasingly recognized plasticity of the adult brain. Nevertheless, it contains a powerful idea that if true would break the vicious circle implicit in the requirement for a network whose job would be to assign other networks to represent each event. As in real life, learning in Edelman's model is an unsupervised, self-organizing process.

Suppose then that the neurons of the fetal cortex, or of the association areas of the adult cortex, are originally connected randomly, as Edelman proposed. Then the fit between an experienced event and an existing neural network may depend on whether the network has been ordered (made to order) by a high enough ratio of canalizing functions. Such a self-organized mapping could be the basis for spontaneous or single pass learning, like language acquisition.

Rote learning, in the brains of mammals at least, requires more than this spontaneous matching. The more laborious aspects of learning may result from the deliberate modification of noncanalizing rules in the matching network. Any Boolean rule can be modified algorithmically by computer to convert it into a canalizing rule (Wuensche and Lesser, 1992). In this procedure, single bit mutations of a rule are examined one by one until the canalizing rule that requires the fewest changes from the original is found. The new rule is not identical to the original, but usually a close approximation to it.

The canalizing procedure inevitably results in the loss of some information contained in the original rule. Logical relations involve canalizing rules exclusively. Most nonscientists and many scientists feel that purely logical descriptions of events are inadequate to represent the varied quality of actual experience. Perhaps it is the inevitable loss of information in the canalizing process that accounts for this widespread feeling. Logical relations imposed by nonspontaneous learning may indeed operate on only rough approximations of the events they purport to represent.

Until very recently, there was an objection to applying this argument at the level of neuron to neuron connections. Most of the evidence in the past had indicated that a neuron emits an impulse when the sum of its thousands of inputs are added to reach a threshold level. The inputs were thought to be indistinguishable from one another; therefore, there would be no pattern to be extracted by the firing mechanism.

We now know that each of the thousands of postsynaptic sites on the dendrites of the neuron can be modified individually.

Thresholds are lowered through new protein synthesis when two neighboring sites are stimulated at the same time. If sites can be recognized individually, their connections can be organized at a higher level than that provided by simple additive thresholds. This is in fact what happens. Vogl, Blackwell, and Alkon (in press) have now shown that the neurons in all layers of the visual cortex respond to patterns of stimulation in groups of dendrites.

The level of organization of the neural networks in the brain does not necessarily determine the level of organization of human thought, however. We know little as yet about the laws that govern the relations between local neural networks and networks of such networks. It seems obvious that the complexity of these relations increases as one approaches the level needed to support conscious thought. It is also clear that what we consider to be rational thought emerges in development long after pattern recognition has been firmly established. Logic is not acquired spontaneously, like language.

When we reach the level of thought, the presence or absence of order generated by canalizing rules may determine what we perceive to be rational or not. If this is so, a thought we experience as rational may be a thought that has been ordered by canalizing rules. The difference between rational and irrational in a given instance could be quantitatively small though qualitatively very large.

Irrational thought would not be a single thing, the antithesis of rational thought. It would be a vast reservoir of disordered Boolean networks whose distance from the ordered state may depend on just a few or very many missing bits or missing rules. Rational thought would float on the surface of this reservoir.

Mutations could be expected to degrade the canalizing rules from time to time or to upgrade the noncanalizing. Some of the noncanalizing rules would be near to being canalizing, easily converted through only a small number of modifications. Other noncanalizing rules would require a great many mutations to become canalizing. The accessibility of an irrational thought of the patient to the analyst's interventions may depend in part on the number of canalizing mutations needed to bring the patient's thinking at that moment into the ordered state.

When Freud spoke of making the unconscious conscious, or of substituting ego for id, he was referring to the analyst's role in making rational sense of the patient's inner conflicts and confusion. The analyst's interpretations were to be the instrument for this transformation. But for Freud the distinction between the rational and the irrational was abrupt. The irrational was the product of a separate *system* of thought, which he called the primary process. He believed that the primary process used its own set of rules that contradicted the rules of rational or secondary process thought.

The implication seemed to be that the analyst's interpretation was the substitution of a rational idea for an irrational idea of the patient. Analysts discovered early on that attempting to make such a substitution directly seldom worked. What was needed was what Freud called the working through process. The patient's irrational idea had to be confronted from many angles, in many contexts, until the recollection of childhood memories and the expression of genuine affect could emerge.

My suggestion is that the canalization of an irrational idea may require many stages, each a little closer to rational order than the previous one. A fully rational thought would not be achieved until the phase transition to order is reached by the canalizing of a sufficient number of input rules in a region of the network. Our tendency to think in polar opposites (to rely on Boolean rules with only two inputs) has worked against our understanding of this alternative.

The visibly successful intervention would cause a mutation that completes the ordering of a nearly ordered network. The effect of an intervention that brings a more disordered network closer to order would not be directly observable. The effect of the intervention in this case could only be judged by the eventual ordering that it contributed to. This may come only after a fairly long interval. A very elaborate research effort would be needed to verify the efficacy of interventions whose visible effects are delayed by periods of time that cannot be predicted.

Kauffman describes a second method of creating order in a random Boolean network that may have little to do with psychoanalysis. Order can emerge in a system when the proportion of input rules producing ones or zeroes is very high. Ordinarily, when rules are selected randomly the output of ones and zeroes is nearly equal. The probability, P, that any rule in the network will output either a 0 or a 1 is 0.5. But P can vary between 0.5 and 1.0 in a given network. If there are many more ones than zeroes or zeroes than ones, the network as a whole becomes ordered. (Islands of components free to vary between 1 and 0 will remain.)

For any network, there is a critical ratio, P_c, such that the network becomes ordered if P_c is exceeded. If P is closer to 0.5 than to P_c, frozen islands appear in a sea of disorder. Order can be created by skewing the outputs to a proportion of ones or zeroes higher than P_c.

The order acquired by a system when its outputs become increasingly homogeneous may have little to do with the coherence or rationality of a patient's thought. However, this may be another way of obtaining order in the brain, through generalized effects such as those obtained with psychotropic drugs. This latter kind of order has an obvious value in treating mental illness. It is likely that the psychoanalytic process itself, apart from specific content, also has a generalized ordering effect of this kind.

There is a possible mechanism for this tonic effect in psycho-analysis. The preponderance of new connections created in psychoanalytic treatment are excitatory, in the sense that they enhance rather than retard communication between the functional units of memory. It is likely that the analytic process increases the ratio of excitatory to inhibitory connections in the memory as a whole. Perhaps there is a critical point, P_c, at which the preponderance becomes great enough to create a percolating web of communicating units. Crossing the threshold at P_c would create a phase transition into a more highly organized structure. We would have to imagine this happening not once for the memory as a whole, but many times over for various local regions of memory.

Greater order in the adaptive organization of the patient's mental contents may be achieved through canalizing changes in the input rules that structure the connections between associations in his long term memory. What would the analyst have to do to facilitate such a transformation?

First, we note that the commonly named logical relations, AND and OR are canalizing Boolean rules with two inputs. NOT is a canalizing Boolean rule with one input. All other logical relations can be formed by combining these three into larger structures. The logical operations of most digital computers use AND, OR, and NOT logic gates exclusively. Logic gates embody the canalizing rules that link the components in a Boolean electronic circuit. Each gate operates according to one of the canalizing Boolean network rules.

Second, canalizing rules are a subset of all rules possible in a Boolean network, that is, a subset of rules with K inputs and a single output that has two possible values. Some of the rules in a random Boolean network of any size are canalizing by chance. As K increases, however, the fraction of canalizing rules occurring at random diminishes very rapidly. Canalizing rules are likely to be preferred for information-processing functions in our brains. They produce unambiguous outputs and take less processing time for execution. I suspect that this preference is independent of scale, so that what works best for genetic regulatory systems also works best for cognitive activity at much higher levels of complexity.

If that is so, it would follow that cognitive activity is also ordered when inputs are few and canalizing functions are numerous. Human thought would be logical when ordered and illogical when chaotic. Two inputs to a cognitive logic gate would be the norm. The first logical relation learned by human beings has only one input, NOT. Thereafter, two inputs become attainable. Reasoning from more than two premises is difficult for the unassisted adult mind. Multipremised logical puzzles like those devised by Charles Dodgson require pencil and paper to sort out.

Cause-and-effect relationships in nature are, ipso facto, canalizing rules. Whether an effect has one cause or many, there is always at least one precondition whose presence or absence assures a predictable outcome. For example, it would be quite astonishing if any natural mechanism were found that produced a foreseeable output when one of two possible preconditions held but not both. When the outcome of a process is chaotic or indeterminate, we do not speak of its having a cause.

The psychoanalyst who suggests that a slip of the tongue is

motivated is introducing a canalizing rule to explain an event that seemed random to the patient. Let us suppose that in general the analytic process converts noncanalizing input rules into canalizing rules. This would reduce the ambiguities in the patient's way of integrating new information, increasing his cognitive efficiency and his self-confidence.

The introduction of canalizing rules into the associative networks of long term memory would increase the accessibility of repressed memories. Perhaps this is the way new associative pathways are opened to consciousness in general. Then it would also be the way that transference distortions are corrected by the creation of accessible associative pathways during analysis. Exploring the differences between the patient's experience of the analyst and of his caretakers when a child would lead to the canalization of the old rules.

We know that the psychoanalytic process reduces old ambiguities and creates new distinctions in the life story of the patient. The conversion of noncanalizing to canalizing input rules in the structure of long term memory is a plausible mechanism for this transformation. This mechanism may be operating whenever new connections are made in analysis between memories that have been isolated from one another in the past.

We can take another look at Richard's first dream, in which his homosexual aggression was being acted out in the room next to his parents' bedroom. His baby brother was in the bedroom with his mother. The relation between the feeling of exclusion by mother and the angry turn to a man for satisfaction was indicated but not stated in the dream. The dream brought these two images together but represented their relation only through spatial contiguity. We could say that the two images were inputs to a rule that failed to produce an unambiguous output, that is, a noncanalizing rule. The analyst suggested that Richard's exclusion from the bedroom was the cause of his aggressive homosexual activity. This is a canalizing intervention.

One objection to this might be to say that the dream was simply disordered. It contained no evidence of a rule at all. I am suggesting, in contrast, that because the analyst's relatively simple intervention gave the dream a clear logical output the dream already embodied a rule on the verge of canalization. This formulation is at the basis of Freud's discovery that dreams are meaningful. Yet Freud was driven by his own polarizing logic to assign the patient's dream and the analyst's interpretation to the mutually exclusive categories of primary and secondary processes. What we see here is that Freud's categories refer more accurately to subsets of ordered and not yet ordered regions in the larger network that encompasses both.

The canalizing effect of the work on Richard's dream is illustrated by the sequence of associations that show his fury over his mother's choosing another male to share her bedroom. I spoke earlier of this sequence as an avalanche. Here we see that in this case the avalanche flows through a rather narrow channel. The channel was opened by the formation of a new rule in Richard's thinking. According to this rule, whenever Richard's rage at his mother is evoked by a current event, any ambiguity in his relations with other important women in his life will be amplified and distorted.

A good example of the distortions caused by an insufficiently canalized associative network is the effect on Richard of his wedding trip with Ellen. Richard tried to assert himself on returning from his honeymoon by reducing his analytic hours. This was a preemptive strike based on an assumption that the analyst, like his father (as he had imagined), would now consider him a dangerous rival. It was a general rule for Richard that good things would be followed by bad things. He had to prepare himself by reducing his expectation that the good things would continue.

Cutting down on his analysis would diminish the analyst's power to retaliate for his success in marriage and would make him less vulnerable to the malevolence of fate. The network of assumptions that led him to this conclusion was disordered. It produced negative or doubtful outputs from an array of positive inputs. Similar fantasies drive the mechanism of *undoing* typical of obsessional patients. If the analyst had reacted passively to Richard's gambit, he would only have confirmed the effectiveness of this defense mechanism. (Richard's failure to reorganize this material on his own was due to the anxiety that evoked the defense mechanism.)

Following Richard's reluctant agreement to continue as before, the analysis focused on his anger with the analyst and the relation of this anger to his feelings about his father. Richard's memories of his father's emotional withdrawal from him now became more accessible. He began to understand his father's behavior as part of a lifelong problem with depression. His rules of inference from his father's behavior were newly canalized in a way that led him to a novel kind of discrimination. He could now begin to tell the difference between his father's defensive withdrawal from him and the punishment of a jealous and vengeful god.

Each patient has a vast set of input rules that specify how information from current and past events interacts to determine a current feeling state or fantasy. When these rules form a disordered network, transference distortions such as Richard's are the consequence. The network can become ordered if enough of the rules are canalized in the course of the analytic work. This requires that the assumptions hidden in the disordered network be brought to light through the recovery of the memories that gave rise to them. Awareness of the transference distortions leads to the recovery of these memories.

Missing Connections

At the neurological level, developmental deficits of many kinds can prevent connections from forming. The neurons of the fetal brain migrate from a point of origin in the wall of the lateral ventricle to their functional locations in the layers of the cortex. Many more synapses exist at this early stage than are needed for later adaptive behavior. Those that perform effectively are selected for preservation, while the superfluous ones are pruned away (Edelman, 1987). Other synapses function at specific stages of early development and then disappear.

Synapses that serve their purpose and disappear are the cause of critical periods in development. Some things have to be learned at just the right time or a permanent deficiency results. The overall plasticity of the human brain makes it difficult to observe such deficits in isolation.

One illuminating exception is the ability of an infant to recognize and produce the sounds of a language. This ability seems
to have little interaction with other linguistic or cognitive skills.
At 6 months, babies can be conditioned to respond to any pho-
neme used in any human language. By the time they are a year
old, however, they react only to the phonemes of the language
spoken around them.

The difficulty of learning the phonemes of a new language
after puberty is familiar to everyone. For all but a very few exceptional people, this ability is permanently lost in the early teens.
Developmental changes in neuron populations create permanent
deficits in normal people.

Complex and subtle abnormalities in neurological development are coming to be recognized with much greater frequency.
Among these are the attention deficit disorders, the dyslexias, and
the malady now known as specific language impairment. Some
varieties of obsessive compulsive disorder fall into this group as
well. These complex kinds of deficit have been hard to isolate
from the more generalized cognitive disorders and from emotional illnesses.

Among the hereditary psychoses, the neurophysiological
deficit in schizophrenia has not been well characterized as yet.
The picture for major depression has been getting clearer in
recent years, however. While many patients with these conditions
can learn to adapt to them through psychoanalysis, psychoanalysis
by itself can only go part way in making up the loss of connection
caused by neurotransmitter deficits.

Even in the case of the major psychoses, the role of biology
in emotional development is poorly understood. The theories of
Freud, Erikson, Mahler, and other psychoanalysts all presuppose
a series of critical periods in the emotional growth of the child,
closely tied to maturation of the brain. Greenspan's (1979) explorations in this area confirm the importance of specific kinds
of input from the mother and other caretakers at these critical
times. Caretaker inputs are needed to evoke the new functions
of the maturing brain at specific periods in infancy and tod-
dlerhood. One can think (rather crudely) of postnatal inputs
from caretakers as the programming aspect of development, as
distinct from hard-wired neurological deficits.

Psychoanalysis is most effective with patients who are missing connections at the programming level. Their experience has led to conflict and confusion about adaptive goals and strategies. Because of this, information they take in from their surroundings is not used purposefully. It is distorted or disregarded. Anna Freud's (1936) catalog of defense mechanisms has proven to be a useful guide to these pathways of evasion. The mechanisms of defense divide the contents of the patient's mind into zones that are not accessible to conscious scrutiny.

Repression is the most representative of these mechanisms. As Breuer and Freud (1893–1895) discovered, repression blocks access to consciousness for specific memories and regions of memory. Information lost to repression is useless to the patient's conscious effort to solve a problem. Yet at the same time it can exert a maladaptive unconscious influence on his feelings and behavior.

Repression is a general term for the mechanisms that prevent new connections from being formed within the associative structure of the patient's long term memory. Psychoanalytic treatment fills in connections that are missing because of repression. What Freud called "memories sunk into the id" are representations of events that are only very sparsely connected in the associative memory network because of repression.

Freud's original term suggests that unacceptable memories are *pushed back* into the unconscious by the defensive mechanisms of the ego. His later idea, that memories *sink* into the id, marked a change in his thinking, but a change whose theoretical implications he did not fully explore. The id in this later formulation is exerting a force, analogous to the force of gravity, to draw the unacceptable memories into itself. If we take the id to be a hierarchical organization of unconscious infantile attractors, Freud's idea becomes much more concrete. Repressed memories are pushed into the unconscious by the mechanisms of defense and pulled into it by unconscious attractors. They are objectionable to the conscious ego but gourmet fare for the id.

Memories sequestered in unconscious attractors are isolated from other memories. The connectedness of repressed memories with one another and with the Freudian preconscious is below the threshold for accessibility. To give this a very simple measure, let us say that E (the number of connections) / N (the number of repressed memories) < 0.5, or some equivalent critical level. As E increases with treatment, while N remains roughly constant, E/N rises eventually to 0.5 (or the equivalent). At this point a phase transition takes place. The repressed memories join the giant component of the preconscious. Where id (disorder) used to be, primitive ego (order) now appears.

At a finer level, the networks that contain these memories may be well enough connected, but still disordered, because they lack a sufficient proportion of canalizing rules. A phase transition would occur whenever this proportion reaches its critical level.

What is true of the preconscious is most likely also true of long term memory. Isolated areas of repressed material in the neurotic patient's long term memory need to be reconnected with one another and with the larger network of memories as well. This may be done by establishing new connections or by ordering disordered networks of existing connections. The analyst's responsiveness to the obscurities in the patient's story acts as a catalyst for this process of reconnection taking place within the patient.

Under the usual circumstances, repressed memories cannot be updated by new information. Either they do not connect with the new data taken in when personal experience broadens and deepens or else they connect with distorted representations of these data after they have already been degraded by an unconscious attractor. The repression has to be circumvented before the new data can be used to revise the memories.

Loss of memory for important events, especially traumatic events, is the best documented form of repression. The recovery of these memories is essential to the reorganization of the patient's self and object representations. During an analysis, many varieties and degrees of repression are typically uncovered and reversed.

For example, a memory that came up earlier in an analysis can appear suddenly in an entirely new context, reconnected to a new set of similar events from which it had been separated. This memory had not been excluded from consciousness. It was simply deprived of its historical associations in long term memory.

Sometimes the recovered memory turns out to have been part of the patient's conscious view of himself for much of his life, but then had been abruptly forgotten after a particular event. Sexual maturation, with its attendant anxieties, and the loss of a parent through death or divorce are typical precipitators of repression on this scale.

Repressed memories of early childhood experience most often appear in the analytic discourse when the patient is giving his associations to the images in his dreams (Palombo, 1978, 1984a,c, 1992b). I think it quite possible that most if not all very remote memories enter consciousness through the process of dream construction.

In one interesting case (Palombo, 1984c), a patient discovered the identity of a childhood experience that had appeared with great vividness in a dream. Despite the identification, however, she never succeeded in recalling the actual experience.

> The patient, Florence, currently in analysis, is a medical illustrator in her mid-twenties. She dreamed she was in a large, old-fashioned bathroom with her former anatomy professor. The professor was sitting on the toilet, obviously very sick, vomiting blood. Florence felt helpless and horrified. Then the professor was inside something that looked like a very large stall shower, or perhaps a swimming pool with a transparent wall. The pool was filled with water, and the professor was near the bottom of it, gasping for breath.
>
> The dream occurred during an episode of angry dissatisfaction with the progress of the analysis. A week earlier, she had sought out the professor, ostensibly for professional reasons, but with conscious fantasies about seducing him. When she actually saw him, she found she had no real interest in pursuing the fantasies. The large bathroom in the dream recalled her rooming house in college, where she had first met the professor, as well as the analyst's office.
>
> My questions about memories associated with the dream imagery reminded her of Father's ulcer operation when Florence was fifteen. The operation had temporarily improved Father's rather sour disposition, but his schizoid character pathology continued to pose an insuperable obstacle to Florence's attempts to reach him emotionally. There was also a very embarrassing incident at a swimming pool, at age twelve, when Father had inappropriately

complimented Florence on her breast development. No other associations were reported. We left the discussion of the dream feeling that something important had been omitted.

About two months later, Florence was talking to an older sister, Julia, who mentioned that their father had her (Julia) take
showers with him regularly until she was about fifteen, "in order
to get her used to the male anatomy." Julia assumed that Florence
had also showered with Father. She was surprised to find that
Florence had no memory of doing so. Although Florence could
not recall ever having seen Father and Julia together in the shower,
many puzzling aspects of her relations with each of them suddenly
came into focus, including previously repressed incestuous fantasies dating to age four [pp. 417–418].

This example illustrates both the richness and the devious-
ness of associative connections in long term memory. Ordinarily,
one would have expected the new connection formed by the
dream and Julia's report to have opened access to the original
experience, whatever it was. But Florence's defenses against the
recall of the memory held fast, even though she felt sure the
dream must have referred to the events Julia described. The new
material was enough to bring about a reorganization of her view
of her father, however, and of her conflicting motives in viewing
her father as a sexual object.

A neurophysiological ground for repression is not known.
One can imagine either a process that destroys already existing
connections or the inhibition of a process that forms context-
defining connections from the outset (these have now been localized to the frontal lobes). The second hypothesis is more econom-
ical and more in accord with the events of an analysis. The
recovery of memories after decades of repression argues against
the destruction of existing connections.

This is not to say that the mechanisms that cause the repression of particular kinds of events are passive mechanisms. The
mechanisms that actively prevent the formation of new connections, especially the unconscious infantile attractors, do not degrade the memory structure that already exists. We can explain
the reorganization that takes place during analysis through either
the addition of new connections or the canalizing of disordered

networks. New connections and new canalizing rules will bring about the transition to a new organizational phase.

Even at the time an event is first registered in long term memory, it may be isolated from a meaningful context of related events. Traumatic situations are well known to degrade the records they leave. The memory of such an event may remain isolated indefinitely from the person's experience of the world as a whole. When that happens, the terrifying affects that originally accompanied the event are preserved intact along with the memory. Their isolation prevents them from being connected to and compared with the memories of later situations in which the sufferer was able to avoid or alleviate the effects of the trauma.

A common form of failed structural connection seen in analytic patients is the absence of affects that others would consider appropriate. There are many gradations in this situation, too. One sees a wide range, from very subtle distortions of unpleasant or unacceptable feelings to blanket denials that the feelings exist. Obsessive patients minimize their feelings, ignore them, or explain them away. Hysterical patients exaggerate and clutch at theirs with dramatic persistence even when evidence of their inappropriateness is apparent on all sides.

For obsessive patients, feelings can be isolated from consciousness by a lack of the needed connections, just as is the case with repressed memories. But for hysterical patients, the means for dealing with unwanted affects is different from that for memories. Affects in hysteria abhor a vacuum. When the appropriate quality or intensity of affect is unacceptable, a less objectionable substitute is chosen from the affects appropriate to other events.

Of course, the substitution by the ego of inappropriate qualities or intensities of feeling may be the result of mood disorders either induced or mediated by biological causes. In severe psychotic states this influence can be overwhelming, but it can be present in lesser degrees even in patients who have been diagnosed as psychoneurotic. Therapeutically, the issue remains the same. The significant event has to be reunited with the feeling appropriate to it, whatever the source of the original discontinuity. This is a critical event in every phase transitional reorganization.

A third basis for missed connections in the minds of psycho-analytic patients is their denial of emotional conflict. Conflict arises when competing desires lead to contradictory inner states and behaviors. The human nervous system was formed to react in real time to changing environmental stimuli, with the most effective emergency behaviors wired in. As the capacity to choose between shorter and longer term goals appeared during evolution, conflict became inevitable. But the capacity to deal gracefully with conflicting aims did not develop so smoothly.

Primitive ways of conflict resolution still come naturally to us, especially the method of suppressing and isolating the less urgent desire. This maneuver clears the decks for immediate action, but it eliminates the opportunity to act later on the suppressed wish. The tendency to repress the less acceptable wish is strongly reinforced when that wish seems to be dangerous in itself. Hence the creation of a dynamic unconscious as the repository for unwanted wishes cut off from the mental information stream.

A more effective strategy for conflict resolution is the setting of priorities for actions to be taken up at a later time. The most urgent impulse is acted on in the knowledge that something else remains to be done. The satisfaction of the secondary wish is postponed in this case. Whether it can be safely implemented in the future is unresolved at the time of the postponement. Neither of these methods supplies the means for taking action on the secondary wish if the action required to achieve the primary wish precludes it.

The third and most effective strategy is to find a new way to conceptualize the conflict so that noncontradictory behaviors can be chosen to achieve each of the conflicting desires. This kind of solution requires that new connections be made at higher levels of organization. It is the only way that a conflict can be resolved and stay resolved over the long term. The opposing wishes are reorganized into a new and more complex structure in which each of them becomes a resource for the other.

This example comes from a session with a young patient who began by saying that he had to decide by today whether to switch over to a new department in his firm. He feared making either choice. There were advantages and disadvantages on both sides.

Either way, he would be "burning his bridges." His old boss or his potential new boss would be furious at him.

During the analytic hour he reviewed his reasons for leaving his last job for the current one. Negative transference attitudes toward his analyst in another city influenced his choice. He discussed his difficulties in relating to his authoritarian father, which he said made him distrustful of any new relationship. His problem with his passive homosexual longings came up in this context. If he moved to the new department his coming to analysis would be easier. But he couldn't make up his mind as to whether that would be an advantage or not.

By the end of the hour it became clear that he was really trying to decide which of his actual or potential masters to serve. When the patient organized his experience in this way, he could only follow one master at a time. No compromise was possible. He had been doing it that way all his life, and had repeated the pattern in his transference relationships with both analysts. Once he had recognized this motif, he was able to think for the first time about making a choice that would be best for him, rather than for his various bosses and therapists. He realized that he could keep his options open by phasing in some work from the new department while completing his assignments on his current accounts with the old.

The emergent properties and behaviors of this new organization were simpler *and more effective* than the sum of the conflicted wishes to please everybody and nobody had been. Conflict resolution by phase transitional change is the concluding stage of an evolutionary path that leads from a direct reaction to external events toward an inner state of reflection and reorganization. Of course, imagining the next stage of the path is only the first step toward achieving it.

Other defense mechanisms described by psychoanalysts tend to be variations on these three basic mechanisms or on combinations of these three. Creating or restoring the missing connections that come to light during the unfolding of the analytic discourse is part of the texture of every analysis. This goal can be achieved sooner or later by a phase transitional reorganization at the appropriate hierarchical level.

5 NETWORKS AND CONNECTIONS IN THE BRAIN

Neural Networks and Genetic Evolution

In this chapter we will look briefly at the system of connections that underlies the activity of the brain and some of its most important components. Although a neuron is a very simple unit compared with an idea or a feeling state, the structures that organize neurons into effective assemblies are similar to the structures that organize ideas and feelings. We cannot translate directly from structures at one level to structures at another, because emergent properties at all levels make this impossible. But we can expect to see the same principles of organization at work at all levels.

Brain activity is the result of a vastly complex interaction among systems containing many interacting parts. The search for computer models of brain activity began with Hebb's (1949) idea for a simulated neural network. McClelland and Rumelhart (1986) laid the foundations for our current understanding of neural network simulations. Mathematically, neural networks are specialized cellular automata. They are complex adaptive systems similar in many ways to the regulatory systems for gene expression. Learning in neural networks has much in common with evolutionary change in organisms, although the time scales they work on are vastly different. The complexity of neural networks in the living brain is also vastly greater than the complexity of those simulated in the computer. What is of great interest is that many functions and properties of the living brain are mimicked on the smaller scale.

A neural network is a layered structure of individual units (neurons or microprocessors) linked together at junction points called synapses. The network operates as a unit, with layers of neurons specialized for input, processing and output. Basic processing units in the human brain appear to contain from 10^5 to 10^6 neurons. An artificial network used in a simulation may contain as few neurons as ten or as many as a thousand.

A synapse transmits a fraction of the excitation it receives to each adjoining neuron. At any synapse, the fraction transmitted is the *connection weight* of that synapse. When the weight of the synapse is higher, the proportion of incoming excitation it transmits is greater. The output of the network at a given moment depends on the pattern of the connection weights of its neurons. A network is said to learn when this pattern is altered by a series of inputs. (The following section is adapted from Palombo, 1992b.)

The basic relation between input and the weighting of synapses was proposed by Hebb (1949). He conjectured that when two neurons were stimulated simultaneously, the weights at the synapses connecting them would be increased. When reinforced in this way, each of the two stimulated neurons would become more likely to fire later when the other was stimulated. With many additions and modifications, Hebb's idea has been shown to describe the learning mechanism of both artificial and natural neural networks. Weightings that reflect the external stimuli impinging on the network during an input cycle are strengthened. Weightings that do not match the input are diminished. Hebb's rule, as it is called, is a form of natural selection.

A neural network is thus a set of neurons linked by connections that provide feedback when the cells are stimulated. When Hebb (1949) proposed this model, scientists knew little about the actual connections in the brain. Computer simulation was their main research tool. Today's neurophysiological research techniques have confirmed that the neural network is the basic structure of brain organization (Nadel, Cooper, Culicover, and Harnish, 1989). Research on the neural network model now uses experiments with mammal brains in vivo. The fundamental importance of neural networks in the human brain is now well established, although the details of their operation are still not clear.

In computer simulations of neural networks, the connections between neurons can be set up in many different ways. Each configuration produces a distinct pattern of output when the network is activated. At most, every neuron in the network may be connected to every other neuron, but usually only a small fraction of the possible connections is needed to carry out a particular function. Most commonly the neurons are organized in layers, as in the brain, with the output of one layer forming the input to the next.

A key relationship is that between the weights at the synapses of a neuron and the threshold of the neuron to external stimulation. As an illustration, we will assume that the threshold to external stimulation of our sample neuron has a value of 1.0. One unit of external stimulation causes the neuron to discharge. Excitation coming from neighboring neurons in the network lowers its threshold to stimulation from the outside to a value less than 1.0. If the neuron receives 0.2 units of excitation from its neighbors, the external threshold decreases to 0.8. This means that the relationship between the weights at the synapses and the threshold is inverse. As the change from neighboring neurons rises, the threshold to an external stimulus goes down.

The functional properties of the neural network are a consequence of this inverse relationship. *If the weights on the synapses of a particular neuron are high enough, the neuron will fire when only its neighbors are stimulated, without having to be stimulated itself.*

What makes the weights change? Lacking biological data, Hebb proposed a *learning rule* that would govern the shifts in the weights when the network is stimulated. The Hebb rule states that *the weight of a synaptic connection between two neurons increases whenever the neurons are activated at the same time by an external source.* Although the Hebb rule has been superseded in computer simulations by more efficient learning rules, it is still a useful first approximation for our purposes here.

As an example of a very simple neural network, let us take a single layered 5 × 9 grid of light-sensitive cells, like those of the human retina (see Figure 5.1). Think of the letter A as projected onto this grid in the following pattern:

	A	B	C	D	E	F	G	H	I
1					X				
2				X		X			
3			X	X	X	X	X		
4		X						X	
5	X								X

Figure 5.1.

Neurons at E1, D2, D4, etc., are activated by matching elements of the stimulus pattern. When the activated neurons fire, the output of the network replicates the original stimulus. Without connections between the neurons, the grid would just be a grid. No trace of the A would be left in it after it was discharged.

The image formed on the cells of the grid without connections would be a *local* representation of the stimulus, a *pictorial* image of it. A local representation reproduces the shape and proportions of the stimulus in the geometry of the sensitive elements that record it. A one to one relationship links the stimulus elements and the recording elements. The output is a replica of the input. Our usual idea of a mental representation is very much like a local or pictorial representation.

Now consider the same one layer light sensitive grid with every neuron connected to every other. This very simple configuration is called an *autoassociator*. According to the Hebb rule, when the A is projected onto this grid each pair of neurons stimulated by the letter will also stimulate each other. The weights of their mutual synapses go up, and the threshold of each of these neurons to further stimulation from the projected A goes down.

In this network the excitation transmitted from one stimulated cell to another is (let us say) 0.15. The increase in weights with each application of the stimulus pattern is small, say 0.01. We begin with all the weights at 0.0. When the complete A is input, the complete A is output as well. After 67 repetitions of the stimulus, the value of the weights at each synapse of the stimulated neurons reaches 0.67. Then the feedback received by each stimulated cell from each of the others is $0.67 \times 0.15 = 0.1$. Each neuron then receives a total of 1.1 from all its neighbors, more than the 1.0 needed for discharge. If only 11 of the 12 neurons in the A are stimulated at this point, all 12 still receive 0.1×10 units and will fire. The network then outputs the whole A even if one of the 12 elements in the projected image is missing.

After 100 or more repetitions, the weights reach the maximum value of 1.0. Each neuron receives the full 1.0×0.15 units from each of the other stimulated neurons. Now all 12 of the A neurons will fire if only seven of them have been externally stimulated ($7 * 0.15 = 1.05 > 1.0$). The whole A will be output when only a fragment of it, one leg and the crosspiece for example, has been projected onto the grid. *This fragment acts as a probe. When input to the network, it retrieves the complete image of which it is a part.*

Transformed into a neural network, the grid remembers the A. It only has to be reminded of the image of the A by the partial stimulus of leg and crosspiece to retrieve all of it. Because it is not a replica of the image itself, the memory trace of the A is not a local representation. The one to one relationship between the elements of the stimulus and the elements of the grid that record them has been overridden. Individual neurons can fire without having been stimulated by an external source. The representation is distributed over the whole network. A *distributed representation* created by a neural network shares many critical properties with a human memory trace.

Like a human memory trace, a distributed representation can be activated and retrieved by a partial stimulus. Proust's famous story of his eating a *petite madeleine* whose taste brings back an intense emotional experience of childhood is a good example of this phenomenon. The neutral madeleine acted as a probe for the recovery of the complete emotion-laden experience of many years before. We see this phenomenon repeatedly in psychoanalysis.

One can address a distributed representation *by its content*. It can be retrieved without knowledge of the actual physical location of the memory trace. A fragment of the content can be used as a probe to retrieve the complete representation, wherever it is physically located in memory.

A distributed representation can reproduce the entire stimulus even when some neurons in the network have been disabled. We see this effect, called *graceful degradation,* in the recovery of human patients with traumatic aphasia. Graceful degradation is not so evident with the single layered autoassociator, where each neuron serves both as input and output device. In the more usual simulated memory network with two or three layers, each input neuron excites several output neurons. Each output neuron is stimulated in turn by several input neurons. The output is a complicated function of the input, not a physical replica of it. The loss of a single neuron in either layer hardly affects the calculation of the output function.

A neural network can be taught many similar but not identical patterns, all variations on a single prototype. It then recognizes the unlearned prototype more accurately than any of the learned variations. Taught to recognize the representations of several breeds of dog, it creates a distributed representation of a generic dog. This property, known as *generalization,* is familiar in human memory.

Distributed representations are not confined to a single region of contiguous neurons, but can be spread out over a large and discontinuous domain. While the input layer may have to mimic the geometry of the input stimulus pattern, as with our autoassociator, other layers are not restricted in the same way.

They may be distributed over large regions of the brain. What matters is the topology of the connections, not the geometry of cell location.

Perhaps the most remarkable property, from the point of view of the psychoanalyst, is the ability of a neural network to store many distributed representations simultaneously. The number that can be stored efficiently in a given network depends on two factors. One is the number of neurons in the network. The other is the degree of differentiation among the patterns being stored. Besides the A stored in our autoassociator, we can store other letters of the alphabet as well. A is an ideal case, since no other letter overlaps it in more than two or three isolated points. A probe made up of the leg and crosspiece of the A retrieves only the A from a network containing the entire alphabet.

If the probe consists of a region unique to one of two similar letters, that letter is retrieved no matter how closely it resembles the other one overall. However, if the probe consists of a region common to both letters, the output of the network may be one, both, or an unpredictable conflation of the two. The more elements contained in the network, the more elements are distinct in each of the two representations. The more distinct elements there are, the easier it is for the network to distinguish between the two patterns.

Is it possible that the entire long term memory of a person can be organized as a single neural network structure? The answer to this is no. With an upper limit of about 10,000 synapses for each neuron in the brain, a fully connected network could have only that number of neurons. Perhaps a more sparsely connected multilayered network could have as many as 10^5.

Actual numbers in the mammalian brain are in this range. For example, the hippocampal region of the rat brain is a set of interacting neural network groups. Estimates based on the functional anatomy of the hippocampus suggest a value between 10^5 and 10^6 neurons per group (O'Keefe, 1989).

With 10^{10} or 10^{11} neurons in the human brain, hundreds of thousands of neuron groups this size would be available for memory. These groups would be organized as a hierarchical system, with higher level neural network groups taking the output of lower level groups as their input (Edelman, 1989; Finkel, Reeke, and Edelman, 1989). Higher level outputs would link the elementary units of image and affect into larger and more meaningful groupings.

The initial registration of a new event in memory most likely involves many neural network units. Each variety of sensory experience and affective toning probably has a separate unit. (PET scan and MRI results indicate a very elaborate distribution over the frontal, parietal and occipital lobes for every word in memory.) No single neural network register can store a complete and fully meaningful psychological event. To achieve that, the outputs of many component network groups have to be integrated.

The difference between the contents of the basic neural network units and the fully integrated representation of the event is like the distinction between a sense datum and a perception. A perception is a very complicated form, including narrative elements and affect as well as imagery. First order neural networks would be responsible for the registration of sense data, but the integration of sense data into perceptions would take place at a higher level (see Edelman [1989] for a theory of higher level integration using a sophisticated neural network model of the brain).

Changes in synaptic weights caused by new stimuli are small and gradual. They are like nearest neighbor mutations in an evolving genome. Such small changes can be modeled on relatively smooth fitness landscapes. The output of a neural network, its "phenotype," as it were, depends on its history as encoded in its pattern of synaptic weights, or its "genotype."

Time is needed to effect a major change in these systems without undermining their historical stability or their current fitness. For genotypes, the time is geological. For neural networks in the human brain, the time depends on the extent of the change. When major aspects of personality structure need to be reorganized, years may be required.

The Hippocampus and the Amygdala

The hippocampus is a small area in the medial temporal lobe, shaped by the distinctive spiral curve of the seahorse. This remarkable organ is the integrator and coordinator of the highest levels of cortical association (Cohen and Eichenbaum, 1993). It creates the spatial context that unifies the experience of the various senses, the basis for representational memory. During REM sleep it is active as the contents of short term memory are transferred into permanent storage in the cerebral cortex.

The hippocampus is the switchboard for the information hierarchy of the brain. Sensory association areas at the highest levels of the cortex communicate through the hippocampus. Connections made by the hippocampus between these cortical association areas form the top level of the information hierarchy. The perception of an event, as distinct from its sensory registration, is made possible by the hippocampus.

Although isolated images can be remembered if focused on, the preferred unit of memory storage is the event. An event is stored in long term memory as a set of integrated higher level sensory images connected by the links established in the hippocampus.

During the initial period when a new event is represented in short term memory (one day to perhaps a week), the integrative processing done by the hippocampus has not yet registered in the cortex. Trauma can still prevent the transfer to long term memory. The cortex already contains the original sensory information, but it is not yet integrated. Information is sent to the hippocampus only after being recorded and processed in the primary and secondary sensory cortex. Short term memory contents are transferred to long term memory storage when the information created by the hippocampal processing of cortical associations is sent on to the cortex. This occurs during the process of dreaming, when hippocampal activity is especially high.

Hippocampal function is among the first to be lost in Alzheimer's disease. The most salient symptom of hippocampal dysfunction is the loss of the transfer function from short to long term memory. We have known since the 1950s that REM time (dreaming) is markedly decreased in Alzheimer's patients.

New events are not stored at random in the cortex. If that were so, they could never be recalled. PET scanning with normal subjects confirms that information is sharply localized even at the level of semantic categories. At a higher organizational level, an event combines many of these items with memories of similar events. The power to recall an item depends on an elaborate associative network that can be entered from many directions, according to the context. This network is created by the hippocampus as it decides where to store the new events it has been processing. How is the decision made? A new event has to be compared with possibly related events already in storage. The event network is formed by associative links between the new events and the events already in storage they resemble. Newell, Shaw, and Simon (1957) showed the need for a matching procedure to construct an associative network.

Since the functional unit of memory is the integrated event, the comparison requires the recall of integrated events already contained in long term storage. This comparison takes place during dreaming sleep, when integrated sensory representations of new and previously stored events are superimposed on each other in the process Freud called condensation. The coherence of the superimposed image is the test of relatedness between the current and past events. This process was described in *Dreaming and Memory* (Palombo, 1978), before I was aware that the hippocampus is the region of the brain specialized to perform exactly this function.

The integration of the sensory imagery of an event is an emergent property of hippocampal function. So also is the creation of the intricate associative web of long term memory. The hippocampus is specialized for phase transitional behavior, that is, the reorganization of associative networks. Hippocampal activity, which is especially intense during dreaming, is required to reorganize the contents of memory at the event level. In the hippocampus of mammals, new phase transitions are created, cultivated, and controlled. This is one of the greatest and, to my mind, least appreciated achievements of evolution.

The almond-shaped amygdala, close to the hippocampus in the mid-brain, is a center of primitive emotional reactivity. The amygdala interacts with short term memory structures to give what Edelman (1992) calls *value* to the transactions carried out by the brain with the outside world. Value is his name for the adaptive payoff for the processing of a particular interaction between the organism and its surroundings. It is experienced in humans and probably in all mammals as good and bad feeling states, or, in Freud's terms, as pleasure and pain.

The amygdala takes part in primitive conditioning events that are not transmitted to the cerebral cortex. Nevertheless, it gives values to experience at higher levels as well. It has a vast network of connections that link it to many areas of the brain, including the thalamus, hippocampus and cortex. The amygdala's idea of value is not solipsistic. The amygdala is especially active in the recognition of affects in others, surely the most highly adaptive activity of the newborn.

The Chemical Basis of Connectivity

Communication occurs in neural networks when electrical impulses cross the synaptic junctions where two neurons meet. This process is itself quite complex. When an outgoing electrical impulse arrives at the tip of an axon branch, it excites the secretion of an active chemical agent into the narrow space at the synaptic junction. This agent, called a neurotransmitter, initiates a new incoming electrical impulse in the dendrite of the receptor neuron.

Dozens of neurotransmitters are now known. Each is specific to a particular population of brain cells. Neurotransmitters form a weak link in the chain of communication between nerve cells and between neural networks. Dysfunction of the neurotransmitter system is implicated in many varieties of mental illness, most clearly in depression.

Effective drugs for depression assist the action of specific neurotransmitters, chiefly norepinephrine and serotonin. In so doing they broadly increase the connectedness of the relevant brain areas. This is different from the increase in connectedness achieved in psychoanalysis by the reinforcement of particular associations. Drug therapy is like a phase transition caused by an increase in the homogeneity of the input rules in a random Boolean network. Psychotherapy is more like a phase transition caused by an increase in the number of canalized rules. This correspondence suggests that the two effects are not necessarily competitive. Neurotransmitter enhancement may facilitate the process of long term restructuralization for which psychoanalytic treatment aims.

Historically, psychoanalysts have been very cautious about treating their analytic patients with drugs. Their reservations were based on two ideas that now appear to have been mistaken and one that has been tragically prophetic. When psychotropic drugs were introduced, their chemical activity was hardly understood. Obvious models for their mode of action were stimulation and sedation. Tranquilizers reduced mental activity, calmed the patient down. Minor tranquilizers worked like the major antipsychotic drugs, dampening down unwanted brain activity.

Psychoanalysts rightly saw their work with patients as demanding a high level of mental effort. Their opposition to medications also had a more theoretical basis. Many analysts believed that a patient's primary motive for remaining in treatment is anxiety. If the anxiety were reduced, the patient would leave. To keep the patient working, the analyst would have to maintain a sufficient level of anxiety in the patient by remaining aloof and only partly accessible. It would be self-defeating for an analyst with this point of view to introduce a substance that might undo his own efforts to keep the patient's discomfort at an optimal level.

When I was in training, I heard a well-respected teacher say that a patient's belief that he was getting better could be a serious obstacle to the success of his analysis. I should add that this analyst advocated an extreme degree of passivity in the analyst's stance toward the patient, extreme even for the traditional analysts of his time. He was quite unprepared to deal with the patient's loss of momentum when the progress of the analysis reached a local optimum.

The problem for the patient who wants to leave treatment too soon is not his lack of anxiety. It is his misinterpretation of his lowered anxiety as a sign that he has used up his chances to get better. The self-organizing momentum of the patient's ego can be restored. The analyst has to display his understanding that the patient is suffering from a lack of imagination caused by a deficiency in his experience. One might call this a negative fantasy, a fantasy that things can't get any better, no matter what happens in the future. Such a fantasy may be due to an inhibition of positive memories that might evoke punishment or retaliation if revived.

Lack of anxiety is not the culprit either when medication seems to abolish the wish for further treatment. The impulse to leave is most often a reaction by the patient to the local optimum experience. It may also be a defense against the grief occasioned when the patient discovers that he has been living most of his life under a cloud. The lifting of the cloud is a painful reminder of losses that either have been denied or else have been accepted with resignation as the price for even a modest level of adaptive functioning.

However, successful medication can make the patient eager for treatment and not at all complacent about it. The initial lifting of Richard's depression was aided by a low dose of a serotonin uptake inhibitor. His reaction, which he articulated in the water-skiing image, demonstrated a new enthusiasm for the analytic process, which did not abate until more than a year later, when he returned from his honeymoon. Richard could experience the improvement he felt with the medication as complementary to the analytic process. This may have been due in part to the fact that the drug treatment was not begun until after the analytic process had already been well established.

Some psychoanalysts have objected to the use of medications as an adjunct to analytic treatment because they claim the role of the medicator is not a neutral role. They believe the analyst must be a neutral observer only. He will be intruding on the patient's autonomy if he takes sides among the various conscious and unconscious forces vying for control of the patient's thoughts and feelings. The medicator, on the other hand, is aligning himself with the patient's executive ego, opposing his unconscious wishes and impulses. So runs the argument.

This objection is based on a misunderstanding of Freud's very useful notion of neutrality. The analyst must be neutral in the sense that he needs to maintain his objectivity about a patient's conflicting desires. He avoids involvement in a solution to the conflict achieved by force rather than by reorganization. He is not neutral about the outcome of the treatment, however. His assignment is to create the optimal conditions for a successful analytic process. When a patient is embarking on an action that interferes with the analytic process, the analyst is obliged to report this to the patient. This is traditionally called analysis of the patient's resistance. Thinking that the analyst is merely informing the patient about the consequences of his choice is foolish, however. If the analyst is not convinced that the treatment is worthwhile, the patient will soon be aware of it and will distance himself from both the treatment and the analyst.

When the patient is in a psychophysiological state that threatens the analytic process, the analyst is simply doing his job by helping the patient deal with the threat. In Richard's case the analyst was well-advised to allow the process to develop before considering the use of medication. The medication should be experienced by the patient as an adjunct to the analysis, not the other way around.

With Richard it became evident after a period of analysis that his ability to participate freely and actively in the process was compromised. His tendency to morbid scrupulosity and self-castigation was part of his lifelong pattern of depression. The medication was suggested as a way to deal with this interference in the process. It was not offered as a cure for the symptoms that had developed as a result of his efforts to control the depression by reducing emotional risk. Richard had to be able to make this distinction before the medication could become an adjunct to the analysis. This would not have been the case earlier on, when Richard's depression was much more acute.

Another important variation of the argument is that when the analyst becomes a medicator, his role changes. This concerns the patient's perception of the analyst as a source of gratification outside the analytic process itself. If the medication is given too early, or if the analyst suggests that it is offered as an alternative to the analytic process, then trouble is likely. This is a countertransference problem in the particular analyst, not a problem caused by the medication as such.

Unhappily for patients and analysts alike, health insurance for psychoanalytic treatment is now routinely being denied. The excuse for this denial is that medication is a cheaper and medically adequate alternative. Analysts were right to fear this opportunistic attack on their work. However, to the extent that they deny the value of medications in analysis, they contribute to the mistaken belief that the two kinds of treatment are real alternatives.

If analysts demand that patients choose between the two, they must realize that the choice will often be for economy and speed rather than quality and durability.

Complexity and the Brain

Although complexity is characteristic of all living things, higher levels of complexity emerge as evolution moves on. Metazoa and their various organs are complex systems with many cellular components. Yet in simple animals like the sponges, interactions between component cells are preprogrammed and limited in their range. A neural network ring opens and closes the mouth of a sea anemone, using a primitive form of experiential knowledge with its genetic programming.

As cognitive capacity increased during the evolution of the vertebrates, new levels of organization beyond that of the single neural network emerged. Many of these are embodied in the evolving anatomy of the vertebrate brain. We can see the development of specialized structures, culminating in the differentiated expanse of the human cortex and its vast array of connections.

Functional organization is harder to specify. Rosen (1991) suggests that the function of a component in any system can be defined as the difference between the functioning of the system with and without the component. This may seem obvious for the brain. Most of what we have learned about brain function comes from the correlation of functional deficits with damage to specific anatomical structures. Noninvasive imaging techniques (CAT and MRI) have opened the way to finer discriminations of structure.

Historically, psychoanalysts have had to rely for their theory on correlations between deficits at various levels of functional organization. Lack of precision in their vocabulary for these functional deficits has horrified some philosophers of science. Certainly, improvements can be made in the description of the coevolutionary functioning of the patient and analyst in the analytic process. But, psychoanalysts have not been remiss in using their clinical experience to develop a self-contained functional theory. As functional theories of mental activity and neuroscientific descriptions of the brain become more precise, we can expect to see a greater and greater convergence of the two.

Functionalism is a movement in cognitive psychology that tries to get around our still meager understanding of brain structure. It seeks functional explanations for human cognition at all scales, from the very large to the very small. The aim is to separate the aspect of mental activity that resembles a computer program from the aspect that resembles the computer itself. The presumption is that the program will be easier to fathom than the workings of the computer. A universal computer can be made from many different materials. Any of these differently realized material computers can run the same programs. To the extent that mental activity is like the programming of a computer, a theory of mental activity could make sense apart from any direct knowledge of the underlying hardware embodiment.

Psychoanalytic theory is a typical example of functionalist theory. Since Freud first elaborated what he called his metapsychology, analysts have been trying to construct a plausible theoretical model to explain psychological changes over the long term. A plausible model is not a biologically accurate model. It is a model that attempts to account in a consistent way for observations made during the analyst's work with patients. It shares the major shortcomings of any functionalist theory. Other consistent theories may explain the same observations as well or even better. The question here is not whether to substitute another functionalist theory for the traditional theory of psychoanalysis. That would not work, and for good reasons. Psychoanalytic theory does not exist in a vacuum. It is deeply embedded in a clinical practice whose aim is to alleviate suffering. A sensible practitioner does not abandon a method that helps his patients until he can be sure a newer method will do at least as much and only then provide something better.

To encourage other psychoanalysts to pay attention to what is new in neurobiology and in science is not to suggest that they give anything up that already helps them help their patients. Knowledge of the brain can be used to narrow down choices between functional theories that are only roughly compatible with observation. We may even discover that a finding in neuroscience can supply the germ of a new model of psychological function, but this is not essential for interdisciplinary research to be useful. It is enough that we can eliminate ideas from our theories that are not compatible with what is known about the human brain.

The brain is superbly equipped to facilitate, optimize, and exploit the opportunities for adaptation created by the complex world in which it lives. Freud was correct when he suggested that psychoanalysis works by freeing this rich potentiality from neurotic inhibition. However, the process that frees the patient to respond optimally to the world is itself highly complex. It enters, in intricate and often very delicate ways, into the self-organizing process already taking place within the patient. This is what we will explore at greater length in the next chapters.

6 THE EDGE OF CHAOS IN THE THERAPEUTIC PROCESS

Phase Transitions and Emergent Properties

For a system near the edge of chaos, a small change in input from the environment can lead to a reorganization of the system's structure at a level of increased complexity. If this were not possible in the psychoanalytic process, the patient would be unable to recover the ground lost over many years of maladaptive living. Without reorganization, every analysis would be like the fictional autobiography of Tristram Shandy in Lawrence Sterne's novel of that name. Shandy set out to write his own history from his birth to the time when he was writing. He spent three days describing the events of his birth. He concluded that his efforts were futile. If he kept up the same pace he would just fall further and further behind.

Reorganization is the bootstrapping procedure that makes evolution possible and makes it progressive. A nonlethal mutation that fails to give an organism (or a species) a better ability to reorganize is biologically irrelevant. In the same way, a psychoanalytic intervention that does not contribute to the potential of the patient's mental contents for reorganization is not therapeutic.

175

Sudden and surprising changes in a patient during analysis are evidence of phase changes in the structure of his mental contents. We have seen some dramatic examples of a phase transitional change in Richard's analysis. One function of the psychoanalytic setting and the therapeutic relationship is to raise or lower what we might call the *temperature* of the patient's mental activity. The aim is to reach an optimal balance of structure and mobility.

Organized systems of components can be found in either frozen or fluid states. Frozen states are uniform in structure, rigid, crystalline, brittle, and predictable. Local deformations do not propagate through a frozen system, unless they are strong enough to destroy it. Fluid states, by contrast, are chaotic. Lacking internal structure, they are in continual flux. Local perturbations may spread over an entire system in the fluid state within a very short time. Since neither frozen nor chaotic states are differentiated, they cannot be configured to represent or carry information.

Differentiation within systems appears only at the phase transition between frozen ice and chaotic fluid states. Complex geological examples are the coastlines of the polar ice caps. Where the uniformly rigid ice cap meets the uniformly chaotic ocean, uniformity disappears. The coastline is a uniquely configured series of promontories, inlets, islands, and icebergs, each with its own finely detailed fractal shape.

So it is with the activities of complex systems overall. Individual forms with stable identities exist only when the system is poised near the edge of chaos, at the phase transition between frozen and fluid states. If a system remains near the edge of chaos, its potential for differentiation and new information content is virtually unlimited.

An example of behavior near the edge of chaos in biology is the growth curve of a species in an ecological system. Growth can be rapid when a species has only a few members, because the balance of the ecosystem is not perturbed by the growth. When a single species spreads across a large area, however, the environment becomes less hospitable. The growth rate of the proliferating species slows. Predators begin to multiply more rapidly than the species itself. Resources needed by the species (food and space) become scarce. Growth is limited by the number of species members already present. As the size of the existing population becomes larger, the growth rate becomes inversely proportional to the size.

This state of things is described by the famous Lotka Volterra equation, $x_{t+1} = r * x_t * (1- x_t)$. Here x_t is the fraction at time t of the maximum size of the population supportable by the environment under ideal conditions. The expression x_{t+1} represents the fraction one generation later. The growth rate is r. At generation $t + 1$, x_{t+1} increases along with x_t until x_t reaches half the maximum. Then x_{t+1} decreases as x increases further toward 1.

The Lotka Volterra equation is a quadratic. It describes a parabola with coordinates x_t and x_{t+1}. At the apex of the parabola, $x_t = 0.5 * r$, and $x_{t+1} = x_t^2 = 0.25 * r$. To give x_{t+1} a range from 0 to 1, r is allowed to vary from 0 to 4.

As x_t increases beyond 0.5, the value of x_{t+1} becomes dependent on r in a very complicated and counterintuitive way. When r is less than 1, x_{t+1} is 0. Between $r = 1$ and $r = 3$, each x_{t+1} has a unique solution. At $r = 3$, however, the value of x_{t+1} bifurcates. Two widely separated valid solutions to the equation suddenly appear. At $r = 3.50$, a second bifurcation occurs. The equation now has four solutions. At $r = 3.54$, it has eight.

The value of x can be any one of the different solutions. For example, from $r = 3$ to $r = 3.50$, x_{t+1} can be either 0.765 or 0.558. On the graph of the equation this appears as a cycle of period 2. Between $r = 3.50$ and 3.54, the values are 0.874, 0.383, 0.826 and 0.500. This is a cycle of period 4. As the r values for each new bifurcation get closer and closer together, the cycles become larger and larger. The series of bifurcations continues at ever decreasing intervals of r, until, at $r = 3.57$, an infinite number of solutions exists. The system is chaotic.

Between $r = 3$ and $r = 3.57$ a zone of differentiation precedes the onset of chaos. Within this zone is a cascade of period doubling bifurcations, a hierarchy of distinct values that depend very sensitively on r. At the limit, no differences or distinctions exist. Beyond $r = 3.57$, in the chaotic realm, things become complicated once again. As r increases further, narrow windows containing no solutions appear in the midst of the chaos. Within these windows, miniature cascades of period bifurcation lead again to chaos. Within that chaos are more windows continuing miniature cascades of period bifurcation, and so on indefinitely.

The series of bifurcations that occurs as x_{t+1} goes from $r = 1$ to $r = 4$ yields the same sequence of behaviors as the cellular automata described by Wolfram (1986). This is quite fascinating. From $r = 1$ to $r = 3$, x_{t+1} is frozen at a single value (Wolfram Class I). From $r = 3$ to $r = 3.57$, x_{t+1} is periodic (Wolfram Class II). Between $r = 3.57$ and $r = 4$, x_{t+1} is chaotic (Wolfram Class III). Just before the onset of chaos near 3.57, the cycles of x_{t+1} are so large that the specific values of r cannot be determined.

Peak and Frame (1994) point out that this behavior is similar to that of Wolfram Class IV cellular automata, which appear between Class II (periodic) and Class III (chaotic) behaviors. Class IV automata exhibit the characteristics of complex systems near the edge of chaos. They have extremely long transients approaching infinity in the limit. These transients are made up of self-similar clusters that retain their identities despite small changes as the automaton cycles.

Kaneko and Suzuki (1994) have conducted a clever simulation in which coevolving agents optimize their performance in a space defined by a growth parameter derived from the variable r in the Lotka Volterra equation. These agents are simulated birds who maintain their spatial and sexual territories through their individually identifiable songs. The ability of one bird to imitate another bird's song allows it to invade the other's territory. Imitation is achieved by an adjustment of the imitating bird's song to make it more like the victim's.

Songs are defined as the set of values given by the Lotka Volterra equation as a growth variable a varies over its range from 0 to 2. The growth parameter a passes through the usual frozen, periodic, and chaotic phases. Each of 200 simulated birds is assigned a random value of a at the start of the round robin tournament. Each bird tries to imitate its opponent's song by incorporating it into its own. Songs with two values, produced after the first bifurcation, are more difficult to imitate than songs with only one. As the value of a increases, the values continue to bifurcate until the onset of chaos. Imitation becomes more difficult as the number of values increases. In each confrontation of the tournament, the bird that comes closer to successfully imitating the other bird's song is the winner. This is the bird whose own song is the more complex.

After each round of the tournament, the birds are assigned a fraction of the total population proportional to their scores on the previous round. This has the effect of natural selection. The fittest birds, as defined by their scores, are the more successful reproductively. During the population update process, random mutations increase or decrease the value of a for individual birds at a rate of one in 10^5.

Kaneko and Suzuki's results confirm that in an environment where complexity as such has an adaptive advantage, coevolution moves toward the edge of chaos. The complex song that protects against imitation is selected for in their tournaments. According to their findings, however, the movement toward the edge of chaos is not smooth. It takes the form of a punctuated equilibrium in which sudden increases in the average value of a are followed by much longer periods where a stays constant.

A close correlation turned up between the peaks in the rate of change of a and the values where the number of solutions increases abruptly. There were some surprises, too. Six major peaks defined the landscape. One was at the bifurcation point between 2 and 4 solutions, another at the bifurcation between 4 and 8 solutions. One was at the onset of chaos, and one at the appearance of the first window in period 3 of the chaotic realm. The population stabilized at $a = 1.94$, far beyond the onset of chaos, which occurred at $a = 1.4$.

These findings (and others) suggest that the ordered and disordered realms do not have a single continuous boundary that can be labeled as the edge of chaos. Where phase space has more complex structure, as in the realm of the Lotka Volterra equation and in many other physical systems, the shape of the edge of chaos is also complex. It is distributed over a set of partitions separating many compartments, even, as here, over infinitely many nested self-similar compartments.

In Kaneko and Suzuki's simulation we see this complicated structure exemplified. Edge of chaos conditions exist at several values of a. For the coevolution of the simulated birds, these values lead to differences in the height and width of the peaks on the evolutionary landscape. The final peak at $a = 1.94$ is unique in one important respect, however. It has a Lyapunov exponent of zero, which means it is at the transition point between periodic and chaotic conditions. One can argue, as Kaneko and Suzuki do, that this finding shows that $a = 3.88$ is *the* edge of chaos *for their system.*

The idea of the edge of chaos is useful for psychoanalysts despite difficulties in finding an exact mathematical definition for the edge. Nor is it necessary to know the precise location of the edge in any particular system. The notion of the edge of chaos gives the psychoanalyst a *normative description* of optimal coevolutionary activity in the psychoanalytic process. It tells him that behavior near the edge of chaos is inherently unstable. Edge of chaos behavior can deteriorate into either a state of rigid periodicity or a state of chaotic disorganization.

Kaneko and Suzuki show that where edge of chaos behavior is adaptive, coevolution drives the ecosystem in that direction. Their experiment suffers from an important limitation, however. The adaptive advantage of increased complexity in their system is wired into their simulation. An increase in the difficulty of imitating a song follows directly from an increase in the length of the song. The length of the song is equal to the number of values of x at parameter a.

But is edge of chaos behavior adaptive in all circumstances? The cases of the crocodile and the cockroach suggest that the answer is "not necessarily." Neither one has changed very much in more than a hundred million years, yet they continue to be quite successful in filling their ecological niches.

Successful organisms and complex adaptive systems overall may not necessarily be driven toward the edge of chaos. However, when change is advantageous, as it is when the ecosystem changes significantly, organisms evolve in a direction that promotes adaptation.

In psychoanalytic treatment, change is desirable. Psychoanalysis itself evolved from other methods that failed to provide lasting change in the neurotic patient. The patient undertakes analysis because he wants to change. Change in psychoanalysis involves increasing the connectedness and complexity of the patient's mental contents. (This is in contrast with pharmacotherapy, which aims for a tonic and temporary change in the patient's overall state of mind.)

Patients in psychoanalysis, especially in the early stages, may not appreciate the adaptive value of working toward the edge of chaos. They may find the hazards of life near the edge of chaos frightening, and may actively seek to avoid them. When this form of resistance is not dominating the analytic process, however, co-evolution leads to longer and longer trains of associations (the songs of the psychoanalytic patient). Finer and finer distinctions appear between emotionally similar events. Kaneko and Suzuki's simulation is a model of the irregular progress through coevolution that leads to stabilization of an ecosystem near the edge of chaos.

Connection and Differentiation: Attractors

In Kaneko and Suzuki's work, the elements of the song are related because they are all generated by the Lotka Volterra equation at a fixed value of a. The associations produced by a psychoanalytic patient, on the other hand, are linked through a particular state of feeling aroused by a particular kind of event. Each train of associations reads out the contents of a particular connected neighborhood in the patient's associative memory structure.

The connections among the related song elements made by the Kaneko birds in constructing their songs can only be adaptive, but the same is not always true for the connections in human memory. One important aspect of the analyst's job is to help the patient overcome the effect of what we might call *pathological connectedness* among his mental contents. Pathological connections short-circuit the systems they infect. When painful experience is repressed, it is sealed off from consciousness by fantasy-based pathological connections. If a patient's husband and father are indistinguishable at a deeply emotional level, for example, she may fail to differentiate her behavior and feelings toward them in her daily life.

A pathological connection is a condensation that fuses relationships formed early in childhood with relationships encountered in adult life. The transference side of the patient's feelings toward the analyst arises from the links between the figure of the analyst and these childhood objects. The analyst's behavior is assimilated to the food set of the attractors that formed around the patient's experience of these objects. It might appear that this kind of connection would have to be broken in analysis for the patient to adapt more successfully in his adult relationships. Freud's military imagery for the analyst's action against these pathological structures is largely based on the idea that they must be broken into or broken down to free the patient.

In fact, we have no reason to believe that pathological connections are ever disconnected by the work of analysis. It is enough that these connections are circumscribed and circumvented by the creation of new connections in the analytic work. These new connections open the painful memories of the past to comparison with later events in the patient's life when viewed realistically, especially with the events of the analysis itself. The analysis builds a new collateral circulation around the pathological blockage to the flow of information within the patient's memory structures.

A pathological connection forms a closed circle of primitive condensations. This closed circle always remains a potential attractor for the patient's feelings during times of stress, even after a successful analysis. Such an attractor may be a fixed point toward which all other values converge under the dynamics of a system, or a cyclic structure from which no easy escape is possible. It may also be a chaotic or strange attractor that never repeats exactly but cycles endlessly within a fixed envelope.

An attractor is surrounded by a *basin of attraction,* the area or volume drained by the pull of the attractor. A basin of attraction is a like local optimum turned upside down. Instead of climbing to a higher level of adaptation, an object is drawn down by a force acting like gravity. Attractors determine the dynamics of the physical world at all scales. Electron shells around an atomic nucleus form a set of attractors for electrons. The positive electrical field of the atomic nucleus is a basin of attraction. Walden Pond is an attractor, and the area in Concord containing the streams that feed it is its basin of attraction. Walden Pond also attracts readers of Thoreau. The recently confirmed black hole at the center of M87, the supermassive elliptical galaxy at the center of the nearby

Virgo galaxy cluster, is an attractor. Its basin is the central region of the galaxy. Within that volume its gravitational pull is greater than the centrifugal force of a star or other orbiting object. Stars are constantly being drawn into the center of the black hole.

For the analytic patient, infantile experiences are caught up and drawn into the primitive condensations that influence his emotional life even while they remain repressed. The basin of attraction here is a region of the patient's adult experience labeled with the emotional value of the infantile fantasies that form the attractor. Richard's experience with Ellen and other potential mates was a basin of attraction for his violent infantile fantasies about his relationship with his mother.

Various streams of new information feed the infantile attractor. These streams are differentiated and individualized, as are most events of adult life. Once drawn into the basin of attraction, however, they lose their individuality and with it the possibility of being responded to with discrimination.

The connections through which new information is drawn into an infantile attractor work in only one direction, like the valves that keep the blood in our veins moving in the direction of that great attractor, the heart. Information about the infantile attractor does not move through these connections in the direction of consciousness. What emanates from the attractor is not information. It is a childhood feeling state, unmodified by current experience and reconstituted repeatedly when triggered by current events. This feeling state may be quite terrifying, even in a well-functioning adult patient.

Freud's picture of the id as a "cauldron of seething excitations" can be viewed as a snapshot of an unconscious attractor. (There must be many unconscious attractors partitioning the unconscious mental contents of each patient.) When Freud said, "Where the id was, there the ego shall be," he was celebrating the opening of unconscious infantile attractors to the adult patient's mature judgment. In analysis, new connections are added to the patient's mental contents that lead back from the infantile attractor to his conscious experience in the present moment.

Attractors in the nonpathological organization of mental contents are strange attractors. This is because the complex interactions among mental contents create nonlinear dynamics, the dynamic basis of the strange attractor. Strange attractors are deterministic but not predictable. The trajectories of two points initially close together in a strange attractor may diverge rapidly. When the patient associates freely in an analytic hour he displays this pattern of diverging trajectories.

Pathological unconscious infantile attractors are more primitive than this. Pathological attractors are not as highly structured in the mathematical sense as the usual psychological attractors of everyday life. In fact, the fixed point attractor of an idée fixe and the closed curve attractor of an obsession are clinically quite pathological though mathematically extremely simple. In a successful psychoanalysis one would surely find an increase in the strangeness of the patient's unconscious attractors.

Strange attractors generated by a computer often have fascinating and even beautiful shapes. They are multilobed objects connected by many bridges. Whether the trajectory of a given point stays in its current lobe or crosses a bridge to another lobe is determined but not predictable. With time all lobes are visited, however. This kind of structure makes a good model for the flexibility required by a healthy mind in a changing environment.

Self-Organization in the Psyche

The mechanism in the psychoanalytic patient that draws his conscious adult experience of the present down into an unconscious region of childhood memories where all subtlety and distinctiveness are lost is effectively a basin of attraction. Unlike the water in Walden Pond or the matter crushed together by a black hole, however, the contents of the infantile emotional attractor are not completely homogeneous. Unlike the seething excitations in Freud's cauldronlike id, they have a primitive but very effective organization.

Mental contents incorporated into the infantile attractor do not simply sink into the attractor. They are transformed through an active process. A basin of attraction in a force field is not a complex enough image to represent this activity. The irregular streams arriving at the amorphous pool that is Walden Pond lose their individuality. The molecules of water they deliver remain the same. They are not reorganized when they enter the pond. The loss of atomic structure in a black hole is disorganizing, not reorganizing. Mental contents are transformed in a more intricate way when drawn into the infantile attractor.

Kauffman (personal communication) suggests that the contents of the infantile attractor form a closed finite autocatalytic set (Kauffman, 1993, p. 373). Those elements of current experiences that enter the attractor make up its *food set*. The infantile fantasies that make up the attractor maintain and reproduce themselves by consuming the food set. Elements of the food set are not only sequestered from the patient's conscious problem solving capabilities when drawn into the attractor. They are also actively resynthesized into emotional facsimiles of the fantasies that form the contents of the attractor.

What happens in that case to the representation of the original experience? At first glance, it might appear that once the autocatalytic attractor is formed, every element of the food set would be transformed into infantile fantasy and permanently lost to memory. We know this is not what happens. The recovery of repressed memories, years and decades old, is basic to the psychoanalytic process.

The product of this transformation is inserted into the stream of information that drives the decision making processes of the psychic apparatus. This can be explained through the workings of the mechanism of displacement described by Freud.

The information stream coursing through the psychic apparatus does not carry blanks. When an item is displaced from the stream by an attractor, a substitute is provided to take its place. The substitute is most likely to be the transformation product of the original experience as it has been generated by the attractor. Repressed experience is drawn into the attractor and transformed into a member fantasy of the autocatalytic set. In this form it can be reemitted into the information stream. Fortunately, a representation of the original, untransformed, experience can often be recovered in analysis from long term memory, where it had been inaccessible to the information stream.

Because sensory input from the real world is continuous, childhood memories cannot be inserted to replace actual new experiences in this cognitive stream unless the patient is psychotic. Affects are not so easily checked against external reality, even in people without significant psychopathology, however. The inappropriate affects generated by an infantile attractor can be introduced into consciousness without being identified by the neurotic patient as inappropriate. To the outside observer, on the other hand, the pathological attractor typically appears to be making emotional mountains out of tiny molehills.

What would the internal structure of an unconscious infantile attractor look like? We have had a good preliminary answer to this important question at least since 1975, when Colby published his remarkable working model of a paranoid patient. His computer simulation, called PARRY, was interviewed for one hour via teletype by the members of a panel of psychiatrists. These psychiatrists could not distinguish PARRY'S responses during such an exchange from those of a group of paranoid humans with whom they also communicated via the teletype.

PARRY is a sophisticated program that matches key words and phrases in the questions asked by an interrogator with preformed output strings. The number of key phrases and output strings needed for a successful simulation like PARRY is only a few thousand. The set of key words and phrases is an attractor. It reduces the infinite array of possible sentences transmitted by the interrogator into a closed finite set that can be matched with PARRY'S small set of output strings.

PARRY preserves the continuity and coherence of the exchange by keeping track of the topics being discussed and the output strings that have already been used. Some outputs are organized as stories, produced in a fixed order. No output is used twice. It is extraordinary that a preformed set as small as PARRY's could successfully counterfeit an adult human being, even a psychotic patient. (This set is large enough only for a single interview. On a second exchange PARRY can be more easily recognized because it runs out of new things to say.)

The attractor sets of actual paranoid patients would be many times larger than PARRY'S. PARRY'S success, however, suggests that they might still be closed and finite, at least during a psychotic episode.

When we come to neurotic patients in psychoanalysis, the situation is more complex, but not necessarily different in principle. First, the neurotic patient has a wide choice of possible verbal expressions for the contents of the attractor set. An unlimited number of possible sentences can express the finite number of items in the attractor set.

Second, the basic units of the attractor set are not ideas but images in multiple sensory modalities with affective coloring and action potential. That is, they are memories of actual events and of fantasies about actual events. The unit of input from current experience, a member of the food set, is also an event.

A neural network takes in information from its environment and emits an output specific to each input of information. The output may be a replica of the input, a partial image of it, or a behavioral response with no formal relation to the input at all. In each case the output is a transformation of the input. When a neural network functions as a recognition device, it can output a whole image it has previously learned when the input to it is an incomplete piece of the previously learned image. An infantile attractor does the same. It returns a whole infantile event when fed a current event that resembles it only in part.

A simulated neural network is usually tuned or updated by a feedback loop that tells it how closely its actual output for a given input compares with the adaptively optimal output. The weights of the network elements can then be changed to reduce the difference between the actual and the optimal. A network is said to be *supervised* by such a feedback loop (which may or may not contain a human observer). Neural networks in the brain are normally updated continuously in the light of current experience. The infantile attractor in the patient has escaped from adaptive supervision at some critical time early in his development.

The infantile output of the attractor replaces (displaces) the input of adult experience in the information stream of the psychic apparatus. The attractor acts as a filter, an early warning system. It extracts and amplifies evidence of danger from the new data impinging on the patient's mind. The output of the attractor is often accompanied by anxiety or pain, sometimes quite intense, which often leads to avoidant behavior maladaptive in adult life.

The neural network model is helpful, but it has its limitations, too. One of them is the stereotypical output of the infantile attractor. Clinical experience suggests that the productions of an infantile attractor are much more diverse than one would predict from a simple neural network model. The infantile attractors encountered in work with patients are devious. Their output is often novel, and even occasionally ingenious. These attractors seem capable of elaborations and manipulations beyond the capacities of a neural network.

PARRY and neural networks with similar properties are simpler in many ways than the autocatalytic sets described by Kauffman and Fontana. The attractor formed by the neural network has a rigid output. It cannot create a novel response under new circumstances. In Piaget's terms, it can assimilate but not accommodate. Thinking of the psychological attractor as an autocatalytic set takes one a step closer to matching theory with observation.

A Fontana Level 1 organization is a closed autocatalytic set, but it can produce infinitely many outputs determined by the same small set of rules. This very simple example presented by Fontana and Buss (1993) shows how this is possible. As in earlier references to Fontana's work, the individual algebraic expressions play the roles of functions and of objects acted on by other functions. When one expression acts on another in this system, one or both of them is transformed into another functional expression.

All objects maintained in this Level 1 organization are characterized by a particular kind of syntactical architecture (see Figure 6.1). In this example, every object is a string of building blocks. Building blocks come in two varieties, A or B, such that i contiguous A's are followed by j contiguous B's with $i > = j$. The organization can, therefore, be visualized in the i, j plane. All actions that occur within the organization can be described by two invariant laws, that is, by two emergent regularities in the behavior of the system. According to the first law, an object acting on another object produces the object immediately below it on the diagonal, as illustrated by the bold arrow in Figure 6.1. This law applies to all objects except those at the lower ends of the diagonals. The second law states that the objects at the lower ends of the diagonals, where $j = 1$, operate on other objects to form

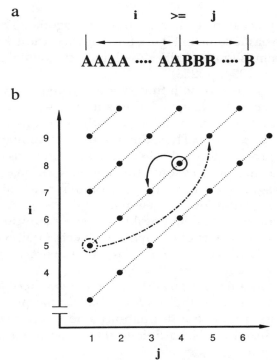

Figure 6.1. A simple Level 1 organization. Objects retained in the system share a grammatical structure (a). They can be represented as strings over two primitive building blocks *A* and *B*. The grammar requires a string to be a juxtaposition of two parts, the first containing only *A*s, the second only *B*s, such that there are at least as many *A*s as *B*s. In λ-notation *A* stands for an arbitrary abstraction, $\lambda x \, i$, and a sequence of *j* *B*s represents the variable *x j*. This illustrates a description of the system by means of an iso-morphism that dispenses with λ-notation. As a result of its grammatical structure, every object can be represented as a point in the plane with coordinates (j, i) (b). Two laws (represented schematically) completely describe the relationships realized in this system. The first law states that the action of every object which is not the bottom object of a diagonal generates its lower neighbor on the diagonal independently of the argu-ment object (solid line). The second law states that the bottom object on a diagonal generates particular objects located up the diagonal de-pending in a simple way on the argument object (dotted line). (Fontana and Buss, 1993, p. 25, from *Complexity* edited by G. Cowan, D. Pines, and D. Meltzer, p. 227. © 1994 Addison-Wesley Publishing Company, Inc. Re-printed by permission of Addison Wesley Longman, Inc.)

new products located further up on the diagonal. This is illustrated by the dashed line in Figure 6.1. Together these laws ensure that the system is syntactically closed and self-maintaining (Fontana and Buss, 1994, p. 228).

The diagonals can be infinitely long. When a new object is formed further up the diagonal, the value of i, which is the number of A units it contains, is the sum of the i's of the two objects that collided to create it. Thus, the number of building blocks in a string may proceed through a long series of additions to infinity. Acting against this progression is the tendency for objects to slide down the diagonal wherever they encounter other objects that are not at the bottom of the diagonal.

Kauffman describes the possible shapes of autocatalytic sets. These are sets of strings of elementary objects (amino acids, nucleotides, words, ideas, and so on). He calls them *Eggs, Jets, Mushrooms, Filigreed Fogs, and Pea Soups.* "[A Jet is] a set of transformations among strings from some *maintained founder set of strings* (analogous to the food set) having the property that, under the algorithmic transformations among the strings, each string is produced only by a unique set of parent strings and is produced in a unique way" (p. 373).

The Level 1 organization in this example of Fontana and Buss is an infinite Jet. The founder set is at the bottom of the diagonal, where j, the number of B units, is one. Interactions between objects with only one B can, given enough time, produce any object on the diagonal. The result is that both the diversity of the objects in the Jet and the length of the longest object tend to increase over time. Although the number of objects that can be created by the Jet is infinite, the Jet is closed to new object types. Only the addition of more A's and B's is possible. Newly created objects have the same structure as the objects in the founder set.

Assume that the infantile attractors operating in the patient are autocatalytic Jets. Then they will produce an increasingly large set of responses to stimuli that have the same emotional structure as the simple fantasies generated by the infantile rules. However, the attractor in Fontana's and Buss's example is a mathematically simple attractor. It has no inhibitions against repeating itself exactly.

Fontana and Buss specify the rules of engagement between their algebraic objects in a notational system called the *lambda calculus*. The lambda calculus is the formal basis for the list processing programming language, LISP, used for many artificial intelligence applications. The structures identified by Kauffman in the transformations of autocatalytic sets are called *grammars*. A grammar is a set of rules that specifies the conversion of one symbol string into another symbol string by the action of one or more additional symbol strings. In the natural world, the laws of chemistry make up a grammar, but not an algebra, which has additional properties. In Fontana's algorithmic chemistry, the laws of the lambda calculus are both a grammar and an algebra.

A grammar and the strings it operates on together make up a *formal language*. The laws of chemistry, along with atoms and molecules, make up a language by this definition. The grammatical rules and the lexicon of a natural human language set a lower limit to what can be expressed in the language. (Many additional constraints, physical, biological, and psychological, influence what can count as meaningful human discourse, however.)

An unconscious infantile attractor and the symbolic strings it generates form a very much smaller and more limited language. The infantile attractor takes in a very diverse set of objects, its food set, which has been presented to it in what we might call the general language of experience. It translates this set into its own private and restricted language. Its utterances or emissions are also in this restricted language, which may be hard to distinguish at first glance from the general language of experience (cf. PARRY).

Grammars can be very complex in themselves. Grammars of natural languages like English have so far proved impossible to describe with a unique set of rules. Many viable but incomplete analyses of English grammar are now competing for primacy among linguists. These grammars seem to produce the same set of English sentences, but disagree on some basic questions of structure. In searching for the rules of an unknown language, one looks for a self-consistent (though not necessarily unique) set that produces the observed output.

An important controversy concerns the extent to which linguistic forms are biologically predetermined. Chomsky and his followers insist that the rules of grammar are universal, an innate function of the human brain. Yet we see evidence that the grammars of individual languages evolve independently, away from any primitive set of the common features they may share.

Bybee, Perkins, and Pagliuca (1994) have shown that grammatical operators in all natural language groups evolve from words with lexical meaning. They list five major mechanisms of semantic change in grammatical forms, which operate at different stages in the evolution of a form. Inference and generalization are the most common. Metaphor, harmony, and binary opposition are the others. The more evolved grammatical forms are more compact phonetically and more likely to be attached to the main verb when written.

Common lexical sources for grammatical operators include verbs like come, go, arrive, verbs of motion in general, know, measure, finish, get, reach, make, have, be, become, desire, wish, and so on. Adverbs of time are sources too.

Contemporary natural languages differ considerably in the lexical derivations of their grammatical forms. The forms of a particular language cover a distinctive region in the space of possible grammatical functions. Every natural language has specific forms for some of its grammatical operations, but uses circumlocutions for others. Of course, what makes human speech in general such a powerful conceptual tool is that circumlocution has no inherent limits in any language.

Circumlocution is basic to the psychoanalytic process. It is the analyst's primary means for getting around the patient's pathological attractors. The patient lacks appropriate forms of expression for his own conflict-ridden experience. Circumlocution makes possible the evolution of a common language that allows the patient to apply the analyst's knowledge to himself.

In everyday speech, circumlocution often implies evasion. The analyst must be careful to keep his circumlocutions focused on the unconscious attractor in control at the moment. Otherwise, he runs the risk of entering into the patient's own evasiveness. Then circumlocution becomes euphemism, rather than a method for extending meaning beyond the previously available verbal forms.

We see the content of infantile experience losing its substantive meaning as it evolves into the rule sets of pathological attractors. These rule sets act as grammatical operators that homogenize and degrade the content of later experience, which becomes absorbed into the food sets of the attractors.

Erik Erikson's description of psychosexual development in the first year of life makes a distinction between the lexical and grammatical aspects of infantile experience. The major theme of his theory is the transformation of the various erogenous zones (lexical) into modalities of information processing (grammatical). This is the process underlying normal development (referred to by Hartmann [1964] as the neutralization of sexual energy). The pathological attractor upsets this sequence of transformational events. It reverses the usual movement in the child's mind toward a more differentiated perception of events.

A pathological attractor appears when a developmental task fails to be completed. The attractor is a futile but endlessly repetitive attempt to complete the task. Its greedy consumption of new information entering the child's experience is motivated by this lack of closure. In psychosomatic illness or conversion hysteria, the result may be a failure to process body contents or body parts physiologically. As Abraham (1955) pointed out, the model of ineffective bodily functioning is easily transferred to mental functioning. Someone who characteristically bites off more than he can chew, or who can't decide whether to shit or get off the pot, is trapped in a maladaptive strategy built around a pathological attractor.

Bybee's five mechanisms of grammatical evolution are much like the mechanisms that seem to operate when a pathological attractor forms. Metaphor, inference, generalization, harmony and binary opposition are all at work in the fantasies that produce the rules of an attractor. The evolution of natural languages is not a rational process. However, it is saved from the fate of the pathological attractor by the process of natural selection operating within the language community. The pathological attractor is isolated in the depths of the patient's unconscious mind. The analytic process draws the content of the attractor into the linguistic community constituted by the analytic discourse.

A survey of the world's natural grammars shows that some rules are common to all of them, others have only a few exceptions, and still others apply only to certain language groups. For example, all human languages have distinct units of expression (though not necessarily single words) for agent, action, and object. For *nearly all* languages, the subject precedes the object in a sentence. In *English,* the passive construction converts the old object into a new subject (a pseudo-agent) to preserve this relationship. Relative clauses precede the nouns they modify in many languages, while in may others they follow. No clear trend can be observed (Greenberg, 1963).

One would expect to have similar gradations of generality in the rule sets of pathological attractors. Some rules of the grammars of unconscious infantile attractors are universal. Take, for example, the rule that a real contemporary experience is transformed by an attractor into a virtual childhood experience. Other rules are circumscribed by the child rearing practices of their culture. Rules that draw a sharp distinction between the caretaking responsibilities of nuclear and extended families are an example. Some rules are specific to particular illnesses. The rule that no good feeling can be expected to last is typical of depression, for example. Idiosyncratic rules make every unhappy family different from every other.

The grammars of infantile attractors are much simpler than the grammars of natural languages. In fact, they are probably closer in complexity to the laws of chemistry than to the spoken language of a competent adult. Nevertheless, the effort required to extract grammatical rules from the output of an attractor should not be underestimated. Much of the time taken by the psychoanalytic process is devoted to the extraction of grammatical rules from attractor driven behavior.

Kauffman's definition of the autocatalytic Jet fits the clinical observation that an unconscious attractor is a transmitter of its output. It takes in the very broad set of inputs permitted by the grammatical rules that translate sensory experience into mental representations. It emits the much narrower set of products defined by the grammar of the attractor. The attractor-transmitter acts as a filter, narrowing down the band width of its input. In this respect it does the work of the traditional Freudian defense mechanism, or Colby's PARRY. It attracts and intercepts new experiences that may signal danger. It then substitutes a small and more predictable set of unambiguously dangerous items in the psychic information stream. Thus we may think of attractor-transmitters as defense mechanisms as well as storehouses of primitive fantasy.

We observe that the output of unconscious attractors in neurotic patients is much richer than the output of PARRY. Since PARRY effectively mimics a neural network, I would argue that the neural network model is not an adequate explanation for the complexities of human thought and behavior. Nevertheless, it provides a *lower bound* on their complexity. The lack of a mapping from neural networks into autocatalytic sets may therefore be due to limitations in the neural network models available to us today. Then again, the lack of a mapping may turn out to be remediable mathematically in the future.

Perturbing the Pathological Attractor

The autocatalytic attractor-transmitter is very resistant to change, since it is designed to respond to a wide range of adult experience without altering its output. Yet the food set of the attractor is still only a small subset of the full range of human experience. The neurotic patient often seeks out situations that mimic the infantile events for which the laws of each attractor-transmitter were devised. Thus, the food sets of the attractors are much smaller than the full set of experiences possible for the patient in his adult life. This distinction is essential to the psychoanalytic process, which operates *within* the patient's experience but *outside* the food sets of his attractors.

What happens when an autocatalytic attractor encounters an object outside its normal food set? Fontana and Buss (1993) simulated this kind of event, with very interesting results:

> The effect of perturbing Level 1 organizations was explored by periodically injecting random objects into an existing organization . . . With one exception, the results were identical. The organization persists without any change in the emergent laws that

characterize it. Level 1 organizations are very robust to small perturbations.

In the exceptional case, a perturbation resulted in the appearance of a new emergent law. This new law did not displace any
of the existing laws. The new system proved robust to continued
perturbations. The exceptional case is relevant in that it illustrates
that Level 1 organizations can be altered by perturbations [pp.
229–230].

In other words, the laws of the autocatalytic attractor can
be expanded or extended, some of the time at least, through
perturbations caused by the taking in of objects outside its food
set. These new objects become members of the reorganized autocatalytic set. They are then maintained and renewed by the expanded organization.

In some instances, the perturbing object has spawned interactions that resulted in a stable extension of the previous set of
objects. Objects that extend the rules of an organization are (by
definition) grammatically distinct from the objects constituting
the organization prior to perturbation. The insertion of a new
string (or rule) may require a recasting of the organization's
grammatical and algebraic description (Fontana and Buss, 1993).

They add (1996): "The algebraic relationships which define
an organization also determine *specific* opportunities for its extension. Biological interpretations are many. As but one example,
Morowitz suggests that nonenzymatic precursor networks of the
cellular core metabolism have evolved via distinct extensions"
(p. 71).

The analyst's job is to extend the rule sets (the grammars)
of the patient's attractors in this way. As shown by Fontana and
Buss, some autocatalytic sets can be enlarged by perturbation with
new strings. A patient's unconscious attractor can be perturbed
by interventions of the analyst that come from *outside* its food set.

If the patient's infantile attractors are modeled as Level 1
organizations, we would expect them to be expanded or extended
by some at least of the analyst's interventions. The attractor is
not broken down or degraded by the intervention. It reorganizes
in a way that incorporates the analyst's intervention to form a
more flexible and comprehensive set of rules. The increased diversity of the attractor's new output brings it a step closer to the

variety and complexity of the patient's contemporary life experience.

In psychoanalysis we find that the input of the attractor-transmitter changes as the attractor becomes reorganized. While its output expands as new rules emerge, the food set of the attractor also grows smaller. As time goes by, fewer and more specific events can trigger the distorting effects of the attractor. For example, when Richard began his analysis, he went into a paralyzing rage whenever his parents visited him or even spoke with him on the telephone. *All* of their actions toward him evoked *a single* overwhelming feeling state. After a period of analytic work, he could react with rage only when they were *particularly* obtuse or offensive. He recognized that sometimes, at least, he was reacting to the memory of a childhood experience evoked by their present behavior, rather than to the behavior itself.

While the food set of a reorganizing attractor becomes more specific, the output continues to differentiate. Richard began to notice that his parents were not as bad as they used to be. His anger was more focused on specific events in the history of his interactions with them. He became aware of differences in the circumstances that influenced some of those events but not others. He discovered that his feelings toward his father and mother were quite different. Although he was angry with both of them, it was for different reasons. Fewer but more specific triggering events evoked a wider diversity of responses. The ghosts turned into ancestors as the food set of the attractor diminished and its output expanded.

The ideal outcome of this evolutionary process would be to integrate the attractor into the overall structure of the patient's mental life. Then the attractor would no longer exist as a separate region with its own closed and limited set of rules. "Where id was, there ego shall be," in Freud's words. Clinical observation suggests that this ideal state is never reached. The attractor may be outgrown as far as its influence on everyday life is concerned, but it seems usually to remain latent in a form that can be revived under sufficient stress.

But perhaps we simply do not know whether this revived attractor is really a reactivation of the old attractor or a new and less powerful attractor reconstituted from memory. Depending on the answer to this question, there may be a difference in the persistence of the reemergent attractor. The typical revival of the original symptoms as the end of an analysis gets closer suggests that, here at least, the attractor reappears in a much attenuated form.

As the attractor-transmitter expands, its output becomes more diversified. The Jet of the original, unmodified attractor may turn into a Mushroom. A Mushroom differs from a Jet in that its products feed back to perturb it further. This is like the feedback loop that develops in the analytic discourse when a new self-observational schema becomes available to the patient.

The output of the unconscious attractor usually gets to the outside world (here the analytic discourse) as an association to a triggering event of the moment. In the external world it may initiate a new round of interaction with another agent (such as the analyst). But the output of an attractor may also be directed inward. The output of one attractor may initially belong to the food set of another. When the output of the first attractor is expanded, it may no longer be completely contained within the food sets of the other attractors it normally feeds. The modified output of the first attractor may then become a perturbing (reorganizing) influence on these other organizations.

This sequence sets up the possibility of a chain reaction among the other attractors, leading to a cascade of new outputs. We see this happening in analysis when an intervention by the analyst opens a cluster of new associations and recollected memories. How far a particular chain reaction of this kind will go is likely to be determined by the power law distribution characteristic of behavior in critical systems near the edge of chaos.

Support for the idea that a change in one attractor causes a ripple effect through the entire system comes from work by Freeman (1995) and Kelso (1996). Freeman showed that the rabbit olfactory cortex is organized into a set of attractors that recognize individual odors. When a new odor is introduced, a new attractor is formed. The already existing attractors do not remain as they were, however. The entire olfactory cortex is reorganized. Each odor previously recognized is now matched with a new attractor similar to the earlier one but different in shape.

Kelso measured phase transitions in finger movement coordination tasks. Subjects moved their index fingers in opposite directions in time with a metronome. When the metronome was gradually speeded up, a phase transition took place in which the fingers suddenly began to move in the same direction. Kelso described this as a movement from one dynamic attractor to another. In a similar experiment, separate metronomes were assigned to each hand. The metronomes were set at a constant speed of one cycle per second. Subjects were asked to follow the right and left metronomes with right and left index finger movements. Intrinsic attractors (peaks in subject accuracy) appeared spontaneously when the beats of the metronomes were either simultaneous or 180 degrees apart. Subjects were then taught to follow the metronomes when the beats were 90 degrees apart, ordinarily a low point in performance.

The shapes of the subjects' attractors were measured in this experiment before and after each of three 90-degree learning sessions. Not only did a new attractor appear at 90 degrees after the new task was learned, but the intrinsic attractors at zero and 180 degrees were modified each time. As Kelso says (1996), "The *entire attractor layout changes with learning*, not simply the coordination pattern being learned" (p. 171). So it is with the unconscious pathological attractors of the analytic patient. A change in the attractor nearest the surface of the analytic discourse affects its nearest neighboring attractors most of all. The neighboring attractors affect their neighbors, and so on. The situation is like that in the Game of Life and in other cellular automata. A change at one point in the layout of dynamic attractors triggers a series of changes in nearby attractors. These changes may in turn lead nowhere or to a reorganization at a larger scale.

What distinguishes the perturbation that causes the large scale reorganization? Perhaps something more can be learned about this from Fontana's and Buss's experiment. Unfortunately, they do not analyze the exceptional combination of Level 1 organizational structure and perturbing object that led to an expansion of the attractor rules. It might be possible for their data to distinguish the characteristics of the organization and perturbing object that led to a reorganization and an expanded rule set.

Something similar occurred when the analyst's response to Richard's homosexual dream expanded the rule set of a prominent infantile attractor. One would like to know whether the mathematics of Fontana's and Buss's system could model the results of such an intervention as well.

After enough perturbations have expanded the rule set of an attractor, we would expect a phase transition to alter its character in a qualitative way that is easily observable. Can we also observe the moment to moment approach of a system to a phase transition? This is, of course, much more difficult to do. Kelso (1996) offers two useful suggestions. He pictures the phase transition as the flipping of a ball from a shallow basin of attraction to a deeper basin adjacent to it. The two basins share a common rim. The ball has to move with enough momentum while inside the shallow basin to permit an escape over the rim into the deeper one.

As random perturbations to the ball push closer to its escape velocity, the effect is to make the shallower basin act as if it were shallower still. Its power to attract decreases. Kelso says: "Imagine a soccer team kicking our little black ball entirely at random. When the slope of the hill is steep, the ball can't be kicked very far away from its equilibrium position. When the slope flattens, however, the same magnitude of kick will cause the ball to move much farther away. As a result, near the critical point the attractor state suffers wild critical fluctuations" (p. 109).

In an analysis, the fluctuations Kelso refers to take the form of richer and more varied free associations by the patient and a correspondingly enriched simulation in the mind of the analyst. The freedom of the patient's associations provides the power that moves him over the rim into the new attractor, like the random kicks of the soccer team in Kelso's illustration. Kelso's wild critical fluctuations are simply the conditions we normally find near the edge of chaos. The wild fluctuations should be distinguished from the avalanche of new material that enters the analytic discourse *after* the phase transition has occurred, however. The avalanche is not a fluctuation within the boundaries of the old attractor, but evidence of a shift in the boundaries themselves.

Kelso's second suggestion for observing the approach to a phase transition is the lengthening of the *relaxation time* after a perturbation. As an attractor undergoes a subthreshold perturbation, it responds to the perturbing influence. This response alters its behavior temporarily, but as it assimilates the perturbation its old behavior returns. As the phase transition approaches, the return to the old behavior (relaxation) takes longer and longer, until at the phase transition, it is infinite. In analysis, the relaxation time is the time it takes a patient to drift back into an old pattern of thought and behavior after reacting to an intervention by the analyst. Away from the edge of chaos, relaxation time is short. The patient's associations to the intervention are brief. He moves back to his old line of thought quite soon. Near the edge of chaos, the patient's trains of associations become longer and longer. At the transition point, the patient seems to take the ball and run with it himself. The process of reorganization going on within him has reached a condition of autonomy. It does not require input from the analyst until the phase transition has been consolidated.

Kelso's simple model suggests that the shallower attractor will eventually be eliminated completely if the disparity between the attractors continues to increase. Pathological attractors in the psyche of a patient never seen to disappear completely, however, no matter how fully integrated his mental organization becomes. What is really described by the basin of attraction in Kelso's model is the attractor's power to attract. The physical (neural) structure of the attractor can persist even when its power of attraction has been neutralized. An organizational malfunction at a higher level can revive the power of a neutralized lower level attractor.

Freud's rule that the analyst must avoid gratifying the patient's neurotic wishes is still the keystone of modern psychoanalytic technique (Stone, 1961). The patient's neurotic wishes mark out the food sets of his pathological attractors. The gratification of a neurotic wish confirms and strengthens the fantasies contained in the attractor that produces it. Fontana's and Buss's findings suggest that the analyst can promote the reorganization of an attractor only if his interventions come from outside its food set. This would be apart from and in addition to the specific content of any of the interventions.

Perhaps this counterintuitive idea can explain the belief of some analysts that the content of the analyst's interventions is only of minor interest. For them the therapeutic relationship is more important than what the analyst actually has to say. We can endorse the importance of the good therapeutic relationship if we define it as one in which the analyst refrains from feeding the patient's pathological attractors. However, the content of the analyst's interventions plays an active and essential role in locating the boundaries of the food sets. These boundaries may be far from obvious at the beginning of an analysis.

The analyst's interventions should help to bring these boundaries into the patient's awareness. The empathic understanding of the analyst leads him to respect the patient's subjective world and its power over him. But it does not confirm the patient's belief that his subjective world is the entire world.

Statements or questions like, "You [must have] felt pretty awful when that happened[?]," "That was [must have been] difficult for you[?]," "It [must have] seemed to you as if . . . ," tactfully distinguish the patient's feelings and perceptions from the facts of the world outside. The analyst takes his stand on the boundary between the patient's subjective reality and the reality defined by the facts agreed on between them.

Some analysts appear to believe that the analyst can work successfully from entirely within the patient's subjective space. Some are skeptical about the possibility of an "objective" reality that anyone could agree on. Others believe that the analyst must stay within the patient's subjective world at least until the patient has achieved a certain degree of self-confidence and trust. More reasonably, the analyst should work with, but not within, the patient's subjective world from the beginning. He needs to keep one foot inside the patient's world and one outside. In particular, he must clearly situate the source of his interventions in the larger world outside the food set of the patient's attractors.

The analyst helps the patient discover the closed set of rules underlying the superficially diverse set of outputs from his attractor-transmitters. The first requirement is to find and recognize the unconscious attractor. This often happens through a process of convergence as the analytic discourse begins to unfold.

The food set of the attractor includes a variety of distinct events of the patient's current life situation. On the surface, these events may have no obvious connection. As the analytic discourse develops, however, the associative pathways that can be traced out from each of these varied events finally meet in the attractor. Richard's current problems with his boss, Ellen, and his mother converged at the infantile preoedipal attractor marked by the image of the urn.

The analytic techniques of free association, dream interpretation, and transference interpretation all work to facilitate the convergence. Analysis of the transference is a critical tool in this endeavor. It gives the most direct indication of the presence of pathological connections between the patient's current way of dealing with his life and his past experience.

Since many attractors are at work in the patient's unconscious, the identity of a single attractor may be difficult to discover. A new event may initiate associative pathways leading to two or more attractors. Nevertheless, one attractor is usually more accessible than any other at a given moment, and this one eventually emerges from the search. It is critical that the analyst allow this attractor to identify itself. His assessment on purely theoretical grounds of the most appropriate attractor to investigate at that moment may be very far off the mark.

An attractor may reveal itself only in stages. Richard's remark about cutting off his foot with a table saw like the one his father had used suggested the presence of an unconscious self-mutilation (or castration) attractor. This attractor was almost certainly related to the oedipal fear of retaliation by the father for the son's sexual interest in his mother. The analyst might also have guessed at the time that the attractor was linked with the matricidal attractor that played a significant role in the first important breakthrough of the analysis.

It was not until several months after the fantasy was reported that this theme returned. Ellen was away on an extended business trip. Richard reported that it was fine with him. He decided to do some work to improve the basement of the new house. He bought a new table saw, without telling either Ellen or the analyst about his intention beforehand. During the next hour, after reporting that he was very pleased with the purchase, he experienced an intrusive fantasy that his older brother was pushing his head into the saw from behind. It occurred to him spontaneously that the fantasy might depict a wish to do the same to someone

else. The analyst mentioned the dream about discovering his
mother's dismembered body in the basement.

Richard said he was angry about his mother's abandoning
him. He was also angry about Ellen's absence. He remembered
his very aggressive sex during his college days with women he
hardly knew or liked. Then he said, "I feel I'm being eviscerated
as I talk about this." The analyst suggested that he might have
imagined himself eviscerating those women during intercourse.
Richard said, "Yes. One of us was going to be hurt."

From this interchange and the earlier material, we can reconstruct a preoedipal attractor based on an unconscious doubt in
Richard's mind about the integrity of his body. This uncertainty
was closely tied to the issue of bodily control. Did his mother
control the functions of his body, or did he? Were the functions
linked internally through his own mind and will, or were they
connected only externally through his mother's control of them?

This attractor seems to have been organized around early
fantasies of dismemberment, mutilation, and evisceration. The
image of the urn that prevented him from moving under his own
power was part of this complex. In order for Richard to become
whole, his bodily functions had to be separated from his mother's
control and reassembled within his own body. They had to be
broken off or extracted from his mother's body, leaving her damaged or destroyed.

During the phallic period, Richard's hypervaluation of his
penis was assimilated to this earlier attractor. Castration became
the most dangerous form of mutilation for him. Evisceration of
the woman during intercourse was its counterpart. The drama of
"One of us was going to be hurt," was focused on the genitals of
both sexes. But the fear of danger to Richard's bodily and personal integrity remained a problem that interfered with his relations to men and women both.

Soon after this session, Richard began to speak of his mother's frequent attempts to draw him out of his social and emotional
withdrawal when he was a child, which he had stubbornly resisted.
The analyst said, "So you weren't only pushed back into the urn
when you tried to get out, but you were also pulled out when you
wanted to stay in." He said, "I did have some control over that."

Here we see an output of Richard's matricidal attractor, his seeking of emotional isolation, serving as an input to the oedipal attractor. If he didn't stick his neck out, he wouldn't have to worry about losing it. His mother's discouragement of his bodily initiatives, so painful to him during the early years, became internalized to form a defensive shell protecting him from his castration anxiety.

What we see in Richard's case is the common situation in which developmental events of the phallic and oedipal periods, ages 3 to 6, are assimilated to an attractor formed even earlier in life. Phallic and oedipal issues were already part of the food set of the mutilated body attractor when they entered Richard's experience. An attractor formed at any stage of development profoundly influences all later stages, as Freud (1905), Erikson (1950), Spitz (1959), and many others were to insist.

Patients are often unaware that particular events occurring in their daily lives have been captured by an attractor. But intense anxiety can arise when an attractor transforms a new experience into the pathological mimic of an infantile fantasy. Phobic patients become hypersensitive to possible triggering events to protect themselves from this kind of surprise. This hypersensitivity is a very costly defensive strategy. It artificially broadens the food set of the attractor until it encompasses larger and larger areas of the patient's experience.

Tracing out the pathways that lead from current experience to the infantile attractor in analysis is a useful alternative to this strategy. The steps already traced (through the analytic discourse) are available in memory for convergence on the infantile condensations that constitute the attractor. The analyst's possession of the analytic discourse in his own memory allows him to function as a backup when the patient's memory of the analytic discourse falters. When the attractor has been located and brought into the analytic discourse, the patient can take a more active role in exploring the attractor's mode of operation.

This chapter was already written when I became aware of Michael Moran's (1991) important paper applying chaos theory to psychoanalysis. Moran anticipated some of what I consider to be the more important ideas developed and elaborated in this work. His ideas about the effect of the analyst's interventions on

the patient's pathological attractors are a case in point. Moran
says:

> This leads to some thoughts about the possible mechanism of
> action of psychoanalysis. Seen within chaos theory, the therapy
> may act as an extended series of well-timed perturbations, which
> serve gradually to disrupt the attractor of the patient's fantasy in
> the direction of increased complexity. One might see the patient
> coming to analysis with a (relatively) simple nearly periodic at-
> tractor that is easily disrupted. Behavior is predictable in certain
> dimensions; that is, it is maladaptive (and adaptive) in a relatively
> predictable manner, with a similar pattern over time. Through
> the well-timed and well-dosed perturbations (interpretations of
> defenses, for example), the strange attractor acquires complexity.
> Analysis would be seen as tuning the attractor to a higher grade
> of structural intricacy. The shape of the attractor changes; espe-
> cially its dimensionality increases. As a consequence, behavior (fan-
> tasy material, thought, cognitive patterns) becomes less rigidly
> determined (less periodic). More of any one phase space is visited
> by the trajectories of the system. That is, more behavior is possible
> as dimensionality of experience increases. Of course, other ways
> of increasing the complexity of the attractor may be posited, and
> could include modeling, internalization of certain ego functions
> of the analyst, and a variety of learning experiences outside the
> analysis (and one could doubtless offer others) [pp. 216–217].

A little further on, he adds, "One mechanism for the route
of change might be through the route of phase transitions" (p.
217). Moran does not directly consider the coevolutionary aspect
of the analytic process, but he hints at it: "Might we see the
therapeutic action of psychoanalysis as the interaction between
the strange attractors of the analyst and the patient?" (p. 218). I
believe Moran's hypothesis is both stronger and easier to grasp
when it is embedded in an evolutionary framework.

I see the unconscious not as a single attractor but as a complex organization of attractors. At any given time, the unconscious of the patient can be approached effectively from only a
small number of directions (often no more than one). The analyst
rarely, if ever, has the opportunity to perturb the patient's unconscious as a whole or all at once. Yet the portion of the unconscious

accessible at any moment seems always to have a closed set of autocatalytic rules and a bounded food set.

The identification of individual attractors and their structural relationships is the key to what Moran calls "well-timed and well-dosed perturbations." That is, the location and identification of individual attractors is what makes the perturbation hypothesis a powerful clinical tool. This will be illustrated in detail in chapter 10. Whether or not the analyst is addressing an attractor accessible at the moment is usually a critical question.

Moran's view of the unconscious as a single attractor may correspond to the analyst's usual view of the patient when an analysis begins. The progress of the analysis can be measured by the level of *differentiation* of the patient's infantile attractors. The unconscious at the beginning of analysis can be thought of as a single entity that bifurcates repeatedly as the analysis proceeds. Chaos theory would predict that the intervals between bifurcations diminish as time goes by. This would be an interesting hypothesis to test empirically.

The Edge of Chaos in Mental Life

We have reason to believe that the ordered realm near the edge of chaos is the optimal condition for human mental activity as well as for the physical and computational systems described earlier. Pathological mental states can be characterized by their location in the frozen and chaotic regimes far from the optimal level of activity at the boundary between them.

In bipolar disorder, the prototypical example, mental activity alternately cycles into frozen and chaotic states, both of them far from the edge of chaos. Histrionic personalities also function on the chaotic side of the optimum, but closer to the edge. Obsessive compulsives are frozen, but not as frozen as severely depressed patients.

Schizophrenic patients can be at either extreme. A psychosis may be thought of as a state that is fixed at a distance from the edge of chaos for relatively long periods. Borderline patients are easily driven away from the edge, but tend to rebound more quickly. In neurotic patients, circumscribed areas of memory structure are sequestered from normal mental activity near the edge of chaos.

The mental life of the borderline or psychotic patient at the beginning of treatment is that of a self-organized system fallen into disrepair. Its components are not communicating or collaborating effectively. It is below the critical level of inner connectedness at which the components of the system come together to form a coherent whole. The patient in this condition does not have a single vantage point from which to view himself as a whole person. (This is the paranoid–schizoid position described by Melanie Klein [1946].)

As the analytic work adds more and more new connections, the organization of the patient's mental contents reaches a critical threshold. A connected component forms within the system which is large enough and coherent enough to impart the power of self-observation. Self-observation is an emergent property of systems well enough connected to have at least one component that communicates with each of the major hierarchical structures of the system. For the patient, this entails at a minimum the acknowledgment that he has unconscious wishes and fantasies with the power to vastly influence his feelings and behavior.

Most patients in analysis have successfully completed this phase transition to inner coherence in early childhood. Piaget and his followers in developmental psychology have described in detail how self-observation emerges in the first years of life (Piaget, 1937). The ratio between structure and chaos is always changing as the child develops, when his experience of the world and his internal processing power increase at different rates. Under these conditions, new structure emerges in a series of discontinuous phase transitions.

Self-Organization and Self-Observation

For the adult patient beginning an analysis, self-observation is limited to the large connected component of his psyche, called the *preconscious* by Freud. Disconnected components are not accessible to the patient's consciousness. During analytic treatment these dissociated components of his mental content are reunited with the large connected component. This is another aspect of what Freud called "making the unconscious conscious." The aim is not simply to have the patient achieve a conscious or rational understanding of his conflicts, however, although this can be helpful. What is needed is an increase in the accessibility of the patient's repressed mental contents. The analyst acts as a catalyst for the movement of the patient's mental activity as it adaptively seeks this optimal state of mind.

Among psychoanalysts, the emergence of self-observation is often regarded as the result of the patient's taking in, or introjecting, a piece of the analyst's functioning. It is often supposed that in the earliest stage of this development a baby is unable to distinguish clearly between the person supplying the nutriment and the nutriment itself. Identification with the analyst's functioning begins, according to this model, as a process of incorporation and assimilation.

What happens inside the patient, after the analyst's function has been introjected, has not been very clearly understood. I suggest that what is taken in is not so much the analyst's observing function as the set of connections he makes between the patient's external behavior and his internal schemata. These connections are sorted and reassembled within the patient's psychic apparatus as a multidimensional representation of the analyst at his work. This image of the analyst is connected in various ways to representations of other internal objects and ultimately to related aspects of the patient's self-representation. Pathological attractors that hinder this process are reopened to the normal flow of information through the various levels of the system.

During normal development, internal representations are continually updated. New connections that link representations of others with the child's representations of himself are added as the internal connectedness of individual representations increases with time. As the patient speaks, the analyst searches for patterns of missing connections to and from areas not ordinarily accessible to the patient's current capacity for self-observation.

All analysts are familiar with patients who are highly connected at a preconscious level but dramatically disconnected from important areas of feeling and experience nevertheless. The connectedness of the preconscious may be used defensively as a labyrinth of escape routes from the warded off unconscious.

Nonetheless, the associative structure of the preconscious contains visible gaps wherever pathways to the unconscious have been sealed off. These gaps are maintained by the unconscious infantile attractors that divert the normal flow of information. The unconscious is approached in analysis through the discovery and repair of the key elements that reflect the structure of the patient's preconscious in the stories he tells.

The stories are sequential, but the internal connectedness of the contents of the patient's mind is hierarchical. High and low level structures may be connected, depending on the size of the pieces and the power of the attractors. Higher level connections are needed to bridge the gaps that isolate large areas of inaccessible material.

Intrapsychic structures that emerge during the psychoanalytic process have to be flexible, but they have to be hierarchical as well. The self-organizational properties of the psyche would, if left to themselves, make this progression very likely, if not inevitable. Psychopathology can be defined as anything inside the patient that inhibits the natural process of self-organization. The analyst's job is to enhance the patient's self-organizational processes. An analyst who does not see himself in this role runs the risk of imposing a much more rigid kind of hierarchy on the patient's mental contents.

Self-organization leads directly to self-observation. The higher the organizational level of the patient's psyche, the wider is his perspective when he looks at and into himself. The analyst, however, cannot intervene directly at the higher levels. The patient has to get there on his own, through the progressive reorganization built from phase transitions that begin at the lowest levels of connectedness. Nevertheless, when a high-level phase transition is *already* taking place, the analyst's identifying and labeling the change are useful to the patient. At such a time, the analyst has an opportunity to link the change itself with the events that led up to it. These events are by this time a part of the analytic discourse.

Freud was concerned with the need for making lower level connections first, in order to bring about a reorganization at higher levels, in his advice to the analyst to stay close to the "surface" of the patient's consciousness. Although this term suffers from vagueness, it is useful as a marker for the boundary between what is and is not accessible to the patient at any moment in the analytic session. To put it in the terms of our discussion here, the analytic surface is a boundary between those attractors that can be effectively perturbed by the analyst's interventions and those that cannot.

The situation is complicated because the analyst's interventions are not the only therapeutic inputs to previously inaccessible attractors. Equally important, perhaps even more important, are the newly diversified outputs of the component attractors that have already been modified and expanded. In combination, these novel outputs can perturb another attractor at the analytic surface, like the elements of the grid that recorded the A in our neural network example. Then again, the analyst's intervention is often the critical factor in bringing together this combination of inputs to effectively precipitate a phase transition in the attractor at the surface. When the analytic process is near the edge of chaos, the combination of internal stimuli may be enough in itself to bring about a phase transition. A chain reaction may be possible, leading to a cascade of new lower level connections that can trigger a reorganization at a higher level.

As mentioned earlier, the Jet of repetitive outputs from an unmodified low level attractor does not perturb a neighboring attractor at a higher level. The output of the lower level attractor may in fact be a regular component of the food set of the higher level attractor. However, when a low level attractor is expanded, its more diversified output may have the power to perturb the higher level attractors it normally feeds. The new output of the lower level attractor will then be working synergistically with the analyst's interventions to perturb the attractor at the higher level. This is what we saw when the analyst connected Richard's fear of having children of his own with his rage at the arrival of a younger brother.

As seen from a point of view inside the patient, the analytic process works from the bottom up. From the analyst's point of view, outside the patient, it works from the surface in. We must distinguish here between the pathological attractor whose food set includes the outputs of other attractors, on the one hand, and the new higher level organization generated by the analytic process, on the other. Though the pathological attractor receives inputs from other attractors, its level of organization is not typically higher than that of the attractors that supply it. Unless the supplying attractors have already been expanded, the analyst's attempted interventions may be overwhelmed by the familiar diet of unexpanded outputs from these attractors.

Thus, we have a network of unconscious infantile attractor-transmitters, similar in many ways to a neural network. Each attractor-transmitter is fed both by external events and by the outputs of other members of the network. The distance from the analytic surface to individual attractors in the network will depend on the attractor's position in the network and its interactions with its neighbors.

Clinical observation suggests that the order in which attractors become accessible to intervention is highly structured though not linearly so. Various issues have to be worked out before other issues can be dealt with. For example, triadic attractors cannot be successfully expanded before the dyadic attractors that feed them have been modified. A patient must have a stable inner representation of another person before he can become concerned about losing that other person to a rival.

The idea that the modified output of an already expanded attractor can perturb other attractors in its neighborhood gives direction to the sequence in which attractors become accessible. The analyst's intervention is successful when the attractor in question has been primed by the outputs of other already modified attractors. When the modified output of an attractor near the surface perturbs another less accessible attractor, the second attractor can be nudged closer to the surface. This movement toward the surface may be an intermediate step that prepares the way for an increase in organization of the attractor. It would be like the addition of a new canalizing rule to the rule set of the second attractor.

Once an attractor has been expanded, it may be replaced at the analytic surface by another attractor, yet unexpanded but no doubt primed by the modified output of the previous attractor at the surface. Observation suggests that most often the expansion of an attractor will require many steps. For example, an attractor may require many excursions to the analytic surface before its output is sufficiently expanded to perturb its neighboring attractors. Still, it may be able to perturb its neighbors before it is completely expanded. This is a problem for further research.

A hypothesis grounded in clinical observation is that the higher the organizational level of the patient's ego, the deeper will be the potential for penetrating into his network of unconscious infantile attractors. In other words, increased powers of self-observation will increase the accessibility of unconscious material through a top-down effect. This seems to contradict the picture of increased accessibility of deeply buried unconscious attractors arising from bottom-up perturbations originating at the analytic surface. We can resolve the apparent contradiction if we assume that the new ego structure is built through the self-organization of newly expanded attractors. Then we would have two functions for the expanded attractor: (1) Its modified output perturbs unmodified attractors, increasing their accessibility to the analytic surface; (2) its expanded structure creates the opportunity for it to be incorporated in the self-organization of similar structures to form higher level organizations.

This seems to me to make good sense. It reveals the building of new structure and the uncovering of unconscious fantasy material to be two consequences of the same sequence of interventions and internal reorganizations. The analyst working in his office with a patient would find it impossible to separate the two. If we think of it in this way, we have a very fine-grained view of the structure building activity of the analytic process. We also have a more balanced alternative to Freud's idea that if only the unconscious fantasies are uncovered, the patient's already competent ego will take over its responsibilities without requiring any modification itself.

How can we learn whether one attractor's output belongs to the food set of another attractor? The place of the attractors in the developmental sequence is an important clue. Attractors developing later in life would naturally take the outputs of lower level attractors as inputs. They would also very naturally have a greater degree of complexity (larger rule sets).

One might imagine that an attractor with more primitive instinctual content would be found further away from the analytic

surface than an attractor that developed later. Attractors organized around preoedipal (dyadic) issues typically appear at the
analytic surface before attractors with oedipal (triadic) content,
however. Preoedipal attractors often screen off oedipal attractors,
in fact, keeping them out of range for interpretation.

The hierarchy of unconscious infantile attractors is, of
course, embedded within the larger hierarchy of adaptive functions normally exposed to conscious review and control. Nothing
in this picture sets a limit in principle to the success of the analytic
process in reorganizing the patient's unconscious structures. It
does appear, however, that the further the process goes, the
greater the need for synergy between the analyst's interventions
and the internal processes of the patient. This synergy is made
possible by the coevolutionary aspect of the therapeutic relationship.

The Edge of Chaos in Psychoanalytic Treatment

The edge of chaos in the clinical situation is the familiar but
hardly ubiquitous state in which the analyst intervenes to open
new pathways to the disconnected aspects of the patient's mental
content. We see it when a patient produces associations that bring
in new material (previously disconnected from the analytic discourse) and create a new context (through new connections) for
old material whose meaning had been obscure. The availability
of the new associations results from the diversification of outputs
from the expanded unconscious attractor-transmitter. These new
outputs act as stimuli for the retrieval of memories previously cut
off from the internal information stream and consequently from
consciousness.

When analysis is working well, Dewald (1972, p. 55) describes
"a spontaneous oscillation in the material between past and present." This is reflected in an easy movement between concerns
about the analyst and about other significant people in the patient's life. This movement is typical of natural processes near
the edge of chaos. The interaction with the analyst reminds the
patient of apparently similar interactions with other people in

the recent and remote past. From such reminders the complex web of the transference is put together.

These oscillations are not smoothly periodic, of course. An avalanche of associations may come tumbling out of the patient without warning. Their sequence is usually not linear, either logically or chronologically. The appearance of these new associations is not predictable from what immediately precedes them. However, the new associations always appear in retrospect to be ordered, as they clarify the meaning of earlier productions of the patient. An avalanche of associations is a clear-cut sign that the analytic process is near the edge of chaos.

Far from the edge of chaos, in the realm of frozen order, the patient's productions are deterministic and predictable. They are deterministic because we can understand in retrospect where they came from. They are predictable because the number and range of the patient's responses to events are stereotyped and limited. In the chaotic realm, the patient's productions are neither deterministic nor predictable. No pattern is discernible in them, even in retrospect.

Near the edge of chaos, what the patient says is deterministic but not predictable. One can easily understand in retrospect how one statement led to another. Still, at the time the patient speaks, neither patient nor analyst can know where it will lead. New associations are about to enter the analytic discourse, fully determined by the sequence of previous statements but never before encountered in the analysis. A deterministic trajectory of associations leads back into the unconscious regions of the patient's mental contents.

Near the edge of chaos in the analytic hour, the patient is receptive to interpretations at a higher level than the immediate level of his associations. His usual resistance to statements that directly attribute causal effects to unconscious fantasies and wishes is much diminished or absent. The patient is a full participant in the analytic work, not a bemused spectator or a naive realist about unconscious motivation.

The analyst's initial instruction to the patient to say everything that comes to mind without editing or withholding is often called the *fundamental rule of psychoanalysis* (Kris, 1982). Most of the time, the fundamental rule is very difficult for the patient to follow literally. It functions primarily as a baseline from which to measure the obstacles that hinder the patient's spontaneity. However, near the edge of chaos, free association may finally be attainable. The patient has for the moment lost his need to control what he tells the analyst. His associative process determines what he says, rather than his fears and fantasies about the analyst's response to him.

Because near the edge of chaos the patient's associations are less restricted, trains of associations can be longer, even lasting through an entire hour. A train of associations is an intelligible sequence, in which one association leads to another by a deterministic (though not predictable) route. A train of associations is to be distinguished from an endless series of meaningless details about a single event or interaction, characteristic of the chaotic realm.

Away from the edge of chaos, trains of associations are short, ending with one kind of interruption or another. Knowing when an interruption to a train of associations is a break in the flow and not simply the appearance of a new association may be difficult for the analyst. This ambiguity is a major source of uncertainty during the analytic process. Interruptions disguised as associations prolong the periods of quiescence that delay reorganization of the patient's mental contents.

As with other systems undergoing evolution, the periods when the analysis is near the edge of chaos may be brief. The patient may retreat in the direction of frozen order. He may feel at such times that he has nothing left to say, or nothing new to say, or that the analyst is not interested in what he says. He finds it difficult to "think of anything." Whatever the analyst has to say seems critical or punitive to him. When the patient's productions become repetitive and predictable in this mode, the analytic situation has moved away from the edge of chaos.

When the productions are unpredictable but no longer cumulative, the situation has moved into the chaotic realm. The patient takes off on a topic that seems unrelated to the issues under discussion. He ignores or evades the analyst's interventions. The analyst may wait for a connection to an earlier topic to appear, but finds himself losing the thread of the associative sequence. He may feel that the patient is putting him down, flooding him with unworkable material, caricaturing the instruction to say everything that comes to his mind.

A shift away from the edge of chaos is usually more subtle than this, however. It may come to the analyst's notice as a modulation in his interest in what the patient is saying. When analysis is working optimally, near the edge of chaos, the analyst is entirely engaged in what the patient is telling him. He experiences the session as flowing in a natural way from topic to topic, each topic illuminating the previous one. New material appears in a meaningful context within the continuous discourse of the analysis. Pauses are brief and lead to new branchings in the patient's associative pathways. In descriptions of the "good analytic hour," such as those of Kris (1951) and Khan (1976), the analytic process is near the edge of chaos.

For the patient, the edge of chaos also has a characteristic feeling. He finds himself discussing thoughts and feelings normally difficult to talk about. Inner resistance is being overcome, with feelings of animation and excitement being generated. The thinking of the analyst and the patient converge. When the analyst intervenes, the patient may feel he was just about to say the same thing. The analyst seems to be taking the words right out of his mouth. He may wonder why he had not thought of them himself, sooner. In the same way, the analyst's planned intervention may be forestalled by the patient's arrival at the same point, just as the analyst was about to speak.

Near the edge of chaos, analyst and patient are in tune. Their contributions, usually complementary, now overlap and reinforce each other. The mother–infant relationship is often evoked to illustrate the attunement of the psychoanalytic process near the edge of chaos. This analogy is misleading, however. It attributes an unrealistic asymmetry to the analytic pair. More apt would be the image of a vocalist and her coach working together at the piano. Viewing the analyst's simulation of the patient's inner life as his accompaniment to the patient's vocalizations would not be so far-fetched.

Because the patient near the edge of chaos remembers events of his early life with revived and often vivid feeling, it is often said that the patient is reliving these early experiences in the analysis. Kris called this reliving of early experience "regression in the service of the ego," a term that makes a useful distinction in psychoanalytic thinking. The idea of the edge of chaos helps us to sharpen the distinction even further.

Regression is the patient's reenacting of childhood strategies for dealing with anxiety to avoid dealing with his conflicts in the present. A patient in regression is not experiencing the childhood events that led him to adopt the maladaptive strategy, however, nor is he experiencing the accompanying affects. Regression in the analytic hour is a movement away from the edge of chaos. In contrast, the patient who is regressing in the service of the ego is *reliving* the traumatic events of childhood with a revival of his original feelings. Either he is moving toward the edge of chaos or he is already close to it. This is a regression in chronological terms, but clearly a progression in the coevolutionary development of the analysis.

The analyst can distinguish the reliving of traumatic childhood events with their original affects from histrionic reenactment with false but exaggerated feeling. A hysterical reenactment is a move away from the edge of chaos. With the hysterical patient, the events being reenacted are the stereotyped traumatic events transmitted by an unconscious infantile attractor. They lack plausible detail and they are unrealistically distorted by the grandiose fantasies incorporated into the attractor.

Unlike memories genuinely relived during an analysis, these hysterical pseudomemories do not open the patient's associations to new material. They only lead back to themselves, and to endless repetition. Sometimes, a hysterical memory can contain nothing but the fragments of events in its food set recently consumed by the attractor. The false memories of childhood seduction in the news today are the products of infantile attractors that have meshed successfully with pathological social structures.

An effective way for the analyst to move the patient back toward the edge of chaos is to link his present chaotic or frozen state with other similar states experienced by him in the recent or distant past. This helps because it locates the patient's difficulty in moving toward the edge of chaos in his entrapment by an infantile attractor.

As Kauffman observes, cells and organisms must remain slightly to the ordered side of the edge of chaos if they are to survive as autonomous agents. New molecules entering the cell must be screened very carefully, to be sure they do not cause avalanches of adverse reactions. If the cell membrane does not perform this function, natural selection will. Cells and organisms are normally in a subcritical state that combines stability with flexibility.

Yet the terrestrial biosphere as a whole is supracritical. New macromolecules and new species are constantly being created. Kauffman suggests that as the organisms in an ecological community coevolve, they evolve individually toward the edge of chaos, from more ordered to less ordered. The ecological community as a whole can approach the edge of chaos from the other direction, becoming less chaotic as it evolves.

As psychoanalytic treatment progresses, the patient's and the analyst's views of each other often become less rigid, while the therapeutic ecosystem moves from chaotic to ordered. Kauffman suggests that in coevolutionary systems generally these movements toward the edge of chaos are mutually enhancing. Any loosening of order within the patient or the analyst (though not complete unraveling) will increase the order of the analytic discourse and the therapeutic ecosystem. Conversely, any increase in the coherence of the analytic discourse will stimulate a loosening of preconceptions and defenses within the patient and the analyst.

Approaching the Edge of Chaos

An unconscious infantile attractor is always an obstacle on the patient's path toward the edge of chaos. It is not just a fantasy that gets in the way, but a fantasy with very sharp teeth. Finding a way around the attractor may be extremely painful for the patient. If the patient feels that he lacks the emotional strength or will to go beyond the attractor, for example, he may misinterpret the analyst's efforts to free him from the attractor. The intervention may appear to him as a destructive attempt to dislodge him from the vital core of his personality.

For example, Harvey, a man who was brought up by a depressed and intermittently suicidal mother, felt irrationally responsible for her survival and well-being. When his wife developed breast cancer and died, Harvey blamed himself for failing to fulfill his responsibilities to her. A tiny shred of truth lay behind this idea, because he had not opposed her procrastination in seeing a doctor about her condition as vigorously as he might have. Harvey continued to blame himself for many years, though he succeeded in living a full and productive life.

Harvey sought analytic treatment when he met another woman, because he found himself filled with self-hatred at the prospect of having a good relationship again. He believed unconsciously that if he stopped blaming himself for his wife's death, he would reveal that his love for her had been inadequate and insincere. This was also what he had believed about his love for his mother when he found himself unable to relieve her agitated depression during his early years.

If he blamed himself, he could at least be a decent and loving though miserable person. If he stopped blaming himself, he would be a cold hearted monster, perhaps even a murderer. In feeling this way Harvey was applying a view of himself he had learned as a child through his interaction with his nearly psychotic mother to the later tragedy with his wife.

Harvey was living with a childish unconscious emotional organization which made him responsible for every misfortune. His value as a human being depended on his keeping everything and everyone safe. When his wife died, he felt that his failure was unforgivable and irredeemable. Although he devoted himself to his work with great intensity and succeeded in accomplishing many difficult professional tasks, he still felt like a very bad person.

Harvey needed help in reorganizing his views of himself and of the world, so that he could give his misfortunes their own independent causes and histories, separate from his own unconscious malice. As it was, all his misfortunes were interchangeable in the attractor built around this fantasy. Everything was his fault, and the distinguishing details didn't matter. Differences in his experiences with the women in his life had been set aside in favor of the pain and humiliation he had suffered with his mother.

One problem in helping Harvey was that he had to become fully aware of his primitive unconscious organization and all the pain it had caused him before he could be motivated to change it. The condensations that make these experiences unconsciously equivalent did not become fully vivid to him until they were re-lived in relation to the analyst. That is, the analyst had to *become* the patient's needy and unreliable, depressed mother before he could be clearly distinguished from her.

When the patient could observe how the analyst had become his mother, he noticed that other people were transformed into his mother too. He could see that he himself caused these trans-formations, and that he had the capacity, previously unused, to reverse them.

His open access to the analyst's responses allowed the patient to test his projections without incapacitating anxiety. Like his mother, the analyst often went off into his own world, leaving the patient feeling angry and unsatisfied. Nevertheless, the analyst did not reject the patient's protests or his expressions of retalia-tory feeling, as his mother had.

Throughout the sorting of the patient's projections, the ana-lyst has to convey to the patient that in facing his pain and loss he is opening himself to a new, more realistic and more satisfying view of his life. Any doubts about this on the analyst's part will be picked up and magnified by the patient.

Another problem for the analyst of this patient was the *second-ary gain* that accompanied his suffering. Like other depressed patients, he had adopted the strategy of avoiding disappointment by always expecting the worst. This made his world completely predictable. He could prepare himself for what was coming. He could not be surprised. Even more powerfully, he could continue to imagine himself responsible for his mother's well-being. He was avoiding the worst by keeping her alive. This feeling of power was a desperate compensation for his fear of losing her. If he stopped blaming himself for his wife's death, he would be relin-quishing the remnants of this grandiose power.

A reorganized ego state is, first, *differentiated* with respect to the previous state. Childhood experience and contemporary events can be differentiated *only after the unconscious identity be-tween them has been recognized by the patient.* For this to happen, the attractor has to be located and expanded by the analyst's interventions. Once the unconscious connections that hold the primitive condensation together have been reconnected with the larger structures mediated through consciousness, the patient can begin to see the important differences between them, but not before.

Differentiation of objects is one primary characteristic of a system near the edge of chaos. Memories of events reduced to equivalence by the more primitive unconscious attractors appear together for the first time when the analysis is close to the edge. Their similarities and differences are then open to further exploration.

7 COEVOLUTION IN COUPLED SYSTEMS: THE THERAPEUTIC RELATIONSHIP

Coadaptation

The patient and the analyst become partners in the task of unlocking the patient's major emotional conflicts. But they don't do the same thing. The role that each performs is the counterpart of the other's role. Together they can do something that neither of them can do separately. We might think of calling them counterpartners in the analytic process. The analyst brings his knowledge and experience to the task, his knowledge and experience with and about people who suffer from many kinds of emotional illness. The patient brings his own problem with him, and with it the only source of data particular to his problem.

Years of training and practice enter into the analyst's professional knowledge and experience. His teachers, supervisors, training analyst, colleagues and patients have taught him what he knows. He has a wide knowledge of his own culture and, to a lesser degree, of others. His personal experience, deepened and articulated by his own analysis, gives him a model for the intricacy and complexity of mental life.

223

The analyst has been through the analytic process before, in the roles of both patient and analyst. A man from the Ozarks was once asked if he believed in baptism. "Believe in it?" he said, "Heck, I've seen it done!" The analyst has seen it done. This experience shapes the analyst's contribution to the analytic process.

Patients often complain that they have much more at stake in the outcome of the analysis than the analyst does. They imagine that because the analyst has less to lose if the analysis fails, he will not work as hard or care as much about the outcome. For the patient, the analysis may be a matter of life or death. At the very least, he expects that it will enhance his emotional well-being for the remainder of his life. The patient is aware that he has only one analyst to rely on, while the analyst has many patients.

The analyst's goals are more limited. He earns his livelihood by working with patients. However, his living does not depend on this patient, or on any single patient. Still, he does have his own goals for the analysis. Making his work with each patient as effective as possible is one of them. Developing his therapeutic skills is another. He knows that to reach these goals in an analysis, he is required to participate in an evolutionary process that takes considerable time and effort.

A coevolutionary relationship, in which both patient and analyst change, is necessary for the analysis to achieve the separate but intersecting goals of the analytic partners. Kauffman's findings are consistent with the clinical observation that optimum adaptation for the patient cannot be achieved without a coevolutionary therapeutic process in which the analyst also evolves.

What is it in the analyst that evolves during the analysis of a given patient? The analyst's understanding of the patient must obviously evolve for the treatment to be effective. Is that enough? Must his skills as a therapist for other patients evolve as well? The answer to this last question must be positive. The treatment of any patient can hardly be optimal if the analyst is not learning something from that patient that will help him with others.

Patients like to think that their analysts have become better people while analyzing them, apart from any improvement in professional skills. Can this be true? I think perhaps it is, sometimes, with much variation from patient to patient and analyst to analyst. Is it essential to a successful analysis? Common sense suggests that something must be amiss if the analyst derives no personal benefit at all from a prolonged and productive interaction with the patient.

Can we estimate the relative stakes of the analyst and patient in the outcome of the analysis? This too will vary for each patient and analyst. A very crude first approximation might be the percentage of the analyst's working time spent with a particular patient. For him the patient is one of many. The analyst is unique to the patient. What he accomplishes in the analysis affects all aspects of his emotional life.

Perhaps a story told by Christopher Standish to his psychotherapy students in the early 1960s can be of help here. In the story, an elderly Bedouin dies, leaving his 17 camels to three sons. His will specifies that half the camels go to the oldest son, a third to the next oldest, and a ninth to the youngest. The sons consult the tribal wise man about how to divide seventeen camels in these proportions. The wise man says, "I'll tell you what. I'll lend you my camel. Then you'll have 18. Half of that is 9 for the eldest. A third is 6 for the middle son. And 2 is a ninth for the youngest. One camel will be left over. I'll take my camel back and everyone will have his share." (The story works with 39 camels also, as in the version given by Eigen and Winkler-Oswatitsch [1975].)

According to Standish, the therapist lends the patient his camel. The wise man in this story is doing what Odysseus did in offering blood to the spirits in Hades. Besides giving a very rough estimate of the analyst's stake in the analysis, this parable raises interesting questions about the nature of the analyst's involvement. Does his camel actually leave the analyst's tent, or can the transaction be done on paper? If the analyst's camel comes out to join the other camels, is he completely unchanged after the distribution has been made?

Simulating the Patient's Mental Life

The patient and analyst each participate in fostering a coevolutionary relationship, although their roles are different. The analyst's attention is directed to the patient and what he says. Peterfreund

(1983) suggests that the analyst constructs and continually revises a complex working model of the patient. Palombo (1981, 1985b) calls this process a continuously updated simulation of the patient's personality and pathology.

At the start of a new analysis, the analyst can only rely on his knowledge of mental disorders as they occur in people generally. This set of broad expectations is narrowed down as he begins to learn who the particular patient is. The original outline is gradually redrawn and filled. The analyst remains consciously alert for data that might confirm or disconfirm the current version of his model, but he takes in many other impressions without being aware of them. He adjusts the model as he goes along, consciously and unconsciously, to assimilate this new evidence.

As the patient reveals more of himself, the model changes. Old contradictions and discontinuities are resolved and new ones develop. Important aspects of the patient's personality and pathology remain obscure. Defensiveness on the parts of both patient and analyst will contribute to this obscurity. Transference and countertransference distortions will be worked and reworked. The analyst uses his knowledge and experience to reduce the effects of his countertransference distortions, but the analytic process cannot go on without his continual conscious reassessment of his view of the patient.

The patient is also modeling the analyst, but in a different way. He has a model, more unconscious than conscious, of the hypothetical person who could understand him perfectly. He monitors the quality of the analyst's understanding, as he perceives it, by comparing him with this hypothetical figure. Idealized representations of parents and other influential caretakers play a prominent role in forming his model. Though his conscious goal is not to understand the analyst as a person separate from the treatment, he may feel driven by curiosity about the analyst's personality and life history.

The patient's conscious attention is directed to the people and events in his current life situation, rather than to the analyst. He expects the analyst to understand him just as his parents did or should have. He often ignores evidence that the analyst understands him in a different way from the important people in his outside life, past and present. Nevertheless, changes take place in the patient's unconscious mental organization as the analysis proceeds. The patient begins to feel that he can be understood in a new way.

Asymmetries in the aims of patient and analyst actually work to enhance their value to each other as partners in the treatment process. The analyst's smaller stake in the outcome helps him maintain greater objectivity. The patient's greater freedom to express himself provides the material for analysis. Coevolution is the meshing through continual feedback of the patient's and the analyst's images of one another and themselves, as they pursue their different but converging aims in the analysis.

Internal Connectedness and Coevolution: The Nash Equilibrium

According to Kauffman, the component systems that form an ecosystem naturally move toward an *evolutionary stable strategy* (ESS), also called a *Nash equilibrium.* (Nash received the 1994 Nobel Prize in economics for this work, done during the 1950s.) A Nash equilibrium "is a combination of actions, such that, for each agent, granted that the other agents do not alter their own actions, its action is optimal" (Kauffman, 1993, p. 240).

A Nash equilibrium in an ecosystem is like a local optimum on the fitness landscape of a single system. At a Nash equilibrium, the fitnesses of the individual systems may be maintained far from their own fitness optima, to keep them in balance with the other component systems of the ecosystem. The equilibrium is adaptive to the extent that it provides stability within the ecosystem. The fitness of the ecosystem as a whole may be much lower than it would be at its optimal disequilibrium state, near the edge of chaos.

An illustration of the Nash equilibrium comes from a famous situation in game theory, called *the prisoner's dilemma* (Axelrod, 1984; Poundstone, 1992). In the anecdote from which the prisoner's dilemma gets its name, two suspects in a serious crime have been caught and imprisoned in separate cells. However, the evidence is inadequate to convict either of them of the crime. The prosecutor offers a plea bargain in return for testimony against the other prisoner. If one prisoner testifies and implicates the other, he will be freed. The other will be sentenced to three years in jail. If neither testifies, they will both be tried on a lesser charge and sentenced to one year. If each testifies against the other, they will both receive two years. What should the prisoners do?

A rational strategy for each prisoner individually is to testify against the other. When either player testifies, he gets a better payoff, whether the other player testifies or remains silent. If the other player keeps quiet, the testifying player goes free. If the other player also testifies, he gets two years in prison instead of the three he would have gotten if he had kept quiet. Both players, if rational, will choose this strategy, which will lead to the Nash equilibrium state for the system defined by these rules and payoffs. Using this strategy, each player minimizes the damage the other could do to him. Each will be sentenced to two years in prison.

However, each would do better if both were willing to take the chance that the other would keep quiet. If both refused to testify, they would be jailed for only one year. This would be a *disequilibrium strategy* with an optimal payoff. However, they have no way of communicating their willingness to take this risk in a single round of prisoner's dilemma.

In psychoanalytic treatment, the equivalents of cooperation and defection are not quite the same for the patient and for the analyst. The patient cooperates by following the analyst's instructions to say everything that comes to his mind. He defects by withholding his thoughts. The analyst cooperates by listening empathically to what the patient says. He defects by substituting his own preconceptions for what the patient is actually telling him. Defection in either case is primarily an unconscious act, although either analytic partner may be aware that he is actively suppressing a wish or idea he does not want to deal with just then. The prison walls in psychoanalysis are the unconscious defensive structures that prevent cooperation and self-awareness.

Unfortunately for the prisoners in the anecdote, they have only the one chance to decide. Whatever they learn from their experience will be wasted, at least until they are out of prison again. Still, if they were to make the same decision repeatedly, each could infer a pattern in the responses made by the other player. From these observations, the two could devise an optimizing strategy. This repetitive game is called the *iterated prisoners' dilemma* (IPD). It gives the players an opportunity to learn from the pattern of moves in previous games, but as we will see, the capacity to learn has to evolve through their mutual experience.

Payoffs can be positive in all cases for both players, or, equally, they can be all negative or mixed. What matters for the dilemma is the payoff ranking for the four possible combinations of defection or cooperation strategies, called D and C. These combinations are DD, DC, CD and CC. In the prisoners' dilemma, the ranking of the payoffs is DC > CC > DD > CD, creating the paradox of a rational strategy for both players, DD, that produces a Nash equilibrium with suboptimal payoffs.

DD is the rational strategy for a single encounter, or, as Nash proved, for a finite number of encounters when the number is known in advance to the players. (Defecting in the last game is best, since the last game is identical to a single round game. A player has nothing to lose at that point if he destroys the other player's trust. Knowing that the opponent knows this, it is also best to defect in the next to last game, and so on down to the first.) Only in an *infinite iterated prisoners' dilemma* (IIPD) do the players have a chance to work out an optimal cooperative strategy for the game. The success of a strategy in the infinite iterated version of the game can be measured by the average payoff for the player who uses it over many rounds.

Researchers in game theory became interested in the infinite iterated prisoners' dilemma, where the players encounter each other repeatedly without knowing that any game will be the final one in the sequence. The success of their strategies in the iterated version can be measured by the average payoff for each round.

Axelrod (1984) arranged a round robin computer tournament of prisoners' dilemma strategies and invited other researchers to submit their programs. Fourteen experts responded. In the first round of the tournament, an equal number of simulated agents used each of the 14 strategies.

Axelrod then ran a second tournament round in which the 14 strategies were represented in proportion to their scores in the first round. The number of agents using the winning strategy in each generation was increased slightly, and the number of

losers decreased, so that the total remained constant. After extensive play it was found that a simple strategy, called Tit for Tat,
had the best average score. In the Tit for Tat strategy, the player
cooperates on his first move, then simply makes whichever move
his opponent made on the previous play. If the other player also
cooperates, the Tit for Tat player cooperates again on the next
move. If the other player defects, he also defects. Two players
using this strategy against one another will achieve an optimal
score. After 200 rounds the Tit for Tat strategy dominated the
population of agents.

Axelrod published his results, then invited entries for another tournament. Sixty-eight strategies competed in this replication study. Although Tit for Tat's secret was known to all, the
results were the same. It became axiomatic that Tit for Tat was
the best practical strategy one could expect to find for the IIPD.

However, in 1992, Kristian Lindgren pointed out that Tit
for Tat did badly when mutations or errors occurred during a
tournament. Any change in either player's performance caused
both players to defect from that point on. Lindgren used a variant
of John Holland's genetic algorithm (Holland, 1975, 1996) to
allow the strategies used by the agents in his experiments to
evolve.

Like Axelrod, Lindgren (1992) applied differential reproduction for the natural selection of strategies in a computer tournament. However, Lindgren introduced point mutation (a
random bit reversed) and genetic recombination to vary the original strategies, in the hope of evolving performance nearer the
optimum. The genome of his automated players was very simple,
consisting of just two binary digits. A zero meant defect, a one
cooperate. The left-hand digit represented the player's response
when the other player defected on his last move, and the right-hand
digit his response *when the other player cooperated.*

A zero on the left instructed the player to defect whenever
his opponent had defected on the previous play. A one in either
position directed the player to cooperate. On the left, a one
meant that the first player cooperated when the other player had
just defected. On the right, a one caused the first player to cooperate when the opponent had cooperated on his previous move.
Four strategies are possible for the first player: 00, always defect;

11 always cooperate; 01, Tit for Tat; 10, reverse Tit for Tat (or Tat for Tit). These are called *memory one strategies,* because the memory of only one previous move is used to carry them out.

Lindgren simulated a round robin tournament starting with a thousand players using the four possible strategies in equal numbers. Each of the thousand individuals played against the 999 others in a single generation. The scores for each strategy were averaged. More individuals using the winning strategies and fewer of the losers were present in the next generation.

Three kinds of mutation appeared at random intervals, averaging about one in 100,000 games per player, or one in 50 tournament rounds. In addition to the point mutation, a genome could double its length during replication or split down the middle to give a half-length genome (one half was randomly discarded). Random errors also occurred in the execution of moves at twice the mutation rate.

A double genome had a length of four digits. It produced a strategy that responded in a different way to each combination of *two* previous moves, the player's last move and the opponent's response to that move. This is a *memory two strategy.* Each doubling of length adds another memory to the sequence of immediately preceding moves that a strategy responds to.

Lindgren compared the number of players of each genome type remaining after the end of each round robin. Graphing this variable against time as represented by the number of generations since the start of the tournament, he found a very intricate pattern of punctuated equilibrium. Brief periods of sharp chaotic fluctuation occurred, with one strategy after another becoming dominant. These typically appeared at the outset of play and during the emergence of the memory two strategies, but also at unpredictable moments throughout each run. Longer periods followed, when either a single strategy or a pair of mutually dependent strategies dominated the population.

In most runs, players evolved to memory four strategies (16 digit genomes) reached a near optimal payoff very quickly. They appeared within 30,000 generations (see Figure 7.1, 7.2). At first a single memory four strategy, 1001000100010001, became dominant. Soon many other equally effective memory four strategies, between 20 and 30, joined in. All were different, but all retained

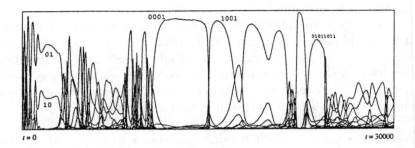

Figure 7.1. The simulation is continued for 30,000 generations, showing that four periods of stasis appear in the evolution. The oscillations observed are damped and the system reaches a period of stasis with coexistence between [01] (TFT) and [10] (ATFT). This stasis is punctuated by a number of memory 2 strategies, and after a period of unstable behavior the system slowly stabilizes when the strategy [1001] increases in the population. This strategy cooperates if both players performed the same action last time. For two individuals using this strategy, an accidental defection by one of the players leads to both players defecting the next time, but in the round after that they return to cooperative behavior. Thus, the strategy [1001] is cooperative and stable against mistakes, but it can be exploited by uncooperative strategies. Actually, one of its mutants [0001] exploits the kindness of [1001], which results in a slow increase of [0001] in the population. This leads to a long-lived stasis dominated by the uncooperative behavior of [0001]. A slowly growing group of memory 3 strategies is then formed by mutations, and the presence of these species causes the fractions of the strategies [0001] and [1001] to oscillate. Two of the memory 3 strategies, $M_1 =$ [10010001] and $M_2 =$ [00011001], manage to take over the population, leading to a new period of stasis. Neither M_1 nor M_2 can handle mistakes when playing against individuals of their own kind, but if M_1 meets M_2 they are able to return to cooperative behavior after an accidental defection. This polymorphism is an example of mutualism which spontaneously emerges in this model. The stasis is destabilized by a group of mutants, and we get a fast transition to a population of memory 4 strategies which are both cooperative and unexploitable. (From Lindgren, 1992, in C. Langton, *Artificial Life:* Volume II, 1992, p. 308. © 1992 Addison-Wesley Publishing Company Inc. Reprinted by permission of Addison-Wesley Longman Inc.)

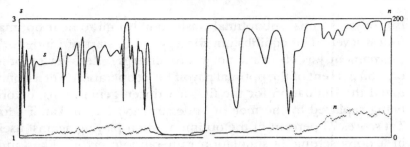

Figure 7.2. The average score s (continuous line) and the number of genotypes n (broken line) are shown for the simulation of Figure 7.1. When the exploiting memory 2 strategy dominates the scene, the average score drops close to 1. The last stasis, populated by the evolutionary stable memory 4 strategies, reaches a score of 2.91, close to the score of 3 achieved by the best strategies in a noise-free environment. Before the transitions and in the periods of unstable behavior, it appears that there are more mutants that survive and the number of genotypes increases, suggesting that most of the evolution takes place in these intervals. (From Lindgren, 1992, in C. Langton, *Artificial Life:* Volume II, 1992, p. 308. © 1992 Addison-Wesley Publishing Company Inc. Reprinted by permission of Addison-Wesley Longman Inc.)

the basic structure of the first successful memory four genome. At that point, the system reached a stable evolutionary strategy at optimal levels of success. No further movement occurred once this level had been reached.

This outcome was not universal, however. About one of ten runs failed to reach a Nash equilibrium within 80,000 generations. One such run reported by Lindgren operated at the same near optimal level, but had occasional lapses when its average score fell sharply for a brief time. The number of evolved strategies during this run reached as many as 200 more than once before crashing and reconstituting. This case is much nearer to the pattern observed in a successful psychoanalysis, where the completely or perfectly analyzed patient is only an ideal.

Lindgren's evolutionary simulation discovered an entire class of only moderately complex strategies that produced near optimal performance. This is one of the best illustrations of the power of a complex computer simulation to produce results completely beyond the anticipation of the scientists who study the natural phenomena being simulated.

Of special interest to the psychoanalyst, Lindgren's experiment shows that, given sufficient time, a coevolutionary system can raise its initial suboptimal Nash equilibrium to near optimal fitness levels. The equilibrium strategy at the start of Lindgren's tournament was 00 (a memory zero strategy). Zero-zero scored only 33 percent of the optimal payoff for cooperation. Yet it dominated the simulation for the first few dozen generations, before being replaced by the memory one strategy, Tit for Tat. Tit for Tat scores 75 percent of the optimum when playing against itself in a noisy setting (a simulation with random errors, like Lindgren's).

The successful memory four strategies operate at a 97 percent level of success. Even more remarkably, they reach a stable equilibrium at this near optimal efficiency 90 percent of the time. The low initial Nash equilibrium is pulled to the higher fitness values by the success of strategies that operate far from the prevailing equilibrium levels.

Can the coevolution of prisoners' dilemma strategies drive the equilibrium state toward the edge of chaos, as Kauffman suggests it might? Similarly, do the successful four memory strategies lock in the Nash equilibrium near the edge of chaos? These questions are difficult to answer definitively. Lindgren does not describe his system as operating in a realm between order and chaos. However, we have good reason to consider the final equilibrium of the memory four strategies to be near the edge of chaos.

Before the first successful memory four strategy appears on the scene, the strategies that compete for dominance have quite different payoffs. The individual strategies that succeed in the competition are either primarily cooperating or primarily defecting strategies. When any strategy achieves dominance, it is at the expense of its predecessors, whose numbers diminish sharply. As a result, the average payoffs for the system as a whole fluctuate widely.

All this changes abruptly when the memory four strategies appear on the scene. The phenomenon of dominance simply disappears. Distinct but equally effective memory four strategies cooperate to share the fitness landscape. Order is preserved at the stable level of successful performance, while variety is achieved in the proliferation of near optimal genotypes. An economy of scarcity is suddenly replaced by an economy of abundance.

These edge of chaos conditions appear at an abrupt phase transition that changes the structure of the entire system, eventually making their behavior fully predictable. The computational basis for the phase transition is quite clear. The addition of new memory capacity to the genome allows an increase in the information about interactions with other members of the ecosystem that can be stored by each component. This makes the strategy of defection completely maladaptive.

We see a similar pattern during the unfolding of a successful psychoanalytic process. The patient entering analysis has a difficult choice to make; the difficulty is usually resolved unconsciously. He can cooperate with the analyst by saying everything that comes to his mind, as instructed, revealing his painful feelings and his doubts about himself. He can also defect by digging himself into his old self-protective but self-deceiving way of operating.

The rational Nash equilibrium strategy in this situation is to defect rather than to cooperate. Most patients unconsciously choose to be safe when faced with the unknown in the person of an analyst of whom they have no first hand knowledge. Of course, the analysis is not a replica of Lindgren's simulation of the prisoners' dilemma. An analysis has only two players, and their roles are not symmetrical. Many other factors determine the course of the analysis than the dynamics of the prisoners' dilemma. These other factors can have a profound influence over the underlying dynamics of the therapeutic relationship, but they cannot completely override them.

However, the patient cannot easily risk accepting the analyst's assurances that cooperation is safe. We know the patient will encounter occasional failures of empathy on the analyst's part. This is an almost unavoidable kind of event that happens despite the analyst's best intentions. In the face of this, the patient begins by unconsciously following the rational strategy that leads to a suboptimal Nash equilibrium.

Some patients try to hide their defection by making a great effort to impress the analyst or to comply mechanically with what they imagine to be his wishes. Others tell their story in a closed and stereotyped way, maintaining tight control over their words and fending off the analyst's attempts to open the analytic discourse. Some simply go through the motions of the analysis without feeling or commitment. More disturbed patients may make little pretense of cooperating, actively fighting off the analyst and blaming him for lack of progress. The patient may take hours, months, or years to realize (unconsciously) that cooperation is safer than defection and potentially much more productive.

Of course, an analysis is not really a prisoners' dilemma situation. It only seems that way to the patient, because he projects his own mistrust onto the analyst. The analyst tries to cooperate, no matter what the patient does. The patient has to play it safe, following a strategy that would lead to the suboptimal Nash equilibrium if the analysis were a prisoners' dilemma.

For the analyst the payoff is positive, whether or not the patient defects. He is not playing by the same rules as the patient. At the least, the patient's defection rewards the analyst with an opportunity to observe his defenses in action. The patient's manner of defecting may also provide the only information available about the unconscious fantasies that motivated it.

However, the analyst may have his own issues to face in responding to the patient's defection. His efforts to be empathic make him vulnerable to being drawn into the patient's game. He can at times be conned into believing that the patient is telling everything. He can also be convinced that the patient's defecting behavior is intractable, no matter what he tries to do to change it. No analyst consciously intends to play Tit for Tat, but unresolved unconscious countertransference feelings may produce a more or less subtle version of defection, which the patient will be quick to pick up and magnify.

I find that inexperienced analysts, when faced with too many defections by the patient, often drastically lower their expectations about how the patient will respond to treatment. At times, they even develop an unconscious conviction that the patient will never change. In spite of this, the patient usually makes some improvement. The analyst's reliable presence and attention can offset other signs that he is empathically withdrawn. But when the patient shows signs of evolving a new and more cooperative strategy, the analyst may react as if the patient is cynically complying with the analyst's wishes. The patient then has a legitimate complaint that the analyst is undervaluing and infantilizing him. The analysis will very likely founder unless the analyst can overcome this countertransference impasse.

Lindgren has shown that an automated coevolutionary process can optimize the fitness level in an open-ended game of prisoners' dilemma. Sufficient time is needed for evolution to take place. Clarity about the difference between cooperation and defection may emerge slowly. As in most real life applications of the prisoners' dilemma, the most difficult question for an observer may be to decide whether a player is actually cooperating or defecting. Both transference and countertransference issues in analysis are likely to show up as difficulties in reaching an agreement about what kind of act amounts to cooperation and what to defection.

Important for our understanding of the psychoanalytic process is the dynamics of interaction that raises a low initial Nash equilibrium to a higher level with a nearly optimal payoff. Lindgren's experiment tells us a good deal about the features of this dynamic pathway. First, the pathway is not smooth. The performance of his system goes through large fluctuations even while genotypic complexity is progressively increasing. Only at the memory four phase transition does the increase in complexity have a definitive influence on future performance. In the psychoanalytic situation, change may come rapidly after a long period of apparent stasis.

Second, it is the extended memory of previous interactions that makes an effective strategy of cooperation safe from exploitation. The corresponding feature of the analytic process is the development of a record in the patient's memory of the analytic discourse. The patient has to learn to overcome the transference projections that make defection seem a rational strategy. He *learns to remember* that his interactions with the analyst have turned out to be different from his fearful expectations when the analysis began. Turned out to be different enough of the time, that is, to generate a memory four strategy.

Lindgren's simulation suggests that the patient's memory of the analyst's interaction with him may evolve through stages in which he can remember and use more information. The patient usually begins analysis with a memory zero strategy. He expects the analyst to react as an authoritarian (indifferent, sadistic, seductive) parent might have, no matter what he, the patient, does. The analyst's actual response may not even be noticed at this point. Gradually it becomes clear that the analyst responds differently at different times. At first it may seem to the patient that these responses have no relation to what he himself says or does.

After a while the patient may enter a stage in which he closely tracks the analyst's statements. He devises a strategy based on what the analyst has said most recently. If the analyst seemed friendly, he speaks more openly; if he does not seem friendly, the patient is guarded. This is a memory one strategy, similar to Tit for Tat. Later the patient may notice that the analyst's response differs according to what he himself has been saying. When he is being open, the analyst's comments may seem more frequent or more focused; when he is guarded, the analyst's responses may be less forthcoming and less specific.

By the memory four stage, or its equivalent in analysis, the patient can recall the response of the analyst to his own reply to the analyst's remarks, if any, about the patient's previous statement. This is enough depth to allow the correcting of misunderstandings, the clarifying of obscurities, and the testing of new hypotheses about the analyst's motives. It makes possible new branchings in the patient's associative pathways without loss of contact with the branching point. Is it enough to support movement toward the edge of chaos?

A memory four strategy is near the human limit of explicit, conscious, immediate memory capacity. Of course, much greater mnemonic depth of implicit and unconscious memory is available through the modification of Nash equilibrium levels. We are dealing with neural network structures that can hold dozens or even hundreds of memory representations simultaneously.

These representations are potentially retrievable if addressed by a matching probe. The interesting empirical question here is whether a relation can be found between the retrieval of unconscious memories and the achievement of a stable evolutionary equilibrium near the edge of chaos. It seems clear enough that unconscious memories can intrude into the analytic discourse at any time or place, near or far from the edge of chaos.

What is at issue here is the degree of correlation between the patient's ability to associate to the retrieved memories and the distance of his current equilibrium state from the edge of chaos. My prediction would be a very strong correlation. In making such a determination empirically, one would have to be careful to keep the measure of the patient's ability to associate to the particular memory independent of the measure of closeness to the edge of chaos, not necessarily an easy thing to do.

Lindgren's work appears to support Kauffman's proposal that there may be a natural tendency for the Nash equilibrium level of a coevolving ecosystem to move toward the edge of chaos. His simulation suggests at the very least that the coevolutionary process must have sufficient time for multiple memory strategies to evolve if it is to achieve this result. Of course, the analytic process must also be open-ended, just like the infinite iterated prisoners' dilemma. Otherwise the patient will correctly believe that he can hold back painful material without ever being called to account for it. So-called brief psychotherapy, whatever virtues it may have, encourages the patient to defect from the first moment of treatment. Multiple memory strategies make it possible to look ahead in responding to a challenge. Chess playing programs that look ahead three moves on each side make powerful opponents for human chess masters.

An important step has been completed when the patient can remember that the last time the analyst defected in the imaginary prisoners' dilemma, he was able to recover on the following move, or at most the one after that. The patient can then look ahead to a recovery from any new misconstrual or misunderstanding. He does not have to be caught in an endless cycle of defection.

The patient is helped when the analyst links the elements of the analytic discourse itself. The analyst can do this by referring explicitly to the relation between what he and the patient are saying now and what they have said before. The analytic discourse provides a record of these connections that is available to both participants. For the record to be effectively connected, it has to be openly self-referential. This will form the solid base for the development of a multiple memory strategy by the patient.

It appears to me that for most analysts the idea of the analytic discourse exists only in the real time of the analytic session. Of course, it leaves a permanent residue in its mutative effect on the patient, but it is not usually understood as an internalized entity with its own coherent structure.

The taking in of the analytic discourse is more likely to be thought of as a process similar to digestion and assimilation. One speaks of the analyst and other objects and parts of objects as internalized, with some pieces of their structures remaining intact after the internalization. But we do not hear much said about the analytic discourse as an internalized entity distinct from self- and object-representations.

Lindgren's work suggests that the history of the interaction between the coevolutionary partners must be incorporated into each partner as a connected structure. This appears to be the case in analysis as well. If it is, we should find a relation between the connectedness of the analytic discourse and its usefulness to the patient for the evolution of a multiple memory strategy.

I believe that analysts usually work in a way that optimizes the connectedness of the analytic discourse, although this is not necessarily a conscious goal. Analysis would be hard to imagine if the analyst were not able to compare what was happening in the session right now with what had happened at other times in other sessions. Much depends on whether what is happening now is a repetition of or a departure from what has happened before.

The analyst should be aware that he has an opportunity to configure the analytic discourse in a way that makes it more useful to the patient. The analytic discourse gives the patient a cumulative sample of alternatives to strategies that fail to get him what he wants and what he needs from the analyst and other people.

The patient often lacks an awareness of the connectedness of his own contribution to the analytic discourse. This is often demonstrated when he introduces a topic as if it were new, when, in fact, he had discussed it at some length in the past.

A typical intervention by the analyst aimed at structuring the analytic discourse might be, "What you're saying now about me sounds like what you said about your mother earlier in the session." Or, "This is the first time you've told me anything about your boss that sounded sympathetic." Or, simply, "You were concerned about this issue last session [last week, last month when you said . . . , when you first came here]." These interventions are the links that hold the analytic discourse together. For example, I find it particularly useful to refer to what the patient has said about one of his parents on a specific occasion in the past, rather than to what I may believe at the moment he feels in general about that parent.

Referring to what the patient has said in the past also keeps it clear that all his statements are taken in context. No particular statement is the final truth about anything. What is revealing is the relationship between what the patient said then and what he is saying now.

What is true for the patient is true for the analyst too. His statements are not final either. They are subject to revision each time the patient opens his mouth to provide new information. The analytic discourse is a possession shared by the patient and the analyst, to which they can each refer in the knowledge that the other also has first-hand experience of it. This is the basis for the development of the analytic equivalent of the memory four strategy in Lindgren's simulation.

My point is not that psychoanalysis can be reduced to a simple game theoretical model. That would be absurd. Nor do I claim that the prisoners' dilemma is the best possible model for the unconscious dynamics of the psychoanalytic process. I am merely suggesting that any useful explanation of these dynamics must be *at least as complex* as Lindgren's simulation of the iterated prisoners' dilemma.

The principle of the Nash equilibrium can be applied to the ecosystem formed by the therapeutic relationship. Kauffman's simulations are relevant here too. For example, let S be the total number of member component systems in an ecosystem. The member systems are said to be *coupled* when changes in one or more components of each member influence the fitness of the other members.

Kauffman finds that when coupled random Boolean networks coevolve, the mean fitness of the individual component networks is highest when S is least, namely 2. For this example of a coevolving ecosystem, 2 is the optimum number of component members. While this result cannot be generalized to other coevolving systems, it offers a suggestive hypothesis for psychoanalytic research.

Kauffman's result is consistent with the clinical experience of psychoanalysts and psychotherapists. Despite many useful contributions from group and family therapies, individual treatment (where $S = 2$) is most often chosen as the optimal setting for improving the fitness of the individual patient.

An analysis reaches a Nash equilibrium state when the patient is safe from major disturbance caused by inadvertent actions of the analyst. By this time, the analyst is also usually safe from serious diagnostic errors. (Not every analytic treatment reaches this point.) Nevertheless, the patient may be making little progress in understanding himself. The analysis may be stalled at an equilibrium where the patient and analyst are in a collusive alliance to keep their boat from rocking.

The analyst's aim must be to move the patient toward the edge of chaos, away from this static equilibrium, without threatening the stability of the therapeutic ecosystem. His interventions are buffered by the natural tendency of the system to return to the equilibrium when perturbed. Although this tendency acts as a useful damper to the destabilizing effects of the analyst's interpretive actions, it also retards the progress of the analysis.

The Nash Equilibrium in Psychoanalysis

In Kauffman's simulation of an ecosystem with coevolving species, not all species interact. Those that do are said to be *coupled*. But not all species are equally coupled. In the simulation, some components of one system (representing a species) are connected with a number of components (representing traits) in a neighboring system. The number of coupled components (C) between systems varies from one coupling to another. When the values of K and C are held constant for all species in an ecosystem, coevolutionary fitness levels depend in part on the ratio of K to C.

Kauffman defines K and C for the simulation as follows: "In the context of the NK model, the natural way to couple landscapes is to assume that each trait in species 1 depends epistatically on K other traits internally and on C traits in species 2. More generally, in any ecosystem with S species, each trait in species 1 will depend on K traits in species 1 and on C traits in each of the S_i among the S species with which it interacts" (1993, p. 244).

Some interesting results follow. The fitness of the species contained in the ecosystem is optimal when $K = C$. A Nash equilibrium is reached very early in the simulation when $K >> C$, but not at all if $C >> K$. Fitness is highest when the Nash equilibrium occurs after a longer but finite time. Most strikingly, when C is high, a low K species can increase its fitness simply by interacting with a high K species (see Figure 7.3).

This last finding corresponds to the situation in psychoanalysis, where C is kept high. (The psychoanalytic situation is intended to maximize the opportunities for communication between the various components of the patient and the corresponding components in the analyst.) The simulation suggests that when a system with low internal connectedness (the patient) interacts under these conditions with a more highly connected system (the analyst in his professional role), then the fitness of the system with a low level of connectedness will increase. This is precisely what we want to happen in an analysis.

Is there some equivalent for the therapeutic relationship of the optimal state of the simulated ecosystem where $K = C$? Is there an optimal degree of coupling between the analyst and the patient? Quantitative estimates for K and C in the analytic ecosystem seem out of the question in our present state of knowledge.

During the analysis, one would expect the change in connectedness for the patient to be much greater than the change in connectedness for the analyst. K will rise sharply for the patient, but only a little for the analyst. Since C must be the same for both, K could not be equal to C for both of them.

K might be equal to C if the patient were coupled to the analyst's simulation of the patient, however. The connectedness of the analyst's simulation can, in principle, increase as fast as the connectedness of the patient's mental organization. But the connectedness of the analyst's simulation depends in large part on the extent to which the increase in the patient's connectedness becomes part of the analytic discourse. Then $K = C$ would hold for the therapeutic relationship if the changes in the patient's inner connectedness were recorded in the analytic discourse.

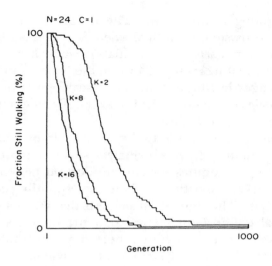

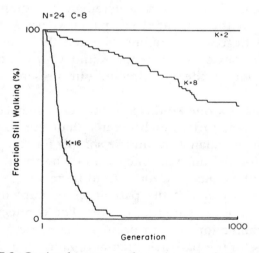

Figure 7.3. Optimal connectedness in coevolution. Fraction of 100 co-evolving pairs of species which have not yet encountered a Nash equilibrium and hence are still walking, as a function of generations elapsed. (From *The Origins of Order: Self-Organization and Selection in Evolution* by Stuart A. Kauffman, 1993, p. 247. Copyright © 1993 by Oxford University Press, Inc. Used by permission of Oxford University Press, Inc.)

Is this possible? Since the changes in the patient's inner connectedness have been stimulated by the events recorded in the
analytic discourse, one might think so. But to make this assumption one would have to ignore the patient's self-organizing capabilities. The patient is, after all, applying what he learns in his
analytic sessions to his life outside the analysis. He learns also
from the feedback he gets from the outside world when his behavior changes. The analyst may be the last to know about these
changes.

Even more significant is the fact that the patient himself may
be unaware of an increase in his inner connectedness until a
new situation arises that requires him to use it. Richard was quite
surprised to find himself much less angry with his parents when
he saw them for the first time after several months of analysis.
Patients are almost always surprised to find themselves dealing
more effectively with troubling situations during analytic treatment. Because so much of the structure building activity in the
patient is unconscious, further analytic work is usually needed to
bring it into the analytic discourse.

On the other hand, it is hardly ever possible to set a clear
boundary to the extent of the analyst's own inner organization
as it participates in the interaction with the patient. His simulation of the patient contains unconscious elements that will eventually be identified, but have not become conscious to him yet.
These unconscious elements of the analyst's simulation are usually in contact with aspects of the analyst's self-image of which he
is unaware just then. While these components of the analyst are
accessible to him under ordinary circumstances, their relevance
to the patient may remain obscure for an extended period.

This uncertainty was probably on Freud's mind when he
spoke of the necessity for the analyst to maintain a state of evenly
hovering attention in listening to the patient. He was trying to
encourage the analyst to expose his own unconscious feelings and
processes to the manifestations in the analysis of the patient's
inner life. No limit exists, a priori, to the kind or number of
the analyst's inner components that may be activated while his
attention hovers. These components cannot yet be included in
the analyst's simulation. Freud's advice was aimed at widening
the scope of the simulation.

Despite these conceptual problems, it appears that an optimal coupling effect can be approximated if the patient is encouraged to express his *thoughts, feelings, and fantasies* about the analyst, that is, to make his model of the analyst as explicit as he can. This allows the patient to increase his own internal connectedness using his model of the analyst as a kind of template for new connections. The analyst certainly makes do with much less feedback from the patient, but at times the analyst would be wise to elicit a response to details of the current state of his simulation.

No doubt the analyst and the patient are actually working simultaneously at multiple levels of K and C, related in ways that have yet to be mapped out. One major issue here is the relation between the connectedness of mental contents accessible to consciousness at the moment of the analytic transaction and the connectedness of the patient's mental contents as a whole.

Kauffman also finds, remarkably, that when C is high in a coevolving system [$N = 24$, $C = 20$], an increase in K for either partner will increase the fitness of both partners. This means that the coevolving ecosystem is autocatalytic, or self-organizing. A coevolving analytic situation seems to have similar properties. An increase in the connectedness of either the patient's mental organization or the analyst's simulation of it can start a chain reaction that may continue for a long time. The fitness of both analyst and patient will be raised by this sequence. Thus, the analysis is driven by the shared self-organizational dynamic in addition to the pressure built up behind the unmet needs of the patient. Changes in the analyst move the patient ahead (toward the edge of chaos and greater fitness), and vice versa. As C increases during the analysis, the capacity of the ecosystem to self-organize will also increase.

This in turn suggests that we think of the analytic situation as a Level 2 Fontana organization, with patient and analyst as interacting Level 1 organizations (autocatalytic sets). The analytic discourse would play the role of the glue in a Level 2 organization. Like the glue, it is produced only by the interaction of the Level 1 components and therefore cannot be replenished independently of those components.

The elements of the glue in a Level 2 organization do not belong to either of the original interacting Level 1 organizations.

Similarly, the analytic discourse does not belong *exclusively* to either coevolutionary partner. It could not have been created separately by either one of them. Like the glue, the analytic discourse disappears when the interacting organizations separate at termination.

The analytic relationship and a Level 2 organization as currently implemented by Fontana are different in one critical respect. The Level 1 components of the Level 2 organization do not change because of their membership in the higher order structure. In contrast, the presence of the analytic discourse leads to a series of reorganizations in the patient's internal structure and in the analyst's simulation of it. Kauffman (personal communication) believes that this difference may be due to a lack of flexibility in the structure of the algebraic expressions that make up the Fontana organizations.

Patients usually feel dissatisfied at the termination of an analysis when the analyst expresses his belief that the patient has internalized the structure of the analytic process sufficiently to carry it on by himself. Yet it seems to the patient that something precious is being lost that requires the presence of the analyst. This reaction is sometimes considered evidence of insufficiently analyzed dependence on the analyst, but it may also be real grief over the discontinuation of the analytic discourse. The patient's newly won independence is the fulfillment of his goals for the analysis, but it is not a direct compensation for the discontinuation of the process that creates the analytic glue. It takes some time for the patient to realize that he actually contains the analytic discourse and that he can rework its contents for his own (not coevolutionary) purposes.

Elizabeth Zetzel (1965) coined the term *therapeutic alliance* to describe an aspect of the analytic relationship that Freud (1912) had included in his concept of the *positive transference* (Kanzer, 1981). The therapeutic alliance is the structure of mutual trust that allows the work of psychoanalysis to proceed. The origins of the therapeutic alliance have been much debated. Zetzel believed the patient's capacity to form a therapeutic alliance was inborn and that it could be ascertained during a brief period of evaluation. Others (Greenson and Wexler, 1969; Curtis, 1979) felt that this capacity could be acquired in the course of analysis.

One must be careful to make appropriate distinctions in using terms like *working relationship* (Greenson, 1967), *therapeutic alliance* (Zetzel, 1965), or *holding environment* (Winnicott, 1965). A therapeutic relationship poised near the edge of chaos is one thing. A therapeutic relationship stalled at a Nash equilibrium with a suboptimal fitness level is quite another. I believe that Greenson and Zetzel both intended to describe a relationship between the neurotic patient and the analyst when poised near the edge of chaos. They were criticized for describing what the critics took to be a stalled Nash equilibrium instead.

Winnicott's point was quite different. He was saying that for many seriously ill patients, the first stage of treatment must be the establishment of a Nash equilibrium. For these patients, movement toward the edge of chaos is possible, if at all, only after the equilibrium has been consolidated. If the achievement of a Nash equilibrium is a precondition for the treatment of a borderline or psychotic patient, however, then the analyst might do better to keep the patient focused in a way that restricts C to a lower value. This will shorten the time needed to reach equilibrium. It may also reduce the potential of the analysis for reconnecting and reorganizing the content of the patient's mind. Some analysts have dreamt of a therapeutic setting for doing analysis with psychotics in which no effort is made to reach an equilibrium "until they are ready for it." In other words, the patient is allowed to regress without limit. Although analysts like Winnicott seem to have succeeded with this strategy on occasion, it seems to me that the dynamics of the therapeutic relationship work against a positive outcome in this situation.

Kohut gives the appearance of believing that the achievement of a Nash equilibrium is all that is necessary for any patient. This seems to me to be as far as treatment can go when the analyst encourages mirroring or idealizing transferences. Movement to the edge of chaos will always be either premature or dangerous if the analysis is approached from this point of view.

These differences in attitude bear on a longstanding controversy among analysts as to the curative factors in analytic treatment. Most analysts adhere to Freud's view that *interpretation* is the key to change for the better in the patient. Others support the idea that the quality of the analytic *relationship* is more important to the outcome of treatment.

Traditional Freudians tend to believe that psychoanalysis is appropriate only for some patients. The advocates of the analytic relationship often work with patients who suffer from character disorders, borderline personality, and psychosis. Object relations theory takes the middle ground in this controversy.

The polarization can be moderated if we understand that two different therapeutic goals are in question. For the severely ill patient, the achievement of a stable evolutionary equilibrium in analysis has enormous benefits. The patient feels steadier and more secure. He feels internally coherent as the analyst mediates among his contending component systems.

These advances are often sufficient for him to restructure his extra-analytic relationships to give himself greater comfort. This positive outcome may be very dramatic, but it can take place with little depth of self-knowledge. Because of this, the patient will continue to have difficulty in facing unpleasant aspects of himself in the analysis. He will resist any movement toward the edge of chaos. Optimal fitness levels may remain far beyond his reach. He remains at considerable risk after the analysis is over.

More lasting change is possible in the neurotic patients who come to analysis already confident that coevolving ecosystems (human relationships) have a strong tendency to reach a Nash equilibrium. These patients can tolerate mutational departures from the equilibrium trajectory without feeling that the path to an eventual equilibrium is endangered. They can postpone the achievement of equilibrium, perhaps even until it inevitably occurs at the end of the analysis.

Obsessive patients with a dependency phobia find the Nash equilibrium state itself to be threatening. They avoid talking about wishes and needs but want to leave treatment whenever they feel that "nothing is happening." Patients with this problem need to be confronted with their warded off anxiety more rigorously than most. Here, the analyst's action to move the patient toward the edge of chaos is not only optimizing but essential to the continuity of the analysis.

Disturbing the Nash Equilibrium

The analyst must be able to judge how much movement away from the Nash equilibrium and toward the edge of chaos can be tolerated by the patient at a given time. This is not something the analyst knows in advance. His judgment depends on the current state of his simulation of the patient, that is, on the current state of the coevolutionary partnership. The analyst is constrained by the danger that the patient may be disorganized by his intervention rather than reorganized. This would result in a stiffening of the patient's defenses (an expansion of the food set of his infantile attractors), lost momentum in the analytic work, or even premature termination of the analysis. With stakes so high, the analyst is more likely to underestimate the patient's capacity for movement away from equilibrium than to overestimate it.

In physical systems, movement away from a local optimum is facilitated by increased randomness. Heat or noise can be introduced to bring this about, in the process called *annealing*. In organic evolution, randomness increases through mutation and genetic crossover. What is the equivalent in psychoanalysis?

Heat and noise play their parts in shaking up the analytic patient's defenses, but pain and loss of control are still more effective. The analyst plays a catalytic role in making these reactions optimally productive. His interpretive interventions fill in the links missed by the patient because of his internal resistances.

Freud discovered that the most useful source of novelty in the patient's experience of himself was the evidence of unconscious mental activity reflected back to him by the analyst. He recognized that dreams are the most reliable and accessible examples of this otherness within the self. By identifying links between these novelties and the patient's ego, he helped the patient incorporate this new data into an enlarged self-schema. This process of interpretation, involving both analyst and patient, has an effect in the coevolving analytic relationship equivalent to the random mutation in biological evolution.

8 DREAMING, SELF-ORGANIZATION, AND THE THERAPEUTIC PROCESS

Dreaming and Memory

Dreaming is an adaptive function of the brain that selects representations of new experiences for storage in long-term memory (Palombo, 1978). The selection process evaluates superimposed images of current events and past events already stored in memory. When the superimposed images form a coherent whole, the new experience is connected in memory with the experience it matches. Freud called the mechanism in dreams that superimposes the representations of present and past events *condensation*. He believed that condensation was a defensive operation that degraded the content of material emerging from the unconscious.

Freud's (1900) original theory of dreams suggested that a dream is initiated when a repressed impulse breaks out of the unconscious. This impulse acts unilaterally to find a means to express itself in consciousness. It takes over other elements of mental activity, the residues of the previous day's experience, and uses them to transport itself into the awareness of the dreamer. Freud's more general theoretical program had defined motivation as a flow of energy from states of higher to lower potential. Pribram and Gill (1976) noted that this choice made it difficult for Freud to imagine any sort of purposefully collaborative or reciprocal intrapsychic process within his metapsychology. In "Some Additional Notes on Dream Interpretation as a Whole" (1925a), Freud expanded his earlier view. He noted a more balanced interaction between the impulse emerging from the past and the dreamer's real life concerns of the dream day. He said:

> It is possible to distinguish between dreams *from above* and dreams *from below,* provided the distinction is not made too sharply. Dreams from below are those which are provoked by the strength of an unconscious (repressed) wish which has found a means of being represented in some of the day's residues. They may be regarded as inroads of the repressed on waking life. Dreams from above correspond to thoughts or intentions of the day before which have contrived during the night to obtain reinforcement from repressed material that is debarred from the ego [p. 111].

The mechanism Freud called *Verdichtung,* or condensation, actually plays an adaptive rather than a defensive role (from *dicht,* cognate with *thick* and *tight*). It brings together separate dream elements so that their relationships and relevance to one another may be drawn out.

Freud did not fully embrace this idea, although he came very close to it when he compared condensation in dreams with Francis Galton's method of constructing family photographs. He said: "[The dreamwork] superimposes, as it were, the different components upon one another. The common element in them then stands out clearly in the composite picture, while contradictory details more or less wipe one another out" (p. 650).

References to Galton's method appear three times in *The Interpretation of Dreams* and again in Freud's essay "On Dreams" (1901). Yet Freud paid little attention to the adaptive goal of Galton's method, which was to discover what the family resemblance consisted of. Galton wanted to know what features were common to the family members, and what relationship existed between these common features and other aspects of the family identity. For Freud, however, the aim of condensation was not cognitive. It was to combine separate charges of psychic energy that were too weak to assault the repression barrier of the unconscious on their own.

This idea of Freud's is consistent with the literal meaning in German of *Verdichtung*, which is *thickening*, as in the thickening of soups and gravies. His use of this culinary metaphor fits in well with his theoretical notion that condensation is a procedure for the concentration of psychic energy. Yet it fails to capture his sense of condensation as the superimposition of entities related but still distinct. This sense is strong in his references to Galton's method, and in the many examples of dream analysis in his publications.

However, the term *Verdichtung* has a punning sense that captures the idea of condensation as superimposition almost exactly. The German word for poetry is *Dichtung* (cognate with *diction*). *Verdichtung* can be read to mean "turning something into poetry." Metaphor in poetry is the verbal form of comparison by superimposition, a linguistic equivalent of dreaming. A dream condensation looks strange because it is a visual metaphor, rather than a straightforward communication (Palombo, 1984b, 1987).

Displacement, the second major mechanism at work in the construction of the dream, is the essential mechanism of defense. Displacement breaks down meaning by intruding new elements into old structures. It acts unilaterally, imposing the substituted items as if by force. Freud's term for displacement, *Verschiebung*, brings with it the sense of violent action missing from the paler English word chosen by Strachey. *Verschiebung* comes from the same Germanic root as *shoving*. It means "pushing or shoving something aside."

The unilateral action of displacement breaks down complex systems. Condensation, on the other hand, works in a bilateral or bipolar mode common to activities that are mutually coordinated. Though condensation is a simple mental operation, it belongs to a larger hierarchy of coordinated activities that create information. At the lower levels of the hierarchy we find such simple biological processes as the recombination of nucleic acid molecules to form novel genetic types. (The oncogene or oncovirus breaks down and disorganizes these genetic combinations by a process we might think of as molecular *Verschiebung*.)

In the *Introductory Lectures on Psychoanalysis* (1917), Freud says: "But although condensation makes dreams obscure, it does not give one the impression of being an effect of the dream-censorship. It seems traceable rather to some mechanical or economic factor, but in any case the censorship profits by it" (p. 173).

I take the "mechanical or economic factor" to be an indication that condensation does work, as opposed to the dream censorship, which interrupts work. Freud is saying here that the mechanism of dream construction has a wider scope than the activity of the censorship. Condensation is part of a basic mechanism, *essential* to the dream in a way that displacement is not.

Condensation binds together the present and the past. It superimposes two sets of sensory images to produce a third composite image that reveals a common aspect of the original two (Palombo, 1976, 1977, 1978). It is like the process of sexual reproduction, which superimposes two genotypes to form a new combination. The composite image produced by the act of condensation shows the family resemblance hidden in the superimposed images, just as Galton's method finds the family resemblance in his superimposed photographs.

Condensations of events, images, and fantasies that comprise an unconscious infantile attractor arise from a similar process. The issue is the same: how is a new event related to an event already experienced? Superimposed images mark a connection that registers an equivalence of some kind. However, both the criteria for establishing a connection and the use to which the procedure is put are very different in the infantile attractor. In dreaming, the criteria are general. Any similarity of meaning, feeling, timing, or sensory quality is a basis for forging a connection in long term memory that could be useful in the future. Neither the use itself nor the set of conditions under which the connection may be useful needs to be known at the time the dream takes place. Moreover, the dream imagery is discarded after it has done its part in making the connection. Only under exceptional circumstances is a dream remembered.

In the formation of an unconscious infantile attractor, the criteria for making a connection are much more focused. The question is whether the new event will lead to a danger already experienced. If the chances are judged to be high, the new event is registered as a repetition of the old danger situation. None of its other features or characteristics matter. Any possibility that the information it carries might be used in the future is shunted aside. The events connected in a dream remain distinct in memory. The new events consumed by an attractor lose their separate identities.

One of Freud's greatest insights was his recognition that unconscious mechanisms in dreaming and symptom formation are *similar*. One of his worst mistakes was to think they are *identical*. Psychoanalytic theory has been off the track for one hundred years because analysts have been unable to notice or acknowledge this error. Hartmann's efforts to promote psychoanalysis as a general theory of mental life had no chance of success because Freud's failure to make this distinction could only turn normal psychology into a branch of psychopathology

The adaptive condensations of the patient's dreams play an essential role in modifying the pathological condensations of his unconscious infantile attractors. The royal road to knowledge of the unconscious is a two-way street. New information enters the unconscious through the patient's dreams. Dreaming is the pathway that leads from the analytic discourse as it takes place in real time during the analytic session to a timeless internal representation within the patient.

In a dream, the condensation is created de novo for an adaptive purpose. It is not itself intended to be stored in long term memory. Consequently, dreams are ordinarily forgotten within minutes of their occurrence. In contrast, images of the undistorted individual events superimposed in the dream are frequently recovered when the dreamer associates to the dream, hours or days later. Images of the individual events are not consumed in the act of superimposition.

However, the dreamer may be awakened during the dream, either by anxiety generated in the dream itself or by an external stimulus. Then the dream imagery becomes part of his waking consciousness. It can be remembered like any other event. When the awakening is caused by anxiety, the dream imagery is often incorporated into the waking fantasy life of the dreamer, especially if the dreamer is a child.

These anxiety-laden dream condensations incorporated during childhood form an important ingredient in the contents of an infantile attractor, contributing to the irrational and often fantastic characteristics it displays. However, the dream imagery does not in itself explain the closure of the attractor set. This is a matter of structure, dictated by the defensive role of the attractor.

The attractor's job is to reduce the overwhelming variety of experience to a few stereotypes that can be handled by the child's undeveloped cognitive capacities. PARRY is a classic illustration of this behavior, reducing the entire vocabulary of the interviewer to 1500 key words. The food set of the attractor must be very large, to take in every possible sign of danger. The output of the attractor is very small, because the number of responses must be limited to assure safety. Condensation in the attractor actually does have the character of a thickening as well as that of a metaphor.

Unconscious infantile attractors and long term memory are different kinds of psychic structure. Memory has its own attractors, motifs that organize and partition the vast compendium of life experience. Unconscious infantile attractors are not part of that compendium. They intercept and redirect new information before it reaches the stage of careful sorting responsible for the fine structure of memory.

When an unconscious infantile attractor is active, access to long term memory is blocked. In Richard's case we saw how the closed set of an unconscious infantile attractor could open up when he recovered an excluded memory. One example was the "bizarre memory" of the family's waterskiing boat that his father was unable to enjoy because he was always focused on the problems it caused. This memory broke through Richard's dominating fantasy that if he followed his father in becoming a man he would have to remain tied to his father's depression.

With the development of the neural network model, the issue of memory structure has received new attention. The question of superimposed representations has become central to the study of memory. In "A Distributed Model of Human Learning and

Memory" (1986), McClelland and Rumelhart put forward their view of memory acquisition:

> We see the traces laid down by the processing of each input as contributing to the composite, superimposed memory representation. Each time a stimulus is processed, it gives rise to a slightly different memory trace—either because the item itself is different or because it occurs in a different context that conditions its representation. The logogen [meaningful event] is replaced by the set of specific traces, *but the traces are not kept separate.* Each trace contributes to the composite, but the characteristics of particular experiences tend nevertheless to be preserved, at least until they are overridden by canceling characteristics of other traces. Also, the traces of one stimulus pattern can coexist with the traces of other stimuli, within the same composite memory trace [p. 193].

How are images of past events selected for superimposition on the day residues to form the composite condensed image experienced by the dreamer? These images represent significant events of childhood, events often associated with repressed wishes and impulses. The events of the dream day (or events within a few days of the dream day) have evoked or stirred them up. In Freud's word, these recent events are the *instigators* of the dream. My research has shown that the day residues appearing in the dream imagery are in fact associated with these instigating events (Palombo, 1978, 1988). The day residue is a displacement from or substitute for the significant but objectionable event of the day that stirs the unconscious.

Past events represented in the dream are related to the day residues by similarities of sensory image, narrative sequence, and affect. The formation of a condensed composite image in the dream would be impossible if this similarity did not preexist the matching. It seems that a vast array of representations would have to be scanned so that only those past events that already had some degree of similarity to the day residue could be chosen for superimposition. Before the two representations could be matched in the sensory projection mechanisms, a minimal relationship between them would have to be found. Whatever stirring may have taken place during the day, *the activation of the repressed wishes to be represented in the dream cannot be completed until the process of dream construction has begun.*

A systematic search of the entire memory for past events related to the day residue would not be feasible. Too many items would have to be sorted through, even using the heuristic search procedures that have become the hallmark of cognitive simulation in artificial intelligence.

Freud used two vivid images to illustrate his views on the storage of new experience. The *mystic writing pad* (Freud, 1925b) represents the normal situation for memory. The *cauldron of seething excitations* is more like the case where repression is dominant. Both images suggest the neural network model.

The mystic writing pad helps us visualize the sinking of the current representation into the composite long term structure, as does the neural network model. Unlike the neural network model, however, the mystic writing pad does not allow us to visualize the intact retrieval of the current representation at a much later date. An individual representation can only contribute to an overall tendency of the system, at the cost of its individual features.

The cauldron of seething excitations (Freud, 1923) is a more subtle case. Although "impressions" sink into it, they are not absorbed into a composite image. They remain separate and intact throughout, though the seething cauldron image suggests a very intense kind of mixing and blending.

Freud was trying to understand the emergence of repressed impulses from the id. He had several ideas about how this might happen, each of which attributed a different degree of autonomy to the impulses. The seething cauldron image suggests that the impulses are truly autonomous. They contain such a charge of restless and unbound energy that they simply overwhelm the repression barrier that holds them in.

Freud's idea that condensation is a method for building up a sufficient charge of psychic energy to penetrate the repression barrier is a variant on this theme. In this version, however, the individual features of the condensed impulses would be lost as the composite was formed.

At the intermediate level of autonomy is Freud's idea that repressed impulses emerge from the unconscious or the id by attaching themselves to the day residues (Freud, 1900, p. 563). Freud tried to reduce the dependence of the impulses on the day residues by declaring the day residues "trivial" and "clear of associations." Their function would only be to provide a disguise from the censor. Still, the day residues are not, in fact, anything like being clear of associations.

Finally, Freud conceived of the repressed impulses as stirred up by specific events of the dream day. This is the sense in which the day residues act as instigators for the formation of the dream (Freud, 1900, p. 561). The recording of events of the present in which fresh impulses are acted out induces the retrieval of specific events of the past associated with similar impulses.

The neural network model offers a biologically plausible mechanism for the last of these three hypotheses of Freud's. A central issue is whether impulses can float freely in the seething cauldron, ready at any moment to begin their attack on the repression barrier. Evidence from both the clinic and the laboratory suggests that impulses are stored as action components of memories. These memories are found in associative structures that must be entered and searched before the action component of a particular memory can be mobilized (Palombo, 1978, 1988).

The Evolution of Dreaming

Neither reptiles nor birds exhibit the rhythmic human pattern of REM sleep, although birds appear to have short, sporadic bursts of something that resembles it. The earliest cloacal mammals, the egg-laying platypus and echidna, are also lacking in the physiological signs of dreaming. Of these, the echidna has been studied at length by Winson (1985). In contrast to the egg-layers, all live-bearing mammals, both marsupial and placental, go through regular cycles of REM sleep.

The brain of the echidna has huge frontal lobes, proportionately larger than any other mammal's excepting only ours. Winson suggests that the echidna needs these extravagant frontal lobes because it has no long term memory. It has to reinvent the wheel every time it wakes up. A famous neurological patient, known as H.M., was inadvertently immersed in an echidnalike state by bilateral temporal lobe surgery for epilepsy (Scoville and Milner, 1957). He could carry on what looked like a normal life during the day, but could not transfer any of his experience into long term memory. He felt that he was starting over from scratch when he awoke each day. H.M. could retain new skills acquired through procedural memory, however. The echidna has similar abilities.

Rats have been deprived of REM sleep immediately after learning a demanding new task. They retain much less of what they had learned afterwards than rats allowed to sleep normally. Having to learn a brand new kind of maze, for example, calls on the rat's *unprepared memory*. This kind of memory is disrupted when the rat is deprived of REM sleep during the following sleep cycle. Tasks requiring only *prepared memory*, like learning a new route through a known maze, are not affected by REM deprivation.

Unprepared memory seems in general to be representational memory, mediated by the hippocampus. Prepared memory in prehuman mammals, like the rats in these experiments, is procedural. This schema is not absolutely watertight, however. Prepared memory in humans may at times be representational. This is an area that needs to be explored further experimentally.

Do the rats dream? We cannot elicit the subjective experience of dreaming in nonhuman animals (or from human infants, for that matter). However, the evidence of hippocampal involvement in their REM sleep strongly suggests that integrated cortical images are present. Our nearest relatives, the great apes, are just on the border of dream awareness. According to Savage-Rumbaugh and Lewin (1995), bonobos or pygmy chimpanzees reach a level of intellectual development equivalent to that of a 30-month-old human. This is just the age at which the idea of a dream becomes meaningful to a child. Koko, a gorilla trained by Patterson (1981), produced sequences of sign language with an incipient narrative quality. Interspersed in these protonarratives were intrusions that read like dream imagery. Patterson interpreted these intrusions as evidence that Koko's mind was wandering. One of them had an unusually vivid and frightening character that suggested a remembered nightmare to me. My 15-month-old daughter awoke in agitation from a nap one day. She said, "Judy fall down,'' referring to our housekeeper. Judy had not fallen down within recent memory. Some time later I remembered that Judy had much earlier been in the habit of playing with the baby while lying on the floor. A plausible explanation might be that the child had been frightened by Judy's posture during their play and had superimposed that experience on her memories of falling while learning to walk.

I believe the onus in this matter is on those who claim a radical discontinuity between adult humans and their nearest relatives in the mental correlatives of REM sleep. The same is true for those who argue that children cannot be said to dream until they actually tell you so. It is hardly likely that REM sleep in human infants is transformed into actual dreaming just at the moment when infants acquire language. Human children become able to identify dreams as such long after they have been reporting fragmented dreamlike experiences.

When pieced together, the various sources of evidence suggest a continuity of dreaming and memory consolidation in all live bearing mammals from the opossum to the person. We can conclude with some confidence that dreaming is a robust function of the brains of the most intelligent of animals over the last 200 million years. The corollary to this theorem is that dreaming performs an essential adaptive function for these animals and for humans.

Dreaming *Is* the Edge of Chaos

We can hardly find a better example than in dreaming of mental activity operating near the edge of chaos. The contents of the dream have neither the predictability of waking thought, taken by many to be the norm of mental activity, nor the randomness that a few sleep physiologists have proposed on and off during the last century.

The outcome of a dream is a reorganization of memory, and the dream itself is a means to this end. When we remember a dream, we have an unusual opportunity to see the images of our past and current experiences being matched and sorted to increase the adaptability of our memory systems. Dreaming is a specialization that creates a continuous phase transitional state, a remarkable invention of the viviparous mammals. It is the biological equivalent of controlled nuclear fusion. Among the many complex adaptive systems we know, nothing else is quite like it.

The physiological cost of maintaining a continuous phase transitional state is very high. Dreaming sleep requires a higher level of cerebral blood flow and consumes more oxygen than either waking thought or nondreaming sleep. Bodily functions necessary for interaction with the environment are diminished (sensory receptivity) or suspended (voluntary muscle action). The ability of mammals to reorganize their memory stores every day of their lives gives them a dramatic adaptive advantage. They are willing to pay the costs in energy and in isolation from the environment in order to dream.

Dreaming and the Therapeutic Process

Dream interpretation has had a central role in psychoanalysis from the beginning. Freud (1900) called dreaming "the royal road to knowledge of unconscious mental activity." However, as for knowledge, dreaming works both ways (Palombo, 1976, 1978, 1980). Dreaming is the neurophysiological gateway to long term memory. It is during the process of dream construction that the significant events of the day are selected for permanent storage in long term memory and represented there for the first time. Among the most significant events for analytic patients are the new connections created by the work of the analytic hour. These connections become a permanent part of the patient's mental structure during the dreams of the nights following the hour.

When new representations are introduced into permanent memory during dreaming, the mind is active. The new material is connected to the previously recorded memories with which it has been successfully matched in the dream. However, the new material also precipitates a reorganization of the region surrounding it in its new location in long term memory. Fresh connections are created that link it with other nearby memories in the associative memory network. This new organization can create associative bridges between related but previously disconnected items, especially those that were actively disconnected by repressive mechanisms.

The introduction of new material into long term memory is a phase transitional process. It reorganizes an already existing structure by adding new connections to it. The extent of the reorganized region for a particular dream varies according to what we might call the bridging potential of the new material. When the patient's experience of the analytic hour is introduced into long term memory, the phase transitional effect of the interpretive work of the hour itself is consolidated. The record of the therapeutic interaction, what I have called the analytic discourse, has an exceptionally high degree of bridging potential.

This intrapsychic reorganization created and consolidated by the dream parallels the reorganization taking place in real time during the analytic hour. The analyst's intervention during the hour and the dream that afterwards incorporates it into the patient's long term memory are counterparts in the overall process of therapeutic reorganization.

Dreaming for the patient is the interior phase of the coevolutionary process of the analysis. The connections made in the common space of the analytic hour, between the patient and the analyst, are reconstructed within the interior space of the patient when he dreams.

One might ask if this interior reconstruction requires the patient to dream about the analyst. This is a complicated question, the cause of much confusion in analytic circles. Transference dreams of the patient (in which the analyst is identified) and countertransference dreams of the analyst (in which the patient is identified) have at times been treated in the analytic world with superstitious awe. Dreams of the patient in which the analyst is identified as himself are thought by some to indicate that the analyst has stepped out of his objective role and gratified the patient's neurotic wishes in some way. Gitelson (1952) suggested that the patient should be referred for treatment to someone else if the analyst appears undisguised in the first dream reported in the analysis.

When Harris (1962) questioned other analysts in a cross-sectional study of reported transference dreams, he found that about 10 percent of reported dreams are transference dreams. In other studies of dreams reported by patients, 3 percent were transference dreams. Nine out of 10 patients reported a transference dream at least once. No evidence has been found of any prognostic significance in the timing or number of transference dreams for a given patient.

Most dreams reported by patients (perhaps all of them) have transference implications that can be discovered through analysis. Unprepared learning is usually difficult to isolate from background information in adult humans. But the analytic hour is a situation where unprepared learning is the rule. We can expect to find the experience of the analytic hour regularly represented in the dreams that follow the hour. The figure of the analyst is superimposed on the various transference figures with whom the patient has connected him.

The composite figure formed by the superimposition may have no identity at all in the dream (a vague or ghostlike figure, "Someone I've never seen before"). It may be identified with someone who has something in common with both analyst and an important object from the past (for example, a spouse, teacher, guide, boss, or monster). Or the dreamer may openly name either the transference object or the analyst. ("I was talking to my cousin the psychotherapist in her office, but I knew it was really you.")

Defensive efforts to reduce anxiety may determine how the identification is made. Most often, the patient is concerned to conceal the references to the analyst, because the analyst is present at the time of the dream report and because his presence is exerting an influence over the patient's current life situation. Sometimes concealing the original transference object is more important to the patient. Naming the analyst as the dream figure may be a way of distracting him from some especially humiliating childhood experience coming close to the surface.

Countertransference dreams are less common than transference dreams. This is what one would expect, since the individual patient is one of many who occupy similar roles in the analyst's professional life. The analyst is also well prepared for the events of the analysis. His simulation of the patient draws on his experience with many patients, and the course of the analysis is familiar to him. His work with the patient relies in large part on his procedural memory, though it characteristically deals with representations.

The relative rarity of the countertransference dream compared with the transference dream is consistent with the differences in the coevolutionary goals of the analyst and the patient. What does this imply about the meaning of the countertransference dream when it does actually occur? Does it indicate, as some have suggested, that the analyst has stepped out of his analytic role?

Lester, Jodoin, and Robertson (1989) have shown that a countertransference dream does indeed indicate a problem in the analytic relationship, but the problem concerns both parties. The analyst's dream reveals that he and the patient are colluding in some way to avoid painful memories of the patient's early life. Analysis of the dream exposes the nature of the collusion and points a way to resolve it. The dream is actually the first step in the resolution.

The countertransference dream brings us back to an earlier question about the extent of the change in the analyst necessary to make the analysis work. A countertransference dream can be seen as an aberration, but the analysis of the countertransference dream is a critical part of the analyst's role as analyst. Whenever he analyzes his countertransference, the analyst is operating near the edge of the analytic relationship, and near the edge of chaos. He is both inside and outside the relationship, dealing with a component of his own personality that is intruding on his work as an analyst. The analyst is improving his analytic technique, but also learning something new about himself.

A pair of interlocking transference and countertransference dreams illustrates some of these issues. The countertransference dream here occurred at an unusual time, on the night following a dream reported during an interview to determine the possible value of an analysis to the prospective patient, Joan. Joan was a depressed woman in her forties who had appeared in the analyst's office earlier in the week heavily bandaged from a recent self-mutilatory attack.

The first hour had seen a continuous stream of rage and invective. Joan complained about her husband's passivity, her daughter's failure in school, her former therapist's incompetence, the cruelty of her parents, and the indifference of the fates. She wanted recognition from the world and could easily imagine committing mass murder to achieve it. In fact, she seemed quite dangerous. The analyst was not enthusiastic about her request for treatment.

In the second hour Joan was much calmer. She reported having a recurrent dream just before coming to see the analyst. In the dream she was left standing on a railway platform. She was supposed to take the train with an unidentified older man, but the man was on the train as it pulled out of the station without her, leaving her feeling devastated. As it usually did, the dream concluded with an orgasm.

Joan reported that at age 9 she had run away from home and her mother's harshness by taking a train to a cousin's house in a city some distance away. She had neither ticket nor money and was treated in a very unfriendly way by the personnel on the train. She was very frightened, but felt good when she was retrieved by her cousin. After four happy months at her cousin's house, she was taken home by her mother. A year later she was taken by her mother on a much longer train trip to another country. This trip initiated a separation from her father lasting more than a year. Her parents did not get together again when her father reappeared. Although she saw him frequently, she was never able to reestablish the close relationship she had with him before the separation. When her mother died three years later she became seriously depressed.

Joan displayed considerable insight in relating these experiences of childhood to the dream and to her present difficulties. That night the analyst dreamed he was on a subway train on the way to his grandmother's apartment when he was a child. The train lost its electrical power and the analyst, along with the other passengers, had to leave it and walk along the tracks in the dark to the next station. The dream was based on a childhood experience of separation. When he was 6, his younger sister was quarantined with scarlet fever. His mother took him on a long subway ride to stay alone for several weeks with his grandmother. Near their destination, the train had stopped between stations. They were without lights for several minutes, but stayed on the train. The analyst was terrified but afraid to express his fear.

Two weeks after being left with his grandmother, while visiting a variety store with her, the analyst saw a toy caboose for an electric train set. On the back of the caboose was a working tail-light. He begged his grandmother to buy him the caboose, although he knew very well that without the rest of the train set he could never get it to light up. When his grandmother refused to buy it, the analyst-to-be was broken hearted. He remained obsessed with the toy and went to the store to see it again several times.

The countertransference dream had located an episode in the analyst's childhood experience that closely matched the patient's. In her dream and in his, the feeling of loss due to separation from an oedipal object was minimized by displacement to an isolated phallic–erotic fantasy. The countertransference dream also contained an additional element not overtly expressed in the patient's dream. This was the wish not to be kept in the dark about the meaning of the separation, to have the painful but obscure experience illuminated. In fact, the countertransference dream did provide the analyst with illumination. He had never before made the connection between his anxiety in the darkness on the train and his later obsession with the light on the caboose.

This countertransference dream was useful in several ways for the analyst. It provided a plausible hypothesis about the patient's psychodynamics based on the match with his own experience. It gave him a sense of being constructively in touch with the patient's unconscious. And it supported the impression he had begun to form during the hour that, despite her apparent lack of ego strength, the patient was able to work psychodynamically. The analysis that followed was long and difficult, but of great benefit to the patient.

The boundary that separates the analyst as an analyst from the analyst as a person must be permeable to some degree. An analyst may be capable in theory of successfully completing the analysis of a particular patient without undergoing personal change himself. In practice, the analyst must be prepared to learn from situations like this, in which an unresolved issue in his own emotional history is evoked by the patient's communications. To the extent that the analyst still has such unresolved issues, the success of his analytic work will depend on the discovery of the points of contact between his issues and the patient's.

The interaction between Joan's dream and her analyst's illustrates important features of the coevolutionary dynamics in analysis. First, the interaction is very specific. It focuses on similar feelings about similar events in the lives of the analytic partners, not on more generalized feeling states. We see such a link being made in the analyst's dream, where the contents of the analytic hour, including the patient's dream and her associations to it, were matched with his childhood memory. Second, the coevolutionary mechanism has access to unconscious cognitive procedures and unconscious memories. It readily calls on them to fill the gaps in the working models being developed. Although as a rule the analyst is less reliant on these unconscious aspects of model building than the patient, their use may be critical when his view of the patient is undergoing a major reorganization.

Phase Transitions in the Creative Process

The associative network built up over years of dreaming is exposed to our view in individual dreams. This network is the foundation of and the prerequisite for logical thinking. The associative network also provides a rich source of data for the continuing discovery of similarities and the creation of new meanings. Dreaming provides a method for combining this material in a way that promotes the recognition of novelty just when it makes an assertion of similarity.

In his book on creativity, Arthur Koestler (1964) refers to this elementary act of creation as *bisociation*. He says: "I have coined the term 'bisociation' in order to make a distinction between the routine skills of thinking on a single 'plane,' as it were, and the creative act, which, as I shall try to show, always operates on more than one plane. The former may be called single-minded, the latter a double-minded, transitory state of unstable equilibrium where the balance of both thought and emotion is disturbed" (pp. 35–36).

As described here by Koestler, bisociation is another name for comparison by superimposition. He sees dreaming as a kind of silent background condition for the individual creative act: "We might say that while dreaming, *we constantly bisociate in a passive way*—by drift, as it were; but we are, of course unaware of it because the coherence of the logical matrices is weakened, and the codes which govern them are dormant'' (p. 178).

Subjective descriptions of the creative process usually refer to a silent or unconscious preliminary phase in which the basic conception of a new work forms itself. Some writers emphasize their waking efforts to approach the involuntary state of mind they experience while dreaming. For most artists and scientists this can happen without conscious prompting, once they have immersed themselves deeply in the material they have chosen to work with.

Perhaps the most famous description of this state comes to us from the French mathematician Henri Poincaré. He says (1913):

> Permit me a rough comparison. Figure the future elements of our combinations as something like the hooked atoms of Epicurus. During the complete repose of the mind, these atoms are motionless; they are, so to speak, hooked to the wall. . . . On the other hand, during a period of apparent rest and unconscious work, certain of them are detached from the wall and put into motion. They flash in every direction through the space (I was about to say the room) where they are enclosed, as would, for example, a swarm of gnats or, if you prefer a more learned comparison, like the molecules of gas in the kinematic theory of gases. Then their mutual impacts may produce new combinations. What is the role of the preliminary conscious work? It is evidently to mobilize certain of these atoms, to unhook them from the wall and put them in swing. . . . However it may be, the only combinations that have a chance of forming are those where at least one of the elements is one of the atoms freely chosen by our will. Now it is evidently among these that is found what I called the *good combination* [pp. 46–47].

When Poincaré writes in this passage of one essential element of the combination as "freely chosen by our will," he appears to mean the element chosen by our wish to solve the problem in the present. The second element of the combination, the one that takes the creator beyond his immediate problem solving ability, comes from some unpredictable location in his store of experience.

Though Poincaré does not specify a relationship between this "unconscious work," as he calls it, and dreaming, the similarity is plain. The combinatorial activity in both cases is critical to the result. But it is possible to make an even deeper connection between dreaming and the creative process than this analogy suggests. The creative process makes use of dreaming in a very particular way.

The recovery of a critical memory in the creative process is similar in form to the retrieval of matching early memories in the dream. But the memories that play this crucial role in the creative process may in fact be the *actual* memories retrieved in dreaming. My hypothesis is that the critical memory in Poincaré's good combination has recently been retrieved by a dream that may not itself be remembered (Palombo, 1982, 1992a).

Artists and scientists have reported from time to time that the creative inspiration for an important project came to them directly from the memory of a dream. Kekule's discovery of the benzene ring through the dream image of a snake swallowing its tail is probably the best known of these anecdotes. However, more often a critical image or idea appears suddenly in waking consciousness after a period of incubation. This image or idea links an aspect of the current problem with the solution to an unexpectedly similar problem buried somewhere in memory.

What is the intrapsychic event that terminates the incubation process? The answer, I believe, is that the missing element has been recovered from the recesses of the memory structure by a recent dream.

Patients who report a dream in analytic therapy spontaneously recall a past event whose imagery is represented in the dream about a third of the time (Palombo, 1984a). If the patient is asked whether the dream image reminds him of a specific past event, the frequency of recall doubles to two out of three. The process of dream construction appears to make these often remote memories accessible to waking consciousness for a week to 10 days after the dream has taken place.

The memories of the distant past activated by the process of dream construction are stored in a short term memory structure from which they can be retrieved voluntarily during this 7- to 10-day period. These early memories are then available for daytime matching, and so for the waking creative process.

The question is whether the memories retrieved *by dreams that have not been remembered* are accessible to waking consciousness in the same way. When a dream is remembered, it serves as a ready-made probe for the recall of these events. The memory of the dream experience connects with the memory of the life event incorporated into the dream and is now temporarily stored in short term memory.

A similar connection is likely to take place when an unexpected and seemingly unrelated memory appears with no apparent source during free association in analysis. Perhaps the analyst's intervention acts like a remembered dream as a probe into the pool of memories revived by the patient's recent dreams. The artist or scientist may be fashioning his own probe into a temporarily accessible pool of dream-generated solutions when he reexamines his previous work on a problem.

This idea would help to explain the subjective feeling that creative inspiration is *involuntary*. The participation of the creator's dreaming in the creative process cannot be called into action by conscious effort. It can only be experienced subjectively as a kind of unexpected gift. Nevertheless, the creator is acutely and sometimes defiantly aware of the contribution to the created work made by the practical skills and conscious intentions that shape the probe.

How does the artist or scientist make his inner vision meaningful to his audience? How does the psychoanalyst convey his insight to the patient in a way that makes an emotional impact? My answer would be that this communication takes place through the matching of the artist's or psychoanalyst's discoveries (his newly created condensations) with those in the unconscious of his audience or patient.

Thus the completed creative act requires a dreamlike superimposition at a higher level than the dream. The dream itself finds a common ground between the dreamer's current interactions with the world (day residues) and the emotionally meaningful experience he has accumulated over a lifetime (childhood memories). The act of creation superimposes the creator's dream products on the traditions and vital forms accumulated during the long and varied history of his culture. The psychoanalyst's intervention superimposes his newly reorganized view of the patient on the shared experience accumulated by the analytic discourse.

9 THE MUTATIVE INTERPRETATION

What Is an Interpretation?

We are ready to understand a psychoanalytic interpretation as any intervention during the analytic session, anything the analyst says or does, that introduces a new connection into the patient's mental contents. An interpretation can be made at many levels, because new connections must be made at different levels in the hierarchy of the patient's mental organization. If we think of the associative memory structure as a tree, then the analyst interprets at the levels of trunk, branch, twig, and leaf and even smaller subdivisions.

Every successful interpretation has a mutative effect on the patient, but the visibility of the effect depends largely on the level of the connection created by the interpretation. At the lowest level, often invisible to casual observation, is an effect that would be roughly equivalent to a single gene mutation in a single component of one system belonging to an ecosystem.

In contemporary psychoanalytic practice, following Freud, an interpretation is usually thought of as a propositional statement with explanatory force. It translates from the language of the unconscious into the language of everyday life. It states, in some variation, that "X (unconscious and obscure) means or stands for Y (conscious and familiar)." An interpretation in this sense implies a causal relationship between unconscious motives and observable thoughts, feelings, and actions.

Strachey (1934) used the term *mutative interpretation* to specify the kind of interpretation responsible for the major changes in the patient's psychic structure. A mutative interpretation, for Strachey, was a transference interpretation; that is, a statement that something currently happening in the patient–analyst relationship was an unconscious reenactment of an earlier event with another influential person.

Strachey did not say that interpretations that are not mutative in his sense have no beneficial effects. But he limited his speculation about these effects to the remark that "you can't make a cake that's all currants." I will use the term *mutative* to refer to the ingredients of the interpretive cake at all levels and scales.

Of course, Strachey's restricted class of mutative interpretations does have its special place in analysis. A successful transference interpretation can cause a major phase transition, leading to a reorganization of some major component of the patient's mental contents. It can be the culmination of a long series of lower level mutative interpretations.

The Analyst Listens

The typical action of the analyst is to listen. Before he can do anything else, he has to get to know the patient. This is not easy, because the patient resists knowing himself. As the patient speaks, the analyst continuously revises his simulation of the patient. This revision happens for the most part in the analyst's unconscious, although the analyst is usually aware of salient issues and ambiguities in the patient's associations. This continuing unconscious revision is Freud's "state of evenly hovering attention." In this state of mind, the analyst is particularly alert to evidence provided by the patient that either confirms or disconfirms his hypotheses. When such evidence appears, he uses it to correct and extend his model of the patient.

The evidence usually takes the form of a story or narrative told by the patient, often punctuated by less organized associations and more direct expressions of feeling. The analyst's model of the patient is constructed from this narrative and from the way the story changes as he and the patient get to know each other better. From the outset, the story contains gaps, distortions and contradictions, all of which stimulate the analyst to listen with closer attention.

The progress of the analysis can often be measured by the gradual transformation of a stereotyped and fragmented story into one that is more coherent and comprehensive, more true to life, flexible and spontaneous. The degree of coherence of the story at any moment provides a rough measure of the inner connectedness of the patient's mental life.

Spence (1982) has suggested that a coherent narrative may be a fiction that does not reflect the historical truth of the patient's experience. According to Spence, the story constructed during an analysis is an artifact that acts as a substitute for a distorted or defective memory of actual events. It is hardly likely, however, that the constructed analytic story could provide a reliable guide to the patient's feelings and behavior if it did not integrate and organize the connections constructed in his mind throughout his lifetime. The story that evolves during the analysis is coherent and consistent because it succeeds in integrating and organizing the patient's inner experience.

Spence appears to think that by introducing external standards of narrative coherence into the analytic discourse, the analyst helps the patient improve the quality of the story, independently of the historical truth of his life experience. The improved story constructed in the space between analyst and patient can then be taken in and used by the patient to replace his own maladaptive structures.

This account falls short in its failure to recognize that the patient's inner structures are transformed, not replaced, by the new connections revealed or reconstructed in the verbal space shared by the patient and analyst.

Transference interpretations are often the culminating mutative events of an analysis. They work at a high level, tying together the neurotic elements of past and present in an especially vivid way. As Loewald (1960) wrote, the analytic situation is like the scene in Hades where Odysseus is required to offer blood to entice the dead spirits to speak. The living person of the analyst is the offering needed to give the patient's internalized objects their chance to speak again in the analytic hour. Loewald suggested that analysis is the process of turning ghosts into ancestors. This is an apt metaphor for reconnecting an isolated and disavowed region of memory content to its historical position in the patient's long term memory.

Preparing the patient for a mutative *transference* interpretation are many lower level interventions that serve to increase the connectedness of his mental contents. These preparatory interventions must be mutative in themselves because they are prerequisites to the phase transitional interpretation. The fact that their effect is cumulative also requires that they be mutative. Any mutative intervention by the analyst has the effect usually attributed to an interpretation.

The Language of Interpretation

While the analyst sees the patient as well as hearing him, most of his information comes through the patient's words. Moreover, the analyst tries to restrict his own communications to the patient to what can be verbalized. Because of its high precision compared with other forms of communication, language is the primary medium of exchange between the coadapting partners in the analytic relationship.

Language has many properties that suit it for this purpose. The first and most important is that language allows the thoughts and feelings of the patient and the analyst to exist outside their bodies in a common space to which both have full access. Thoughts and feelings are private; spoken language is public. Although the analytic exchange is private as far as the outside world is concerned, within the analytic process itself communications are public.

In its public aspect, a language is a system of conventional signs known to both parties in a dialogue or conversation. As far as the partners to an ordinary conversation are concerned, the conventions of the language are given to them from outside. The speakers of the language have no part in creating its basic syntactic and semantic elements. As the units of discourse increase in size they increase in complexity, however. It is not difficult to compose a sentence in any natural language that has never existed before. The combinatorial possibilities are sufficiently vast to make creativity at this basic level almost inevitable in spoken and written language.

The analytic discourse is a highly complex language structure, comparable to the longest written compositions. It is unique to each analytic partnership. Whenever the language of an analysis becomes routine or stereotyped, one can be sure the analysis is far from the edge of chaos. A stereotyped use of the language of the analytic discourse can usually be detected in units much smaller than that of the discourse itself. Differences in the context of an oedipal interpretation, for example, should be reflected in the language in which each interpretation is made. No two oedipal interpretations in an analysis should sound the same, not to mention interpretations made in different analyses by the same analyst.

The cerebral mechanisms of language production are designed to publicize thoughts and feelings that originate privately. Language is a device for transforming hierarchical structures of meaning within the individual brain into one-dimensional sequences that can be transmitted easily between brains. The mapping from thought to spoken language is not one to one. Many spoken sentences can translate the same structure of meaning, each providing a different emphasis or nuance. Many complexes of meaning can be modified by the hearing of a single sentence, as we saw with Richard.

These properties make spoken language a rich medium for the creation of new connections in the mind of another person. Language is inherently transparent, although it can be easily corrupted to deceive. The cumulative effect of language in an extended discourse is to generate finer and finer distinctions of meaning, without limitation other than the skill and imagination of the speakers.

The analyst's use of language is designed to increase the connectedness of the patient's mental contents. The analyst never tries to tell all he knows. He says only as much as he believes the patient can use at the moment. To say more would place an unnecessary burden on the patient. To say less would be to abandon him. It is easy for the analyst to swing too far in one direction or the other. His usual heuristic is to risk saying too little to a patient with a strong ego and too much to a patient with little ego strength.

Natural languages evolve, though not always for the better. One line of Shakespeare is enough to convince most of us of that. It is possible that modern English is easier to read than the English of Shakespeare's time, though translations of the King James Bible into modern English do little to support this idea. The invention of the printing press, and the dispersion of literacy that followed, seem to have created a steady pressure for the simplification of the written language. Whatever the aesthetic sacrifice, this change might be considered an adaptation for the culture as a whole.

Nevertheless, languages evolve at a fairly constant rate. One can date the division of an older language into two or more recent ones to a good approximation by quantifying the differences between them. These divisions create branching family trees similar to the taxonomic charts that illustrate biological evolution. Darwin (1859) believed that this correspondence was no accident. He said: "If we possessed a perfect pedigree of humanity, a genealogical arrangement of the races of man would afford the best classification of the various languages now spoken throughout the world. If all extinct languages, and all intermediate and slowly changing dialects, were to be included, such an arrangement would be the only possible one" (pp. 562–563).

Using the method known as glottochronology, we can tell that Old English split from the Germanic language group in the middle years of the first millennium A.D. Proto-Germanic is probably two thousand years older. The trail begins to cool just a bit when we look for the earliest Indo-European languages from which Proto-Germanic evolved. The conventional view is that Proto-Indo-European originated at about 4000 B.C. This date has been challenged by new research suggesting 6500 B.C. as more likely.

Despite the steady rate of linguistic change, the evolution of human language is punctuated by the emergence of superfamilies, families, and individual languages. Dante was acutely aware that Italian was not just a dialect of Latin. Among the superfamilies, some are more divergent in their membership, therefore older than others. The Eurasiatic superfamily seems to have displaced an even older and more diverse group, called Dene Caucasian, from most of the Eurasian continent.

Surprisingly, the twelve linguistic superfamilies share a small portion of their basic vocabularies (Ruhlen, 1994). Words for *milk, man, knee, digit, pair,* and *pudenda* are present in some languages of each superfamily. At present 30 or more of these universal cognates have been identified.

Thus, the languages we speak today probably contain memories of the most ancient of human languages, as Freud enthusiastically believed. As language has evolved and continues to evolve, it has reflected changes and divergences in geography and climate and in the technology developed in response to change in the natural world. In so doing, language gives us a useful model of evolutionary changes in our cognitive capacities generally.

Like all the evolutionary processes we have examined, the process of language evolution is active at every moment. Changes in English have been dramatic during the last century. The slang of our childhood is long since dated, and often obscure to us even in retrospect. Neologisms tumble out of the daily newspaper, some becoming instant fads. Most fade away within a few months, but others will become a permanent part of our linguistic culture.

The language of the patient's unconscious is a private language, but it deals with common developmental issues. As Freud suggested, the analyst's interpretations can be seen as a translation from the patient's private language into another language, public and familiar. However, at a deeper level, the analyst's interpretations are part of the evolutionary process through which the language of the analytic discourse itself is developed.

The patient and the analyst have to evolve their own common language if they are to communicate effectively. Ancient words from deep in the linguistic past form the basis for the commonality, but the language is brand new nevertheless, since it develops out of their work together, which has no exact precedent. The language of the analytic discourse is shared only by the two of them, but it is a language that describes aspects of the patient's experience that have never been put into words before.

The analyst's interpretations are a living response to the patient's personal meanings, rather than stereotyped formulas. They refer first to what the patient has been saying, only secondarily to the analyst's knowledge of other people. They contribute to the creation of the unique common language that connects intelligibly with the patient's unconscious.

Mental Spaces

The ability of language to set up distinct but interconnected mental spaces in which relations hold only locally is a linguistic property especially important in the analytic process. Fauconnier (1985) describes in detail how this property allows a variety of hypothetical situations to be treated with a flexibility impossible for the simpler logical analysis of the propositional calculus, often taken as a model for scientific discourse.

This example is from Fauconnier: "In Len's painting, the girl with blue eyes has green eyes" (p. 12). This statement, which appears quite illogical at first glance, makes perfect sense if the mental space of Len's painting is distinguished from the mental space of reality. The girl with the blue eyes, the model *in reality*, is represented *in Len's painting* by an image with green eyes. The theory of mental spaces is an essential constituent of any adequate theory of mental representations.

Fauconnier shows that the same analysis would apply in the previous example if the word *mind* were substituted for the word *painting*. "In Len's mind, the girl with blue eyes has green eyes." Len's artistic vision has become a delusion. In a similar vein, *what the patient believes* is a mental space distinct from the space of *reality*. The two spaces may correspond at many points, but not everything the patient believes is likely to hold in reality. In the sentence, "The patient believes his father wanted him to fail," three mental spaces are represented. One has to consider the reality of the speaker, the belief system of the patient, and the space of the father's wishes.

THE MUTATIVE INTERPRETATION 281

The patient has different attributes in each of these spaces. In the speaker's world, he has a definite and substantial belief about his father's wishes. The speaker raises some doubt about the truth of what the patient believes, however. In the space of the patient's beliefs, he is the victim of his father's wishes. He believes that his father wants him to fail, perhaps with the corollary that what his father wants he usually gets. The content of his belief space may or may not correspond with the content of the speaker's world, or of the real world. In the space of his father's wishes, almost anything could be the case. The representation of the patient in his father's unconscious may be confused with other people important to his father. Opposing wishes can coexist without either one being true to life. The patient's father may want him both to fail and to be President. Perhaps each of his father's conflicting wishes deserves a space of its own. But the patient's belief about his father may also be delusional.

Ambiguity often results when mental spaces are not clearly specified in a statement. Fauconnier gives this example: "Oedipus realizes that his mother hates him, but he doesn't know that she's his mother" (p. 150). This statement makes sense if we understand that the phrase "his mother" refers to two different objects of the same description in separate noncommunicating mental spaces. Fauconnier continues: "The noun phrase *his mother* points to an element *a* ("Jocasta") in *R* [reality] and identifies its counterpart *a'* (also "Jocasta") in *R(S)* [Oedipus's reality]; *a* is the value of the role "mother of Oedipus" in *R*, but its counterpart *a'* is not the value of the role "mother of Oedipus" in *R(S)*. "Mother of Oedipus" refers to Jocasta in *R* but not in *R(S)*" (p. 150).

The ambiguity of many grammatically well formed sentences, like Fauconnier's example here, suggests that mental spaces are *underdetermined* by the grammars of natural languages. Grammars give useful information about mental spaces, in auxiliary and modal verb forms, for example, and in prepositions, but not enough to differentiate them in a general way. This raises a question about the power of grammars ever to specify a complete range of meanings.

Perhaps the grammar of a language is like the genetic code, creating a potentially infinite set of particular sentences. The grammar of a sentence is like the DNA sequence of a gene. It specifies the structure of a particular protein. Mental space structures are like the apparatus of RNA molecules and ribosomes that construct the protein within the three-dimensional world of physical reality. The analogy is imperfect because neither the grammar of the sentence nor the mental space structures specify the meaning of the sentence. But then again, neither the structure of the gene nor the RNA apparatus specifies the function of the protein.

In an evolving organism, a particular protein is not assembled until a need for its function arises. This need is created by what we might call *the semantics of the organism,* laid out during the development of the embryo. What a sentence means depends on the semantics of the speaker's mental organization, which also has powerful historical sources. The role of spatial organization in the physical realization of a coded message can hardly be underestimated.

At the level of brain function, it cannot be a coincidence that the hippocampus, a tiny region in the medial temporal lobe, performs three important but superficially unrelated functions. It is the integrator of the highest level of sensory association areas of the cortex (Cohen and Eichenbaum, 1993). It is the location of short term memory and the agent of long term memory formation in the cortex during dreaming (Winson, 1985). It is also the constructor of spatial representations for the brain as a whole (O'Keefe, 1989). The simplest of these functions, spatial representation, must be the foundation on which the other two are built.

Coming back to mental space confusion in the clinical situation, we would like to know whether we can find a consistent relation between such confusion and the outputs of infantile attractors. What we do know is that confusion of mental spaces is a cardinal sign that an unconscious attractor is influencing the patient's associations. A confusion of mental spaces is similar in this respect to a logical contradiction, but at a more subtle level. The most obvious and significant anomaly of this kind is confusion about the boundaries of the analytic discourse.

The analyst can help the patient clarify the boundaries of his mental structures by calling attention to the ambiguities they create. For example, a patient was describing his father's violent behavior throughout his childhood. The analyst was preparing a comment about the difficulty of living with an insane parent. His aim was to reinforce the patient's shaky perception that it was safe to expect a different kind of response from the male authority figures in his current life.

Just as this point the patient said, "There was a lot of insanity in my house." The analyst replied, without thinking, "Literally." The brief reply was an acknowledgment that his thoughts and the patient's were intersecting, but also a statement that the term *insanity* was not simply a metaphor meaning *wild* or *exaggerated.* The patient continued with a story about how his father's verbal attack against him in a parking lot had caused the horrified on-lookers to lodge a complaint to the local government child abuse office. A social worker arrived at the scene and a very embarrassing investigation was initiated. The patient mistakenly believed he had already told this story to the analyst.

The analyst's comment affirmed that the abnormal behavior of the patient's father belonged to the space of reality, rather than the space of imaginative reconstruction and embellishment. This affirmation would be controversial for some analysts who believe that the role of the analyst precludes a judgment about the reality of any event reported by the patient. They reason that the distortions in fantasy of the child are due to purely instinctual influences, which they assume to be well known. They therefore believe that comparing the patient's fantasies with the reality of his childhood experience is unnecessary. The reality of childhood experience is something they consider to be unknowable anyway.

The distortions in childhood fantasies are distortions of real experience, however. Distortions of different experiences during childhood are themselves different, and the difference makes a difference. The analyst must be able to affirm that the present life of the patient is not *in reality* a replication of his childhood, despite what may be powerful feelings to the contrary. In particular, the analyst himself is not a reincarnation of the patient's parent, as he demonstrates throughout the analysis by his objective approach to the patient, in reality.

The analytic discourse is itself a mental space as described by Fauconnier. It is unusual in being a space shared by two people. Questions of truth apply to the analytic discourse with respect to what was said, by whom, and on what occasion. These are facts that can be disputed. But the content of what is said by the patient is treated by the analyst as the indirect expression of his wishes. It does not matter whether the patient is making a disinterested report on something actually happening or expressing a bizarre fantasy. Within the analytic discourse, the patient's communication is always motivated.

Not everything said during an analysis is said within the space of the analytic discourse, however. The decision to begin treatment, for example, is meant to be taken literally by both parties, as are the analyst's statements about the practical conditions for treatment, including scheduling and payment. Of course, these practical issues will become part of the analytic discourse if the patient uses them to disrupt the analysis, as a nonverbal means of expressing ambivalence and anger. But the analyst must also deal with them outside the analytic discourse, for example, by tactfully insisting that he be paid on time.

The patient has many other ways of expressing feelings nonverbally. Silence during analytic sessions, conscious withholding of unpleasant or frightening material, somatization, acting out of transference wishes away from the analysis, these must be put into language that can be shared in the analytic discourse. The analyst cannot assume, however, that what happens outside the analytic discourse is exclusively a symbolic communication. A patient with somatic symptoms, for instance, should be checked by the appropriate medical specialist.

Within the boundaries of the analytic discourse, the patient is prone to a persistent confusion between the mental spaces of past and present. The unconscious infantile attractor is a pathological mechanism that creates and sustains such confusion in a misguided effort to avert dangers that no longer threaten. But the patient's past itself consists of many interconnected spaces, not all of them accessible to the others.

Typically, the patient sees and responds to something happening in the present as if it were a repetition of an earlier trauma. The analyst can make the patient aware of this confusion by saying, "It's as if your [father, mother, sister, brother] were doing [whatever it is] to you again." Specificity about both the actor and the action are necessary to define the particular mental space of the past that is now the scene of the attractor.

Temporal mental spaces can be of any size or shape. "When you were a child, the day your sister came home from the hospital, in college, just before you had your period, just before you reached your climax, whenever you're feeling depressed, since you've been in analysis, in our last session, just a minute ago," are all mental spaces in which roles, actors, and actions may assume special properties. Ghosts and ancestors occupy different mental spaces within the larger space of the past. By making the patient aware of incongruities in his verbal construction of mental spaces, the analyst helps him locate the attractors that have created the confusion.

The scene of an attractor may, of course, be several scenes superimposed on one another, at times including among them the scene of an event that happened just the other day. It is the rule, not the exception, for example, for the scene of infantile sexual curiosity and conflict to be superimposed on the toilet training scene. This kind of confusion seems so natural that parents often reinforce it by telling a child that its new sibling is "in mommy's tummy." This anticipates the almost universal wish that the new sibling be flushed down the toilet when it arrives.

Naturally, the analyst's interventions often have the aim of helping the patient differentiate and distinguish his erogenous zones. These zones, which may be the most salient of all mental spaces in adulthood, are the easiest for a child to confuse. It is of considerable interest that although the erogenous zones are constituted by basic biological facts, in analysis (and very likely in development) they achieve the status and function of distinct mental spaces only through the conceptual powers of language.

When confused mental spaces are differentiated, new psychic structure is built. This is the same process as the expansion of the laws that govern the input–output conditions of an infantile attractor, though looked at from a different direction. This is why the analyst's efforts to expose the confusion of mental spaces are met with resistance. The confusion is the outward sign of an unconscious attractor pulling the patient away from the diversity and complexity of the real world.

The analyst does not have privileged access to the contents of the real world, as Spence (1982) emphasizes. But, compared with the patient, he does have a privileged perspective on the coherence and comprehensiveness of the patient's story. He has a better opportunity than the patient to notice the mental space confusions that appear in the patient's contribution to the analytic discourse. He can recognize more readily than the patient the intrusion into the discourse of an attractor that necessarily compresses and distorts the patient's input from the real world.

Fauconnier's analysis of the space set up by the phrase "In Len's painting," applies not only to Len's mind, but to his thought, belief, expectation, wish, hope, fear, fantasy, dream and hallucination as well. An element in any one of these spaces may have different properties from its counterpart in any of the others, like Jocasta in the example we examined earlier.

Analysts often assimilate these various kinds of mental space to the categories of wish and fantasy. An unacceptable wish is rendered inaccessible to consciousness, repressed. But the wish is likely to reappear, often in a disguised version, in the patient's fantasies. In the space of a fantasy, a wish has no consequences, no necessary counterpart in the real world. Neurotic patients can usually distinguish a wish from an action, once they can recognize and acknowledge the wish.

However, patients with more severe forms of pathology often have difficulty in making the distinction between wishes and actions even after years of treatment. For these patients, becoming conscious of a wish is the same as acting out the wish, and has the same consequences. Although they may do very well in everyday tasks, they cannot distinguish wishes from actions when feeling is high. They live in constant fear of their own impulses. This very primitive defense is a serious (though not necessarily insuperable) obstacle to psychoanalytic treatment.

The confusion or conflation of mental spaces and their accompanying affects is characteristic of the supracritical phase of mental organization, on the chaotic side of the edge of chaos. In the subcritical phase, on the ordered side, mental spaces and their affects are often separated artificially, with an unnecessary proliferation of spaces creating the paralytic situation described in Zeno's paradox.

In the obsessive or depressive patient, ideas and events are partitioned off from the feelings they produce. At times the events are retained in consciousness only if the feelings become unconscious. The space of reality is divided by this defensive maneuver into cognitive spaces whose contents are conscious and acceptable and affective spaces whose contents are unacceptable and unconscious. However, representations of events that arouse the most objectionable feelings can also be denied access to consciousness. Unacceptable feelings enter consciousness if they are separated from the events that caused them and displaced onto other events.

Here the analyst's task is to help the patient reconnect the divided spaces. For example, "Maybe you felt that way about your mother, too." This task is more direct (though not necessarily met with less resistance) than the analyst's task with conflated and confused spaces. When spaces are conflated, they must be separated by being reconnected with other spaces that are unambiguously different from one another. An example of this (said to a male patient) might be, "But your mother not only paid a lot of attention to the other kids in the house [as your wife does], she also went to bed with your father."

Diverting the Stream of Consciousness

Can we specify the simplest action by the analyst that can be called a mutative intervention? The word *intervention* is itself problematical. It presupposes that the patient lives in a self-contained intrapsychic world, a world the analyst may enter only through an act of self-assertion. This picture gives a one-sided view of the therapeutic interaction, which relies on a degree of openness between the coevolutionary partners. Nevertheless, it underlines the fact that the patient can take the analyst's words in a variety of ways, or leave them, if he chooses.

The simplest intervention must be small enough, but it must also illustrate the process of change through increased internal connectedness. Even the mere repetition by the analyst of a significant word or phrase spoken by the patient can fulfill these criteria. The repeated word or phrase can create a new nodal point in the stream of the patient's associations. (Nods and grunts may need to be included here.)

The analyst's repetition of a word connects what the patient is saying right now with the cumulative structure of associations built up during the analytic process as a whole. It transforms the patient's soliloquy into a dialogue with a known history. The repeated word, including its context in the current train of the patient's associations, is fitted into an open slot in this larger structure. With longitudinal connections along the time line of the analysis, the slot also has many lateral connections to other related elements of meaning and experience. When the analyst connects the significant word of the moment with the overall structure of the analytic discourse, he is connecting the patient's associations in the present to the cumulative structure of associations they already share.

The analyst's decision to intervene, even in such a simple way, is determined by the current fit between the patient's associations and the analyst's simulation. The analyst intervenes when he is faced with evidence (a discontinuity of some sort) that confirms or disconfirms the hypotheses generated by the simulation. He recognizes that at these moments something new is being added to the analytic discourse.

With the repetition of the word, a new associative pathway running through the patient's associative networks intersects the stream of his spoken associations previously recorded in the analytic discourse. These intersections mark a set of nodal points in the patient's memory structure. The analyst's intervention facilitates exploration from these nodal points into new associative territory.

It also transfers a piece of the analyst's internal simulation of the patient into the shared discourse of the analysis. The analyst is informing the patient that the word or phrase is significant to him, that it has a meaningful place in his model of the patient and his behavior. He is telling the patient that what the patient is saying now, right now, is linked in a significant way to other meaningful statements he has made earlier in the analysis. Because the simulation is a hypothesis and may be wrong in its details, it can only be shared when it is supported by evidence provided by the patient.

The analyst is connecting the associations being explored within the patient's own memory structure right now with the cumulative structure of associations built up within the analytic discourse. The connection may be with a significant statement made by the patient just a moment ago, at the beginning of the hour, in the previous session, when his father died, or when he first entered the analyst's office.

Associations are never free in the sense of being random. They appear only along pathways that lead to and from other quite specific associations that form their context in memory. The number of possible associative pathways leading from a given nodal point at any moment is therefore limited. However, an observer, whether the patient himself or the analyst, cannot predict the direction of movement of the patient's associations from that point. Local motivational forces make this choice, outside the patient's awareness and usually beyond the analyst's powers of simulation.

In practice we find a partial exception to the indeterminacy of the associative pathway. When the analytic interaction is taking place near the edge of chaos, the motivational forces at work may be well known to both patient and analyst. Moments of uncanny anticipation by the patient or the analyst can occur near the edge of chaos.

Thus, the mutative potential of the analyst's intervention is already in evidence with the repetition of a single word. The analyst simply marks the point of connection, leaving it to the patient to find the items to be connected. This is, in a way, the ideal intervention. It minimizes the intrusion of the analyst's thoughts into those of the patient.

However, the patient often needs more help than this from the analyst. The patient is suffering from anxiety and repression. His spontaneity and curiosity have been inhibited. He is seeking treatment for symptoms caused by blocked or failed connections that have plagued him for most of his life. He has adapted to the lack of functionality caused by the loss of these connections. His emotional investment in maintaining himself at this unsatisfactory local optimum is considerable. For these and other reasons he may resist making the needed new connections on his own.

Omissions and obscurities in the patient's story are usually motivated, as in the familiar example of the Freudian slip. These gaps in the story may be filled if the analyst simply asks how one apparently disconnected item relates to another. Clarifying questions of this kind often explore the syntax of the patient's utterance. The analyst may ask about chronology or spatial configuration. He may ask who is doing what to whom, with what, or why. The connection established by a clarifying question may provide access to a new associative pathway.

At a more complex level of mutative intervention, the analyst specifies where he thinks the patient's current associations fit into the associative structure of the analysis. He says, "This [word, phrase, feeling, event] reminds me of what you said [just now, at the beginning of the hour, in our last session, etc.] about [such and such]."

How this intervention is worded is not important, of course. Reference to the patient's saying what he said or when he said it might be superfluous in a given instance. However, I find the patient much less resistant to reminders of what he has said previously than to statements that appear to originate entirely with the analyst.

The analyst may also effect small and gradual changes in the patient's inner connectedness by paraphrasing statements that are already close to making a new connection. A paraphrase makes explicit a link that was implicit in the original statement but was not expressed directly. For example, if the patient uses an unusual word to refer to both her mother and the analyst, the analyst may say, "Your mother and I seem to have something in common." He may add, "Although we usually seem so different to you."

A paraphrase is a hypothesis. The analyst may make this explicit by saying, "It sounds as if . . . ," or, "Perhaps you're telling me that. . . . " The patient may continue with her train of thought, comment on the hypothesis or respond with new associative material. Her thoughts may move in parallel with the analyst's or intersect them.

The hypothesis behind the analyst's paraphrase must be supported implicitly by evidence provided earlier by the patient. If the same point has been gone over more than once during the analysis, the labeling may be unnecessary, as in this example. A patient said, "We haven't turned on the new air conditioning yet. I'm afraid I won't be able to go outside again." The analyst said, "You're afraid it will soften you up." Her efforts to harden herself to deny unpleasant feelings had become a recurrent theme in the analytic discourse by this time.

A paraphrase is usually most effective when it stays close to the patient's words of the moment. Still, the patient's words about similar situations spoken earlier in the analysis can often be fruitfully recalled in the paraphrase.

A paraphrase refers to something the patient has said, but the patient may be sending a message through his actions instead. The analyst may describe these actions to the patient. For example, "There seems to be a pattern in your coming to the hour five minutes late every time." He may point out that a message is being sent, as in, "You must be telling me something by paying me late every month." Content in the message may also be identified: "You must have been very angry to skip an appointment without calling me first." The analyst will usually begin with the plain description, but he generally becomes more explicit if the patient remains unresponsive after several go arounds.

When the patient is resistant to these attempts to draw him out, even after repeated effort, the analyst may have to identify specific elements in the patient's discourse that the patient cannot acknowledge openly. For many patients, especially obsessive patients, difficulty in expressing feelings is a paramount symptom. The analyst may say, "You must have felt [angry, sad, tempted, frustrated] when that happened." Or, "Maybe you [were, are] feeling the same way about me [when I said that, right now]."

Recognizing the analyst's impression of his feelings is often easier for the patient than noticing how he is feeling himself. As long as this remains true, however, the patient will remain at a distance from the edge of chaos. The analyst's intervention must always be considered as transitional to the patient's taking over this function on his own.

When he offers a hypothesis about what is happening in the patient's mind the analyst runs a risk, especially if the patient himself is unaware of it. Unless the analyst supports his interpretation with evidence from the patient's previous statements, his

suggestion can be misinterpreted. A borderline patient may believe that the analyst is imposing a misguided fantasy of his own.
A neurotic patient may try to convince himself that the analyst is
correct whether or not he is.

Perhaps the most familiar intervention by the analyst is the
identification of unconscious conflict. The patient tries to decide
whether he is feeling one way or another. The analyst suggests
that he may be feeling both ways in spite of the apparent logical
contradiction. Sequestered memories of events in which both
feelings were prominent may then become accessible. Conflict
can be identified at many levels, from clashing feelings of the
moment to apparently incompatible life goals. The analyst is concerned here primarily with the identification of localized conflicts
in the here and now.

An important but often neglected intervention is the identification of the patient's unused capacities. For defensive reasons,
the patient presents himself as disabled in a variety of ways. When
he provides evidence that under certain circumstances he is quite
able to perform, this should be noted by the analyst. His disavowal
of the function has the same significance as the repression of a
fantasy. The patient is helped to reconnect the missing function
when he is reminded that the alleged disability must be due to
an unconscious inhibition of a capacity that works perfectly well
when he is not anxious.

The interventions listed above do not directly attribute a
causal effect to unconscious motives. Interventions that directly
impute unconscious motivation are only successful when the patient is already near the edge of chaos. Such direct interventions
must be used sparingly at other times. Resistance is greatest when
the analyst claims privileged knowledge of the deepest levels of
the patient's psyche. The patient will have more conviction about
the value of interpretations of unconscious causality if he is in a
position (near the edge of chaos) to make them himself.

However, the patient may resist making connections on his
own, especially if he believes that the analyst is overstepping his
role in the coevolutionary process. If this belief is due to a transference distortion, if the patient has been unresponsive to less
direct measures, and if the patient is near the edge of chaos,

then the identification of unconscious motives is the appropriate intervention.

When the analyst says, for example, "I think you feel that way about me now *because* your mother always turned away from you when you achieved anything out of the ordinary," he is sharpening this issue. When he says "because," he assumes the stance of "the one who knows," in Lacan's phrase, calling attention to the patient's persistent confrontation with authority. The analyst is the authority in the patient's current life who helps him uncover earlier abuses of authority. If he can help the patient acknowledge this paradox, he builds an important bridge to disavowed memories of positive interaction with dysfunctional parents.

The causal interpretation must be used sparingly, however, and with care. It diminishes the patient's initiative in the connection making process, creating an excessive asymmetry in the co-evolutionary relationship. If used too often, it will exacerbate rather than relieve the patient's difficulty in optimizing the benefits he gains from the collaboration with a knowledgeable professional.

The Patient Changes

In Richard's analysis, scattered over a period of about two years, we saw a sequence of unconscious infantile attractors explored and modified by the analytic process. These examples were chosen to illustrate the phase transitional events during which the attractors were uncovered and then restructured by the analytic process. The powerful image at the center of each attractor was the nucleus of a powerfully destructive self-representation.

The culminating phase transitional interpretation takes place when the patient–analyst system is momentarily poised near the edge of chaos. The interpretation acts like a seed crystal dropped into a supersaturated solution. Of course, an interpretation is a more differentiated object than a seed crystal, because in the structured system of the patient's mind it has to fit each of the specific components it links together with precision. When the new organizational state emerges, the cumulative changes in the patient become visible for the first time to patient and analyst alike.

A crystal dropped into a supersaturated solution causes an avalanche of precipitate on the bottom of the flask. Like Bak's sandpile (1996), this avalanche creates a structured heap of particles that behaves according to complex dynamics.

The huge variation in the magnitudes of possible avalanches is due to tiny differences in the structure of the sandpile. These differences are produced by the series of random events that constitute the history of the sandpile. The hierarchy of possible avalanches in the mind of the analytic patient is multidetermined. It is organized by a concatenation of biological and emotional imperatives, frequently in conflict with one another. The point of impact of the analyst's intervention on the patient's associative structures is no doubt much more critical than the location of the grain of sand that sets off the sandpile.

In analysis, culminating interpretations that open a large region of memory appear infrequently. Small avalanches that reorganize a localized area of memory are common. This pattern creates a serious hardship for researchers who try to find linear causal relationships in the sequence of utterances produced by patient and analyst.

Take, for example, the problem of describing the magnitudes or intensities of the phase transitions described in Richard's analysis. A handful of major turning points emerged dramatically during the three years of work discussed in chapter 2. In the next rank we would probably find dozens of significant phase transitions, many of them ignored in the discussion. At the level of smaller phase transitions barely visible to the patient and the analyst, up to a dozen or more may have occurred during each hour of the analysis. Only a tiny fraction could be analyzed in chapter 2.

A phase transition precipitated by a culminating interpretative sequence can be observed to increase the patient's inner connectedness, to move his overall functioning in the analysis nearer the edge of chaos, to improves his fitness, to open sequestered areas of long term memory, and to allow new, more effective, behaviors to emerge. This is a large scale effect, easy to observe.

A significant research effort could be made to count and classify phase transitions at all levels of a complete analysis. At the least, this would require an analysis of associative pathways and their intersections. Since the components of a single middle level phase transition may be widely separated in their times of appearance during an analysis, a concordance of related transitions will have to be constructed as the analysis proceeds. This in itself presents a considerable methodological problem.

As the analyst's simulation of the patient is made more accurate by a new phase transition, his fitness as the analyst of his patient increases. When the analytic ecosystem drifts back again between phase transitions toward a Nash equilibrium, it is likely to move *to a new equilibrium level, higher than the previous one.* While the ecosystem oscillates between the edge of chaos and a Nash equilibrium, its overall fitness will increase and its average distance from the edge of chaos will decrease.

The Emergence of Self-Analytic Capabilities

At least three stages of high level emergence occur in every successful analysis. Each stage must be completed before the next can be reached. The first of these is the achievement by the patient of the ability to imagine a level of fitness above his best level prior to the crisis that brought him into treatment. The patient can begin to plan ahead to reach this new level at this point or soon after. Failure to achieve this capacity often leads to premature termination of the treatment, often within six months to a year.

The second stage is the emergence of a capacity for self-observation sufficient to allow the patient to recognize that important areas of his experience are stored in a region ordinarily outside his awareness. This stage is reached when a critical mass of unpleasant unconscious material has been recovered without intolerable damage to the patient's self-esteem. When this happens, the patient begins to take a more active initiative in the analytic work. He feels less frightened of competing with the analyst in making new connections to previously isolated areas of his mental contents. He may feel that he now knows the very worst about himself, and that the analysis will become less and less painful in the future.

This conviction may be long postponed by unconscious re-sistances. An individual patient may not reach this point until long after the increased connectedness of his mental contents has been amply demonstrated to him through the analytic process.

Usually the patient recovers from his presenting symptoms and starts thinking about leaving treatment before he under-stands in depth how his unconscious fantasies and resistances have contributed to his emotional problems. In Richard's case the sequence was more elaborate. Richard was already working effectively with unconscious material before he returned to his best premorbid level of functioning.

He was already well beyond that level when he started talking about reducing his hours. But it was not until another year had gone by that he reached the stage of knowing that the worst was over. This was when the connection was finally made between his fantasies of self-mutilation and his murderous rage at his mother, when the self-mutilation attractor was linked with his identifica-tion with the hated aspect of his mother and her various surro-gates. The premature wish to leave or reduce the treatment always precedes the patient's discovery that the worst is over.

The third critical phase transition is marked by the emer-gence of self-analytic capacities. The patient begins to imagine that he can simply take over the functions of the analyst and continue the analysis on his own. This is in part a utopian fantasy. Nevertheless, the patient has by this time acquired a considerable measure of independence in his capacity for self-analysis.

At this point in the analysis, the isolated areas of his mental contents have been reconnected with his preconscious sufficiently to be accessible *with work*. Not all such isolated areas become accessible during an analysis. However, at this critical point the patient comes to believe that all such areas are accessible in prin-ciple.

This stage of emergence marks the beginning of the termina-tion period of the analysis. The patient becomes involved in sort-ing out the issues relating to his dependence on the analyst. Real dependence on the analyst's skills has diminished sufficiently for the patient to distinguish it from illusory transference depen-dence carried over from earlier caretaking figures. The fear of ending the analysis also diminishes as this sorting out takes place.

The patient becomes able to mourn for the loss of the analyst's helpful influence without feeling deeply threatened by the loss.

Unless the second and third stages of emergence are reached successfully, an analysis can become interminable. If this happens, it will end only with an intrusion from the external world, to which the patient surrenders without concern for his autonomy. Premature attempts at termination by the patient, motivated by defiance and denial, are a hazard in many analyses. A patient is always relieved when the analyst resists such attempts.

10 THE BEGINNING OF AN ANALYSIS: A CASE ILLUSTRATION

Introduction

Richard's case was chosen to illustrate my thesis because it presented an unusually clear picture of the psychoanalytic process as I see it. One would like to know how well the new theory can be applied to an analysis not preselected for this purpose. An appropriate case to examine would be one recorded and published independently of this book. A case written up before I even began to think about complexity theory would be especially suitable. Of course, the question of my having been influenced by the case would come up, but that would be a less troublesome issue.

The analysis should have been recorded in chronological order, without a bias derived from the analyst's later judgment about the significance of the material. Moreover, it should be published where it is easily accessible. For many reasons, clinical data that meet these criteria are hard to find.

I have made what I think is an obvious choice, the record of an analytic case published in 1972 by Paul Dewald in his book,

The Psychoanalytic Process. Like many other analysts, I read and admired *The Psychoanalytic Process* when it appeared. It includes process notes for each of the sessions that took place during seven selected months of a brief but successful two-year analysis. These 105 sessions include the first, third, and final two months of the analysis. Other sessions (242) are summarized in a few paragraphs each. Dewald provides comments on each of the verbatim sessions, which he says were lightly edited to make them easier to read.[1]

While it was Dewald's aim to keep this clinical material as free as possible of theoretical bias, his own ideas at the time of the analysis naturally influenced the course it took and his comments on it. Nevertheless, I believe he succeeded admirably in providing a representative sample of the events of a psychoanalysis during its beginning, middle and ending phases.

Limitations of space make it impossible to examine more than a few of the published sessions. My original plan was to review individual sessions at one-month intervals starting with the first session of the analysis. Because verbatim notes of the sessions during the second month were not published, I included sessions 1.1, 1.17 (the last of the first month), and 3.1 on my list.

This method is unbiased, but it is not necessarily the best way to locate and examine the critical moments of change in the analytic process. Some compromise was necessary. When I found that a major change had occurred between session 1.1 and session 1.17, which both patient and analyst attributed to an event in the previous session, 1.16, I added 1.16 to the list that already included 1.1, 1.17, and 3.1. (My notation gives the month of the analysis and the number of the session during the month in order to keep the reader better informed about the chronological order of the sessions. Session 3.1 is Dewald's session 35.)

Session 1.1: The Opening Moves

In the first session of an analysis, one often finds the patient telling a fairly well-rehearsed story that precludes a very strong

---

[1] The four sessions analyzed in the text are reproduced with permission in the Appendix.

interaction with the analyst. If the patient has had some experience in therapy, as she does here, she will usually try to recreate the kind of situation that seemed most productive with the previous therapist. Because of this, the interaction with the analyst in the first session may seem to be picking up where the previous therapy left off. However, the fact that the patient is dealing with an unknown analyst, based on limited knowledge about the analyst's role, makes the situation inherently unstable. This factor is ameliorated here because the patient had met with the analyst several months before for a two-session evaluation of her suitability for psychoanalytic treatment.

In session 1.1, the analytic process appears to be close to the edge of chaos, somewhat unusual for a first session. The patient moves easily from thoughts and fantasies about the analyst to thoughts and fantasies about her previous therapist and other important men in her life. Her associations are meaningful, clear in their relationships to other associations, and accompanied by appropriate affect. The sequence in which the associations appear shows this positive movement.

The patient refers in turn to her analyst, her former therapist, her analyst again, her husband, her father(?), her analyst, her former therapist, her father, her former therapist, her analyst, her adolescent boyfriend, her father, her adolescent boyfriend, her father, her adolescent boyfriend, her husband, her analyst, her father(?), and her analyst again. Each association follows in a meaningful way from the one that precedes it. The associations are not repetitive or predictable.

This session begins with the immediate situation of the analysis, switches quickly to the former therapist and then back to the analyst. It goes from there to the patient's current situation with her husband, to the past with her father, and finally back to the analyst. She avoids mentioning her father explicitly. He appears in the associations only when the patient is reminded of him by a previous thought about her analyst, therapist or husband. Thoughts about her father appear more frequently as the hour progresses.

The patient's therapist, her analyst, an adolescent boyfriend, and her father are all linked by the dream she reports and by her associations to it. She says that her husband, the only man mentioned in the hour who is not in the dream, is "the only one to really love me" (p. 23).

Silences in this session last no longer than two minutes. Two of the three silences of that length are deliberately terminated by the analyst, the other spontaneously by the patient. The patient's husband is mentioned for the first time after the analyst's reference to her fear of saying what is on her mind early in the hour. A direct reference to her father appears for the first time after the analyst mentions the patient's anger with himself.

The mobility and motivational coherence of the patient's associations are what we would expect to see when the analytic process is near the edge of chaos. However, the movement leading from her boyfriend to her father in her associations to the dream is the only instance of an association from one past event to another. As the analyst remarks in his notes to the hour, this is the only time she is free from a preoccupation with her current reality and her conflicted wishes to please and defy the analyst. Because of this, the impression that the analytic process in this session is close to the edge of chaos should be qualified. The process is not far from the edge of chaos, but perhaps in the near reaches of the zone of hysteria at the beginning of the chaotic realm.

In this session, a salient unconscious infantile attractor is operating. This attractor has a food set consisting of positive or potentially positive interactions with significant males in the patient's current life situation, including the patient's new analyst, her previous therapist, and her husband.

The autocatalytic rules of the attractor reduce these good experiences with men in her current life to replications of frightening childhood experiences with her father. The products of the attractor are distorted perceptions of the men in her current life, perceptions that take on the negative affects connected with the childhood experiences. The patient finds reasons to feel bad about her analyst, her former therapist, and her husband, to match her experience of the events that originally produced the rules of the attractor.

The session includes four clear examples of such a transformation taking place, under the rules described above. In the first, at the beginning of the hour, the food set of the attractor includes the beneficial effects of the patient's therapeutic interactions with her analyst and with her former therapist. These interactions have occurred in the past, are happening now, and are anticipated. These benign interactions are transformed by the infantile at-tractor into seductions as experienced or imagined in the past with her father, with expectations by the patient that she will be exploited and abandoned subsequently.

The immediate product of this attractor is the fantasy that by becoming pregnant and ugly she can avoid the forbidden grati-fications of sex with her husband and of the therapeutic relation-ship with her analyst. The patient mentions that she has already acted out part of this fantasy by becoming frigid with her husband and by feeling herself repelled by conscious sexual thoughts. She invites the analyst to postpone the analysis until after her preg-nancy is completed.

While she feels repelled by conscious thoughts of sex, how-ever, she has dreams with orgasm, which very likely include imag-ery derived from memories of childhood interactions with her father. The dream she reports later in the session is linked to her father through memories of desperate adolescent sexual activity stimulated (she says) by his abandonment of the family.

The food set in the second example includes all evidence of caring behavior from men. She refers to the analyst's willingness to take her on as a patient and to her husband's willingness to go steadily with her and to really love her when she first met him. This behavior in men arouses her own longings for love.

The infantile attractor transforms these feelings of longing and desire into what seems to her to be an excessive demanding-ness for which she can only expect to be punished. She cites her therapist's "reaction" when she was silent during her hours with him. She thought this was punishment by him for her hiding of her unacceptable wishes toward him. This reminds her of her father's demands that she "jump" whenever he wanted some-thing from her. If she failed to jump, he called her "stupid."

The products of the transformation here are the hostility she feels toward the men who care for her and her fear of showing her positive feelings for them. These transformed feelings are manifest by her silences in the session with the analyst, by her withdrawal from sex with her husband, and perhaps by the impasse that led to her decision to leave her therapist and enter analysis.

When the food set includes evidence that the men in her life reciprocate her feelings of need for them, the rules of transformation become more stringent. In her dream, she was going to show her loving feelings to the analyst, but then ran back to the therapist in fear. This made her feel sorry for the analyst. After her father left, when she was dating, she became promiscuous. "I would conquer something [sic] and then I would immediately start with someone new but it always made me so tired" (p. 23). Then she expresses guilt about not being satisfied with her loving husband.

The experience of a man's reciprocating her own feelings of need was transformed into a conquest. A conquest gives her the opportunity to be the strong one and to dish out the punishment she believes she received from her father for her own feelings of desire.

The products of the attractor in this situation are complex. Along with her sadistic withholding behavior she experiences contempt for and devaluation of those she depends on, like her husband. The dream anticipates a similar situation with the analyst, if he succumbs to her wish for a caring relationship. Her fear of losing her men in this way leads her to cling to "terrible" people (the adolescent boy associated with the man in the dream) who are invulnerable to her demands. It also leads to the fantasy that her children would be taken away from her by the avengers of the men she diminishes, in particular her mother-in-law.

At the end of this fruitful first session the patient has a premonition of success in the analysis. The analyst has listened to her expressions of desire, anger, and fear without either giving in to her or rejecting her. This premonition, now based on a new experience with the analyst, adds to the food set of good but dangerous things to be expected from a man.

The good feeling about the analysis is transformed by the attractor into a defiant act toward her parents, who she is sure will find the analysis unacceptable. She will be punished by their withholding emotional and financial support for the analysis. She is afraid to start the analysis, afraid to "turn my back on my family" (p. 23).

The chief product of this transformation is doubt about proceeding with the analysis. She wonders if she should abandon her wish to overcome her neurotic illness. Is she capable of it, or deserving of it? The only solution is to place herself completely in the hands of the analyst, although she is aware she doesn't even know him. The implication is that she can take this risk because the analyst can always be transformed into another of the terrible people she clings to. She seems quite willing to give up the exercise of her own judgment to enter this Faustian pact with the analyst.

This attractor produces the typical responses expected of a patient suffering from the distortions of experience caused by the Oedipus complex as described by Freud. Her guilt over a forbidden wish to eliminate her mother and become her father's primary romantic object causes her to deny and devalue her positive feelings for men. One can expect that in later sessions the transformation rules of this attractor will be elaborated in much greater detail.

Attractors from the preoedipal period of development are also likely to appear in the analysis. In fact, it is unlikely that the oedipal attractor we see operating in this session will be modified significantly until after the preoedipal attractors have been explicated and their grammars modified. Clues to the nature of these very early attractors appear in her statement, "He was a horrible boy . . . but I would cling to him just as I clung to my life," and in her final assertion of the hour about being in the hands of the analyst, "I feel as if I'm in a vise and I'm caught. It's as if there are all kinds of holes and I'm about to fall through . . . " (p. 24).

Session 1.16: A Conflict of Attractors

The movement of this session appears on the surface to be close to the edge of chaos, as was session 1.1. The patient's associations range over the present and the past, linking the analyst with other figures in the patient's life. However, in contrast to session 1.1, there is a noticeable lack of attunement between the patient and the analyst. This persists despite the patient's efforts to comply with the analyst's wish to continue the exploration of the basin of attraction of her oedipal attractor.

The patient begins the session by saying, "I feel absolutely nothing" (p. 91). A five-minute silence follows. After a prompt from the analyst she reports that her friend Jean may be moving, setting her in a panic. Jean was "the only person I can talk to" (p. 91), a mother-image for her. The analyst responds by suggesting that the loss of Jean would intensify her feelings of dependence on him. He cites her references to feeling panicked and her wanting to block off every feeling as having been caused by her fear of relating to him.

She associates to her dream of the previous night, in which "I felt completely alone in the midst of a terrible disaster" (p. 91). She rushed with her children to the basement because "there were millions of tornadoes all around" (p. 91). Her husband was at work. An older woman came in. Her associations lead her to a painting of a tornado she had seen as a girl. "There was a mother leaning over her children and the clothes were being ripped off her back, and I know it impressed me" (p. 91).

The analyst asks what comes to her mind concerning her trying to get under something in the basement to hide from the storm. She says, "That was in case the house came down, so it wouldn't come down on us" (p. 91). Then, in a state of obvious discomfort, she says, "I want to run back to Harris [her previous therapist] because he knows me. I feel as if I'm being forced to stand alone by myself. No one in the world is going to give me what I want and I have to accept the fact" (p. 91).

Here the patient gives a clear indication that she feels out of attunement with the analyst. She wants to leave him to go to a therapist who knows her, suggesting that the analyst doesn't. She feels forced to stand up alone, as she was in the dream. The analyst is clearly the one who is forcing her. She won't get what she wants. Her imagery suggests that what she wants is to be supported against her fears of abandonment and isolation when her feelings are storming. She laughs and says she feels as if she is falling off the couch.

Despite this imagery, and other references by the patient to a failing dyadic relationship with an unfeeling maternal figure, the analyst now makes an elaborate oedipal interpretation. He ignores the issue of force raised by the patient and focuses on the erotic significance of the painting of a mother with her clothes torn off her back by a tornado. He says, "I wonder if you have a fantasy of getting undressed here, and if you have both a wish and a fear of exciting me sexually" (p. 92).

The patient confirms the interpretation, both explicitly and through associations. She says, "I've thought that I wanted to stand up and take all of my clothes off but that is as far as I can think" (p. 92). She remembers feeling excited during a recent gynecological examination, the first time she allowed herself to have sexual feelings in the examining room. She hoped the gynecologist felt the same. She says, "I've been thinking about being madly in love with you and it makes me excited to come every day and I feel like a schoolgirl with a new boyfriend" (p. 92). But she is shocked by these feelings. They're silly, stupid, embarrassing, and idiotic.

She says, "I want to have feelings and have it not happen. But I'm afraid that you're not strong enough to resist" (p. 92). She used to dress carefully for her sessions with Harris, but has made a point of not doing it with the analyst. She remembers an occasion when she deliberately provoked her father sexually but didn't get a reaction from him. "When my parents used to visit after I got married I would parade around in front of my father in nightgowns or a slip. I was conscious of wanting to attract him . . . It was like I was suddenly saying, 'I'm a woman, Daddy, look at me and realize it.' It never fazed him" (p. 93).

She then reports that she is having great difficulty distinguishing the fantasy of an affair with the analyst from the reality. "How can I go home and love my husband and be sexually responsive? I'd feel guilty, as if I was having an affair" (p. 93). This statement is followed by a three-minute silence. She ends the session by saying, "I can picture it really happening and that I'm not only thinking about it" (p. 93).

From the time of the analyst's interpretation on, the patient's associations provide new oedipal material in response to the analyst's promptings. However, the patient's movement from her preoccupation with an unfeeling mother to the oedipal themes introduced by the analyst appears more compliant than spontaneous. The emotional opposition to the analyst she showed at the beginning of the hour continues despite the thematic shift. Although she tries to stay with the oedipal interpretation, she becomes increasingly uncomfortable with it. Her confusion during the last few minutes about fantasy and reality in her feelings for the analyst is quite atypical of the analytic patient near the edge of chaos.

My impression here is that the patient is simulating compliance with the analyst's clearly and repeatedly expressed opinion about the oedipal significance of her dream and of the transference overall. In simulating her compliance with the analyst's view of the appropriate content for her associations, she also simulates the form of a well-conducted analysis.

This observation, if accurate, is important. It shows that edge of chaos behavior cannot be affirmed from the pattern of the patient's associations alone. Attunement between the patient and analyst is an essential ingredient. We see that the responsibility for attunement is mutual. If either partner is insensitive to the analytic dialogue, and the other doesn't know what to do about it, the analysis can drift away from the edge of chaos. The early weeks of an analysis, when neither partner has a clear picture of the other's ability to recover from such a situation, are especially vulnerable to this sort of disruption.

When the patient is simulating the kind of behavior she knows the analyst wants to see, the analyst is often very cautious about casting doubt on its authenticity. Patients have many ways of camouflaging their output to look like spontaneous associations to the analyst's interventions. Some of these are quite subtle, and difficult for the analyst to recognize, especially if his countertransference feelings obscure the patient's lack of engagement with him. By understanding in detail exactly what are the conditions for an optimal development of the analytic process, the analyst can respond more effectively to the patient's subtle deviations.

In session 1.16 we have another instance where the analytic process, especially in its earliest stages, resembles the prisoner's dilemma. Along with the decision to say whatever comes to mind, the patient must also decide whether to follow the analyst when he tries to channel her associations in a particular direction.

While some analysts might say that the analyst should never try to determine the direction of the discourse, this prescription is impractical when the patient is strongly and persistently resisting the uncovering of unconscious material.

The analyst here is not struggling with a persistent resistance in the patient, however. It is too early to evaluate either the strength or the stubbornness of the patient's resistance. The analyst may be in a countertransference position governed by a need to prove his ability to resist the patient's seductiveness and carry on the analysis in spite of it. At this point, the patient has only two strategies for dealing with this possible defection by the analyst. One is to attempt to comply with his view of the situation and be "a good analytic patient." The other is to change the direction of the analytic discourse by a massive defection of her own. In this session the strategy of compliance wins out over the strategy of disruption.

This struggle to maintain one strategy over the other is evidence of a conflict between attractors. The oedipal attractor that dominated the first session of the analysis is still in control here, but, even with the support of the analyst, barely so. The hour begins in the basin of the dyadic maternal attractor of the pre-oedipal years. This attractor appeared only on the periphery of session 1.1. Here it creates the setting for the analytic hour. The patient is appealing to the analyst to respond to her feelings of loneliness and abandonment. She hopes that his doing so will prevent her feelings of identity loss and annihilation from taking her over completely.

When the analyst interposes the oedipal issues raised in sessions 1.1 and later, the patient tries to follow him. She readily admits to feeling attracted to him and to wishing for a sexual and emotional relationship. She produces evidence that she has felt that way toward other men in authority, her gynecologist in the recent past, and her father in the more distant past. She relates how she provoked her father to respond to her sexuality, and how disappointed she was when he failed to react. She appears to hope that by cooperating in this way she can induce the analyst to be sympathetic to her emotional plight. She asks, "Why don't you ever say, 'I'm sorry, I understand, I'll try to help, and there's no reason for your fear?' " (p. 96).

At the beginning of the session, the dyadic maternal attractor transforms the patient's feeling out of tune with the analyst into anticipations of abandonment and annihilation. However, since she believes the analyst capable of soothing her, these fears remain anticipations only. When the analyst interprets her dream as an expression of an oedipal desire for him, the analysis shifts into the basin of the oedipal attractor again. The patient's positive feelings for the analyst are transformed into feelings of embarrassment, humiliation, childishness, and stupidity, as in session 1.1.

We see the dyadic maternal attractor more clearly than previously in the opening stages of session 1.16. After the dream interpretation it is displaced by the oedipal attractor, although the patient's later confusion about fantasy and reality in her feelings toward the analyst seems to emanate from this preoedipal source. Under the influence of the patient's wish to please the analyst, the analysis moves into the domain of the oedipal attractor. The success of the competing attractors depends powerfully on the analyst's activity and the patient's response to it.

The analyst appears to be reacting to the dialogue about separation anxiety in the early part of the hour as evidence that the analysis was stalled at an unproductive Nash equilibrium. He may have thought the equilibrium had to be upset for the analysis to get closer to the edge of chaos. Perhaps for him, as for many other analysts, the optimal state of the analytic process always includes content at the oedipal level. The patient's response to his oedipal interpretation would have seemed to him like a move in the right direction. However, the nearest thing to a Nash equilibrium here is the collusion between patient and analyst to stay within the basin of the oedipal attractor, despite the disorganization that results.

The return of the oedipal attractor after the interpretation in session 1.16 makes it clear that what might have been behavior near the edge of chaos in session 1.1 was actually a Nash equilibrium state. Both partners were acting according to their preconceptions about the optimal conditions for an analysis. They could produce a reasonable facsimile of analytic work, though not the mutual engagement required for optimal movement. By the end of the hour the patient's discomfort with this situation breaks through. She says, accurately, that she was putting herself entirely in the analyst's hands without even knowing him.

This collusive equilibrium cannot be very stable after only one month of analysis. As we have begun to see at the end of 1.16 and will see quite definitively in 1.17, it collapses with an explosion that drives the analysis further away from the edge of chaos. This is the opposite of what one would hope to see when the analyst intervenes to move the interaction away from a Nash equilibrium. However, although this Nash equilibrium state is unstable at this point in the analysis, it may become stable later, especially if the analyst continues to sustain it.

Session 1.17: Regression

In this session the analysis is far from the edge of chaos throughout, deep in the chaotic realm. The patient states explicitly at the beginning of the hour that this disorganization was caused by the analyst's disruptive interpretation in the previous session. The analyst acknowledges his agreement with this assertion in his written comments, but does not tell the patient during the session that he believes he has made a mistake or that he regrets doing so.

Session 1.17 begins with a three-minute silence, followed by the patient's statement, "I've had a horrible feeling that I was going to pop ever since I was here yesterday" (p. 95). As the session proceeds, she makes more than two dozen references to panic, horror, terror, killing, and destroying. The session is interrupted frequently by long silences: four last two minutes, two more three minutes, and one five-and-a-half minutes.

The patient is almost totally preoccupied with her feeling state since the analyst's interpretation 24 hours earlier. In 1.17 she has only one association to feelings or events before the previous analytic session, "I'm thinking about the time when I was very little and I hallucinated . . . My mother wouldn't come" (p. 96).

She states explicitly that she will not cooperate by following the rule to say everything that comes to mind. She says, "I will not let myself know anything . . . I don't remember . . . I just don't recall . . . The only way to survive is not to feel it . . . I just don't want to talk . . . I just can't do it . . . It's all so horrible I just can't think . . . I can't stand it" (p. 95). These refusals are accompanied by dramatic expressions of suffering and helpless victimhood, and by murderous fantasies directed against the unfeeling analyst and her own (unfeeling?) children.

A thread of continuity links the patient's remarks, supplied by the oedipal attractor. In the previous session, 1.16, the analyst "humiliated" and "destroyed" her by encouraging her to express sexual feelings that he would not reciprocate. She insists that she will not expose herself to further humiliation now. However, expressions of rage, fear, and frustration appear suddenly and explosively to interrupt this train of thought. The only positive feelings for the analyst she expresses during session 1.17 take the form of maternal longings. She says, "I just want to hold on to you and know that you're there" (p. 96).

The patient and analyst are at a coevolutionary impasse. The patient says, "You don't accept my fear because you're afraid yourself. You ignore it or you'll get mad at it but you won't understand" (p. 96). The analyst says in his commentary, "To have avoided these issues or to have indicated my awareness that the interpretation yesterday was premature, or to have actively attempted to reassure her would possibly have interfered with the developing transference situation and therapeutic alliance. She might have experienced such tactics as a sign of weakness or anxiety in me. This would have further mobilized her anxiety" (p. 97). The word *possibly* suggests the analyst's priorities here. His fear of showing ordinary human weakness by admitting a mistake seems to me to underestimate the patient's ability to work with him as indicated in the opening minutes of session 1.16. Her defection in 1.17 may be, among other things, a caricature of his unwillingness to take her into his confidence.

In his comments, the analyst does not propose an explanation for his premature interpretation. It appears to me that although he had noted the intellectualized manner in which the patient presented the workings of the oedipal attractor in session 1.1, he seems unprepared for the strength of the preoedipal attractor on display in this session. The reaction of the patient to his mistake is a massive defection from her agreement to follow the fundamental rule. This is her response to the analyst's retreat from his therapeutic role in the previous session.

After only a month of analysis, the patient has not yet had an opportunity to devise an effective strategy for dealing with the analyst's defection. She can only respond with a defection of her own, a defection so intense that it appears for the moment to deny any hope for further collaboration. Nevertheless, the patient expresses her wish to restore the therapeutic relationship when she says she would just like to hold on to the analyst and know that he's there. This wish is similar to the wish expressed in 1.1, when she fearfully put herself in the analyst's hands. Her willingness to stay with the analysis at this point appears to be based on gratification received in submissive relationships to authority figures in the past, rather than on her current experience of the analysis.

In this hour, the oedipal attractor that dominated session 1.1 appears to have been fused with or overwhelmed by a preoedipal attractor whose presence in 1.1 was indicated by the patient's isolated remarks at the end of the session. It was also out of sight during most of 1.16. The food set of the oedipal attractor consisted of good feelings about men, which were transformed by oedipal guilt into bad feelings about those and other men.

In 1.17, the food set of the now dominant dyadic attractor consists of the patient's bad feelings about a man, the analyst. These bad feelings concern shame and humiliation about sexual wishes. In fact, it appears that they are the same bad feelings previously *produced* by the oedipal attractor, but this time raised to a new level of urgency by the analyst's defection. The patient imagines that the analyst rejects her wishes for a sexual relationship as well the actual relationship she wishes for. That is, she transforms the analyst's therapeutic role into a humiliating rejection of her desire for a more intense and emotional relationship.

The transformation rule of this dyadic attractor transmutes her defensive feelings of rejection and shame into a state of terror, accompanied by a loss of subjective identity, a loss of self-control, and a global state of helpless incompetence. "You said that I wanted to undress in front of you. That's a horrible thing to say! If I let myself go and start feeling, I just can't stand it!" (p. 95). Later on, "You're trying to destroy me. You want to bring out feelings and you don't want to help, but you are just going to sit and watch me suffer and I'm not going to!" (p. 96).

The products of this transformation are feelings of abandonment and annihilation more typical of the second year of life
than of the later oedipal period. The primary object of desire
and frustration for a girl at this time is still her mother. Defection
by a mother at this age is threatening to a child's basic identity
as an independent being. This threat is verbalized by the patient
in 1.17 as a threat to her very existence.

The setting for this fear is purely dyadic. In the operation of
the oedipal attractor, the patient's guilty rejection of her husband, who has been substituted for her father, was to be avenged
by another woman, her mother-in-law. In that case she remained
attached to the male oedipal object as a source of comfort and a
bulwark against the attacks of the maternal rival. In 1.17 there
are only two participants, engaged together in a zero sum game.
Only one can survive. The threat comes directly from the primary
object, leaving nothing in its place if the child succeeds in destroying her. This is a more primitive game than the prisoner's dilemma. Cooperation here is not merely difficult but
inconceivable.

In 1.17, the output of one attractor, the oedipal, has become
the input for another, the dyadic maternal attractor. But this
primitive preoedipal attractor does not take over the patient's
mind on its own initiative. A disorganizing perturbation by the
analyst raises the activity of the preoedipal attractor to the point
at which it dominates the patient's experience. The result is a
transformation that moves the patient from a more organized to
a less organized state, further away from the edge of chaos. This
movement, of course, is in the opposite direction from the movement desired in analysis.

A psychoanalyst looking only at the transcript of this session
would seriously consider a diagnosis of borderline personality
disorder, with discouraging implications for the outcome of the
analysis. Since Dewald's reasons for publishing the analysis include its success and its unusual brevity, however, the reader must
assume that the session represents a temporary hysterical regression rather than a fixed developmental deficit.

However, Dewald's data show very clearly that at this moment
of the analysis, with the patient's current level of overall personality organization as it is, the dominance of one pathological attractor rather than another greatly depends on the state of her

relationship with the analyst. Put more abstractly, the organization of the components of the patient's personality is highly correlated with the organization of the analytic ecosystem. The evolution of the patient's personality structures will depend on the evolution of the therapeutic relationship.

We would certainly like to know in detail how the coevolutionary system of the analysis recovers from this impasse. The analyst says in his comments on session 1.17 and subsequent sessions that his strategy to promote a recovery will be to encourage the patient to give the details of her associations, but postpone any interpretations until later. We do not see this strategy working well in session 1.17. Another approach seems to be required.

Nevertheless, a recovery does take place. We would like to know whether it involves a phase transition, precipitated by a reorganizing perturbation of the preoedipal attractor by the analyst. Unfortunately, the following sessions are not among those presented in detail.

The analyst's summary of these sessions indicates that he narrowed his interventions to inquiries about the patient's resistance to expressing her *conscious* thoughts to him. He did not interpret the content, even when the patient "tested" him in session 2.1 by presenting a "directly Oedipal sexual dream." This allowed the patient to talk in 2.2 about her anxiety as a child when masturbating. She reported a feeling of conscious relief when she left that session, because the analyst had not mocked her account of her masturbating (which she said she had never discussed with anyone else).

By 2.3, "She was able to associate somewhat more freely, and there were spontaneous oscillations between past and present thoughts and experiences, and the analytic situation was progressing" (p. 99). In 2.4, "The patient presented a dream which indicated a growing sense of confidence in me [the analyst] and in my ability to control myself and the analytic situation between us" (p. 99). These remarks seem to describe the revival of a coevolutionary interaction, even though the analyst is still concerned with proving his strength. The analyst's remarks are compatible with either a reinstatement of the earlier Nash equilibrium or a movement closer to the edge of chaos.

We note that the revival is more gradual than the collapse of confidence manifest in 1.17, and that there is no single event to which the analyst attributes this positive change. The reader does not know how the two attractors met with in earlier sessions interact during the segment of the analysis from 2.1 to 2.4. What we seem to see is that the products of the oedipal attractor are rerouted away from the maelstrom of the dyadic maternal attractor and into productive work in the recovery of emotionally significant memories and associations.

One is drawn to the hypothesis that the patient's psychic organization is elastic at its lower boundary. By this I mean that it naturally rebounds from disorganizing perturbations without a major shift in organization. This is perhaps another way of saying that the patient is psychoneurotic. The severe symptoms seen in session 1.17 represent only a temporary regression from her normally more advanced level of organization.

Then the rebound seen in sessions 2.1 to 2.4 would simply be the system returning to its normal level of functioning after being dislodged. We might take this as an indication that what the analyst is describing here is a return to the Nash equilibrium state rather than a strong move toward the edge of chaos. Given the presence of this much self-organizing capacity in the patient, however, one would predict that as her memories of successful cooperation with the analyst accumulate, the depth and frequency of her losing control to this preoedipal attractor will decrease.

We can compare the Nash equilibrium as we see it here with the Nash equilibrium state in the prisoners' dilemma. In the game, a Nash equilibrium results when both agents choose to defect consistently. This would happen in any series that begins with a defection, if both players are using the tit for tat strategy. The payoff to both sides would be minimal. This appears to be what we are seeing in the oedipal exchanges here. However, the all-D situation under tit for tat is extremely stable, while the oedipal equilibrium in the analysis breaks down easily when either the patient or the analyst is dissatisfied with it.

Perhaps a Nash equilibrium in analysis has a history. Then we would be seeing only the beginning stages of it here. We would expect it to become more stable as the analysis progresses. Or it may be that the stability of the all-*D* equilibrium in the prisoners' dilemma is an artifact due to the simplicity of the tit for tat strategy. When strategies using more memory evolve in Lindgren's experiment, the pattern becomes more varied.

Then again, we may feel awkward calling the analytic exchange at the Nash equilibrium mutual defection. The traditional term, *transference-countertransference bind,* may be a little less harsh-sounding, but it has an awkwardness of its own. Thinking about the optimal conditions for making psychoanalysis effective, and about specific deviations from those optimal conditions, has not been overwhelmingly popular among analysts. The need to do justice to the individuality of each patient makes any attempt to define a norm seem dubious. The analyst and the patient are engaged in a task that requires collaboration, although the task may be different in detail for every analytic partnership. An analyst needs to be able to say whether, when, and in what particular areas he and the patient are successfully collaborating, and what obstacles exist to the improvement of their performance together.

One further question needs to be asked about session 1.16. Why the sharp discontinuity between the patient's state of mind at the end of session 1.16 and the beginning of session 1.17? From the patient's account, it appears that the full force of the maternal dyadic attractor appeared as soon as she left the analyst's office. Why not while she was still there? We have seen that the analyst's presence during 1.16 allowed the patient to maintain her hope that he might respond to her in the way she desired, even though the evidence of this was quite meager at that moment, from the patient's point of view.

The separation at the end of 1.16 was the final trigger for the dyadic attractor. The lack of any opportunity for the patient to influence the analyst in his absence from her immediate surroundings completed the movement to despair initiated by the premature interpretation. We would expect to see this theme returning as the maternal attractor comes under closer analytic scrutiny.

Session 3.1: Recovery

Session 3.1 has all the characteristics (until a few minutes before the end of the session) of a good analytic hour in which the therapeutic interaction remains close to the edge of chaos. Until the last few minutes, the patient and the analyst are closely in tune and clearly collaborating in the analytic task. The result is a notable productivity in the patient's associations. Each successive exchange between the two follows from and illuminates the previous exchange. The analyst does his part, staying with the patient's material and fostering her efforts to observe and understand herself. He does not intrude his own agenda until the final moments of the hour.

As a result, the flow of the patient's associations has the quality of deterministic unpredictability typical of the edge of chaos. Although she stays with a single theme for the entire session, and each association leads to the next in an orderly way, at the same time the material that comes up is fresh and unanticipated. Where she had complained about her feelings of abandonment in a dramatic but repetitive way in session 1.17, here she provides a variety of memories that help to make the feelings understandable. Her affect is appropriate to these unhappy disclosures, as she cries through most of the session, which was unusual for her during the first month. As she cries, she speaks of her fear as a child that crying would arouse her parents' anger and push them even further away from her.

The patient's story in 3.1 includes the recollection of events from both the recent and distant past. The effect is different from sessions 1.1 and 1.16, however, where there was little feeling accompanying the memories evoked by the analyst's statements. Here the affects are strong and to the point. The patient and the analyst work together to build and maintain the patient's sense that although the feelings of her childhood do not apply literally to the analytic situation, the recovery and reexperiencing of those feelings is a major part of the analytic work.

Something happens in this session that is not usually mentioned in accounts of the good analytic hour. This is the effort by both participants to relate the contents of this session to events and feelings reported during the sessions immediately preceding. The patient and the analyst are for the first time in a recorded session collaborating to structure the analytic discourse in a way that heightens the continuity of issues and feelings over the course of their work.

The session begins with a clear statement of the patient's feelings, her fears, and her need to keep up her defenses. She says, after an initial 90-second pause, "I'm afraid to talk. . . . I'm afraid that I'm being deserted. I have my defenses of independence and I'm afraid they'll crumble if I talk about it" (p. 112). She is thinking about the analyst's month-long vacation, still three months away. She is sick to her stomach. "It's like I felt on Friday [when the analyst told her he would have to cancel the hour on the following Friday]. Everything is all right if I see you every day, but if there is any break then I fall apart, and I'm unsure I'll ever see you again" (p. 112). This is the feeling violently acted out in session 1.17, but presented here in a way that invites analytic discussion.

When the analyst asks for associations, she says "It's not logical; it's just a feeling" (p. 112). The analyst suggests that she look at the details of her associations without being concerned about their logic. She says, "It's just like when my parents went out. I was always afraid that they'd leave us forever." She says again, "It's just a feeling" (p. 112). The analyst says, "You're repeating with me a feeling that you once had with your parents" (p. 112).

The patient is able to accept this statement as an accurate reflection of her state of mind. She recognizes that the feelings she is having in the present, with the analyst, are transference feelings. They originated in her experience with her parents but are now being applied irrationally to her present situation, which is quite different in reality from her childhood. Nevertheless, she realizes, for the moment at least, that the feelings must be respected, shared, and understood, if she is to be free from their irrational hold over her.

As a result of this coming together, the patient feels able to talk about what it felt like for her as a child. She says, "I went through a terrible phase of fear about my parents. For a while they went out every day and I'd be sick and feel that I couldn't breathe and I thought I'd die. There was a person who stayed with us and she was up in the attic, and I felt we were in the house by ourselves, just us three girls" (p. 112). She tells about the time she had a terrible headache that led to a week-long hospitalization. Her parents just gave her some aspirin and went out.

After the hospitalization she was sent to her grandmother's. She says, "My mother didn't take care of me. For instance, when I had pneumonia when I was three months old I was sent to my grandmother's. My parents never took care of me! . . . I can't let myself depend on them or on you. . . . I want not to be afraid when I'm not with you, and to feel that you will return and that I'm capable until you return. But I can't depend on you. No one ever knew the fear that was inside of me" (p. 113).

In this moving passage we see the patient oscillating between her transference identification of the analyst with her neglectful parents and her more mature identification of her adult self with the analyst's realistic position in her current life. The analyst asks about the fear inside her now about him. She replies by describing her fear that he will desert her. But then she indicates her recognition of the way her feelings are oscillating.

The analyst says, "So we can see that the situation is different today but that the feelings are the same as when you were a little girl" (p. 113). This statement expresses sympathy for the patient's dilemma, while also reinforcing her effort at self-observation. This allows the patient to express her anger at the analyst for not seeing and doing something about her irrational feelings of neediness. The analyst says, "This is like the feeling Monday when you had the urge to walk out and slam the door and you were afraid that I wouldn't see you again if you did. And it's also like Sunday when you were angry at me and then had the fantasy that you were going to cut your own wrists" (p. 113).

Here we have a reconstruction of the sequence of events of the last few days as reported by the patient in a piecemeal fashion. The idea is being established that feelings arise from events in an orderly but not necessarily a straightforward or obvious way. The analytic discourse, although it evolves in what seems like a helter-skelter fashion, eventually provides the material for reconstruction and reconnection as new pieces of the puzzle appear.

The patient says, after a two-minute pause, "I want to ask you like a little child, 'Are you going to be back on Monday?' I really know the answer." And then, "I never had the nerve to ask my parents if they were going out. . . . I wonder why did I never cry and say it to my parents?" She answers the question by saying, "But if I ever cried, then I'd be by myself. . . . I get a sense of panic to be left alone to die for the rest of my life" (p. 114). As she answers the question she stops crying.

The analyst now says, "And this was your feeling when Harris [her former therapist] abruptly said he wasn't going to see you anymore?" (p. 114). In his comments, the analyst explains this intervention as an attempt to help the patient distinguish him, with his assurances to her that he will continue to see her as long as she needs him, from the therapist who was incapacitated by his countertransference feelings. One can also see it as an effort to increase the continuity of the analytic discourse by connecting her feelings about him at the moment with her feelings about Harris when he stopped her treatment.

The patient does not respond to this reference to Harris. She goes back to her fear of being overwhelmed by her feelings of helplessness and anger. Before the sessions ends, there is a three-and-a-half minute silence. She say "I'm waiting for dooms-day. . . . I'm waiting for you to say that it's time to go. I have a sense of panic and I just can't stand it. I just sit and wait" (p. 114).

My impression is that the reference to Harris's abrupt termi-nation evoked the patient's fear of punishment for sexual long-ings. This was too much for her to handle so late in the session, just as her separation anxiety was mounting. In this state, she could not appreciate that the reality with the analyst was different, although her feelings toward him were similar to those she felt when her relationship to Harris became endangered.

The maternal dyadic attractor that dramatically dominated session 1.17 is at work in this session too. But in this case it shares control of the patient's associations with the observing ego of the patient in an effective working alliance with the analyst. The attractor provides the subject matter of the session, the patient's devaluation of her thoughts and feelings about herself and the analyst. But, at the same time, the major topic of the *dialogue* between the patient and the analyst is the transformation rules of the attractor itself.

This duality is present from the patient's opening statement of the session. She says, "I'm afraid to talk. . . . I'm afraid that I'm being deserted. I have my defenses of independence and I'm afraid they'll crumble if I talk about it" (p. 112). Here she reports a fear, then observes how she defends herself against the fear, then reports a secondary fear that her defenses against the original fear will break down if she engages in a dialogue with the analyst. Of course, she is already engaged in a dialogue with the analyst when she reports all of this to him. She hopes he will comfort her rather than undermine her defenses, that he will resist the transforming power of her infantile attractor.

When the analyst indicates that he wants to hear more before making a substantive comment, the patient goes on with her exploration of the transformational rules. She says, "Everything is all right if I see you every day, but if there is any break then I fall apart, and I'm sure I'll never see you again" (p. 112). This is the rule that transforms any absence of the analyst (or hint of emotional distance) into an infantile experience in which the patient feels punished and loses control of both her feelings and her judgment.

The patient tries to defend herself against her fear of this irrational disruption of her mental functioning by saying, "It's not logical; it's just a feeling." The analyst comforts her by saying, in effect, "There is no punishment here for being illogical. We're trying to find out *how* you feel, no matter what kind of feeling it is." This allows her to identify the infantile experience recreated by the attractor. She says, "It's just like when my parents went out. I was always afraid that they'd leave us forever" (p. 112).

The hour proceeds in this way. The dialogue is a delicate balance between conflicting feelings and wishes on several levels of meaning. It allows the maternal dyadic attractor to demonstrate its manner of operating, so that it can be observed and understood, but does not allow it to control the patient's feelings and judgment. One has the sense that the balance is fragile. A small push could move the interaction away from the edge.

And, in fact, a very small push does it. The analyst's miscalculation in bringing Harris into the picture late in the hour is very slight compared with his premature probing for the oedipal transference material in 1.16. But it is enough to lift the dialogue off the tracks for the last few minutes of the hour. The effect on the patient is also slight when compared with the regression of 1.17.

Whether the analyst intended to bring the oedipal material back into this session or was misunderstood by the patient, however, the patient appears to be extremely sensitive to his preference for one attractor rather than another. Her ability to observe the maternal dyadic attractor from a more objective viewpoint in this session does not appear to be transferrable to the oedipal attractor. Whether the analyst imposes a shift away from the currently accessible attractor, as in 1.16, or merely hints in the slightest way at such a shift, as in 3.1, the effect is disorienting to the patient.

Session 3.1 also gives us a glimpse at the inner structure of the patient's maternal dyadic attractor. In her first statement of the hour, quoted above, she appears to be describing an attractor with two levels of functioning. At the first level, stimuli that evoke her longings for maternal comfort and support are transformed into threats to her independence. These threats must be avoided through various kinds of evasive action. When she fails to turn the threats away, a new set of rules comes into play. The elements of the food set are transformed by these new rules into instances of betrayal and abandonment.

We might want to describe the dyadic maternal attractor as having one food set but two sets of transformational products. Which products are created would seem to depend on external conditions (for example, the force behind the threat). However, a closer look indicates that the food set we see transformed into the two sets of products are similar but distinct from one another.

The set of events transformed into threats to the patient's independence seems to include only those events that take place at some emotional distance and have an impersonal quality. She has room to maneuver around them and to escape from them. The anticipated loss of the friend who may be leaving town in 1.16 is an example of this kind of event. In contrast, the food set at the second level of transformation includes events that are more intimate and more emotional. A particular person, who is very close by, is generating an emotional state that cannot be ignored. The analyst's dream interpretation in 1.16, identifying the patient's sexual wishes toward him, is an example of the second kind.

Two separate attractors are evident here. We see a large overlap in the thematic content of their food sets, but very little overlap in the emotional force of the interpersonal events they
encompass. In both of the examples just mentioned, the patient
feels she can't manage without an important person in her life.
However, the action of the friend who may be leaving is not directed toward the patient. The patient's feeling of loss is inciden-
tal to the friend's marriage. The analyst's interpretation, on the
other hand, is aimed directly at her.

I think the evidence is strong enough to assume at this point
that there are two distinct attractors making up what I have been
calling the maternal dyadic attractor. The events that form the
food sets of both attractors involve dyadic relationships with a
nurturing figure. But the food sets, the transformation rules, and
the products of each attractor are different. Their basins of attraction are different.

As we have seen, the two attractors have a dynamic relationship. One acts as a *defense* against the other. The patient says
clearly that she collapses into helplessness and isolation only
when the attempt to maintain her independence by distancing
herself breaks down. Defecting from her agreement to tell the
analyst what she is thinking is her final, pathetically ineffective
effort to maintain her feelings of independence.

Our account of the distinction between the food sets of the
two attractors may be complicated by another factor, however.
This is the possibility that the food set of the second attractor
includes only events that arouse forbidden feelings in the patient,
feelings she expects to be punished for, particularly sexual feelings for men. In favor of this hypothesis is the fact that the patient
clearly expects to be punished by the analyst for her wanting so
much from him. Her inability to respond to the analyst's attempt
to connect this expectation to the breaking off of her treatment
with Harris supports this idea.

Against the hypothesis are a number of considerations. One
is the fact that in 1.16, 1.17, and 3.1 the patient expects to be
punished by the person she loves, not by a third person who is
jealous. Second, the punishment she expects corresponds with
the terrible fears of a child whose primary attachment is still to
her mother. Third, the childhood events she recalls in connection

with the fear of punishment in 3.1 have to do with the unwillingness of both parents to be caretakers.

When the patient remembers in 1.16 that her father failed
to respond to her exhibitionism with an affirmation of her attrac-
tiveness as a woman, her complaint seems to be more about his
failure to provide a particular kind of paternal caring than about
a rejection of her oedipal wishes or about his loyalty to her
mother. On the whole, it appears that the second dyadic attractor
is indeed a dyadic attractor, with male figures found to be at fault
when they fail to provide paternal care or fail to compensate for
the lack of maternal nurturance.

The traditional psychoanalytic view that in a neurotic patient
the reactivation of preoedipal conflicts is ultimately an evasive
action to disguise an even more threatening oedipal conflict may
be applicable in these early sessions of the analysis. But in trying
to understand the individual sessions and their role in the analytic
process, this would be missing the trees for the forest.

The patient's displaying of her preoedipal conflicts to the
analyst as a way of evading her oedipal guilt requires the independent existence of preoedipal attractors that suit the role. The
transformations of the preoedipal attractors must be analyzed in
their own terms before their defensive role in the oedipal conflict
can become intelligible to the patient. Dewald's case material
through session 3.1 illustrates the patient's tendency to move
away from the edge of chaos when this natural progression is disrupted.

The fact that the maternal dyadic attractor could be recognized in session 3.1 as a set of two attractors with overlapping
food sets is of considerable practical and theoretical importance.
A major methodological problem confronting research on the
psychoanalytic process is the lack of systematic criteria for identifying the operations of particular attractors in the data generated
by an analytic session.

In session 3.1, we saw the emergence of two distinct maternal
dyadic attractors where only one had been recognized previously.
Clinical observation indicates that this pattern is typical. Attractors do not appear out of nowhere as an analysis proceeds.
They emerge through the discovery of new and finer distinctions

within the rule sets of attractors already identified earlier in the analysis.

Session 3.1 also shows us the necessary conditions for distinguishing new attractors from old. When the transformation rules in operation at the moment themselves become a topic in the dialogue between the patient and the analyst, new data that make such a distinction possible become available. That is, when the analysis is close to the edge of chaos, the data emerge that make it feasible to further subdivide the food sets and the product sets of the attractors previously indistinguishable in the analytic discourse.

As the coevolutionary process of an analysis moves forward, one expects to see the progressive emergence in the analytic discourse of previously unrecognized unconscious infantile attractors and of their structural relations with one another. The emergence of a particular attractor during the analytic discourse indicates the creation of a new connection between that attractor and the patient's observing ego. This new connection is itself evidence of a reorganization in the patient's mind of the transformation rules of the attractor and of its products.

When such a connection is made, a new rule that makes the transformation rules of the attractor reversible is added to the set of rules. We see the new rule operating in session 3.1 with regard to the first dyadic attractor. At this point in the analysis the patient can move backward from the output of this attractor, her feeling alone and abandoned, to the original food set, the childhood experiences that gave rise to the transformation rules. The patient's failure to respond to the mention of her former therapist near the end of 3.1 is evidence that neither the second dyadic attractor nor the oedipal attractor has yet become reversible in this sense.

The reorganization that makes it possible for the patient to discuss the transformation rules of the first dyadic attractor with the analyst marks a phase transition in an important region of her mental organization. When a phase transition of this kind occurs, we would expect to find a fairly abrupt transition point at which the new view of the patient's unconscious behavior enters her awareness. The quality of the patient's opening remarks in 3.1 indicates that the transition must already have occurred before this session began, probably in the later hours of the second month.

Because these hours are only briefly summarized, we cannot expect to locate a phase transition point precisely. However, there is an interaction described in the summary of session 2.14 that meets many of the criteria for such a transitional event. In this session, according to the analyst, the patient felt anxious about reporting two overtly sexual dreams. She reiterated her fantasy that if she were to fully express her feelings to the analyst, it would result in an overt sexual seduction between them. This time she was receptive to the analyst's observation that this fantasy itself is seductive, and that it is an example of her recurrent attempts to tease and seduce men sexually. When men respond to her sexually, however, she feels hostile and destructive toward them. The analyst suggested that this pattern might apply to her behavior toward him also. She was able to respond by saying, "I want to prove that every man is my father" (p. 106).

In his comments on the hour, the analyst wrote, "It has become clear from the material that this patient uses sexuality for a variety of nonsexual aims including: the expression of her needs to control the other person; the expression of hostility and depreciation of the man; the repetitive reenactment of her disturbed relationship to her father; and expression of her needs to reassure herself of her own value, while at the same time expressing contempt for herself as a woman" (p. 107). This statement indicates an important discovery for the analyst. His view of the patient underwent a significant evolutionary change as a result of this hour.

The next day, in session 2.15, the patient said, "I was thinking of how nice you are and that you really want me to come here and that you really want to help me. It's all so good, the way you said it, about laughing at me about my sexual feelings. When you said: 'Why would I laugh?' it was as if you were saying: 'I'm not going to and there is no reason to.' I feel if I tell you this you'll get flustered, but I should know better than that. You're the first man that I was ever able to talk to about me and not laugh and not have you take advantage of me. It's wonderful, and I love this. I feel very close and I feel as if you really care about me" (p. 109). This appears to be a sincere expression of feeling about the patient's experience in the analysis, rather than an intellectu-alized act of compliance.

This transitional moment is characterized by changes in both of the coevolutionary partners. The analyst realizes that the pa-tient uses sexuality for a variety of nonsexual aims. The patient realizes that it is safe to talk about sex because the analyst cares for her welfare more than he desires her sexually. This amounts to an agreement to proceed with the issues that are ready for analysis without allowing the as yet unresolved oedipal issues to derail the dialogue.

Of course, this agreement is not complete and fully guaran-teed. It will naturally be subject to further stresses and strains. We have seen in session 3.1 that at the moment it applies to the first dyadic attractor, but not, as far as we can tell, the second. While it indicates a full recovery from the mutual defection of sessions 1.16 and 1.17, it goes further, moving the analysis well beyond the status quo in the relationship before these defections took place.

Each of the partners has learned something valuable about how not to misinterpret the behavior of the other. One would be surprised if another session as painful as 1.17 occurred at a later point in the analysis. The agreement reached in 2.14 and 2.15 defines an area in which they can collaborate successfully at this stage of their work together.

The analysis is on a new plateau at which their mutual expec-tations have been stabilized. The inner world of the patient also has a more solid feeling at this point. Of course, much will depend on their ability to follow the implicit agreement made in session 2.14. (The analyst does not actually observe the agreement in session 3.2. He takes up the line he began with his mention of Harris at the end of 3.1. The patient once again reacts badly, but does not lose control as in 1.17.)

The First Reorganization

As an analysis begins, the analytic partners know very little of each other. They proceed by extrapolating from what they already know about the roles of patient and analyst. In this case the pa-tient knows quite a bit about what it means to be a good patient.

Some, but not all, of this knowledge is distorted by her transference fantasies and her experience with her previous therapist. The analyst has his own more sophisticated ideas about what he can expect from a patient. But neither knows enough to keep the analysis close to the edge of chaos all the time.

Opportunities for misunderstanding can arise, often without apparent warning. One can see the trouble coming in retrospect, however, much more easily than in the real time of the analysis. We see both participants working hard to reach the edge of chaos, but pulling back (defecting) when the response they hope for doesn't materialize. The analysis moves toward and away from the edge of chaos in small steps and large. We see a serious but transient disorganization in the patient and organizing interactions at different levels. The organizing interactions appear to be cumulative. The patient's ability to withhold judgment about the analyst's apparent defections is certainly improved by session 3.1.

Some of these shifts are quite subtle. We would like to have a measure for the distance traveled in phase space as well as for the direction of motion. This is not a distance to be measured along a single linear dimension, of course. Nonlinear dynamics may be applicable to this problem in the next stages of research. (A qualitative measure, a rank ordering, will emerge from our discussion later on.)

One complication to be overcome in measuring this distance is the patient's inclination to fabricate edge of chaos behavior in order to satisfy the analyst's therapeutic expectations. We saw that the patient in Dewald's analytic material could reproduce the associational pattern typical of what we expect to see near the edge of chaos, even when there was a lack of emotional attunement in the analytic relationship.

We have observed that the regular updating and restructuring of the analytic discourse plays an important role in keeping the interaction between the analytic partners coherent and the analysis near the edge of chaos. All four elements of edge of chaos behavior, the associational pattern, attunement, a workable strategy for recovery from defections, and the restructuring of the analytic discourse, must be present for a judgment that the analytic process is close to its optimum. If any of these is lacking, the analyst would be right to suspect that the patient is acting out a wish to comply with the analyst's expectations.

In these sessions, the operation of the patient's unconscious infantile attractors was evident from the very beginning. We saw the content of each session spiraling in toward an infantile theme created by an attractor. When more than one attractor was operating in a session, the transition, sometimes quite sudden, could be traced to a particular interaction between the patient and the analyst that shifted the analytic process onto a new track (and into a new basin of attraction).

We see here how a basin of attraction manifests itself verbally as a mental space in Fauconnier's sense. An event that belongs to the food sets of several attractors will have different cognitive and emotional values in the distinct mental spaces defined by each of the attractors. The evidence that critical events in the analysis occur when elements of feeling can be located in more than one food set is suggestive. An analyst who wishes to connect a particular event with the appropriate region of the patient's unconscious mental structures will have to stay within the mental space defined by the currently accessible attractor.

The event by itself may contain very little information about which attractor is the one to work with in the moment at hand. This most accessible attractor can only be identified through an understanding of the context of the event in the ongoing analytic discourse. For this reason, the analyst's "going by the book" can be very hazardous to the analysis.

At a given moment the patient will be more comfortable working near the edge of chaos with the transformation rules of one attractor than with the rules of another. The degree of attunement between the patient and the analyst depends in large part on the analyst's awareness of the appropriate attractor to work with. When he fails to notice that the patient is unable to work with the issues created by a particular attractor, the analytic process moves in the direction of chaos or frozen order.

Many of the technical issues traditionally subsumed under the rubric of tact and timing on the analyst's part actually concern his accuracy in staying within the limits of the appropriate attractor. One of the major problems for students of the analytic process (practicing analysts included) has been the lack of systematic criteria for identifying the operations of particular attractors in the data generated by an analytic session.

We might ask whether there is always one and only one attractor the patient can be comfortable with at a given moment in the analysis. The answer to this must be no. For a more disturbed patient, there may be no attractor accessible to the analytic discourse at a given moment. For the neurotic patient traditionally treated with psychoanalysis, however, it would be exceptional for there to be no accessible attractor at all.

An example of an exception that was only apparent occurred when one neurotic patient was silent for 11 consecutive analytic hours. She let the analyst know she was feeling all right during this time, however. When she returned to the analytic discourse again, she told him she had been imagining herself during the entire time swimming among vicious sharks, which she identified with her mother. The fact that both the patient and the analyst had survived this period of silence had resolved a major issue about trust in her transference feelings. In this case the analytic process continued while the analytic discourse was temporarily suspended.

Can there be more than one accessible attractor? This certainly seems to be possible when the analytic process is at the edge of chaos. In fact, the accessibility of more than one attractor may be another criterion for deciding that the process is at the edge rather than close to it. In Richard's case, his ability *to observe himself in transition from one attractor to another* was a striking feature of the analytic process at the edge of chaos. Is this typical of every analytic process near the edge of chaos? Is the edge of chaos a fault line between attractors? My conjecture would be that the answer to these questions is yes.

We were not far enough along in Dewald's case to begin to answer the questions in a more definitive way. However, in session 3.1, we saw the emergence of two distinct maternal dyadic attractors where only one had been recognizable earlier. My clinical observations again suggest that this pattern is typical. Attractors do not appear out of nowhere as an analysis goes on. They emerge through the discovery of new and finer distinctions within the food sets and transformation rule of attractors already identified earlier in the analysis.

Session 3.1 also illustrates one of the conditions necessary for distinguishing new attractors from old. When the transformation rules in operation at the moment become an explicit topic in the patient's associations, new data emerge spontaneously from the patient's unconscious that make such a distinction visible. This makes it possible to further subdivide the food sets, transformation rules, and product sets of the attractors previously indistinguishable in the analytic discourse.

The analyst must be aware that a transition between attractors is in process. Otherwise, the moment may be lost and the analysis recede quickly from the edge of chaos. I believe the analyst must confirm the opening to the new attractor by noting the different ways in which the current material can be viewed. The essential point to be made is that the events to which the patient is responding belong to the food sets of more than one attractor.

The order in which the attractors appeared in the analytic discourse is of great interest. In the first session examined here, 1.1, the only recognizable attractor was the one that transformed the positive interactive content of the session into manifestations of oedipal guilt in the patient. By the end of the first month, a dyadic attractor emerged that transformed the patient's anxiety about the actions of the analyst into threats of annihilation and identity diffusion (1.17).

By the end of the second month, 2.14 through 3.1, this dyadic attractor divided into two distinct attractors, each concerned with separation and loss. The patient was able to work effectively with one of these attractors but not with the other. As long as the analyst's interventions were directed at the first dyadic attractor, the patient was able to work productively, near the edge of chaos. When he changed the subject of the discourse to the content of the second dyadic attractor, the patient became troubled and backed away.

Although the data of these two months is not conclusive, it correlates well with clinical observations indicating that the progress of an analysis can be measured by the fineness of the discriminations made by the patient in the organization of her inner world and the world she constructs around her. This may be an indication that there is a general recursive pattern in which each unconscious infantile attractor bifurcates into a component that can be worked with at the moment and another component that must bifurcate again before its contents become accessible to analysis.

This is a description of the traditional *working through* stage of the analytic process, the lengthy middle stage of an analysis when the patient keeps finding new partial solutions to her conflicts but never seems to reach the heart of the matter. The partial solutions are possible because a series of distinct attractors is being spun off by an original, more inclusive attractor. (The unconscious appears to change from a single global attractor to a hierarchy of lower level attractors.) Each partial solution restricts the domain of the global attractor, so that it finally becomes a single member in a large set of closely related attractors. The inaccessible residue has lost its power over the domains of its split off and now accessible daughter attractors. This sequence is the pathway along which the unconscious becomes conscious in analysis, the path through which id becomes ego.

Attractors that emerge through the bifurcation of a preexisting attractor have overlapping food sets, like the first and second dyadic attractors in Dewald's case. We have also seen the products of the patient's oedipal attractor acting as the food set for what we now recognize as the second dyadic attractor. This is surely just a bare beginning in the discovery of relationships among attractors. One can expect the oedipal attractor in this case to divide into a set of more differentiated daughter attractors with more distinct characteristics. The patient's remarks in session 2.14 and 2.15 suggest the beginnings of such a differentiation.

The orderly emergence of attractors during the analytic process would severely limit the actual freedom of the patient's associations, if one considers the range of possible topics to be a measure of freedom. (Freedom to say whatever is conscious at the moment is a more realistic use of this term.) It also circumscribes the range of appropriate interpretations by the analyst. To be germane, an interpretation must refer to events in the food set of the currently accessible attractor. But it must also refer to events outside the food set.

How does the analyst help the patient move from one basin of attraction to another, then? His contributions to the analytic process include his capacity to make distinctions between food sets, transformation rules, and transformation products. He helps the patient distinguish events in the food set of the current attractor that trigger the transformation rules of other attractors as well. He notices differences in these rules and in their products.

The analyst can make these distinctions unobtrusively, by saying, for example, "You didn't seem to feel the same way about this when [a similar event] happened. I wonder what was different this time." Or, "Maybe it feels different now, when I seem to be [doing something unpleasant to you], from the way it felt when your mother did it when you were a child."

Interventions of this kind give rise to the small changes that accumulate before the precipitation of a phase transition, here marked by the splitting of the attractor. An analysis is *at* the edge of chaos when such a phase transition actually takes place. The bifurcation of the current attractor is achieved when the patient is able to observe that she has been until now under the control of the newly split off attractor. The rule of reversibility added to the transformation rules of this attractor separates it from the inaccessible residue of the original attractor and from the conglomerate of still inaccessible attractors that make up his unconscious.

Even with this relatively small sample of clinical data, we can see how our understanding of the psychoanalytic process can be increased when we approach it from the point of view of coevolution and complexity theory. Psychoanalytic treatment is a fully dynamic process, moving at any moment toward or away from the optimal level of coevolutionary interaction. The events of the analysis that mark the turning points along this route come quickly into focus for the observer. Their significance in promoting or retarding the optimal movement of the analysis can be recognized with little difficulty.

Changes in the course of the analytic process are accompanied by changes in the level of organization of the patient's view of herself in relation to the analyst. The analyst's views of the patient and of his work with her change at the same time. The progression is not smooth. It takes the form of relatively abrupt phase transitional shifts after the accumulation of many smaller modifications.

A phase transitional shift stabilizes the analytic process at a new level of coadaptation. The turning point of the phase transition can be recognized by the changes that occur in the organization of the patient's world and in the analyst's view of the patient's capacity for change.

Near the edge of chaos, the associations of Dewald's patient are varied and mobile. She moves easily from one related topic to another; that is, from one item to another in the food set of the most accessible attractor. At the edge of chaos, the associations converge to reveal the structure of the attractor itself. A rule of reversibility appears in the set of transformation rules of the attractor, a rule that allows the patient to move backwards in thought from the products of the attractor to the observation of its transformation rules in action.

This increase in the patient's powers of self-observation reflects a bifurcation of the attractor into separate parts, one accessible to the patient's self-observation, the other visible, if at all, only to the analyst. The rule of reversibility creates a boundary that encompasses the newly accessible attractor, protecting further exploration of its contents in the analysis from the disruptive effects of attractors still under the control of the unconscious. The newly accessible attractor now belongs to the shared domain of the analytic discourse.

If the analysis stays within the boundaries of the newly emergent attractor for some time, it will stabilize in a new Nash equilibrium at a higher level of adaptation than the previous one. This new level of adaptation will bring the new equilibrium state closer to the edge of chaos than the previous one had been. In this way the Nash equilibrium state of the coevolutionary system will naturally evolve toward the edge of chaos. The order of emergence of the bounded attractors will correlate with the order of increase in the levels of adaptation reached by successive Nash equilibrium states and correspondingly with their closeness to the edge of chaos.

This does not mean, of course, that the analytic process moves unidirectionally toward the edge of chaos. Setbacks along the way are common, as we saw illustrated in Dewald's sessions

1.16 and 1.17. We may ask whether any Nash equilibrium state is ever farther from the edge of chaos than the equilibrium states that precede it in the course of an analysis. My conjecture at this point is that such a regression to a stable equilibrium state far from the edge of chaos is very infrequent in neurotic patients, but fairly common in patients who are severely ill. I think the dividing line here corresponds to the distinction often made between patients who are analyzable in theory and those who are not.

The disruption in session 1.17 did not result in a new equilibrium state farther from the edge, but in a chaotic situation that gradually resolved to a new and higher equilibrium level in 2.3 and 2.4. The Nash equilibrium states we are discussing at this point are states in which work is being done preliminary to the next phase transition that lies ahead. They must be distinguished from the pseudo-equilibrium we observed earlier when the patient and analyst were joined in their premature attempt to explore the oedipal attractor. The associative pathways opened by the patient in such a pseudo-equilibrium state may advance the analytic process, however, since they become part of the analytic discourse. The analyst may acquire information in this way that will be useful later in the analysis, even though it may be disruptive to reflect it back to the patient at the moment.

These features of the analytic process, among others, were observed in this brief sample of Dewald's recorded analysis. Success in analyzing this data lends confidence to the hope that, given enough clinical material, the theoretical assumptions made earlier in this book can be confirmed. A special cause for hope is the way the theory interacted with the sample to emerge with new ideas and finer distinctions. This is the first step in a coevolutionary interaction between theory and data that one would like to see in every case.

11 CONCLUSION

The Implications for Psychoanalytic Treatment

A rule of thumb for most psychoanalysts is that "activity" by the analyst should be minimized except for the quintessential analytic function of "interpretation." I hope *The Emergent Ego* leads to some important expansions and modifications of this heuristic. The act of interpretation is not limited to explanation by the analyst of possible unconscious meanings behind what the patient tells him; this function of interpretation is not its most important. Interpretation, or, more broadly, intervention by the analyst, is the analyst's way of fulfilling his function as a coevolutionary partner in the analytic process. It is essential to the progress of the analysis. A major part of the analyst's job is to track the progress of the analysis and to organize and update the analytic discourse. These tasks are as much a part of the analytic enterprise as the identification of unconscious fantasy. They require a kind of activity on the part of the analyst that has not been traditionally conceptualized as interpretation.

Any activity by the analyst is a potential intrusion into the patient's own thoughts. This is a serious issue, since many patients have had difficulty in separating their own thoughts from those of their primary caretakers. Analysts are rightly wary of activity that is not interpretive. The problem has been that their definition of interpretation was so narrow that it excluded activity of the analyst needed to make the analytic process succeed. Freud and other traditional analysts reacted vehemently to Ferenczi's misappropriation of the term *active* as a description of the analyst's role. In doing so they closed off the investigation of their own activity as traditional analysts.

Complexity theory and modern evolutionary theory are useful because they demonstrate that the analyst cannot help being active if the analysis is to work. The real question is not whether he should be active, or how active he should be, it is how he should be active. Is he active in the constructive way necessary to facilitate the analytic process or is he active in a way that opposes and diminishes it? The theory helps to answer this question by mapping out the process and locating many of the points at which the analyst's constructive intervention is essential to the unfolding of the process.

Making the unconscious conscious is essential to the success of any psychoanalysis. But this way of describing what happens leaves out the contextual aspects of unconscious fantasy. Unconscious fantasy is a major issue in psychopathology because unconscious fantasy shapes the pathological infantile attractors whose dynamics distort the patient's experience of himself and the world around him. Unconscious fantasies exert their influence through the structure of the attractors in which they are embedded. They cannot be "interpreted" outside this context.

The need to interpret unconscious fantasies in context, through the dynamics of the attractors in control of the patient's thoughts of the moment, is one of the most difficult things for a beginning analyst to learn. Many expedients have been used to curb the beginner's tendency to interpret out of context. Without an understanding of the dynamics of the attractor, however, most of these are unconvincing to the student. Perhaps the worst advice to the beginner is to say as little as possible. This cuts down on inappropriate interpretations, but it also prevents the analyst from doing his job as the patient's coevolutionary partner. The result, besides a poor analysis, is significant damage to the beginning analyst's self-image and self-esteem.

The Implications for Psychoanalytic Theory

The theory of emerging properties in complex self-organizing systems offers an opportunity for a systematic reconceptualization of psychoanalytic theory. A scientific understanding of relations between mind and body, central to the psychoanalytic enterprise, has always seemed problematic to the analyst because of the threat of reductionism as the ruling philosophy in natural science. Complexity theory neutralizes the threat of reductionism. The advantages of a scientific foundation for psychoanalysis are available without the drawback of oversimplification. Complexity theory also counterbalances Freud's overly pessimistic view of mental activity as a discharge phenomenon that necessarily increases the entropy in the psychic apparatus.

As I have mentioned before, a particular area of vulnerability in traditional psychoanalytic theory is its rudimentary understanding of the therapeutic action of psychoanalytic treatment. Freud believed that once the patient's defenses have been reduced and his psychic energy mobilized, his adaptive ego would take over and provide a cure, without specific attention from the analyst. Besides its limiting effect on the analyst's work with patients, this formula has discouraged investigation of the analytic process as process. The theories of coevolution and self-organized systems provide a new framework for investigations into the nature of the process.

Freud believed that the ego is constructed through the taming by the environment of biologically unrestrained instinctual energies. Despite much significant work on ego psychology by analysts since Freud, this idea is still influential. Complexity theory offers a comprehensive basis for understanding the adaptive ego as an emergent product of evolution rather than a relic of frustrated biological urges.

One important obstacle to a theoretical understanding of the therapeutic process has been the lack of a common language for describing both the interaction *between* the patient and the analyst and the resulting changes taking place intrapsychically *within* the patient. Because of this deficit, analysts have found it difficult to conceptualize the specific effects of the therapeutic interaction on the intrapsychic structures of the patient. Complexity theory provides a common conceptual language through the *connectedness* of components within a system, externally coupled through further *connections* with other systems in its ecosystem. Kauffman's demonstration that these inner and outer connections have direct causal effects on one another is the crucial finding here.

I leave for last the replacement through complexity theory of scientific anachronisms at many levels of Freudian metapsychology. One such anachronism is Freud's divorcing of human motives from the adaptive context of all biological activity (the psychic energy theory). No organism as complex as the human could have evolved without a highly structured set of internalized restraints on behavior. An antagonistic environment working against an organism whose behavior is unconstrained would not merely enforce adaptive behavior, it would destroy the organism.

More has to be built in than restraint, however. An intricate synergy between action and structure is necessary for the organism to take advantage of its limited and changing opportunities in the environment. Hartmann's (1939) effort to introduce the adaptive point of view into psychoanalytic theory had little effect, if any, on Freudian metapsychology. As much as he may have been influenced by Darwin in his pessimistic view of human nature, Freud's basic stance was antievolutionary. His espousal of Lamarck was motivated in part by the shortcomings of Darwin's original theory, but it also indicated a resistance to the idea of innate structures channeling the "forces" that drive people to irrational thoughts and acts.

Hartmann's work, although influential in many areas, failed to promote the idea of adaptation to a prominent role in psychoanalytic theory. There were many reasons for this. Hartmann was reluctant to confront Freud's antievolutionary bias directly. He tried to smuggle adaptation into psychoanalytic theory without drawing out the implications of evolution as a model for human development or for the psychoanalytic process itself. But, as I have tried to make clear, evolutionary theory in its early scientific incarnations was of little help in understanding the nature of process in general.

Complexity theory reveals the intimate relation between action and structure. Structure develops from the affinities that bring about the interactions of smaller structures. This principle operates at all scales. It describes the moment to moment interaction of the patient and the analyst and it describes the therapeutic effect of the analysis as a whole. While this principle of structure formation holds at all scales, the affinities that link the entities at any particular level of organization may be quite different from those at other levels. Hence the futility of postulating "psychic forces" that determine the activities of the psychic apparatus at all levels. Freud understood that desire is a compound of many ingredients. But he was not able to formulate this insight in his archaic metapsychology.

There are many such anachronisms in traditional psychoanalytic theory. Some have been ameliorated by object relations theory, but object relations theory confines itself to a narrow range of organizational phenomena, that of object representations. Object relations theory must be embedded in a larger theory that takes account of the body and the brain as well as the manner in which people internalize their relations to one another.

I have only sketched out a few of the possibilities for reorganizing psychoanalytic theory in the light of the new developments in complexity theory and modern evolutionary theory. I hope the reader will agree with me that this is only the beginning of a very extensive project.

Some Possibilities for Further Research

The application of the current findings of complexity theory to the psychoanalytic process can be extended far beyond the areas sketched out in *The Emergent Ego*. Computer modeling of complexity theory can be adapted specifically to the psychoanalytic situation, a very simple example of this research technique would be to repeat Lindgren's work with the prisoners' dilemma using a game more nearly like psychoanalysis, incorporating the asymmetrical payoffs for the patient and the analyst in the psychoanalytic relationship. The patient always has more at stake (and more at risk) than the analyst. This asymmetry may lead to a different set of optimal strategies for the two participants in an analysis.

In other words, a result in complexity theory can be made more specific to psychoanalysis by introducing constraints that are particular to the psychoanalytic situation. Random Boolean networks (RBNs) spontaneously organize into structures. This is the minimum for what is possible in Boolean networks. As we have seen, canalizing Boolean networks are more structured than RBNs. Associative structures in the human mind are certainly more structured than RBNs. The more we learn about the affinities in associative networks, the better able we will be to assess the kinds and degrees of structure in the human mind generally. This in turn will help us improve our strategies for modifying pathological structures (infantile attractors). Elvin Semrad, the charismatic teacher at the Massachusetts Mental Health Center in the nineteen fifties and sixties, told his residents, "If you think schizophrenics have weak egos, try to change them."

Reviewing and reorganizing the clinical data of the analytic process according to these ideas and results would still be a vast and daunting enterprise. To begin with, the data are difficult to collect. All data collection methods intrude destructively into the therapeutic relationship. The guarantee of confidentiality is essential to the patient's ability to speak freely to the analyst about his thoughts and feelings. Any violation of this guarantee, no matter how well intended or how well insulated from the analysis, will have inhibiting effects on the patient. Complexity theory cannot help with this problem.

On the other hand, complexity theory can help reduce the mountains of data produced by the process itself. Efforts to study these data have been hampered because so much of it is produced in the course of an analysis. The data appear during a session in a linear sequence that flattens out their hierarchical structure. The profile of the mountains of data has no connection with the unfolding structure of the process. The researcher must be able to identify nodal points in these hierarchical structures as they appear unmarked in the liner sequence of the data. Complexity theory offers the best hope we have had as yet for an objective way to reconstruct the inner structure of the patient's psyche using the linear data of the therapeutic interaction.

An Overview

In *The Emergent Ego* I have suggested answers to a number of long-standing questions about the psychoanalytic process. I list just a few here. What do the patient and the analyst actually *do* in an analysis? In the traditional view, the patient tries to say whatever comes to his mind and that the analyst tries to interpret what the patient says in order to bring about a therapeutic change. We can see now why this description is incomplete. The patient and the analyst are doing something *together*. They are *collaborating* on a task that changes each of them, leading to a convergence of results beneficial for both. They are *coevolving*.

Is there anything intrinsic to the process that makes it so difficult and time consuming, apart from the individual patient's resistance? Yes. The analytic discourse is a cumulative structure that can only be built from the ground up. The therapeutic effect comes not from the sudden release of dammed up instinctual energies, as Freud suggested, but from the reorganization of experiences, feelings, and beliefs into new and more complex systems at many levels of structure.

What is the analyst's role in this? Does he only interpret? Does he do anything besides interpreting? Taking the traditional view of interpretation, the answer to both these questions is no. The hidden assumption behind them is that interpretation is sporadic and opportunistic. In reality the analyst processes what the patient says and does from the first minute of the analysis, to simulate as best he can what is happening in the patient's mind. His interventions follow systematically from what he learns as he processes. A more relevant question would be: How does the analyst decide when to convey the results of his processing to the patient? The answer is not mysterious. The analyst communicates what he learns to the patient when the patient presents him with feelings, ideas, and images that the analyst recognizes as being connected. The patient shows he is ready for the analyst's intervention by bringing his ideas and feelings into juxtaposition in the analytic discourse, but without actually making the connection himself.

The juxtaposition may be temporal, but it may also be created through similarities of image, metaphor, or verbal style that bridge a span of time. Then the analyst makes the connection by matching what the patient is saying right now to what he has said previously. The analyst may feel greater confidence in the timing of his intervention when the patient makes the same juxtaposition more than once, as he most often does.

What do we mean by an interpretation, then? What makes an interpretation mutative? Any communication by the analyst that makes a new connection in the patient's mind is mutative, and, as such, an interpretation. A connection is mutative when it links the contents of the patient's mental organization in a new way, at any level. For example, "You must have felt bad about that," is an interpretation when the patient reports an unpleasant experience *without affective expression.* Interpretation at this basic level, connecting experience with feeling, is often necessary before the patient can even begin to sort out the nature of the feeling, not to mention the unconscious guilt that led him to deny the feeling in the first place.

Thinking about the analytic process in this way allows one to move quickly and easily from the larger task of the coevolutionary partners in the analysis as a whole to the details of their everyday interaction. This is because the larger task and the daily details all fit within the same conceptual framework. The same principles of collaborative interchange apply at all scales of the analytic process.

The same is true for typical questions at an intermediate level. Why does the progress of an analysis take so many twists and turns, with sudden advances following long periods of apparent stasis? This is simply the way organization evolves. Turning points occur at large and small scales. They are the organizational phase transitions from which new states of mind emerge.

Why does the patient's feeling a little better so often make him seem to lose interest in feeling much better? Freud thought patients are motivated to change by anxiety, and become less motivated when their anxiety is reduced. We have seen that anxiety about descending from a local optimum on his fitness landscape *prevents* a patient from risking a new search for a higher peak.

Then what moves the analytic process forward, in general? According to the Freudian tradition, the main motive force behind progress in analysis is the patient's discomfort. The patient wants to be relieved of anxiety and frustration. The analyst obliges by analyzing him. The impetus for the analysis comes from the patient exclusively. While it is true that every analysis is initiated by the patient's complaints, it is not true that the analysis must be reinitiated at every moment by these complaints and those that succeed them. Once the analytic process gets under way, it awakens the patient's desire to act on his own behalf for the improvement of his situation in life. That is, it restores his ability to function as a complex adaptive system.

When this happens, when the patient begins to function as an independent agent, his need to adapt becomes a motivational force that operates effectively in the absence of any immediate discomfort. The phase transition to this level of autonomy does not depend entirely on the patient, although the patient must be able to collaborate. A patient will become an agent only if the analyst can adapt successfully to the psychological disabilities that bring him into treatment. The analyst must demonstrate that he can learn from what the patient tells and shows him. The change in the analyst's understanding of the patient creates the opportunity for the patient to change through a reciprocal coevolutionary movement. And vice versa.

These are the conditions for the analytic process to work. Once it is working it is self-maintaining. This does not mean that the patient's resistances disappear. His commitment to the analytic process may be threatened at various times. But if the analyst successfully adapts his own behavior to the patient's difficulties in following the fundamental rule, then a mutually satisfying outcome is likely. Without a coevolutionary process, no amount of suffering on the patient's part can make an analysis work. With a coevolutionary process, no experience of success by the patient should prevent the process from continuing to completion.

This is only a small sampling of questions we can ask about the psychoanalytic process. Many other issues have been addressed in *The Emergent Ego*. What is psychic structure, for instance? How does it change? How can a linear sequence of the analyst's words alter the multidimensional structure of the patient's long term memory? How can dreaming be an essential part of the therapeutic process even when the patient doesn't remember his dreams? Why are psychoanalysis and psychophar-macology complementary rather than competing methods of treatment?

We now have good enough answers to these and many other questions that affect psychoanalytic technique. Good enough, that is, to provide an immediate benefit for patients in analysis today. We also have a new set of testable hypotheses, sufficient, I believe, to distinguish psychoanalysis from methods of psychic healing that disavow the complexity of the human brain and spirit or the significance of the coevolutionary interaction between patient and analyst.

EPILOGUE

The publication of any part of an analytic discourse affects the nature of the analytic relationship. It introduces a new set of possibly divergent goals for the partners in an already very complicated ecosystem. The analyst's interest in learning from the patient ordinarily converges with the patient's interest in being understood. This is not true of publication. While the analyst has both altruistic and selfish motives for communicating what he has learned to his colleagues, neither of these motivations has much to do with benefiting the patient directly.

Analysts respond differently to this dilemma. Many avoid publication altogether. Others make great efforts to disguise the material, hoping that the patient will not become aware that his analytic experience has appeared in print. This may work for brief excerpts, but it nonetheless violates the confidentiality of the relationship. I am doubtful that the countertransference of an analyst who undertakes such a unilateral action can ever be successfully analyzed within the context of the analytic relationship.

Still other analysts delay publication until the analysis is completed, with the expectation that the analysis will not be affected retroactively. I think this is a large and for the most part unwarranted assumption. If anything needs to be analyzed, it is the patient's disappointment on discovering that the analyst is concerned about other things than the patient's welfare. What is to be done?

For the patient to have an opportunity to analyze his feelings about this departure from the original analytic contract, the analyst's plans for publication must be announced during the analysis. This is a delicate matter, because the analytic relationship has to be sufficiently consolidated to withstand the introduction of the analyst's ambition into the analytic discourse. Even in a successful analysis, like Richard's, a considerable amount of work is required to accommodate this modification. Here is what happened when Richard heard about the analyst's plan.

Richard was asked by his analyst to review chapter 2 of this manuscript, with an explanation of its role in the book. He was very curious. He agreed to look at it without thinking twice. On the way home, however, he thought, "I'm sure reading this will change the analysis forever. Maybe I'd better not read it." But he read it immediately, although, he said, keeping his distance from it. As he read the chapter, he found himself becoming angrier and angrier. He made notes, suggesting changes that would improve the disguising of his identity. None of these were of great significance, however, and nothing explained the anger he was feeling. He spent many hours trying to understand his reaction.

He told the analyst that he had come up with two things that bothered him. One was the presence of the analyst as a *subject* in the written description of the analysis. "In here, I'm the subject 99 percent of the time. That's what I'm used to. I wanted to say, 'Fuck you! I'm moving on' " After a silence, the analyst said, " 'Fuck you!' usually means that your mother's subjective feelings and problems are intruding on you and burdening you. Perhaps your awareness of me as a subject makes you feel that you have to put your own feelings aside to please me."

Richard said, "Well, maybe therapy doesn't really have to change." The analyst said, "One thing that has changed is that it may be easier for you to anticipate what I'm thinking, so that you may be more tempted to say what you think I'm expecting to hear." Richard said, "Yes, it's like there will be two of me here. I have the image of a balloon slowly leaking. It makes me want to put the analysis behind me as if it were part of my experience with my family. I feel manipulated."

The second issue was the "clinical" tone of the case report. "All those abstract words that we never use in here." It was as if it were about someone else. "I like the fact that the therapy happens right here in this room. Now it will be out in the world somewhere where I can't control it. It won't have anything to do with me anymore." The analyst asked if the possibility that other people might benefit from the use of his case in the book meant anything to him. Richard said he hadn't thought about it. The analyst said, "Perhaps you're angry that you'll be sharing what you've worked so hard for without getting anything directly in return. Maybe this connects with the situation you experienced with your younger brother." Richard said that sounded plausible to him, but that he didn't feel anything about it.

On the weekend he attended a family gathering. He was asked to bring a guest to the party who lived at a distance. He agreed to do it, although it required considerable effort and kept him away from the party for some time. His good deed was appreciated, but he couldn't make up his mind whether he was a hero or a chump for doing it. He wondered if his motive was merely to impress his relatives.

That night he dreamed that he was standing on the platform of a train station. He was throwing people off the platform onto the electrified rail, killing them. Only one of the victims was identified, a child in the family. The other victims were adults he didn't know. In his associations to the child he mentioned some differences he felt with the child's father, a very assertive person. The analyst suggested that the father might not have been so easy to throw off the platform. Richard said it was odd that there was no resistance to his own aggression from anyone in the dream.

The analyst said, "Maybe this is a case of taking out your anger at an older male on a younger one who can't defend himself. That would tie in with your anger at your younger brother for taking your mother away, when your father was your main rival." Richard then mentioned fantasies he had entertained of hurting the man he was bringing to the party. "It would have been easy," he said. The analyst asked about the nameless adult victims in the dream. Richard said, "They didn't even try to defend themselves from me."

The analyst said, "They make me think of the nameless people who might benefit from the publication of your story. They would have no recourse if you decided to hold it back." Richard replied, "You told me that one neurosis is very much like another one. I wonder if one recovery from a neurosis is like every other one, too. You seem to be suggesting that mine might actually be better than somebody else's. The analyst said, "I wanted to use your story to illustrate the process of recovery because I think it shows how it works with unusual clarity." Richard agreed to make notes on the items he wanted changed.

Several weeks went by without any mention of the manuscript chapter. Richard spoke mostly about his ambition at work and his impatience with inept subordinates. When Richard was discussing his resentment of some assignments he received at work, the analyst suggested that he too had given Richard an assignment he might resent. At work, the problem was that Richard often felt obliged to do more than his own assignment, to make up for the others who were not as conscientious. The analyst said he thought the chapter must have contained a lot more than Richard could have digested in a single reading.

Richard said it was strange to see his analysis from someone else's point of view. The analyst said, "It was strange to find out what I was thinking." Richard said, "Yes, it was disillusioning to find out that you had to think at all. I imagined that you just knew everything."

A week later Richard reported that he had reread the chapter. He was making notes about the changes he wanted, and would bring them in. He noticed that during his first reading of the chapter he had missed something important, the extent of his own aggression. He related this to his situation at work, especially his impatience with his colleagues lower down in the hierarchy. He really wanted to "smash them" when they failed to do their work effectively. He saw that this was interfering with his ability to motivate them, as well as being inappropriate.

He had just had his yearly evaluation, which went very well. His boss's assistant wasn't there this time, just his boss and himself. This meant that he was being treated as more on the assistant's level, not just a beginner, as he was the year before. He then remembered a fantasy he had in the seventh grade which he had reported several times before. He was doing really well in his woodworking class at school, and imagined himself as the teacher's assistant. His mother had encouraged him to ask the teacher if he could actually be his "assistant." He was mortified when he was turned down, but secretly admired the teacher for sparing him from the extra responsibility.

The analyst said, "By asking for your comments on the manuscript I was in a way making you *my* assistant." Richard said, "Yes, I felt that when you gave me the chapter, our relationship changed forever. By accepting this other role I was giving up my assurance of being taken care of by you." The analyst said, "As if my willingness to be your doctor depended on your inhibiting all your aggression toward me." Richard said, "That's what I've been doing all my life."

Here we see Richard moving toward a new conceptualization of the analytic partnership. He is still caught up in his idealization of the analyst as the good parent of childhood who takes care of everything. But this is the same parent who demands strict obedience as the price for his caretaking. Richard's position as the subservient but protected child represents a local optimum in his development away from the isolated and depressed little boy he was. His pain at leaving this behind is evident. Yet it is essential for him to realize that parents have to learn and think, that they sometimes need assistance, and that they have personal goals apart from the welfare of their children. Without this realization, the next mountain on Richard's horizon would always seem insuperable.

The beneficial outcome of this departure from the original analytic contract raises a more general question about the state of the relationship when the analysis ends. Many analysts believe that the relationship can become more nearly symmetrical while remaining within the constraints defined when the analysis began. Much anecdotal evidence suggests that this possibility enters the patient's consciousness only when circumstances force him to see the analyst outside the professional analytic role.

As far as I know, these moments of recognition and disillusionment occur accidentally. The analyst plays no part in either planning or predicting them. Richard's analyst was not looking ahead to possible benefits of the discussion of the chapter, either. He was too concerned with the risk he was taking in disturbing Richard's privacy. Perhaps we might say that at a phase transition the patient is necessarily a little bit ahead of the analyst. This is

quite different from the situation when the patient is stuck at a
local optimum and the analyst has to anticipate the next move.
Here the patient arrives at his new viewpoint on the analytic process on his own. The analyst cannot anticipate such a reorganization of the patient's mental contents or what will emerge from it.

APPENDIX

Session 1.1

The patient came in prepared to begin analysis. While still sitting up in a chair, we discussed and set the times of her four hours per week, and also the financial arrangement in which I would give her the bill on the first session of each month and she was to bring the check in prior to the tenth of the month. I explained to her the basic rule of free association, after which she lay down on the couch and the analysis began.

P: What will I do if I'm pregnant?

A: In analysis there will be times when you will have questions that you want to ask. But before answering them it's important for us to try to understand what's behind the question and see if it has other meanings than the question itself.

P: I don't think I have any special reason to be pregnant, but I do wonder if maybe it would be detrimental to my treatment. If I am pregnant I also wonder whether maybe I did have a reason?

The material in the appendix is from *The Psychoanalytic Process: A Case Illustration* by Paul Dewald, Basic Books, 1972 and is reprinted here with permission. (Each dash represents 30 seconds of silence.)

A: What comes to your mind?

P: There can't be any other reasons and yet maybe I wondered that if I were to get pregnant that I wouldn't have to do this. (Elaborates the conflict.) I know that I did get pregnant within a month after I started my counselling with Mr. Harris.

A: Rather than jump to conclusions as to whether or not there is a reason, let's just look and see what comes to your mind.

P: Maybe I had the wish that it would make me ugly. I think I have a desire for that.

A: What's the detail?

P: I'm not sure whether that's my own thought or whether it is something that I was told. But I think that it would be an escape from any kind of sexual feelings. If I were pregnant and ugly then no one would be sexually attracted to me. I think that that is my biggest problem.——

A: You seem to have some fear of talking about it.

P: Yes, I can feel that. I've been completely frigid for the last three weeks and I can't even stand the thought of anything sexual. And yet, at the same time I've had a lot of dreams with orgasm.——

A: What comes to your mind about the hesitation in your thinking?

P: I have a sense of fright about my feelings toward you.——I was hoping that you could do my analysis. (Elaborates.) Then . . . I felt as if I had found someone who cared and that somehow I would get a relationship here even though I know that that's ridiculous and that I'm just a patient.——

A: Try to pursue what comes to your mind about this.

P: ——I have the feeling that you'll be mad at me if I don't say something, and so I just can't say anything. But the longer the silence lasts the worse it gets.

A: What comes to your mind about the idea that I would be mad at you?

P: I think of the way Mr. Harris used to react if I didn't say anything. It also makes me think of my father and the way he would say "jump" and I'd have to jump or else he would call me "stupid."—I have a sense of hostility about it. I know when I'm feeling love but I don't know when I'm being hostile. And it scares me most to show my hostile feelings. But I wonder if maybe I have that turned around.

A: What comes to your mind?

P: Maybe I'm really afraid to show my love feelings. I have quite a bit of hostility that I'm aware of, and it's like my mother's. She takes it out on sales people. Last night I dreamed that I was going to do this but then I ran back to Harris instead of to you. Somehow I felt so sorry for you. The person in the dream had a mustache so I figured it must be you. In the dream I thought "I'm so sorry that I didn't go to him and when I didn't, he cried." But then in the dream I said to myself, "You're not the first one and he's probably been hurt before."—

A: Dreams are frequently useful in analysis, but we use them in a special way. After you've told me the dream itself, try to take each of the elements in the dream as it occurred and see what your associations are to each part.

P: The man in the dream somehow reminded me of a boy that I used to go with. He got upset when I left him but he also got over it almost immediately. Somehow there was a feeling of many women being in the dream and that reminds me of my father and all of his affairs.

A: What are the details of your thoughts about the boy that you went with?

P: That was really the worst time in my life and I turned into a terrible person. He was a horrible boy and he came from a very bad family but I would cling to him just as if I clung to my life. I had lost all of my feeling of security when we moved to Springfield and so I grasped the nearest straw that I could find. I did lose that security that I had.

A: What was the detail?

P: My father had left us just before we moved and I always had the feeling that my mother and father didn't care about me.——I feel sick to my stomach just thinking of this. I grabbed hold of boys and I'd go steady but then we had to leave Evanston and I felt as if half of my life was gone. It was all something new for me but I felt so estranged and I also knew that what I was doing was wrong. I've never talked about this before. I would conquer something and then I would immediately start with someone new but it always made me so tired. Every time I grasp hold of somebody he slips away from me. That's the reason I felt so upset this morning about Tom's mother. Tom is my only stronghold and he was really the only one who would go with me steadily and he was the only one ever to really love me.

A: What comes to your mind about the upset this morning?

P: I got the feeling that somehow she would think me an unfit mother and then the whole thing began to snowball. I felt as if I had to call her and be sure that everything was all right. I had to convince myself that no one could take my children away from me.—I wonder if maybe it was my own fear. I hadn't even thought about it until she suggested that maybe she should take the children for awhile. I felt as if I wanted something this morning, but I don't know what.

A: What comes to your mind?

P: I felt so anxious as if I couldn't stand it.—I was afraid to start my analysis and I felt as if I was going to lose something.

A: What are your associations to your fear of the analysis?

P: (Laughs.) I felt as if through starting analysis that I'd turned my back on my family and that somehow I would never return to my old world and that I would be dependent for my whole life. It all frightens me.—I'm on my own for the first time in my life and I have to do this all by myself. My family are really opposed to it and I've never had to do anything by myself before.

A: What was the detail of the fright itself?

P: I feel like crying. I wonder what I'm thinking of?—It's so hard to do something that you're not sure of yourself, especially when everybody else is trying to talk you out of it. My parents object. I tried to break away from them but I haven't. But then they didn't even contact me about this. I know that I'm going to be mad if they don't help me, but I also know that they won't help.

A: What's the detail?

P: I think probably I'm going to change in some way, but I wonder is this the right thing for me to do? I don't know anyone who has ever been through analysis, and I wonder what about the results of analysis. I can't run away and yet I think that maybe my parents are right. I just don't know. I feel as if I'm hanging and I'm being pulled by both sides.

A: Let's look at the details of your fears of analysis and your doubts about starting. What comes to your mind?

P: I just don't know anything about it and I keep wondering what am I going into? I wonder will I be able to take it? At the same time I wonder what can be so frightening? But I sure do get frightened. I feel as if I'm completely placing myself in your hands and I don't even know you. I know that I'll probably be very dependent on you. (Elaborates.) I'm not sure that I'm strong enough for this and I know that I got awfully upset even while I was waiting to start.

A: So you feel as if you are starting on something new that's completely unknown and frightening, and you are doing it with someone that you don't know.

P: I feel as if I'm in a vise and that I'm caught. It's as if there are all kinds of holes and I'm about to fall through and yet I really do know that this is the only way. I've tried religion and I've tried running away and neither of them works. I'm so easily suggested to. (Elaborates.) I just have no mind of my own. (Elaborates.)

A: We'll stop here for today.

Session 1.16

P: ——I feel absolutely nothing. (Elaborates.) I'm not happy or angry at home.——

A: What comes to your mind about the silence?

Cry   **P:** —Jean called me. She's marrying a social worker at Veteran's Hospital and she's not sure of it, but she may be moving. It set me in a panic because I'm really dependent on Jean.

A: What's the detail?

P: We've always been good friends and very close and I stood by her through her divorce and we both went to Harris for a while. We used to call each other "the only person I can talk to." I can't even talk to Tom about some things and she was always a mother-image for me.

A: I wonder if you're worried that if she leaves this will intensify your feelings about me because she won't be around any more to dilute it. As a result, you have a sense of panic and so you are blocking off every feeling because of your fear of relating to me.

P: —It's like a dream that I had last night. I felt completely alone in the midst of a terrible disaster. In the dream I was at home with my two children and there were millions of tornadoes all around. I grabbed the children and we rushed to the basement, and I tried to get under something to protect us and Tom was at the office. Then an older woman came in. I've always had fears of tornadoes. (Elaborates.) The basement in the dream was a combination from the one we have now and from the one in the house where I grew up. It was like the dream of the world burning up or coming to an end. But this time I was all by myself and I had to protect my children because no one else was there.——

A: What are your thoughts about tornadoes?

P: I've been afraid of them ever since I was a girl. I saw a painting of one once as a girl and of how it hit. There was a mother leaning over her children and the clothes were being ripped off her back, and I know it impressed me.——

A: You were trying to get under something in the basement. What comes to your mind?

P: That was in case the house came down, so it wouldn't come down on us.—I want to run back to Harris because he knows me. I feel as if I'm being forced to stand up alone by myself. No one in the world is going to give me what I want and I have to accept the fact.——(Laughs.)—

A: What was the laughter?

P: I heard a noise and I feel as though I'm falling off the couch. I had a sensation of rocking.

A: The dream came to your mind in connection with the idea of intensifying your feelings about me. In the dream there is a lot of violence from the tornadoes and in the painting of the woman with the two children, her clothes were torn off. I think this represents you with your clothes off. You've described before how Tom gets excited and wild when you get undressed, but he wasn't in the dream. I wonder if you have a fantasy of getting undressed here, and if you have both a wish and a fear of exciting me sexually.

P: I have thought about that.

A: What was the detail?

P: I've thought that I wanted to stand up and take all of my clothes off but that is as far as I can think.——

A: Do you mean, "can think," or do you mean, "let yourself think?"

P: Let myself. I'm embarrassed thinking about that. Why would I think of it? It's silly. In January I went to see my O.B. man and I know that I was sexually attracted. It was the first time that I ever allowed myself to have sexual feelings in the examining room. I hoped that he would, and I immediately ate when I got home and I wouldn't stop eating for a week, I was so shocked at myself.——I've been thinking about being madly in love with you and it makes me excited to come every day and I feel just like a schoolgirl with a boy-friend. So I immediately say it's all silly, because I don't want to get into it, it's stupid.——All of my life I've hidden my feelings of love and attraction for boys and it's the same way with you. I'd die of embarrassment if you knew.——

A: What's the detail of the feeling?

P: Why wouldn't you accept it? I want to have feelings and have it *not* happen. But I'm afraid that you're not strong enough to resist. I feel as if you'll think, "This idiot."

A: What's the detail?

P: It's like I'd be bothering you and that I'm not capable of getting either love or sexual feelings from you. I'd be like a love-sick little girl pestering you and it shouldn't happen.

A: So you feel that it would be upsetting either way, whether you get a response or whether you don't get a response, and so you are choosing to block everything.

P: It would be frightening if I get a response and humiliating if I wouldn't.——I used to dress very carefully when I'd go for my sessions with Harris. I've made a point of *not* doing it with you.

A: What comes to your mind?

P: No matter what I'd look like, your reaction would always be the same.——When my parents used to visit after I got married I would parade around in front of my father in nightgowns or a slip. I was conscious of wanting to attract him. (Elaborates.) It was like I was suddenly saying, "I'm a woman, Daddy, look at me and realize it."—It never fazed him. He'd come into the room when I had the cramps and he'd talk to me and I used to feel that he was sexually attracted to me. Now I don't feel that he ever was. Somehow this makes me feel good.——How can I *really feel* sexual feeling for you and still remain a wife to my husband? I can't possible handle both.——

A: What comes to your mind?

P: I can imagine myself absolutely an idiot in love with you and wanting everything and being completely involved in it. How can I go home and love my husband and be sexually responsive? I'd feel guilty, as if I was having an affair.——

A: Your associations stopped suddenly and now there is silence. It's as if you don't want to go into something. What comes to your mind about not wanting to go further?

P: This is such a comical situation. The idea of having an affair! It's all so one-sided. It's not funny at all. But that's what I wanted. That was the way I felt before I saw Harris. It was all very exciting and yet I felt guilty. (Elaborates.)——

A: What comes to mind as to why you wanted to hold that back?

P: I can picture it really happening and that I'm not only thinking about it.——

A: We'll stop here for today.

Session 1.17

P: ——I've had a horrible feeling that I was going to pop ever since I was here yesterday. (Elaborates.) It's been ferocious. I had a dream and I was in a panic but I don't remember it.—

A: What was the detail of the feeling itself?

P: It was the same feeling of anxiety as if the whole world was going to crash in on me. I can't think at all and I will not let myself know anything.

A: You seem to be afraid of feeling anything, and of not thinking but just letting yourself feel.

P: I was trying to relax and was lying in the sun and my thoughts were wandering and I had a sudden sense of panic. I can hardly remember now but I caught myself plotting to destroy you. I was terribly afraid of the thoughts to follow.—

A: What was the detail of the plot to destroy me?

P: I don't remember.——It's like that dream, I just don't recall. I was frustrated with my child and I had the thought that she should be dead, and I started to cry and she wouldn't go to sleep and I felt as though I would like to kill her.—How mean you are to me. I thought about the things I would say to you but I don't remember.—I'm thinking about yesterday and my dream. You said that I wanted to undress in front of you. That's a horrible thing to say!——If I let myself go and start feeling, I just can't stand it! This way I can.

A: How do you mean that you can't stand it?

P: I can't function; I can't take care of my children, my home or anything. I'm so hostile at home and I hate it. So I'm not going to show anything. That's the only way I can survive. I've never been this way! I'm suddenly so afraid of my anger toward my children. I feel as if I'll die.

A: You've been having all of these feelings and fears at home. What are your associations to the feelings that you have there and the lack of feeling that you are having here in the analysis?

P: It's all going toward my husband and my children. The emotion should be directed toward you. I have so many feelings for you. But the only way to survive is not to feel it.

A: What's the detail of your thought that you wouldn't survive if you felt what you know you already feel here?

P: I don't know.—You put out no feeling at all, so how can I?——Sometimes I feel like . . . my emotions come up and I have such a fright and I just want to hold on to you and know that you're there. They overpower me and they kill me.———

A: What are your associations to the silence?

P: —I just don't want to talk.

A: Well, what comes to your mind?

Cry   **P:** —You're trying to destroy me. You want to bring out feelings and you don't want to help, but you are just going to sit and watch me suffer and I'm not going to!

A: What comes to your mind about me sitting here and watching you and not helping at all?

P: I'm so frightened! I'm really frightened! I feel like a child screaming in the dark and my parents won't come. With a child you can sit and reason with it. But I can't. I know there are no boogy men or ghosts or witches, but I just can't do it.

A: You have the feeling that I'll try to destroy you. What comes to your mind about that?

P: I'm thinking about my own needs and how you're not going to satisfy them but you'll see them and you won't help me. You enjoy seeing me frightened. Why don't you ever say, "I'm sorry, I understand, I'll try to help, and there's no reason for your fear?"

A: And what would it mean to you if I did say all of that?

P: I'd collapse. I just don't know. It's like there is something wrong with me for being afraid. You think I have no reason for fear, but I am afraid and so there is something wrong. I'm thinking about the time when I was very little and I hallucinated. (Elaborates.) My mother wouldn't come. I thought that things were trying to destroy me. She finally came at the end. I was never so scared! And they knew it!——

A: You have the thought that I'd feel there is something wrong with you if you're afraid. What are your associations?

Cry　　**P:** ——You don't accept my fear because you're afraid yourself. You ignore it or you'll get mad at it but you won't understand.——

A: What's the detail of the idea that I'm afraid?

P: —It's like . . . if I feel hostility it scares me and you know. It's all so horrible I just can't think.

A: If you can convince yourself that I'm afraid, then in a way you would be justified in trying to control your own feelings. I think you're using this as an excuse and as a defense against your own feelings.

Cry　　**P:** ——(Sigh.)—If I just knew what I was going to do.

A: What's the fantasy?

P: There is none. I picture myself lying here with my arms and legs flaying around and screaming and doing it for the rest of my life.——Whenever I have this anxiety feeling, I am afraid of the physical movements and motions. I think I'd run out on the street and scream and tear my hair and I'd act like an idiot.——

A: See if you can develop that fantasy further.

Cry　　**P:** —I can't stand it!——

A: We'll stop here for today.

Session 3.1

P: ——I'm afraid to talk.—I'm afraid that I'm being deserted. I have my defenses of independence and I'm afraid that they'll crumble if I talk about it.

A: What's the detail of the fear of being deserted?

P: —I'm thinking about your vacation for a whole month this summer. I feel sick to my stomach. I keep wondering if I can make it. It's like I felt on Friday. Everything is all right if I see you every day, but if there is any break then I fall apart, and I'm unsure if I'll ever see you again.

A: What are your associations to that?

P: —I don't know. It's not logical; it's just a feeling.

A: Let's just look at the details of your associations without too much concern about the logic of them.

Cry **P:** —It's an emotional separation. If I'm not with you I'm never sure that you'll be there. It's just like when my parents went out. I was always afraid that they'd leave us forever.

A: What do you remember about that feeling?

P: I was so insecure. I could see them when they were there. It's just a feeling.

A: That's the very reason to look at it without so much emphasis on the logic. You're repeating with me a feeling that you once had with your patents.

Cry, Sob **P:** ——I went through a terrible phase of fear about my parents. For a while they went out every day and I'd be sick and feel that I couldn't breathe and I thought I'd die. There was a person who stayed with us and she was up in the attic and I felt as if we were in the house by ourselves, just us three girls. I felt all alone and I thought there was nobody I could depend on and I knew that I couldn't live. I was sick once and I had a terrible headache and they just gave me some aspirin and went out and there was nobody there but my sisters. I knew that something was wrong with me. Finally they took me to a hospital.——They never were sure whether it was polio or meningitis, but I was in the hospital about a week. That was the only time that I was ever sick, and afterwards I went to my grandmother's. My mother didn't take care of me. For instance, when I had pneumonia when I was three months old I was sent to my grandmother's. My parents never took care of me! They left me alone all the time!——I can't let myself depend on them or on you. You'll not always be there. I want not to be afraid when I'm not with you, and to feel that you will return and that I'm capable until you do. But I can't depend on you. No one ever knew the fear that was inside of me.

A: What about the fear that is inside you now about me?

Cry, Sob   **P:** —It's obvious to me how much I depend on you! If I admit it then I'm helpless. Then I'd beg you to take care of me and love me and I'm unsure if you will and I'm mad at myself that I need you so much!—It's so hard to admit this but my whole security lies in you. I'm afraid that you are not going to give me the security I need. I want and *need* you to take care of me. Then I try to deny it and I'll take care of myself.

A: So we can see that the situation is different today but that the feelings are the same as when you were a little girl.

P: —It's a hopeless feeling to look to others for security and never get it. It makes me mad!

A: What comes to your mind?

P: I'm mad at you, and then at myself for needing it. And then I get mad to the point that I don't need you. I'm mad that you don't see it and do something about it.

A: So we can see how angry you are at me but you are also afraid that I'll desert you if you ever express the anger and so you turn it back against yourself. This is like the feeling Monday when you had the urge to walk out and slam the door and you were afraid that I wouldn't see you again if you did. And it's also like Sunday when you were angry at me and then had the fantasy that you were going to cut your own wrists.

P: ——I want to ask you like a little child, "Are you going to be back on Monday?" I really know the answer.——

A: Let's look at your associations to the question.

Cry!   **P:** I don't like to ask it. I never had the nerve to ask my parents if they were going out, and I always sent my sister in to ask. It was silly, but I can't admit it.——It would be like saying, "Please stay, I'm helpless and I don't want you to go."—I wonder why did I never cry and say it to my parents? I just couldn't. It put the reality right in front of me.

A: What comes to your mind?

Cry   **P:** I could talk myself into not needing anyone and survive. But if I ever really say, "I need you," then I have no defenses. I can at least survive if I don't admit this. But if I ever cried, then I'd be by myself. If I hold my head and my chin up then I feel stronger. But if I cried I'd just die there right on the floor.—I get a sense of panic to be left alone to die for the rest of my life. That's my biggest fear.

A: And this was your feeling when Harris abruptly said he wasn't going to see you any more.

P: —Ha! There is no defense for this. I feel that I'll die and that's no defense. To say that I don't care would be all right if it was honest. But I keep having these spells of not being able to breathe or being afraid I'm going to die or wanting to cut my wrists, and that's just no way to live.—

A: One problem comes up when you try to *fool* yourself about not caring.

P: I can't fool myself, and so what do I do?——What if I ever allow myself to need you? I know that I do, but what will happen if I ever drop my defenses about not needing you and not loving you?

A: What comes to your mind about it?

P: I'm afraid of being left alone and emotionally not satisfied. I can't live that way. I want to be capable of taking care of myself really and not do it by fooling myself. But how do I get to this?———I'm waiting for doom's day.

A: What are your associations to the feeling?

P: I'm waiting for you to say that it is time to go. I have a sense of panic and I just can't stand it. I just sit and wait.—

A: We'll stop here for today.

At the door the analyst hands her the bill for the previous month.

REFERENCES

Abraham, K. (1955), *Clinical Papers and Essays on Psychoanalysis.* New York: Basic Books, 1956.

Ackley, D., & Littman, M. (1994), A case for Lamarckian evolution. In: *Artificial Life,* Vol. 3, ed. C. G. Langton. Reading, MA: Addison-Wesley, pp. 3–10.

Axelrod, R. (1984), *The Evolution of Cooperation.* New York: Basic Books.

Bak, P. (1994), Self-organized criticality: A holistic view of nature. In: *Complexity: Metaphors, Models and Reality,* ed. G. A. Cowan, D. Pines, & D. Meltzer. Redwood City, CA: Addison-Wesley, pp. 477–496.

——— (1996), *How Nature Works.* New York: Springer-Verlag.

——— Tang, C., & Wiesenfeld, K. (1988), Self-organized criticality. *Physical Rev. A.,* 38:364.

Berlecamp, E., Conway, J., & Guy, R. (1982), *Winning Ways,* Vol. 2. New York: Academic Press.

Breger, L. (1967), Function of dreams. *J. Abnormal Psych. Monograph,* 72:1–28.

Breuer, J., & Freud, S. (1893–1895), Studies on Hysteria. *Standard Edition,* 2. London: Hogarth Press, 1955.

Buss, L. (1987), *The Evolution of Individuality.* Princeton, NJ: Princeton University Press.

Bybee, J., Perkins, P., & Pagliuca, W. (1994), *The Evolution of Grammar: Tense, Aspect and Modality in the Languages of the World.* Chicago: University of Chicago Press.

Campbell, D. T. (1965), Variation and selective retention in sociocultural evolution. In: *Social Change in Developing Areas: A Reinterpretation of Evolutionary Theory,* ed. H. R. Barringer, G. I. Blanksten, & R. W. Mack. Cambridge, MA: Schenkman.

Casti, J. L. (1993), The cognitive revolution? Santa Fe Institute Working Paper 93-05-30.

Cohen, N. J., & Eichenbaum, H. (1993), *Memory, Amnesia and the Hippocampal System.* Cambridge, MA: M.I.T. Press.

Colby, K. M. (1975), *Artificial Paranoia: A Computer Simulation of Paranoid Processes.* New York: Pergamon.

Crutchfield, J. P. (1994), Is anything ever new? Considering emergence. In: *Complexity: Metaphors, Models and Reality,* ed. G. A. Cowan, D. Pines, & D. Meltzer. Redwood City, CA: Addison-Wesley, pp. 515–538.

Curtis, H. C. (1979), The concept of the therapeutic alliance: Implications for the "Widening scope." *J. Amer. Psychoanal. Assn.,* 27(Suppl.):159–192.

Darwin, C. (1859), *The Origin of Species by Means of Natural Selection or the Preservation of Favored Races in the Struggle for Life.* Facsimile reprint. Cambridge, MA: Harvard University Press, 1964.

Davies, N. B., & Brooke, M. (1991), Coevolution of the cuckoo and its hosts. *Sci. Amer.,* 270:92–98.

Dawkins, R. (1976), *The Selfish Gene.* Oxford: Oxford University Press.

———— (1982), *The Blind Watchmaker.* New York: W. W. Norton.

Depew, D. J., & Weber, B. (1995), *Darwinism Evolving: Systems Dynamics and the Genealogy of Natural Selection.* Cambridge, MA: M.I.T. Press.

Dewald, P. (1972), *The Psychoanalytic Process.* New York: Basic Books.

Domingo, E., Sabo, D., Tanaguchi, T., & Weissmann, C. (1978), Nucleotide sequence: Heterogeneity of an RNA phage population. *Cell,* 13:735.

Durham, W. (1991), *Coevolution: Genes, Culture and Human Diversity.* Stanford, CA: Stanford University Press.

Edelman, G. (1987), *Neural Darwinism*. New York: Basic Books.

——— (1989), *The Remembered Present*. New York: Basic Books.

——— (1992), *Bright Air, Brilliant Fire*. New York: Basic Books.

Ehrlich, P. R., & Raven, P. H. (1964), Butterflies and plants: A study in coevolution. *Evolution*, 18:586–608.

Eigen, M. (1992), *Steps Towards Life*. Oxford: Oxford University Press.

——— McCaskill, J., & Schuster, P. (1988), The quasi-species. *J. Phys. Chem.*, 92:6881.

——— Schuster, P. (1977), The hypercycle. A principle of natural self-organization. Part A: Emergence of the hypercycle. *Naturwissenschaften*, 64:541–565.

——— Winkler-Oswatitsch, R. (1975), *Laws of the Game*. New York: Knopf, 1981.

Eldredge, N., & Gould, S. J. (1972), Punctuated equilibria: An alternative to phyletic gradualism. In: *Models in Paleobiology*, ed. T. J. M. Schopf. San Francisco: W. M. Freeman.

Erikson, E. (1950), *Childhood and Society*, 2nd ed., rev. & enlarged. New York: W. W. Norton, 1963.

Fairbairn, W. R. D. (1946), Object relationships and dynamic structure. *Internat. J. Psycho-Anal.*, 27:30–37.

——— (1958), On the nature and aims of psychoanalytical treatment. *Internat. J. Psycho-Anal.*, 39:374–385.

Fauconnier, G. (1985), *Mental Spaces: Aspects of Meaning Construction in Natural Languages*. Cambridge, MA: M.I.T. Press.

Finkel, L. H., Reeke, G., & Edelman, G. (1989), A population approach to the neural basis of perceptual categorization. In: *Neural Connections, Mental Computation*, ed. L. Nadel, L. Cooper, P. Culicover, & R. M. Harnish. Cambridge, MA: M.I.T. Press, pp. 146–179.

Fontana, W. (1992), Algorithmic chemistry. In: *Artificial Life*, Vol. 2, ed. C. Langton, C. Taylor, J. D. Farmer, & S. Rasmussen. Redwood City, CA: Addison-Wesley, pp. 159–210.

——— Buss, L. (1993), The arrival of the fittest: Toward a theory of biological organization. Santa Fe Institute Working Paper 93-09-055.

——— ——— (1994), What would be conserved if 'the tape were played twice'? In: *Complexity: Metaphors, Models and Reality*, ed.

G. A. Cowan, D. Pines, & D. Meltzer. Redwood City, CA: Addison-Wesley, pp. 223–236.

———— ———— (1996), The barrier of objects. In: *Boundaries and Barriers: On the Limits of Scientific Knowledge,* ed. J. L. Casti & A. Karlqvist. Reading, MA: Addison-Wesley, pp. 55–84.

Freeman, W. J. (1995), *Societies of Brains: A Study in the Neuroscience of Love and Hate.* Hillsdale, N.J.: Lawrence Erlbaum.

Freud, A. (1936), *The Ego and the Mechanisms of Defense.* New York: International Universities Press, 1946.

Freud, S. (1900), The Interpretation of Dreams. *Standard Edition,* 4 & 5. London: Hogarth Press, 1955.

———— (1901), On dreams. *Standard Edition,* 5. London: Hogarth Press, 1955.

———— (1905), Three Essays on the Theory of Sexuality. *Standard Edition,* 7:123–143. London: Hogarth Press, 1953.

———— (1911), The handling of dream interpretation in psychoanalysis. *Standard Edition,* 12:89–96. London: Hogarth Press, 1958.

———— (1912), The dynamics of the transference. *Standard Edition,* 12:97–108. London: Hogarth Press, 1958.

———— (1914), Remembering, repeating and working through. *Standard Edition,* 12:145–156. London: Hogarth Press, 1958.

———— (1915), The unconscious. *Standard Edition,* 15:159–204. London: Hogarth Press, 1957.

———— (1917), Introductory Lectures on Psychoanalysis. *Standard Edition,* 16. London: Hogarth Press, 1961.

———— (1920), Beyond the Pleasure Principle. *Standard Edition,* 18:1–64. London: Hogarth Press, 1955.

———— (1923), The Ego and the Id. *Standard Edition,* 19:1–59. London: Hogarth Press, 1961.

———— (1925a), Some additional notes on dream-interpretation as a whole. *Standard Edition,* 19:123–138. London: Hogarth Press, 1961.

———— (1925b), A note upon the 'Mystic Writing-Pad.' *Standard Edition,* 19:225–232. London: Hogarth Press, 1961.

———— (1937a), Analysis terminable and interminable. *Standard Edition,* 23:209–253. London: Hogarth Press, 1964.

———— (1937b), Constructions in analysis. *Standard Edition,* 23:255–269. London: Hogarth Press, 1964.

Fromm, E. (1941), *Escape from Freedom*. New York: Rinehart.

Gelfand, A. E., & Walker, C. C. (1984), *Ensemble Modeling*. New York: Marcel Dekker.

Gell-Mann, M. (1992), Complexity and complex adaptive systems. In: *The Evolution of Human Languages,* ed. M. Gell-Mann & J. A. Hawkins. Reading, MA: Addison-Wesley.

———— (1994), *The Quark and the Jaguar*. New York: W. H. Freeman.

Gitelson, M. (1952), The emotional position of the analyst in the analytic situation. *Internat. J. Psycho-Anal.,* 33:1–10.

Gould, S. J. (1989), *Wonderful Life: The Burgess Shale and the Nature of History*. New York: W. W. Norton.

Grant, P. R., & Grant, B. R. (1992), Hybridization of bird species. *Science,* 256:193–197.

Graubard, S. R., Ed. (1988), Artificial Intelligence. *Daedalus* (whole issue) 117:1–312.

Greenberg, J. (1963), Some universals of grammar with particular reference to the order of meaningful elements. In: *Universals of Language,* ed. J. Greenberg. Cambridge, MA: M.I.T. Press.

Greenberg, J. R., & Mitchell, S. A. (1983), *Object Relations in Psychoanalytic Theory*. Cambridge, MA: Harvard University Press.

Greenson, R. R. (1967), *The Technique and Practice of Psychoanalysis*. New York: International Universities Press, 1958.

———— Wexler, M. (1969), The non-transference relationship in the psychoanalytic situation. *Internat. J. Psycho-Anal.,* 50:27–40.

Greenspan, S. I. (1979), *Intelligence and Adaptation*. New York: International Universities Press.

Gumerman, C., & Gell-Mann, M. (1994), *Understanding Complexity in the Prehistoric Southwest*. Redwood City, CA: Addison-Wesley.

Guntrip, H. (1961), *Personality Structure and Human Interaction. The Developing Synthesis of Psychodynamic Theory*. New York: International Universities Press.

Harris, I. D. (1962), Dreams about the analyst. *Internat. J. Psycho-Anal.,* 43:151–158.

Hartmann, H. (1939), *Ego Psychology and the Problem of Adaptation*. New York: International Universities Press, 1958.

———— (1964), *Essays on Ego Psychology*. New York: International Universities Press.

Hawkins, D. (1966), A review of psychoanalytic dream theory in the light of recent psycho-physiological studies of sleep and dreaming. *Brit. J. Med. Psychol.*, 39:85–104.

Hebb, D. O. (1949), *The Organization of Behavior.* New York: Wiley.

Hendrick, I. (1943), Work and the pleasure principle. *Psychoanal. Quart.*, 12:311–329.

Holland, J. H. (1975), *Adaptation in Natural and Artificial Systems.* Ann Arbor: University of Michigan Press.

——— (1996), *Hidden Order: How Adaptation Builds Complexity.* Reading, MA: Addison-Wesley.

Huberman, B. A. (1989), The adaptation of complex systems. In: *Theoretical Biology: Epigenetic and Evolutionary Order from Complex Systems,* ed. B. Goodwin & P. Saunders. Edinburgh: Edinburgh University Press, pp. 124–133.

Kaku, M. (1994), *Hyperspace.* Oxford: Oxford University Press.

Kaneko, K., & Suzuki, J. (1994), Evolution to the edge of chaos in an imitation game. In: *Artificial Life,* Vol. 3, ed. C. G. Langton. Reading, MA: Addison-Wesley, pp. 43–54.

Kanzer, M. (1981), Freud's 'Analytic Pact': The standard therapeutic alliance. *J. Amer. Psychoanal. Assn.*, 29:69–88.

Kauffman, S. (1993), *The Origins of Order: Self-Organization and Selection in Evolution.* Oxford: Oxford University Press.

——— (1995), *At Home in the Universe.* Oxford: Oxford University Press.

Kelso, J. A. S. (1996), *Dynamic Patterns: The Self-Organization of Brain and Behavior.* Cambridge, MA: M.I.T. Press.

Khan, M. (1976), The changing use of dreams in psychoanalytic practice. *Internat. J. Psycho-Anal.*, 57:325–330.

Klein, M. (1940), Mourning and its relation to manic-depressive states. *Internat. J. Psycho-Anal.*, 21:125–153.

——— (1946), Notes on some schizoid mechanisms. *Internat. J. Psycho-Anal.*, 27:99.

——— Heimann, P., & Money-Kyrle, R. (1955), *New Directions in Psychoanalysis.* New York: Basic Books.

Koestler, A. (1964), *The Act of Creation.* New York: Macmillan.

Koza, J. R. (1992), Genetic evolution and coevolution in computer programs. In: *Artificial Life,* Vol. 2, ed. C. Langton, C. Taylor, J. D. Farmer, & S. Rasmussen. Redwood City, CA: Addison-Wesley, pp. 603–630.

—— (1994), *Genetic Programming*. Cambridge, MA: M.I.T. Press.

Kris, A. (1982), *Free Association: Method and Process*. New Haven, CT: Yale University Press.

Kris, E. (1951), Ego psychology and interpretation in psychoanalytic therapy. *Psychoanal. Quart.*, 20:15–30.

Kuhn, T. (1961), *The Structure of Scientific Revolutions*. Chicago: University of Chicago Press.

Lakoff, G., & Johnson, M. (1980), *Metaphors We Live By*. Chicago: University of Chicago Press.

Langton, C. G. (1989), Artificial life. In: *Artificial Life*, ed. C. G. Langton. Reading, MA: Addison-Wesley, pp. 1–48.

—— (1992), Life at the edge of chaos. In: *Artificial Life*, Vol. 2. ed. C. G. Langton, C. Taylor, J. D. Farmer, & S. Rasmussen. Redwood City, CA: Addison-Wesley, pp. 41–92.

—— Taylor, C., Farmer, J. D., & Rasmussen, S., Eds. (1992), *Artificial Life*, Vol. 2. Redwood City, CA: Addison-Wesley.

Lester, E. P., Jodoin, R.- M., & Robertson, B. M. (1989), Countertransference dreams reconsidered: A survey. *Internat. Rev. Psychoanal.*, 6:305–313.

Lindgren, K. (1992), Evolutionary phenomena in simple dynamics. In *Artificial Life*, Vol. 2, ed. C. G. Langton, C. Taylor, J. D. Farmer, & S. Rasmussen. Redwood City, CA: Addison-Wesley, pp. 295–312.

Loewald, H. (1960), On the therapeutic action of psychoanalysis. *Internat. J. Psycho-Anal.*, 41:16–33.

Lynch, G., Granger, R., Larson, J., & Baudry, M. (1989), Cortical encoding of memory: Hypotheses derived from analysis and simulation of physiological learning rules in anatomical structures. In: *Neural Connections, Mental Computation,* ed. L. Nadel, L. Cooper, P. Culicover, & R. M. Harnish. Cambridge, MA: M.I.T. Press, pp. 180–224.

Maynard Smith, J. (1982), *Evolution and the Theory of Games*. Cambridge, U.K.: Cambridge University Press.

—— (1994), The major transitions in evolution. In: *Complexity: Metaphors, Models and Reality,* ed. G. A. Cowan, D. Pines, & D. Meltzer. Redwood City, CA: Addison-Wesley, pp. 457–470.

Mayr, E. (1963), *Animal Species and Evolution*. Cambridge, MA: Harvard University Press.

McClelland, J. L., & Rumelhart, D. E. (1986), A distributed model of human learning and memory. In: *Parallel Distributed Processing*, Vol. 2, ed. J. L. McClelland & D. E. Rumelhart. Cambridge, MA: M.I.T. Press, pp. 170–215.

Monod, J. (1971), *Chance and Necessity*. New York: Knopf.

Moran, M. (1991), Chaos theory and psychoanalysis. *Internat. Rev. Psychoanal.*, 18:211–222.

Morowitz, H. (1992), *Beginnings of Cellular Life*. New Haven, CT: Yale University Press.

Nadel, L., Cooper, L., Culicover, P., & Harnish, R M., Eds. (1989), *Neural Connections, Mental Computation*. Cambridge, MA: M.I.T. Press.

Newell, A., Shaw, J. C., & Simon, H. A. (1957), Empirical explorations of the Logic Theory Machine. *Proceedings of the 1957 Western Joint Computer Conference*. New York: Institute of Radio Engineers.

Nunberg, H. (1931), The synthetic function of the ego. *Internat. J. Psycho-Anal.*, 12:123–140.

Olds, D. (1994), Connectionism and psychoanalysis. *J. Amer. Psychoanal. Assn.*, 42:581–612.

O'Keefe, J. (1989), Computations the hippocampus might perform. In: *Neural Connections, Mental Computation*, ed. L. Nadel, L. Cooper, P. Culicover, & R. M. Harnish. Cambridge, MA: M.I.T. Press, pp. 225–284.

Packard, N. H. (1988), Adaptation at the edge of chaos. Technical Report CCSR-88-5, Center for Complex Systems Research, University of Illinois.

Padel, R. (1992), *In and Out of the Mind: Greek Images of the Tragic Self*. Princeton, NJ: Princeton University Press.

Palombo, S. R. (1973), The associative memory tree. *Psychoanal. & Contemp. Sci.*, 2:205–219.

———— (1976), The dream and the memory cycle. *Internat. Rev. Psychoanal.*, 3:65–84.

———— (1977), Dreams, memory and the origin of thought. In: *Thought, Consciousness and Reality: Psychiatry and the Humanities*, Vol. 2, ed. J. H. Smith. New Haven, CT: Yale University Press, pp. 49–83.

———— (1978), *Dreaming and Memory: A New Information-Processing Model*. New York: Basic Books.

———— (1980), The cognitive act in dream construction. *J. Amer. Acad. Psychoanal.*, 8:185–201.

———— (1981), Emanuel Peterfreund on information and systems theory. *Psychoanal. Rev.*, 68:168–173.

———— (1982), How the dream works: The role of dreaming in the psychotherapeutic process. In: *Curative Factors in Dynamic Psychotherapy*, ed. S. Slipp. New York: McGraw-Hill, pp. 223–242.

———— (1984a), Recovery of early memories associated with reported dream imagery. *Amer. J. Psychiatry*, 141:1508–1511.

———— (1984b), The poet as dreamer. *J. Amer. Acad. Psychoanal.*, 12:59–73.

———— (1984c), Deconstructing the manifest dream. *J. Amer. Psychoanal. Assn.*, 32:405–420.

———— (1985a), Can a computer dream? *J. Amer. Acad. Psychoanal.*, 13:453–466.

———— (1985b), Emanuel Peterfreund: The information revolution. In: *Beyond Freud: A Study of Modern Psychoanalytic Theorists*, ed. J. Reppen. New York: Analytic Press, pp. 109–134.

———— (1985c), The primary process: A reconceptualization. *Psychoanal. Inq.*, 5:405–435.

———— (1987), Hitchcock's *Vertigo:* The dream function in film. In: *Images in Our Souls: Cavell, Psychoanalysis and Cinema: Psychiatry and the Humanities*, Vol. 10, ed. J. H. Smith. Baltimore: Johns Hopkins University Press, pp. 44–63.

———— (1988), Day residue and screen memory in Freud's dream of the botanical monograph. *J. Amer. Psychoanal. Assn.*, 36:881–904.

———— (1992a), The Eros of dreaming. *Internat. J. Psycho-Anal.*, 73:637–646.

———— (1992b), Connectivity and condensation in dreaming. *J. Amer. Psychoanal. Assn.*, 40:1139–1159.

Patterson, F. (1981), *The Education of Koko.* New York: Holt, Rinehart, Winston.

Peak, D., & Frame, M. (1994), *Chaos under Control: The Art and Science of Complexity.* New York: Freeman.

Peterfreund, E. (1971), *Information, Systems and Psychoanalysis.* New York: International University Press.

———— (1983), *The Process of Psychoanalytic Therapy.* Hillsdale, NJ: Analytic Press.

Piaget, J. (1937), *The Child's Construction of Reality.* New York: Basic Books, 1954.

Poincaré, H. (1913), Mathematical creation. In: *The Foundations of Science*, ed. G. Bruce Halstead. New York: Science Press, 1960.

Poundstone, W. (1985), *The Recursive Universe: Cosmic Complexity and the Limits of Scientific Knowledge*. Chicago: Contemporary Books.

——— (1992), *Prisoner's Dilemma*. New York: Doubleday.

Pribram, K., & Gill, M. (1976), *Freud's "Project" Reassessed*. New York: Basic Books.

Prigogine, I., & Stengers, I. (1984), *Order Out of Chaos: Man's New Dialogue with Nature*. New York: Bantam Books.

Rapaport, A. (1962), The use and misuse of game theory. *Sci. Amer.*, 187:108–114.

Raup, D. M. (1992), *Extinction: Bad Genes or Bad Luck?* New York: W. W. Norton.

Ray, T. (1992), An approach to the synthesis of life. In: *Artificial Life*, Vol. 2, ed. C. G. Langton, C. Taylor, J. D. Farmer, & S. Rasmussen. Redwood City, CA: Addison-Wesley, pp. 371–408.

——— (1994), Evolution and complexity. In: *Complexity: Metaphors, Models and Reality*, ed. G. A. Cowan, D. Pines & D. Meltzer. Redwood City, CA: Addison-Wesley, pp. 161–176.

Reiser, M. (1990), *Memory in Mind and Brain: What Dream Imagery Reveals*. New York: Basic Books.

Rosen, R. (1991), *Life Itself: A Comprehensive Inquiry into Nature, Origin and Fabrication of Life*. New York: Columbia University Press.

Rosenblatt, A. D., & Thickstun, J. T. (1977), *Modern Psychoanalytic Concepts in a General Psychology*. New York: International Universities Press.

Rubinstein, B. (1980), The problem of confirmation in clinical psychoanalysis. *J. Amer. Psychoanal. Assn.*, 28:397–418.

Ruhlen, M. (1994), *The Origin of Language*. New York: Wiley.

Savage-Rumbaugh, E. S., & Lewin, R. (1995), *Kanzi: The Ape at the Brink of the Human Mind*. New York: Wiley.

Schafer, R. (1976), *A New Language for Psychoanalysis*. New Haven, CT: Yale University Press.

Schroedinger, E. (1944), *What Is Life?* Cambridge, U.K.: Cambridge University Press.

Scoville, W. B., & Milner, B. (1957), Loss of recent memory after bilateral hippocampal lesions. *J. Neurol. & Neurosurg. Psychiatry*, 20:11–12.

Simon, B. (1978), *Mind and Madness in Ancient Greece. The Classical Roots of Modern Psychiatry.* Ithaca, NY: Cornell University Press.

Spence, D. (1982), *Narrative Truth and Historical Truth: Meaning and Interpretation in Psychoanalysis.* New York: W. W. Norton.

Spitz, R. (1959), *A Genetic Field Theory of Ego Formation.* New York: International Universities Press.

Stone, L. (1961), *The Psychoanalytic Situation.* New York: International Universities Press.

Strachey, J. (1934), The nature of the therapeutic action of psychoanalysis. *Internat. J. Psycho-Anal.,* 15:127–159.

Taylor, F. J. R. & Coates, D. (1989), The code within the codons. *Biosystems,* 22:177–187.

Turchin, V. F. (1977), *The Phenomenon of Science.* New York: Columbia University Press.

Vogl, T. P., Blackwell, K. T., & Alkon, D. L. (in press), Self-organization of cortical information processing. In: *Brain and Values,* ed. K. Pribram & J. King. Hillsdale, NJ: Erlbaum.

von Neumann, J. (1966), *Theory of Self-Reproducing Automata.* Chicago: University of Illinois Press.

——— Morgenstern, O. (1944), *Theory of Games and Economic Behavior.* Princeton, NJ: Princeton University Press.

Weiner, J. (1994), *The Beak of the Finch.* New York: Knopf.

White, R. W. (1953), *Ego and Reality in Psychoanalytic Theory.* New York: International Universities Press.

Winnicott, D. W. (1965), *The Maturational Processes and the Facilitating Environment.* New York: International Universities Press.

Winson, J. (1985), *Brain and Psyche: The Biology of the Unconscious.* Garden City, NY: Anchor/Doubleday.

Wolfram, S. (1986), *Theory and Applications of Cellular Automata.* Singapore: World Scientific.

Wright, S. (1931), Evolution in breeding populations. *Genetics,* 16:97.

Wuensche, A., & Lesser, M. J. (1992), *The Global Dynamics of Cellular Automata: An Atlas of Basin of Attraction Fields of One Dimensional Cellular Automata.* Reading, MA: Addison-Wesley.

Zetzel, E. (1965), The theory of therapy in relation to a developmental model of the psychic apparatus. *Internat. J. Psycho-Anal.,* 46:39–52.

NAME INDEX

SUBJECT INDEX